P9-CCJ-729

JOHN WILLIS

SCREEN WORLD

1984

Volume 35

CROWN PUBLISHERS, INC.

ONE PARK AVENUE

NEW YORK, NEW YORK 10016

Copyright © 1984 by John Willis. Manufactured in the U.S.A.
Library of Congress Catalog Card No. 50–3023
ISBN 0–517–55437–2

TO

JOAN BENNETT

whose beauty, charm and talent on stage, screen and television have endeared her to millions of fans. . . .

SHIRLEY MacLAINE IN "TERMS OF ENDEARMENT"
© *Paramount Pictures*
1983 ACADEMY AWARDS FOR BEST ACTRESS AND BEST FILM

CONTENTS

EDITOR: JOHN WILLIS

Assistant Editor: Stanley Reeves

Staff: Joe Baltake, Marco Starr Boyajian, Terence Burk, Mark Cohen, Mark Gladstone, Miles Kreuger, John Sala, Van Williams
Designer: Peggy Goddard

Acknowledgments: This volume would not be possible without the cooperation of Ward Ableson, Tom Allen, Sasha Alpert, Chris Anderson, Jane Alsobrook, Pamela Austin, Fred Baker, Henry Baker, Nina Baron, Sharon Behn, Eric Belcher, Mike Berman, Ian Bernie, Jim Bertges, Denice Brassard, Joseph Brenner, Susan Brockman, Barry Cahn, John Calhoun, Fabiano Canosa, Karen Capen, Eileen Nad Castaldi, Philip Castanza, Jerry Clark, Sandy Cobe, Bill Coleman, Ann Cochran, Craig Cox, Alberta D'Angelo, Francene Davidoff, Cindy DePaula, Donna Dickman, Ira Deutschman, Dennis Doph, Robert Dorfman, Helen Eiseman, Bill Elsor, Suzanne Fedak, Mary Lou Finnin, Lynn Fishoff, Tim Fisher, Andrew Fox, Don Francella, Dore Freeman, Renee Furst, Kathryn Galan, Roul Gatchalian, Carolyn George, Ted Goldberg, Joseph Green, Elissa Greer, Elizabeth Hager, Allison Ahaau, Ron Harvey, Tom Haskins, Richard Hassanein, Fred Hift, Dennis Higgins, Beverly Inus, Tina Jordan, Gail Joseph, Andy Kaplan, Richard Kraft, Don Krim, Jack Kurnes, Christine LaMont, Clare Larson, Maryanne Lataif, Jack Leff, Lloyd Leipzig, Wynn Lowenthal, Peter Lowy, Arlene Ludwig, William Lustig, Jeff Mackler, Steven Maklin, Kathy Madden, Howard Mahler, Leonard Maltin, Harold Marenstein, Louis Marino, Priscilla McDonald, Peter Meyer, John Miller, Rich Miller, Susan Mills, Paul Mowry, Barbara Mudge, Michael Myers, Joanna Ney, Sue Oscar, Lillie Padell, Tom Patricia, Janet Perlberg, Paula Pevzner, Jerry Pickman, John Quinn, Jerald Rappoport, Ruth Robbins, Reid Rosefelt, Ed Russell, Suzanne Salter, Les Schecter, Richard Schwarz, Barbara Schwei, Mike Scrimenti, Eve Segal, Jacqueline Sigmund, Marcia Silen, John Skouras, Stephen Soba, Fran Speelman, David Sprigle, Alicia Springer, John Springer, Laurence Steinfeld, Stuart Strutin, Ken Stutz, Deborah Taylor-Bellman, Maureen Tolsdorf, Bruce Trinz, Mark Urman, Don Velde, Bill Velsor, Sherrie Wallace, Wendy Whitescarver, Bob Winestein, Christopher Wood, David Wright, Stuart Zakim, Mindy Zepp, Michael Zuker, Paul Zul

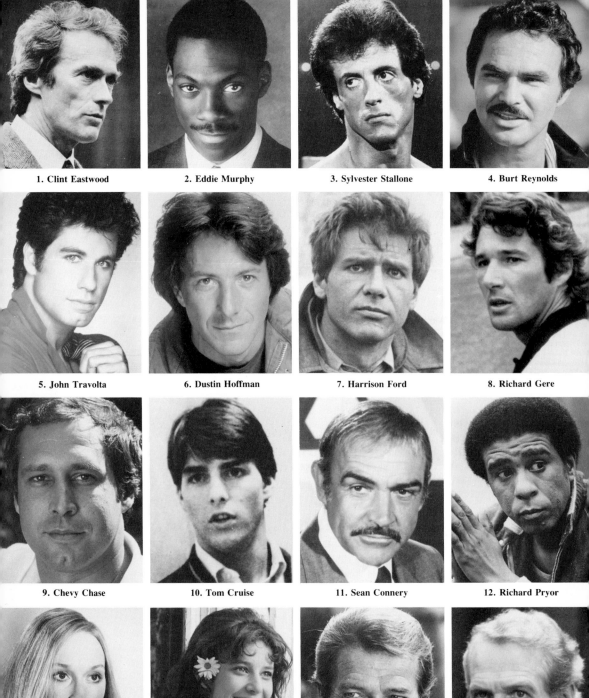

1. Clint Eastwood

2. Eddie Murphy

3. Sylvester Stallone

4. Burt Reynolds

5. John Travolta

6. Dustin Hoffman

7. Harrison Ford

8. Richard Gere

9. Chevy Chase

10. Tom Cruise

11. Sean Connery

12. Richard Pryor

13. Meryl Streep

14. Debra Winger

15. Roger Moore

16. Paul Newman

TOP 25 BOX OFFICE STARS OF 1983
(Tabulated by Quigley Publications)

17. Teri Garr

18. Dudley Moore

19. Barbra Streisand

20. Goldie Hawn

1983 RELEASES

January 1 through December 31, 1983

21. Lou Gossett, Jr.

22. Al Pacino

23. Mark Hamill

24. Jane Fonda

25. Dan Aykroyd

Brooke Shields

Mel Gibson

Sissy Spacek

LIANNA

(UNITED ARTISTS CLASSICS) Producers, Jeffrey Nelson, Maggie Renzi; Directed, Written and Edited by John Sayles; Photography, Austin de Besche; Music, Mason Daring; Art Director, Jeanne McDonnell; Assistant Director, Carol Dysinger; Associate Producers, Lauren Wingate, Douglas McKenna; Wardrobe, Louise Martinez; Choreographer, Marta Renzi; A Winwood Production; In color; Rated R; 115 minutes; January release

CAST

Lianna	Linda Griffiths
Ruth	Jane Hallaren
Dick	Jon DeVries
Sandy	Jo Henderson
Theda	Jessica Wight MacDonald
Spencer	Jesse Solomon
Jerry	John Sayles
Bob	Stephen Mendillo
Cindy	Betsy Julia Robinson
Kim	Nancy Mette
Sheila	Maggie Renzi
Mrs. Hennessy	Madelyn Coleman
Job Applicant	Robyn Reeves
Lighting Assistant	Christopher Elliott
Dancers	Marta Renzi, D. David Porter
Betty	Rochelle Oliver
Liz	Nancy-Elizabeth Kammer
Rose	Jean Passanante
Evelyn	Maggie Task
Dick's Students	Marisa Smith, Amanda Carlin
Supermarket Customer	Madeline Lee
Receptionist	Deborah Taylor

Linda Griffiths, Jane Hallaren
Above: Jon DeVries, Linda Griffiths

Jo Henderson, Linda Griffiths Above: Jon DeVries,
Jessica Wight MacDonald, Jesse Solomon Top:
Jane Hallaren, Linda Griffiths © *United Artists*

THE STING II

(UNIVERSAL) Producer, Jennings Lang; Director, Jeremy Paul Kagan; Screenplay, David S. Ward; Photography, Bill Butler; Designer, Edward C. Carfagno; Editor, David Garfield; Original Music, Lalo Schifrin; Costumes, Burton Miller; Assistant Directors, L. Andrew Stone, Ross Brown, Robert Engelman; Boxing Choreography, Ron Stein; Choreographer, Alton Ruff; Songs, Scott Joplin; In color; Rated PG; 103 minutes; January release.

CAST

Gondorff	Jackie Gleason
Hooker	Mac Davis
Veronica	Teri Garr
Macalinski	Karl Malden
Lonnegan	Oliver Reed
Kid Colors	Bert Remsen
Blonde with Kid Colors	Kathalina Veniero
Carlos, Lonnegan's guard	Jose Perez
Gallecher, Lonnegan's guard	Larry Bishop
Lonnegan's Thugs	Frank McCarthy, Richard C. Adams
Eddie	Ron Rifkin
Bandleader	Harry James
Lady Dorsett	Frances Bergen
Band Singer	Monica Lewis
Messenger	Danie-Wade Dalton
O'Malley	Val Avery
Gertie	Jill Jaress
Man in ticket line	Paul Willson
Ticket Clerk	Sidney Clute
Redcap	Al Robertson
Cab Driver	Hank Garrett
Clancy	Bob O'Connell
Doc Brown	John Hancock
Handicap	Larry Hankin
Page Boy	Jerry Whitney
Big Ohio	Michael D. Alldredge

and Danny Dayton, Corey Eubanks, Mike Raden, Tim Rossovich, Fred Dennis, Sam Theard, Marty Denkin, Rex Pierson, Angela Robinson, Elaine Goren, Iva Rifkin, Lise Kristen Gerard, Lenetta Kidd, Joe Monte, Carl Gottlieb, David Ankrum, Tony Giorgio, T. Max Graham, Melodie Bovee, Cynthia Cypert, Lesa Weis, Jacqui Evans, Max Wright, Carolyn Carradine, Benny Baker, Bob Minor, Terry Berland

Top: Jackie Gleason, Teri Garr, John Hancock
Below: Mac Davis, Dave Cadiente Right: Mac
Davis, Teri Garr Below: Jose Perez, Oliver Reed
© Universal City Studios

Karl Malden, Teri Garr, Jackie Gleason

9

Fred Ward, Belinda Bauer

TIMERIDER
The Adventure of Lyle Swann

(JENSEN FARLEY) Executive Producer, Michael Nesmith; Producer, Harry Gittes; Director, William Dear; Screenplay, William Dear, Michael Nesmith; Art Director, Linda Pearl; Photography, Larry Pizer; Music, Michael Nesmith; Editors, Suzanne Pettit, Kim Secrist, R. J. Kizer; In color; Rated PG; 93 minutes; January release

CAST

Lyle Swann	Fred Ward
Claire Cygne	Belinda Bauer
Porter Reese	Peter Coyote
Claude Dorsett	Richard Masur
Carl Dorsett	Tracey Walter
Padre	Ed Lauter
Ben Potter	L. Q. Jones
Daniels	Chris Mulkey
Dr. Sam	Macon McCalman
Jesse	Jonathan Bahnks
Terry	Laurie O'Brien
Third Technician	William Dear

Top: Peter Coyote Left: Belinda Bauer
© *Jensen Farley*

INDEPENDENCE DAY

(WARNER BROS.) Producers, Daniel H. Blatt, Robert Singer; Director, Robert Mandel; Screenplay, Alice Hoffman; Music, Charles Bernstein; Photography, Charles Rosher; Designer, Stewart Campbell; Editor, Dennis Virkler; Costumes, Julie Weiss; Assistant Directors, Jerry Sobul, Herb Adelman, Joseph Kontra; Additional Songs, Jim Messina; In Technicolor; Rated R; 110 minutes; January release.

CAST

Mary Ann Taylor	Kathleen Quinlan
Jack Parker	David Keith
Carla Taylor	Frances Sternhagen
Les Morgan	Cliff DeYoung
Nancy Morgan	Dianne Wiest
Sam Taylor	Josef Sommer
Red Malone	Bert Remsen
Evan	Richard Farnsworth
Shelly	Brooke Alderson
Andy Parker	Noble Willingham
Rose Parker	Anne Haney
Janis	Judy Brown
Billy Morgan	Jeff Polk
Joey Morgan	Zachary DeLoach
Youngest Morgan Child	Scott and Lane Simpson
Ginny	Cheryl Smith
Minister	Kenneth E. Reynolds
Ticket Taker	Buz Sawyer
Delivery Man	Donovan R. Sparhawk
Uncle Sam	Jacky Martin
Nurses	Bunny Summers, Susan Ruttan
Orderly	David Dunnard
Linda	Mary Ann Smith

and Lauryl Kays, Lance Gordon, Hurschel G. Dunn, Kenny Studer, Glenn E. Gray, Bruce Flanders, Adrienne Hampton, Don Slatton, Steve Whipple, Mack Jones

Right: Dianne Wiest, Cliff De Young
Top: Kathleen Quinlan, Dianne Wiest
© Warner Bros.

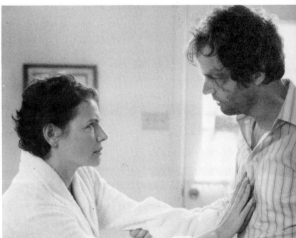

David Keith, Cliff De Young

Kathleen Quinlan, David Keith

TABLE FOR FIVE

(WARNER BROS.) Producer, Robert Schaffel; Director, Robert Lieberman; Screenplay, David Seltzer; Photography, Vilmos Zsigmond; Designer, Robert F. Boyle; Editor, Michael Kahn; Assistant Directors, Newton Arnold, Russ Harling; Art Director, Norman Newberry; Costumes, Vicki Sanchez; In Deluxe Color; Rated PG; 122 minutes; February release

CAST

J. P. Tannen	Jon Voight
Mitchell	Richard Crenna
Marie	Marie Christine Barrault
Kathleen	Millie Perkins
Tilde	Roxana Zal
Truman-Paul	Robby Kiger
Trung	Son Hoang Bui
Mandy	Maria O'Brien
Old Man	Nelson Welch
Bickering Husband	Bernie Hern
Bickering Wife	Moria Turner
Newlywed Husband	Kevin Costner
Newlywed Wife	Cynthia Kania
Rodessa	Marion Russell
Twins	Gustaf Unger, Bertil Unger
Captain	Erik Holland
Ventriloquist	Helle Franz
Blonde	Peggy Kubena
Communications Officer	James Lawrence
Girl on airplane	Ora Rubinstein
Frank	Robert Schaffel
Ship's Officer	Rupert Sykes
Ugo	Hugo Valentino
Maitre d'	Ronald Hoiseck
Taxi Driver	Enrico Pini
Jeep Driver	Said

Jon Voight, Richard Crenna, Millie Perkins, Roxana Zal, Robby Kiger
Top Left: Marie-Christine Barrault, Jon Voight
© CBS Inc.

THE PIRATES OF PENZANCE

(UNIVERSAL) Producer, Joseph Papp; Direction and Screenplay, Wilford Leach; Executive Producer, Edward R. Pressman; Co-Producer, Timothy Burril; Music, Sir Arthur Sullivan; Lyrics, Sir William Gilbert; Additional Music, William Elliott; Choreography, Graciela Daniele; Costumes, Tom Rand; Designer, Elliot Scott; Editor, Anne V. Coates; Photography, Douglas Slocombe; Assistant Director, Barry Langley; Art Directors, Ernest Archer, Alan Cassie; Associate Producers, Andrew Tribe, Stephen Katz; Based on New York Shakespeare Festival production; In Panavision, Technicolor and Dolby Stereo; Rated G; 112 minutes; February release

CAST

Pirate King	Kevin Kline
Ruth	Angela Lansbury
Mabel	Linda Ronstadt
Major-General	George Rose
Frederic	Rex Smith
Sergeant	Tony Azito
Samuel	David Hatton sung by Stephen Hanan
Edith	Louise Gold sung by Alexandra Korey
Kate	Teresa Codling sung by Marcia Shaw
Other Daughters	Leni Harper, Clare McIntyre, Louise Papillon, Tilly Vosburgh, Nancy Wood
Pirates	Anthony Arundell, John Asquith, Mohamed Aazzi, Tim Bentinck, Ross Davidson, Mike Grady, Simon Howe, Tony Millan, G. B. Zoot Money, Andrew Paul, Ken Leigh Rogers, Mohamed Serhani, Mike Walling
Policemen	Peppi Borza, Nicolas Chagrin, Frankie Cull, David Hampshire, Phillip Harrison, Maurice Lane, Neil McCaul, Jerry Manley, Rhys Nelson, Garry Noakes, Chris Power, Kenny Warwick
Pinafore Captain	Romolo Bruni
Pinafore Company	John Bett, Lennie Byrne, Jo Cameron-Brown, Zulema Dene, Marta Eitler, Carole Forbes, Jack Honeyborne, Carol Macready, Brian Markham, Valerie Minifie, Linda Spurrier, Ursula Stedman

Top: Rex Smith, Angela Lansbury
© Universal City Studios

Angela Lansbury, Linda Ronstadt, George Rose,
Rex Smith, Kevin Kline

THE KING OF COMEDY

(20th CENTURY-FOX) Producer, Arnon Milchan; Director, Martin Scorsese; Screenplay, Paul D. Zimmerman; Executive Producer, Robert Greenhut; Photography, Fred Schuler; Designer, Boris Leven; Editor, Thelma Schoonmaker; Music, Robbie Robertson; Associate Producer, Robert F. Colesberry; Costumes, Richard Bruno; Assistant Directors, Scott Maitland, Lewis Gould; Art Directors, Edward Pisoni, Lawrence Miller; An Embassy International Picture in DeLuxe Color; Rated PG; 108 minutes; February release

CAST

Rupert Pupkin	Robert De Niro
Jerry Langford	Jerry Lewis
Rita	Diahnne Abbott
Masha	Sandra Bernhard
Ed Herlihy	Himself
Band Leader	Lou Brown
Stage Door Guard	Whitey Ryan
Chauffeur	Doc Lawless
Young Girl	Marta Heflin
Autograph Seekers	Katherine Wallach, Charle Kaleina
Caricaturist	Richard Baratz
Rupert's Mom	Catherine Scorsese
Dolores	Cathy Scorsese
Man in Chinese restaurant	Chuck L. Low
Liza Minelli	Herself
Roberta Posner	Leslie Levinson
Receptionist	Margo Winkler
Mr. Gangemi	Tony Boschetti
Cathy Long	Shelley Hack
Cabbie	Matt Russo
Woman in phone booth	Thelma Lee
Dr. Joyce Brothers	Herself
Mystery Guest	George Kapp
Victor Borge	Himself
Raymond Wirtz	Ralph Monaco
Security Guard	Rob-Jamere Wess
Jonno	Kim Chan
Cook	Audrey Dummett
Audrey	June Prud'Homme
Bert Thomas	Fred De Cordova
TV Director	Martin Scorsese
Tony Randall	Himself

and Loretta Tupper, Peter Potulski, Vinnie Gonzales (Fans), Alan Potashnick, Michael Kolba, Robert Colston, Ramon Rodriguez, Chuck Coop, Sel Vitella (Men at telephone), Mick Jones, Joe Strummer, Paul Simmion, Kosmo Vynil, Ellen Foley, Pearl Harbour, Gaby Salter, Jerry Baxter-Worman, Dom Letts (Street Scum), Edgar J. Scherick (Wilson), Thomas M. Tolan (Gerrity), Ray Dittrich (Giardello), Richard Dioguardi (Capt. Burk), Jay Julien (Lawyer), Harry Ufland (Agent), Scotty Bloch (Secretary), Jim Lyness (Ticket Taker), Jeff David (Announcer), Bill Minkin (McCabe), Diane Rachell (Mrs. McCabe), Jimmy Raitt (Stage Manager), Charles Scorses, Mardik Martin (Men at bar)

Top Left: Robert De Niro
Below: Robert De Niro, Diahne Abbott
© 20th Century-Fox

Jerry Lewis, Robert De Niro

Robert De Niro, Jerry Lewis
Top: Robert De Niro, Sandra Bernhard

THE LORDS OF DISCIPLINE

(PARAMOUNT) Producers, Herb Jaffe, Gabriel Katzka; Director, Franc Roddam; Screenplay, Thomas Pope, Lloyd Fonvielle; Based on novel by Pat Conroy; Photography, Brian Tufano; Designer, John Graysmark; Editor, Michael Ellis; Music, Howard Blake; Associate Producer, Basil Rayburn; Assistant Directors, Michael Murray, Roger H. Lyons; Art Director, Alan Cassie; Costumes, John Mollo; In color; Rated R; 103 minutes; February release

CAST

Will	David Keith
Bear	Robert Prosky
General Durrell	G. D. Spradlin
Abigail	Barbara Babcock
Alexander	Michael Biehn
Pig	Rick Rossovich
Mark	John Lavachielli
Trado	Mitchell Lichtenstein
Pearce	Mark Breland
Poteete	Malcolm Danare
Macabbee	Judge Rienhold
Braselton	Greg Webb
Gilbreath	"Wild" Bill Paxton
Gooch	Dean Miller
Commerce	Ed Bishop
McIntyre	Stuart Milligan
Teresa	Katharine Levy
MacKinnon	Jason Connery
Rowland	Rolf Saxon
Bobby	Michael Horton
Cadet Colonel	Ian Tyler
TAC Major	Tony Sibbald
TAC Captain	Norman Chancer
TAC Officers	Ronald Fernee, Michael Fitzpatrick, Richard Oldfield
Mrs. Durrell	Sarah Brackett
Mrs. Bear	Mary Ellen Ray
Librarian	Helena Stevens
General's Secretary	Valerie Colgan

and Matt Frewer, Williams Hope, Peter Hutchinson, Peter Merrill, Sheridan Earl Russell, Simon Shepherd, Aaron Swartz, Graham Cull, Mark Eadie, Tom Fry, Lee Galpin, Dean Lawrence, Martin Phillips, Joe Searby, Christopher Warrick, Nicola King, Sallyanne Law, Elizabeth Morton, Kim Thomson, Sophie Ward, Natasha Fraser

Right: David Keith, Michael Biehn
Above: G. D. Spradlin, David Keith
© *Paramount Pictures*

Mark Breland, David Keith
Top Right: David Keith, Robert Prosky

Mitchell Lichtenstein, Rick Rossovich,
David Keith, John Lavachielli

WITHOUT A TRACE

(20th CENTURY-FOX) Producer-Director, Stanley R. Jaffe; Screenplay, Beth Gutcheon from her novel "Still Missing"; Photography, John Bailey; Designer, Paul Sylbert; Associate Producer, Alice Shure; Music, Jack Nitzsche; Editor, Cynthia Scheider; Costumes, Gloria Gresham; Assistant Directors, Terry Donnelly, Robert E. Warren; Art Director, Gregory Bolton; In DeLuxe Color; Rated PG; 121 minutes; February release

CAST

Susan Selky	Kate Nelligan
Al Menetti	Judd Hirsch
Graham Selky	David Dukes
Jocelyn Norris	Stockard Channing
Margaret Mayo	Jacqueline Brookes
Phillippe	Keith McDermott
Ms. Hauser	Kathleen Widdoes
Alex Selky	Daniel Bryan Corkill
Pat Menetti	Cheryl Giannini
Eugene Menetti	David Simon
Polygraph Operator	William Duell
Vivienne Grant	Joan McMonagle
Malvina Robbins	Louise Stubbs
Naomi Blum	Deborah Carlson
Sachs	Charles Brown
Anna	Sheila M. Coonan
Mr. Garrett	Peter Brash
Janet Smith	L. Scott Caldwell
Martina	Ellen Barber
Dr. Sorel	Theodore Sorel
Schoyer	Sam J. Coppola
Production Assistant	Elaine Bromka
Makeup Man	Roger Kozol
Makeup Woman	Caroline Aaron
Coffee Shop Owner	Lee Sandman
Officer Coffin	Fred Coffin
Justine Norris	Marissa Ryan
Baker	Dan Lauria
Ward	Donny Burke
Marcia Menetti	Stephanie Ann Levy

and Peggy Woody, Kathrin King Segal (Girls on movie line), Marcella Lowery (Sgt. Rocco), Luke Skckle (Hank), Jane Cecil (Mrs. Applegate), Todd Winters (Technician), Timothy Minor (Soundman), Lynn Cohen (Woman with dog), Kymbra Callaghan (Hairdresser), Ronald Barber (Guard), Carlotta A. DeVaughn (Officer), Parents: Robert Ott Boyle, Joseph M. Costa, Elizabeth Lathram, Terrance K. O'Quinn, Angela Pietropinto, Tory Wood, Police: Don Amendolia, Tony Devon, Thomas Kopache, Lou Leccese, Mark McGovern, Steve Mendillo, Bob Scarantino, Martin Shakar, Bill Smitrovich, Reporters: Ashby Adams, Hy R. Agens, MacKenzie Allen, Peter Burnell, Bruce Carr, Maria Cellario, Gregory Chase, Paul Collins, Ken Cory, William Fowler, Edmund Genest, Roxanne Gregory, Gracie Harrison, Richmond Hoxie, W. H. Macy, Freda Foh Shen, James Storm, Brenda Thomas, Allan Weeks, Hattie Winston

Top: Kate Nelligan, Danny Corkill Right: Nelligan, David Dukes, Judd Hirsch Below: Hirsch, Nelligan
© *20th Century-Fox*

David Dukes, Kate Nelligan
Above: Kate Nelligan, Stockard Channing

LOCAL HERO

(WARNER BROS.) Producer, David Puttnam; Written and Directed by Bill Forsyth; Music, Mark Knopfler; Associate Producer, Iain Smith; Editor, Michael Bradsell; Designer, Roger Murray-Leach; Assistant Directors, Jonathan Benson, Joel Tuber, Melvin Lind, Matthew Binns; An Enigma production for Goldcrest; In color; Rated PG; 111 minutes; February release

CAST

Happer	Burt Lancaster
Mac	Peter Riegert
Ben	Fulton Mackay
Urquhart	Denis Lawson
Moritz	Norman Chancer
Oldsen	Peter Capaldi
Geddes	Rikki Fulton
Watt	Alex Norton
Marina	Jenny Seagrove
Stella	Jennifer Black
Victor	Christopher Rozycki
Rev. MacPherson	Christopher Asante
Cal	John Jackson
Donaldson	Dan Ammerman
Roddy	Tam Dean Burn
Baby	Luke Coulter
Mrs. Wyatt	Karen Douglas
Skipper	Kenny Ireland
Fountain	Harlan Jordan
Peter	Charles Kearney
Gideon	David Mowat
Anderson	John Poland
Linda	Anne Scott Jones
Bulloch	Ian Stewart

and Tanya Ticktin (Russian), Jonathan Watson (Jonathan), David Anderson (Fraser), Mark Winchester, Alan Clark, Alal Darby, Roddy Murray, Dale Winchester, Brian Rowan (Ace Tones), Caroline Guthrie (Pauline), Ray Jeffries (Andrew), Willie Joss (Sandy), James Kennedy (Edward), Buddy Quaid (Crabbe), Edith Ruddick (Old Lady), John Gordon Sinclair (Ricky), Sandra Voe (Mrs. Fraser), Jimmy Yuill (Iain), Betty Macey, Michele McCarel, Anne Thompson (Switchboard Operators)

(standing) Burt Lancaster, Fulton MacKay, (kneeling) Peter Capaldi, Peter Riegert, Chris Rozyki, (front) Denis Lawson, Jennifer Black Top Left: Burt Lancaster
© Warner Bros.

Peter Riegert, Burt Lancaster, Peter Capaldi
Top: Peter Capaldi, Peter Riegert

BAD BOYS

(UNIVERSAL) Producer, Robert Solo; Director, Richard Rosenthal; Screenplay, Richard Di Lello; Photography, Bruce Surtees, Donald Thorin; Designer, J. Michael Riva; Editor, Antony Gibbs; Music, Bill Conti; Associate Producer, Martin Hornstein; Assistant Directors, Tom Mack, Pat Kehoe, Bill Elvin, Katterli Frauenfelder; Set Designer, Maher Ahmad; In Technicolor; Rated R; 123 minutes; February release

CAST

Mick O'Brien	Sean Penn
Ramon Herrera	Reni Santoni
Gene Daniels	Jim Moody
Horowitz	Eric Gurry
Paco Moreno	Esai Morales
J. C. Walenski	Ally Sheedy
Viking Lofgren	Clancy Brown
Tweety	Robert Lee Rush
Wagner	John Zenda
Carl Brennan	Alan Ruck
Warden Bendix	Tony Mockus
Terrell	Erik Barefield
Perretti	Dean Fortunato
Ricky Lee	Lawrence Mah
Carlos	Jorge Noa
Pablo	Ray Caballero
Mrs. Moreno	Martha De La Cruz
Mr. Moreno	Ray Ramirez
Robert Walenski	Eugene J. Anthony
Detective Moran	Andrew Gorman
Pacito	Marco A. David
Black Gang Leader	Donald James
Woman Victim	Jane Alderman
Judge	Richard L. Rosenthal
Vicki O'Brien	Fran Stone

and Omar S. Saunders (Johnson), Kevin Springs (Roberts), Eric David, John San Juro (Lineup Boys), Adam Pelty (Gun Dealer), Robin Coleman (Squad Car Cop), Marvin Townes, Aaron Holden (Bad Dudes), Bill Martin, Jr. (Truck Driver), Myles O'Donnell (Worker), Edward Kearns (Lineup Sgt.), Brenda Joyce Minor (Policewoman), Richard Lee Padget (Guard), Peter Kirkpatrick, David Barrett (Mess Hall Supervisors), Peter Kobernik (Food Supervisor), Dick Sollenberger (Van Driver)

Top Right: Esai Morales, Ray Caballero, Ally Sheedy, Sean Penn, Alan Ruck Below: Eric Gurry, Sean Penn
© *Universal City Studios*

Reni Santoni, Sean Penn

Ally Sheedy, Sean Penn

10 TO MIDNIGHT

CANNON GROUP) Producers, Pancho Kohner, Lance Hool; Director, J. Lee Thompson; Screenplay, William Roberts; Executive Producers, Menahem Golan, Yoram Globus; Editor, Peter Lee Thompson; Photography, Adam Greenberg; Story, J. Lee Thompson; Music, Robert O. Ragland; Assistant Directors, Barbara Michaels, Terry Buchinsky; Art Director, Jim Freiburger; Set Director, Cecilia Rodarte; In Metrocolor; Rated R; 101 minutes; March release

CAST

Leo Kessler	Charles Bronson
Laurie Kessler	Lisa Eilbacher
Paul McAnn	Andrew Stevens
Warren Stacey	Gene Davis
Dave Dante	Geoffrey Lewis
Capt. Malone	Wilford Brimley
Nathan Zager	Robert Lyons
Mr. Johnson	Bert Williams
Bunny	Iva Lane
Ola	Ola Ray
Doreen	Kelly Palzis
Dudley	Cosie Costa
Lab Technician	Paul McCallum
Karen	Jeana Tomasina
Betty	June Gilbert
Judge	Arthur Hansel
Minister	Sam Chew
Tina	Katrina Parish
Peg	Shawn Schepps
Mrs. Johnson	Sydna Scott
Mrs. Byrd	Barbara Pilavin
Desk Sergeant	Beau Billingslea
Jerry	James Keane
Medical Examiner	Jerome Thor

Top: Andrew Stevens, Charles Bronson, Lisa Eilbacher
Below: Geoffrey Lewis, Gene Davis
© Y & M Productions

Charles Bronson
Top: Gene Davis

HIGH ROAD TO CHINA

WARNER BROS.) Producer, Fred Weintraub; Brian G. Hutton; Screenplay, Sandra Weintraub Roland, S. Lee Pogostin; Based on book by Jon Cleary; Executive Producer, Raymond Chow; Photography, Ronnie Taylor; Designer, Robert Laing; Editor, John Jympson; Associate Producer, Frederick Muller; Music, John Barry; Aerial Photography, Peter Allwork; Assistant Directors, Bert Batt, Chris Carreras; Art Director, George Richardson; Costumes, Betsy Heimann, Franco Antonelli; A Golden Harvest/Jadran Film in Technicolor; Rated PG; 120 minutes; March release

CAST

O'Malley	Tom Selleck
Eve	Bess Armstrong
Struts	Jack Weston
Bradley Tozer	Wilford Brimley
Bentik	Robert Morley
Suleiman Khan	Brian Blessed
Alessa	Cassandra Gava
Charlie	Michael Sheard
Lina	Lynda Marchal
Officer	Timothy Carlton
Ahmed	Shayur Mehta
Ginger	Terry Richards
Silversmith	Jeremy Child
Franjien Khan	Peter Williams
Satvinda	Dino Shafeek
Zura	Robert Lee
Alessa's Mother	Peggy Sirr
General Wong	Anthony Chinn
Wong's Aide	Chua Kah Joo
Kim Su Lee	Ric Young
Alec Wedgeworth	Timothy Bateson
Von Hess	Wolf Kahler
Henchman	Marc Boyle
Countess	Zdenka Hersak
Chauffeur	Domagoj Mukusic
Khan's Nephew	Sime Jagarinas
British Officers	Simon Prebble, Daniel Clucas, John Higginson

Jack Weston, Tom Selleck, Bess Armstrong
Top Left: Tom Selleck
© *Golden Communications/Warner Bros.*

22

Bess Armstrong, Tom Selleck Top: (L) Armstrong, Selleck, (R) Bess Armstrong

THE OUTSIDERS

(WARNER BROS.) Producers, Fred Roos, Gray Frederickson; Director, Francis Coppola; Screenplay, Kathleen Knutsen Rowell; Based on novel by S. E. Hinton; Music, Carmine Coppola; Photography, Stephen H. Burum; Designer, Dean Tavoularis; Editor, Anne Goursaud; Associate Producer, Gian-Carlo Coppola; Assistant Directors, David Valdes, Jamie Freitag; Costumes, Marge Bowers; In Panavision, Technicolor and Dolby Stereo; Rated PG; 94 minutes; March release

CAST

Dallas Winston	Matt Dillon
Johnny Cade	Ralph Macchio
Ponyboy Curtis	C. Thomas Howell
Darrel Curtis	Patrick Swayze
Sodapop Curtis	Rob Lowe
Two-Bit Matthews	Emilio Estevez
Steve Randle	Tom Cruise
Tim Shephard	Glenn Withrow
Cherry Valance	Diane Lane
Bob Sheldon	Leif Garrett
Randy Anderson	Darren Dalton
Marcia	Michelle Meyrink
Jerry	Gailard Sartain
Buck Merrill	Tom Waits
Store Clerk	William Smith

Top: C. Thomas Howell, Diane Lane
© Pony Boy Inc.

Matt Dillon, C. Thomas Howell, Ralph Macchio

THE BLACK STALLION RETURNS

(MGM/UA) Producers, Tom Sternberg, Fred Roos, Doug Claybourne; Director, Robert Dalva; Screenplay, Richard Kletter, Jerome Kass; From novel of same title by Walter Farley; Photography, Carlo DiPalma; Editor, Paul Hirsch; Music, Georges Delerue; In color; Rated PG; 103 minutes; March release

CAST

Alec Ramsay	Kelly Reno
Raj	Victor Spano
Kurr	Allen Goorwitz
Meslar	Woody Strode
Abu Ben Ishak	Ferdinand Mayne
Tabari	Jodi Thelen
Alec's Mother	Teri Garr
Tiny Man	Doghmi Larbi
Raj's Father	Angelo Infanti
Scarface	Luigo Mezzanotte
Foreign Legion Officer	Franco Citti

Right: Kelly Reno

Kelly Reno, Vincent Spano

TENDER MERCIES

(U/AFD) Producer, Philip S. Hobel; Associate Producer, Mary-Ann Hobel; Director, Bruce Beresford; Screenplay, Horton Foote; Co-Producers, Horton Foote, Robert Duvall; Photography, Russell Boyd; Art Director, Jeannine Oppewall; Assistant Directors, Richard Luke Rothschild, Kelly Wimberly; Editor, William Anderson; Choreographer, Nick Felix; An Antron Media Production in Movielab Color; Rated PG; 96 minutes; March release

CAST

Mac Sledge	Robert Duvall
Rosa Lee	Tess Harper
Dixie	Betty Buckley
Harry	Wilford Brimley
Sue Anne	Ellen Barkin
Sonny	Allan Hubbard
Robert	Lenny Von Dohlen
Reporter	Paul Gleason
Lewis Menefee	Michael Crabtree
Rev. Hotchkiss	Norman Bennett
LaRue	Andrew Scott Hollon
Jake	Rick Murray
Bertie	Stephen Funchess
Steve	Glen Fleming
Henry	James Aaron
Nurse	Suzanne Jacobs

and Jerry Biggs, Sheila Bird, Robert E. Blackburn III, Eli Cummins, Tony Frank, Berkley H. Garrett, Helena Humann, Barbara Jones, Jerry Jones, Harlan Jordan, Robert P. Kelley, Ray LePere, Pat Minter, Terry Schoolcraft, Oliver Seale, Denise Simek, Robert Stewart, Susan Aston, Vicki Neff, Pamela Putnam, Jerry Abbot, Bobby Hibbitts, Buddie Hrabal, Jerry Matheny, Wayne Milligan

Left: Tess Harper, Robert Duvall, Allan Hubbard
© *Universal City Studios*

*1983 Academy Awards for Best Actor (Robert Duvall),
Best Original Screenplay*

Robert Duvall, Tess Harper

Robert Duvall, Tess Harper, Lenny Von Dohlen

Robert Duvall, Allan Hubbard Top: Wilford Brimley, Ellen Barkin, Betty Buckley

TRENCHCOAT

(BUENA VISTA) Producer, Jerry Leider; Director, Michael Tuchner; Screenplay, Jeffrey Price, Peter Seaman; Associate Producer, Joel Morwood; Music, Charles Fox; Photography, Tonino Delli Colli; Designer, Rodger Maus; Editor, Frank J. Urioste; Assistant Directors, Carlo Cotti, Michael Kissaun, Mark Schilz, Doug Metzger; Costumes, Gloria Mussetta; Art Director, John B. Mansbridge; In Technicolor and Dolby Stereo; Rated PG; 91 minutes; March release

CAST

Mickey Raymond	Margot Kidder
Terry Leonard	Robert Hays
Inspector Stagnos	David Suchet
Eva Werner	Gila Von Weitershausen
Nino Tenucci	Daniel Faraldo
Princess Aida	Ronald Lacey
Marquis DePina	John Justin
Lizzy O'Reilly	Pauline Delany
Sean O'Reilly	P. G. Stephens
Estaban Ortega	Leopoldo Trieste
Cpl. Lascaris	Brizio Montinaro
Afro-Dite	Martin Sorrentino
Taxi Driver	Luciano Crovato
Boss Arab	Massimo Sarchielli
Laurie	Jennifer Darling
Arab	Kevork Malikyan
Achmed	Vic Tablian
Burly Salt	Brian Coburn
Mother	Fifi Moyer

and Marcello Krakoff, Philip Alexander, Brian Eubanks, Saviour Tanti, Nadine Azzopardi, Emanuel Abela, Charles Saliba, Margaret Von Brockdorff, Ruth Borthwick, Freda Camilleri, Lilly Harding, Nancy Calamatta, Anthony Spiteri, Joe Quattromani, Eddie Baldacchino, Joe Coppini, Harry Jones, Michael Kissaun, Charles Darmanin, Joe Abela, Benny Farrugia

Top: Margot Kidder, Robert Hays, and below
with Gila von Weitershausen, John Justin
© Buena Vista Distribution Co.

Margot Kidder, Robert Hays, also above
Top: Ronald Lacey, Margot Kidder

THE HUNGER

(MGM/UA) Producer, Richard A. Shephard; Director, Tony Scott; Screenplay, Ivan Davis, Michael Thomas; From novel by Whitley Strieber; Photography, Stephen Goldblatt; Music, Michel Rubini, Denny Jaeger; Editor, Pamela Power; Designer, Brian Morris; Costumes, Milena Canonero; Assistant Directors, David Tringham, Michael Stevenson, Debbie Vertue; Additional Photography, Hugh Johnson; Art Director, Clinton Cavers; In Panavision and Metrocolor; Rated R; 98 minutes; April release

CAST

Miriam	Catherine Deneuve
John	David Bowie
Sarah Roberts	Susan Sarandon
Tom Haver	Cliff DeYoung
Alice Cavender	Beth Ehlers
Lt. Allegrezza	Dan Hedaya
Charlie Humphries	Rufus Collins
Phyllis	Suzanne Bertish
Ron	James Aubrey
Disco Couple	Ann Magnuson, John Stephen Hill
Jelinek	Shane Rimmer
Disco Group	Bauhaus
TV Host	Douglas Lambert
Lillybelle	Bessie Love
Phone Booth Youths	John Pankow, Willem Dafoe
London House Couple	Sophie Ward, Philip Sayer
Waiting Room Nurse	Lise Hilboldt
Interns	Michael Howe, Edward Wiley
Skater	Richard Robles
Eumenes	George Camiller
Egyptian Slave	Oke Wambu

Right: Catherine Deneuve, David Bowie
© MGM/UA Entertainment Co.

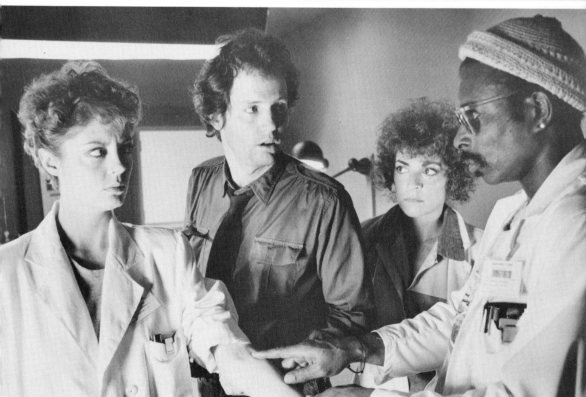

Susan Sarandon, Cliff De Young, Suzanne Bertish, Rufus Collins

FLASHDANCE

(PARAMOUNT) Producers, Don Simpson, Jerry Bruckheimer; Director, Adrian Lyne; Story, Tom Hedley; Screenplay, Tom Hedley, Joe Esterhas; Executive Producers, Peter Guber, Jon Peters; Photography, Don Peterman; Designer, Charles Rose; Editors, Bud Smith, Walt Mulconery; Music, Giorgio Moroder; Choreography, Jeffrey Hornaday; Associate Producers, Tom Jacobson, Lynda Rosen Obst; Costumes, Michael Kaplan; Assistant Directors, Albert Shapiro, Marty Ewing; Soundtrack on Casablanca Records; In Movielab Color and Dolby Stereo; Rated R; 96 minutes; April release

CAST

Alex Owens	Jennifer Beals
Nick Hurley	Michael Nouri
Hanna Long	Lilia Skala
Jeanie Szabo	Sunny Johnson
Richie	Kyle T. Heffner
Johnny C	Lee Ving
Jake Mawby	Ron Karabatsos
Katie Hurley	Belinda Bauer
Cecil	Malcolm Danare
Frank Szabo	Phil Bruns
Rosemary Szabo	Micole Mercurio
Secretary	Lucy Lee Flippin
Pete	Don Brockett
Tina Tech	Cynthia Rhodes
Heels	Durga McBroom
Margo	Stacy Pickren
Sunny	Liz Sagal
Normski	Norman Scott
Mr. Freeze	Marc Lemberger
Frosty Freeze	Wayne Frost
Prince Ken Swift	Kenneth Gabbert
Crazy Legs	Richard Colon
Welders	Larry John Meyers, David Dimanna
Dancers at repertory	Helen Dexter, Mark Anthony Moschello, Debra Gordon
Blonde Skater	Erika Leslie
Icerink Officials	Jim McCardle, Ernie Tate
Strippers	Bettina Birnbaum, Deirdre L. Cowden
Maitre d'	Colin Hamilton
Waiter	Tony de Santis
Woman in restaurant	Marjean Dennis
Priest	Bob Harks
Woman at Hanna Long's	Ann Muffly
Racquetball Player	Hank Crowell
Harry	Frank Tomasello

Miss Beal's dances performed by Marine Jahan

Left: Jennifer Beals, Sunny Johnson Top: Michael Nouri, Jennifer Beals © *Paramount Pictures*

1983 Academy Award for Original Song
(Flashdance—What a Feeling)

Lilia Skala, Jennifer Beals

Michael Nouri, Jennifer Beals

Jennifer Beals (also top)   Don Brockett, Michael Nouri

MAN, WOMAN AND CHILD

(PARAMOUNT) Producers, Elmo Williams, Elliott Kastner; Director, Dick Richards; Screenplay, Erich Segal, David Z. Goodman; From novel by Erich Segal; Photography, Richard H. Kline; Designer, Dean Edward Mitzner; Editor, David Bretherton; Executive Producer, Stanley Beck; Associate Producer, Stacy Williams; Music, Georges Delerue; Costumes, Joseph G. Aulisi; Assistant Directors, Tommy Thompson, Francois Moullin, Richard Henry; A Gaylord Production in DeLuxe Color; Rated PG; 101 minutes; April release

CAST

Bob Beckwith	Martin Sheen
Sheila Beckwith	Blythe Danner
Bernie Ackerman	Craig T. Nelson
Gavin Wilson	David Hemmings
Nicole Guerin	Nathalie Nell
Margo	Maureen Anderman
Jean-Claude Guerin	Sebastian Dungan
Jessica Beckwith	Arlene McIntyre
Paula Beckwith	Missy Francis
Davey Ackerman	Billy Jacoby
Nancy Ackerman	Ruth Silveira
Louis	Jacques Francois
Shakespeare Student	Randy Dreyfus
TWA Clerk	Dennis Redfield
TWA Host	Frederick Cintron
TWA Stewardesses	Anne Bruner, Eve Douglas
Woman at Bar-B-Que	Lorraine Williams
Soccer Players	Mark E. Boucher, David E. Boucher
Basketball Player	Homer Taylor
Students	Lisa Figueroa, Frank Koppola, David O. Thomas
Faculty	Jan Stratton, John Wyler, Gwil Richards, Lila Waters, James Beach, Richard McGonagle, Grace Woodard, Louis Plante

Top: Nathalie Nell, Martin Sheen Below: David Hemmings, Blythe Danner Top Right: Danner, Maureen Anderman
© *Gaylord Production Co.*

Martin Sheen, Blythe Danner, and above with Arlene McIntyre, Missy Francis, Sebastian Dungan

SOMETHING WICKED THIS WAY COMES

(BUENA VISTA) Producer, Peter Vincent Douglas; Director, Jack Clayton; Screenplay, Ray Bradbury from his novel; Photography, Stephen H. Burum; Music, James Horner; Designer, Richard Mac-Donald; Editor, Argyle Nelson; Costumes, Ruth Myers; Editor, Barry Mark Gordon; Assistant Directors, Dan Kolsrud, Lisa Marmon; Art Directors, John B. Mansbridge, Richard James Lawrence; Associate Producer, Dan Kolsrud; Animation, Michael Wolf, Ron Stangl; In Technicolor; Rated PG; 94 minutes; April release

CAST

Charles Halloway	Jason Robards
Mr. Dark	Jonathan Pryce
Mrs. Nightshade	Diane Ladd
Dust Witch	Pam Grier
Tom Fury	Royal Dano
Will Halloway	Vidal Peterson
Jim Nightshade	Shawn Carson
Little Person #1	Angelo Rossitto
Little Person #2	Peter D. Risch
Teenage Couple	Tim Clark, Jill Carroll
Young Ed	Tony Christopher
Young Miss Foley	Sharan Lea
Cooger as a young man	Scott DeRoy
Townswoman	Sharon Ashe
Narrator	Arthur Hill
Miss Foley	Mary Grace Canfield
Mr. Crosetti	Richard Davalos
Mr. Tetley	Jake Dengel
Dr. Douglas	Jack Dodson
Mr. Cooger	Bruce M. Fischer
Mrs. Halloway	Ellen Geer
Cooger as a child	Brendan Klinger
Bartender	James Stacy

Right: Jason Robards, Jonathan Pryce

Top: Pryce, Vidal Peterson, Shawn Carson, Pam Grier
© *Walt Disney Productions*

Pam Grier

Jason Robards

ANGELO MY LOVE

(CINECOM INTERNATIONAL) Direction and Screenplay, Robert Duvall; Associate Producer, Gail Youngs; Photography, Joseph Friedman; Editor, Stephen Mack; Assistant Directors, Carl Clifford, Jeffrey Silver, Christopher Stoia; In color; Not rated; 115 minutes; April release

CAST

Angelo Evans	Himself
Michael Evans	Himself
Ruthie Evans	Herself
Tony Evans	Himself
Debbie Evans	Herself
Steve "Patalay" Tsigonoff	Himself
Millie Tsigonoff	Herself
Frankie Williams	Himself
George Nicholas	Himself
Patricia	Katerina Ribraka
School Teacher	Timothy Phillips
Student Reporter	Lachlan Youngs
Student Reader	Jennifer Youngs
Hispanic Student	Louis Garcia
Old Woman	Margaret Millan Gonzalez
Country Singer	Cathy Kitchen
Mother	Jan Kitchen
Peaches	Debbie Ristick
Opera Singers	William Duvall, John Duvall
Godparents	Nick Costello, Diana Costello
Bride's Parents	Johnny Ristick, Yelka Ristick
Greek Dancer	John Williams

and Toma Lakataca, Jimmy Italiano Mitchell, George Apples Thompson, Fat Harry, Potatoes, Big Bob Stevenson, Baby Nicky, Jay Boya Stevenson, Miller Nicholas, Sam Uvanowich, Tony Vlado, Johnny Mitchell, Steve Mitchell, Marko Cristo

Left: Angelo and Michael Evans
© *Cinecom International*

Angelo Evans (C)

BREATHLESS

(ORION) Executive Producer, Keith Addis; Producer, Martin Erlichman; Director, Jim McBride; Screenplay, L. M. Kit Carson, Jim McBride; Based on film "A Bout de Souffle" from screenplay by Jean-Luc Godard; Story by Francois Truffaut; Photography, Richard H. Kline; Music, Jack Nitzsche; Designer, Richard Sylbert; Editor, Robert Estrin; Assistant Director, Jack Baran, Debra Michaelson; Costumes, J. Allen Highfill; Set, George Gaines; In DeLuxe Color; Rated R; 105 minutes; May release

CAST

Jesse	Richard Gere
Monica	Valerie Kaprisky
Birnbaum	Art Metrano
Lt. Parmental	John P. Ryan
Paul	William Tepper
Sgt. Enright	Robert Dunn
Berrutti	Garry Goodrew
Salesgirl	Lisa Persky
Grocer	James Hong
Tolmatchoff	Waldemar Kalinowski
Highway Patrolman	Jack Leustig
Dr. Boudreaux	Eugene Lourie
Kid	Georg Olden
Carlito	Miguel Pinero

and Henry G. Sanders, Bruce Vilanch, Robert Mark Quesada, Nora Gaye, Andres Aybar, Isabel Cooley, Jerry Greenberg, Javier Grajeda, Robert Snively, John Wyler, Jeni Vici, Carl Munoz, Christopher White, Brien Varady, Keith Addis, Martin Erlichman, Peggy Ann Stevens, D. Lee Carson

© *Orion Pictures*

Valerie Kaprisky, Richard Gere, also above

Roy Scheider

BLUE THUNDER

(COLUMBIA) Producer, Gordon Carroll; Director, John Badham; Screenplay, Dan O'Bannon, Don Jakoby; Executive Producers, Phil Feldman, Andrew Fogelson; Associate Producer, Gregg Champion; Photography, John A. Alonzo; Art Director, Sydney Z. Litwack; Editor, Frank Morriss, Edward Abroms; Music, Arthur B. Rubinstein; Assistant Directors, Jerry Ziesmer, Danny McCauley, Chris Soldo, Tom Davies; Special Effects, Chuck Gaspar; Set Designer, Catie Bangs; Costumes, Marianna Elliot, Norman Burza; A Rastar production in color; Rated R; 110 minutes; May release

CAST

Murphy	Roy Scheider
Braddock	Warren Oates
Kate	Candy Clark
Lymangood	Daniel Stern
Icelan	Paul Roebling
Fletcher	David S. Sheiner
Montoya	Joe Santos
Cochrane	Malcolm McDowell
Sgt. Short	Ed Bernard
Mayor	Jason Bernard
Himself	Mario Machado
Alf Hewitt	James Murtaugh
Matusek	Pat McNamara
Kress	Jack Murdock
Allen	Clifford Pellow
Holmes	Paul Lambert
Colonel Coe	Phil Feldman
Tough Mechanic	John Garber
Grundelius	Anthony James
Diana McNeely	Robin Braxton
Nude Lucy	Anna Forrest
Timmy	Ricky Slyter
Chief of Police	Reid Cruickshanks
Fighter Pilot	John Gladstein

and Billy Ray Sharkey, Fred Slyter, Ross Reynolds, Karl Wickman, James W. Gavin, Tom Friedkin, James Read, Mickey Gilbert, Bill Lane, Lolly Boroff, Patti Clifton, Ernest Harada, Frances E. Nealy, Jose Pepe R. Gonzales, Jerry Ziesmer, Tom Lawrence, John Ashby, Tony Brubaker, Norman Alexander Gibbs, Bill Ryusaki, Gary Davis, Tom Rosales, Larry Randles, Kevin P. Donnelly, Peter Miller, Mike McGaughy, Calvin Brown, Lucinda Crosby

Top: Malcolm McDowell, Paul Roebling, Ed Bernard,
Warren Oates, Roy Scheider
© Columbia Pictures

Candy Clark, Roy Scheider
Top: Roy Scheider, Daniel Stern

TRADING PLACES

(PARAMOUNT) Producer, Aaron Russo; Director, John Landis; Screenplay, Timothy Harris, Herschel Weingrod; Executive Producer, George Folsey, Jr; Photography, Robert Paynter; Costumes, Deborah Nadoolman; Associate Producers, Sam Williams, Irwin Russo; Designer, Gene Rudolf; Editor, Malcolm Campbell; Music, Elmer Bernstein; Assistant Directors, David Sosna, Joseph Ray, Linda Montanti; In Technicolor; Rated R; 106 minutes; May release

CAST

Louis Winthorpe III	Dan Akyroyd
Billy Ray Valentine	Eddie Murphy
Coleman	Denholm Elliott
Randolph Duke	Ralph Bellamy
Mortimer Duke	Don Ameche
Heritage Club Doorman	P. Jay Sidney
Ophelia	Jamie Lee Curtis
Beeks	Paul Gleason
Barney	Bo Diddley
Whittington	Alfred Drake
King Kong	Jim Belushi
Penelope	Kristin Holby
Ezra	Avon Long
Attendant	Robert Earl Jones
Cellmates	Giancarlo Esposito, Steve Hofvendahl
President of Heritage Club	Gwyllum Evans
Bank Manager	W. B. Brydon
Doctor	Philip Bosco
Newscaster	Bill Boggs

and Maurice Woods, Jim Gallagher, Bonnie Behrend, Jim Newell, Bonnie Tremena, Richard D. Fisher, Jr., Anthony DiSabatino, Sunnie Merrill, Mary St. John, David Schwartz, Tom Mardirosian, Charles Brown, Robert Curtis-Brown, Nicholas Guest, John Bedford-Lloyd, Tony Sherer, Robert E. Lee, Peter Hock, Clint Smith, Ron Raylor, James D. Turner, James Eckhouse, Frank Oz, Eddie Jones, John McCurry, Michele Mais, Barra Kahn, Bill Cobbs, Joshua Daniel, Jacques Sandulescu, Margaret H. Flynn, Kelly Curtis, Tracy K. Shaffer, Susan Fallender, Lucianne Buchanan, Paul Garcia, Jed Gillin, Jimmy Raitt, Kate Taylor, Deborah Reagan, Al Franken, Tom Davis, Don McLeod, Stephen Stucker, Richard Hunt, Paul Austin, John Randolph Jones, Jack Davidson, Bernie McInerney, Maurice D. Copeland, Ralph Clanton, Bryan Clark, Afemo Omilami, Gary Klar, Shelly Chee Chee Hall, Donna Palmer, Barry Dennen

Left: Don Ameche, Eddie Murphy
© *Paramount Pictures*

Jamie Lee Curtis, Dan Aykroyd

Dan Aykroyd, Jamie Lee Curtis,
Eddie Murphy, Denholm Elliott

Don Ameche, Eddie Murphy, Ralph Bellamy
Above: Kristin Holby, Dan Aykroyd Top: Michele
Mais, Eddie Murphy, Barra Kahn

Eddie Murphy, Jamie Lee Curtis, Dan Aykroyd
Above: Denholm Elliott Top: Paul Gleason,
Jamie Lee Curtis, James Belushi (in costume)

RETURN OF THE JEDI

(20th CENTURY-FOX) Producer, Howard Kazanjian; Director, Richard Marquand; Screenplay, Lawrence Kasdan, George Lucas; Story, George Lucas; Co-Producers, Robert Watts, Jim Bloom; Executive Producer, George Lucas; Designer, Norman Reynolds; Photography, Alan Hume; Editors, Sean Barton, Marcia Lucas, Duwayne Dunham; Costumes, Aggie Guerard Rodgers, Nilo Rodis-Jamero; Makeup/Creature Design, Phil Tippett, Stuart Freeborn; Music, John Williams; Assistant Directors, David Tomblin, Roy Button, Michael Steele; Art Directors, Fred Hole, James Schoppe; Art Director, Joe Johnston; In DeLuxe Color and Dolby Stereo; Rated PG; 133 minutes; May release

CAST

Luke Skywalker	Mark Hamill
Han Solo	Harrison Ford
Princess Leia	Carrie Fisher
Lando Calrissian	Billy Dee Williams
C-3PO	Anthony Daniels
Chewbacca	Peter Mayhew
Anakin Skywalker	Sebastian Shaw
Emperor	Ian McDiarmid
Yoda	Frank Oz
Darth Vader	David Prowse
Voice of Darth Vader	James Earl Jones
Ben (Obi-Wan) Kenobi	Alec Guinness
R2-D2	Kenny Baker
Moff Jererrod	Michael Pennington
Admiral Piett	Kenneth Colley
Bib Fortuna	Michael Carter
Wedge	Denis Lawson
Admiral Ackbar	Tim Rose
General Madine	Dermot Crowley
Mon Mothma	Caroline Blakiston
Wicket	Warwick Davis
Paploo	Kenny Baker
Boba Fett	Jeremy Bulloch
Oola	Femi Taylor
Sy Snootles	Michele Gruska
Fat Dancer	Claire Davenport
Teebo	Jack Purvis
Logray	Mike Edmonds
Chief Chirpa	Jane Busby
Nicki	Nicki Reade

1983 Academy Award for Special Visual Effects

Carrie Fisher, Mark Hamill

Top: Harrison Ford, Mark Hamill, Peter Mayhew © *Lucasfilm Ltd.*

Harrison Ford (c) Top: Nien Nunb,
Billy Dee Williams

Mark Hamill Above: Carrie
Fisher, Harrison Ford

41

HEART LIKE A WHEEL

(20th CENTURY-FOX) Producer, Charles Roven; Director, Jonathan Kaplan; Screenplay, Ken Friedman; Executive Producers, Rich Irvine, James L. Stewart; Photography, Tak Fujimoto; Designer, James William Newport; Editor, O. Nicholas Brown; Costumes, William Ware Theiss; Associate Producer, Arne Schmidt; Music, Laurence Rosenthal; Song "Born to Win" by Tom Snow; Performed by Jill Michaels; Assistant Directors, Steve Lim, Alice West; Sets, Tom Duffield; Choreographer, Bob Banas; In CFI Color; Rated PG; 113 minutes; May release

CAST

Shirley Muldowney	Bonnie Bedelia
Connie Kalitta	Beau Bridges
Jack Muldowney	Leo Rossi
Tex Roque	Hoyt Axton
Don "Big Daddy" Garlits	Bill McKinney
John Muldowney (Age 15–23)	Anthony Edwards
Sonny Rigotti	Dean Paul Martin
Carlos	Jesse Aragon
Bass Player	Bruce Barloe
NHRA Guard	Michel Barrere
Chef Paul	Paul Bartel
Angela	Missy Basile
Photographer	Creed Bratton
Little Shirley	Tiffany Brissette
Matt	Paul Bryar
Guitar Player	James Burton
John's Girlfriend	Jill Carroll
Reporters	Martin Casella, Paul Linke
NHRA Boss	Michael Cavanaugh
Fan	Sandy Chanley
Mrs. Marianne Kalitta	Ellen Geer
Nurse North	Nora Heflin
Sam Posey	Himself
Shirley's Sister	Diane Delano
Good Joe	Leonard Termo
Mrs. Good Joe	Catherine Paolone
Jack's Friend	Terence Knox

Left: Bonnie Bedelia, and above
with Beau Bridges
© *Aurora Film Partners/20th Century-Fox*

Bonnie Bedelia

Beau Bridges

Shirley Muldowney, Bonnie Bedelia

WARGAMES

(MGM/UA) Producer, Harold Schneider; Director, John Badham; Screenplay, Lawrence Lasker, Walter F. Parkes; Photography, William A. Fraker; Editor, Tom Rolf; Music, Arthur B. Rubinstein; Executive Producer, Leonard Goldberg; Design, Angelo P. Graham; Art Director, James J. Murakami; Assistant Director, Newton D. Arnold; In color; Rated PG; 113 minutes; May release

CAST

David	Matthew Broderick
McKittrick	Dabney Coleman
Falken	John Wood
Jennifer	Ally Sheedy
General Beringer	Barry Corbin
Pat Healy	Juanin Clay
Cabot	Kent Williams
Watson	Dennis Lipscomb
Conley	Joe Dorsey
Richter	Irving Metzman
Beringer's Aide	Michael Ensign
Mr. Lightman	William Bogert
Mrs. Lightman	Susan Davis
Wigan	James Tolkan
Stockman	David Clover
Ayers	Drew Snyder

Top: Barry Corbin, Dabney Coleman
Below: Ally Sheedy, Matthew Broderick,
John Wood
© *United Artists*

Howie Allen, Matthew Broderick
Above: Broderick, Ally Sheedy
Top: Broderick, William Bogert

Dabney Coleman, Matthew Broderick, Duncan Wilmore, Ally Sheedy
Top: Dabney Coleman, Duncan Wilmore, Juanin Clay Below: Ally Sheedy, Matthew Broderick,
John Wood (R) Michael Ensign, Barry Corbin

45

TWILIGHT ZONE - THE MOVIE

(WARNER BROS.) Executive Producer, Frank Marshall; Producers, Steven Spielberg, John Landis; Associate Producers, George Folsey, Jr., Kathleen Kennedy, Michael Finnell, Jon Davison; "Twilight Zone" created by Rod Serling; Designer, James D. Bissell; Photography, Stevan Larner, Allen Daviau, John Hora; Editors, Malcolm Campbell, Michael Kahn, Tina Hirsch, Howard Smith; Music, Jerry Goldsmith; Assistant Directors, Pat Kehoe, Dan Attias, Elie Cohn, Alan Smithee; Set Decorator, Jackie Carr; Set Designer, William J. Teegarden; Art Director, James H. Spencer, Richard Sawyer; In Dolby Stereo and Technicolor; Rated PG; 102 minutes; June release

CAST

SEGMENT 1 and PROLOGUE: (Written and Directed by John Landis) Dan Aykroyd (Passenger), Albert Brooks (Driver), Vic Morrow (Bill), Doug McGrath (Larry), Charles Hallahan (Ray), Remus Peets, Kai Wulff (German Officers), Sue Dugan, Debby Porter (Waitresses), Steven Williams (Bar Patron), Annette Claudier (French Mother), Joseph Hieu, Albert Leong (Vietnamese), Stephen Bishop (Charming G.I.), Norbert Weisser (Soldier #1), Thomas Byrd, Vincent J. Isaac, William B. Taylor, Domingo Ambriz (G.I.'s), Eddie Donno, Michael Milgram, John Larroquette (K.K.K.)

SEGMENT 2: (Director, Steven Spielberg; Screenplay, George Clayton Johnson, Richard Matheson Josh Rogan) Scatman Crothers (Bloom), Bill Quinn (Conroy), Martin Garner (Weinstein), Selma Diamond (Mrs. Weinstein), Helen Shaw (Mrs. Dempsey), Murray Matheson (Agee), Peter Brocco (Mute), Priscilla Pointer (Miss Cox), Scott Nemes (Young Mr. Weinstein), Tanya Fenmore (Young Mrs. Weinstein), Evan Richards (Young Mr. Agee), Laura Mooney (Young Mrs. Dempsey), Christopher Eisenmann (Young Mr. Mute), Richard Swingler (Grey Panther), Alan Haufrect (Conroy's Son), Cheryl Socher (Conroy's Daughter-in-law), Elsa Raven (Nurse)

SEGMENT 3: (Director, Joe Dante; Screenplay, Richard Matheson from story by Jerome Bixby) Kathleen Quinlan (Helen), Jeremy Licht (Anthony), Kevin McCarthy (Uncle Walt), Patricia Barry (Mother), William Schallert (Father), Nancy Cartwright (Ethel), Dick Miller (Paisley), Cherie Currie (Sara), Bill Mumy (Tim), Jeffrey Bannister (Charlie)

SEGMENT 4: (Director, George Miller; Screenplay, Richard Matheson from his story) John Lithgow (Valentine), Abbe Lane (Senior Stewardess), Donna Dixon (Junior Stewardess), John Dennis Johnston (Co-Pilot), Larry Cedar (Creature), Charles Knapp (Sky Marshal), Christina Nigra (Little Girl), Lonna Schwab (Mother), Margaret Wheeler (Old Woman), Eduard Franz (Old Man), Margaret Fitzgerald (Young Girl), Jeffrey Weissman (Young Man), Jeffrey Lambert, Frank Toth (Mechanics)

Top Left: Scatman Crothers
© *Warner Bros.*

Vic Morrow

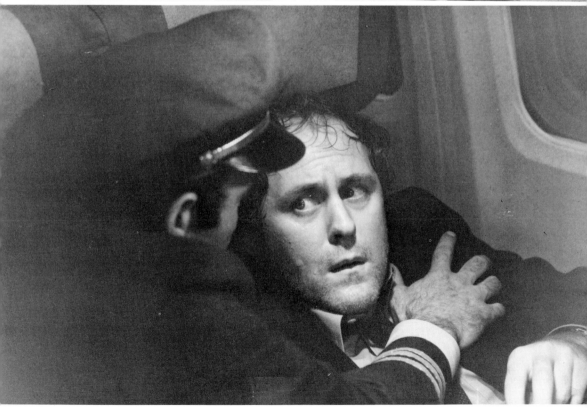

John Dennis Johnston, John Lithgow
Top: Jeremy Licht, Kathleen Quinlan

SUPERMAN III

(WARNER BROS.) Executive Producer, Ilya Salkind; Producer, Pierre Spengler; Director, Richard Lester; Screenplay, David Newman, Leslie Newman; Music, Ken Throne; Songs, Giorgio Moorder; Associate Producer, Robert Simmonds; Editor, John Victor Smith; Photography, Robert Paynter; Designer, Peter Murton; Assistant Directors, David Lane, Dusty Symonds; Art Directors, Brian Ackland-Snow, Charles Bishop, Terry Ackland-Snow; Costumes, Vangie Harrison; In Panavision and Dolby Stereo and color; Rated PG; 123 minutes; June release

CAST

Superman/Clark Kent .... Christopher Reeve
Gus Gorman .... Richard Pryor
Perry White .... Jackie Cooper
Lois Lane .... Margot Kidder
Lana Lang .... Annette O'Toole
Vera Webster .... Annie Ross
Lorelei Ambrosia .... Pamela Stephenson
Ross Webster .... Robert Vaughn

Left: Christopher Reeve
© *DC Comics Inc.*

Margot Kidder (c), Christopher Reeve

Christopher Reeve, Richard Pryor Top: (L) Robert Vaughn, Richard Pryor,
(R) Richard Pryor

THE MAN WITH TWO BRAINS

(WARNER BROS.) Producers, David V. Picker, William E. McEuen; Director, Carl Reiner; Screenplay, Carl Reiner, Steve Martin, George Gipe; Photography, Michael Chapman; Designer, Polly Platt; Editor, Bud Molin; Music, Joel Goldsmith; Assistant Directors, Michael Grillo, Stephen P. Dunn; Art Director, Mark Mansbridge; Set Designer, Robert Sessa; Gorillas, Kevin Brennan; In Technicolor; Rated R; 93 minutes; June release

CAST

Dr. Michael Hfuhruhurr	Steve Martin
Dolores Benedict	Kathleen Turner
Dr. Necessiter	David Warner
Butler	Paul Benedict
Dr. Pasteur	Richard Brestoff
Realtor	James Cromwell
Timon	George Furth
Dr. Brandon	Peter Hobbs
Dr. Conrad	Earl Boen
Gun Seller	Bernie Hern
Olsen	Frank McCarthy
Inspector	William Traylor
Fran	Randi Brooks
Gladstone	Bernard Behrens
Juan	Russell Orozco
Ramon	Natividad Vacio
Desk Clerk	David Byrd

and Adrian Ricard, Sparky Marcus, Perla Walter, Mya Akerling, Don McLeod, Peter Elbling, Diane Peterson, Kate Sarchet, Wendy Sherman, Warwick Sims, Breck Costin, Tom Spratley, Estelle Reiner, Art Holliday, Jeffrey Combs, Jenny Gago, Elma V. Jackson, Oceana Marr, John Easton Stuart, Haunani Minn, Mel Gold, Stephanie Kramer, George Fisher

Right: Steve Martin
© *Warner Bros.*

Kathleen Turner, Steve Martin

KRULL

(COLUMBIA) Producer, Ron Silverman; Director, Peter Yates; Screenplay, Stanford Sherman; Executive Producer, Ted Mann; Photography, Peter Suschitzky; Designer, Stephen Grimes; Editor, Ray Lovejoy; Music, James Horner; Special Makeup, Nick Maley; Costumes, Anthony Mendleson; Associate Producer, Geoffrey Helman; Assistant Director, Derek Cracknell; Art Directors, Tony Reading, Colin Grimes, Norman Dorme, Tony Curtis; Costumes, Bermans and Nathans Ltd.; In Metrocolor and Panavision; Soundtrack available on Southern Cross Records; Rated PG; 126 minutes; July release

CAST

Colwyn	Ken Marshall
Lyssa	Lysette Anthony
Ynyr	Freddie Jones
Widow of the Web	Francesca Annis
Torquil	Alun Armstrong
Ergo	David Battley
Cyclops	Bernard Bresslaw
Kegan	Liam Neeson
Seer	John Welsh
Titch	Graham McGrath
Turold	Tony Church
Eirig	Bernard Archard
Vella	Belinda Mayne
Bardolph	Dicken Ashworth
Oswyn	Todd Carty
Rhun	Robbie Coltrane
Merith	Clare McIntyre
Nennog	Bronco McLoughlin
Darro	Andy Bradford
Quain	Gerard Naprous
Menno	Bill Weston

Top: Ken Marshall, John Welsh, Freddie Jones
Below: Marshall, Battley, Anthony, Armstrong
© *Columbia Pictures*

Lysette Anthony, Ken Marshall, also above

51

STAYING ALIVE

(PARAMOUNT) Producers, Robert Stigwood, Sylvester Stallone; Executive Producer, Bill Oakes; Director, Sylvester Stallone; Screenplay, Sylvester Stallone, Norman Wexler; Based on characters created by Nik Cohn; Photography, Nick McLean; Editors, Don Zimmerman, Mark Warner; Songs, The Bee Gees; Design, Robert F. Boyle; Art Director, Norman Newberry; Costumes, Thomas M. Bronson, Bob Mackie; Choreography, Demnon Rawles, Sayuber Rawles; Associate Producer, Linda Horner; Assistant Director, William Beasley; In Metrocolor; Rated PG; 96 minutes; July release

CAST

Tony Manero	John Travolta
Jackie	Cynthia Rhodes
Laura	Finola Hughes
Jesse	Steve Inwood
Mrs. Manero	Julie Bovasso

Left: Cynthia Rhodes, John Travolta
© *Paramount Pictures*

John Travolta

Finola Hughes, John Travolta
Above: John Travolta, Cynthia Rhodes

Finola Hughes, John Travolta Above: Cynthia
Rhodes, Frank Stallone Top: Rhodes, Travolta

John Travolta, Sylvester Stallone

NATIONAL LAMPOON'S VACATION

(WARNER BROS.) Producer, Matty Simmons; Director, Harold Ramis; Screenplay, John Hughes; Photography, Victor J. Kemper; Designer, Jack Collis; Editor, Pem Herring; Music, Ralph Burns; Associate Producer, Robert Grand; Assistant Directors, Robert P. Cohen, Ross Brown; In Technicolor; Rated R; 100 minutes; July release

CAST

Clark Griswold	Chevy Chase
Ellen Griswold	Beverly D'Angelo
Aunt Edna	Imogene Coca
Cousin Eddie	Randy Quaid
Rusty Griswold	Anthony Michael Hall
Audrey Griswold	Dana Barron
Roy Walley	Eddie Bracken
Kamp Komfort Clerk	Brian Doyle-Murray
Cousin Catherine	Miriam Flynn
Motorcycle Cop	James Keach
Car Salesman	Eugene Levy
Grover	Frank McRae
Lasky	John Candy
Girl in red Ferrari	Christie Brinkley
Cousin Vicki	Jane Krakowski
Cousin Dale	John Navin
Man Giving Directions	Nathan Cook
Pimp	Christopher Jackson
Mechanic	Mickey Jones
Assistant Mechanic	John Diehl
Dodge City Cashier	Jeannie Dimter Barton
Wyatt Earp	Randolph Dreyfuss
Indian	Virgil Wyaco II
Davenport	Gerry Black
Motel Desk Clerk	James Staley
Car Hop	Adelaide Wilder
Motel Guest	Tessa Richarde
Neighbors	Fritz Ford, Eric Stacey, Jr.
Swat Leader	Scott Perry
Policeman	Dennis Freeman
Cowboy	Michael Talbot

Left: Chevy Chase, Beverly D'Angelo, Imogene Coca
Top: Beverly D'Angelo, Chevy Chase, (above)
Dana Barron, Anthony Michael Hall
© *Warner Bros.*

Chevy Chase

Eddie Bracken, Chevy Chase

Beverly D'Angelo, Chevy Chase (also above)

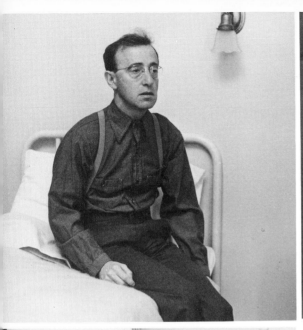

ZELIG

(ORION/WARNER BROS.) Producer, Robert Greenhut; Direction and Screenplay, Woody Allen; Photography, Gordon Willis; Editor, Susan E. Morse; Music, Dick Hyman; A Jack Rollins and Charles H. Joffe production in black and white and color; Rated PG; 84 minutes; July release

CAST

Leonard Zelig	Woody Allen
Dr. Eudora Fletcher	Mia Farrow
Dr. Sindell	John Buckwalter
Glandular Diagnosis Doctor	Marvin Chatinover
Mexican Food Doctor	Stanley Swerdlow
Dr. Birsky	Paul Nevens
Hypodermic Doctor	Howard Erskine
Experimental Drugs Doctor	George Hamlin
Workers Rally Speaker	Peter McRobbie
Martin Geist	Sol Lomita
Sister Ruth	Mary Louise Wilson
Actress Fletcher	Marianne Tatum
Actor Doctor	Charles Denney
Actor Koslow	Richard Liff
Martinez	Dimitri Vassilopoulos
Paul Deghuee	John Rothman
Sister Meryl	Stephanie Farrow
City Hall Speaker	Francis Beggins
Dr. Fletcher's Mother	Jean Trowbridge
On-Camera Interviewer	Ken Chapin
Hearst Guests	Gerald Klein, Vincent Jerosa
Lita Fox	Deborah Rush
Lita's Lawyer	Stanley Simmonds
Zelig's Lawyer	Robert Berger
Helen Gray	Jeanine Jackson
Zelig's Wife	Erma Campbell
Wrist Victim	Anton Marco
House-Painting Victim	Louise Deitch
Vilification Woman	Bernice Dowls

and John Doumanian (Greek Waiter), Will Holt (Chancellor), Bernie Herold (Carter Dean), Marshall Coles, Sr. (Calvin Turner), Ellen Garrison (Older Dr. Fletcher), Jack Cannon (Mike Geibell), Theodore R. Smits (Ted Bierbauer), Sherman Loud (Older Paul), Elizabeth Rothschild (Older Sister Meryl), Kuno Spunholz (Oswald), Themselves: Susan Sontag, Irving Howe, Saul Bellow, Bricktop, Dr. Bruno Bettelheim, Prof. John Morton Blum, Ed Herlihy, Dwight Weist, Gordon Gould, Windy Craig, Jurgen Kuehn

Top: Mia Farrow, (L) Woody Allen
© *Orion Pictures*

Woody Allen, Mia Farrow

DANIEL

(PARAMOUNT) Producer, Burtt Harris; Director, Sidney Lumet; Screenplay, E. L. Doctorow from his novel "The Book of Daniel"; Photography, Andrzei Bartkowiak; Editor, Peter Frank; Executive Producers, E. L. Doctorow, Sidney Lumet; Designer, Philip Rosenberg; Costumes, Anna Hill Johnstone; In color; Rated R; 130 minutes; August release

CAST

Daniel Isaacson	Timothy Hutton
Jacob Ascher	Edward Asner
Paul Isaacson	Mandy Patinkin
Rochelle	Lindsay Crouse
Selig Mindish	Joseph Leon
Susan Isaacson	Amanda Plummer
Phyllis Isaacson	Ellen Barkin
Linda Mindish	Tovah Feldshuh
Robert Lewin	John Rubinstein
Lise Lewin	Maria Tucci
Frieda Stein	Julie Bovasso

Left: Tovah Feldshuh, Colin Stinton, Timothy Hutton
Top: Maria Tucci, Timothy Hutton, Ellen Barkin,
John Rubinstein
© *Paramount Pictures*

Lindsay Crouse, Mandy Patinkin Above: Lindsay
Grouse, Ilan Mitchell-Smith, Rosetta LeNoire

Timothy Hutton, Amanda Plummer Above: Ilan
Mitchell-Smith, Edward Asner, Jena Greca

THE STAR CHAMBER

(20th CENTURY-FOX) Producer, Frank Yablans; Director, Peter Hyams; Screenplay, Roderick Taylor, Peter Hyams; Story, Roderick Taylor; Photography, Richard Hannah; Designer, Bill Malley; Music, Michael Small; Associate Producers, Kurt Neumann, Jonathan A. Zimbert; Costumes, Patricia Norris; Assistant Directors, Bill Beasley, Duncan Henderson; Art Director, Robert "Bo" Welch; Editors, Jim Mitchell, Charles Tetoni; In Dolby Stereo, Panavision, DeLuxe Color; Rated R; 109 minutes; August release

CAST

Steven Hardin	Michael Douglas
Benjamin Caulfield	Hal Holbrook
Detective Harry Lowes	Yaphet Kotto
Emily Hardin	Sharon Gless
Dr. Harold Lewin	James B. Sikking
Arthur Cooms	Joe Regalbuto
Lawrence Monk	Don Calfa
Detective James Wickman	John DiSanti
Stanley Flowers	DeWayne Jessie
Hingle	Jack Kehoe
Detective Kenneth Wiggen	Larry Hankin
Detective Paul MacKay	Dick Anthony Williams
Louise Rachmil	Margie Impert
Martin Hyatt	Dana Gladstone
Robert Karras	Fred McCarren
Albert Beamer	James Margolin
Dawson	Hexin E. McPhee
Adrian Caulfield	Diana Douglas
Assassin	Keith Buckley
Hector Andujar	Domingo Ambriz
Mrs. Cummins	Frances Bergen
Detective Serkin	Charlie Stavola
Sgt. Spota	Robert Costanzo
Garreth	Paul Brennan
Judges	Robin Gammell, Matthew Faison, Michael Ensign, Jason Bernard, Jerry Taft, Mike Austin, Sheldon Feldner

Top: James Sikking, Michael Douglas (also below)
Right: Yaphet Kotto Top: Hal Holbrook, Michael Douglas
© *20th Century-Fox*

Sharon Gless, Michael Douglas

Tom Cruise

RISKY BUSINESS

(WARNER BROS.) Producers, Jon Avnet, Steve Tisch; Direction and Screenplay, Paul Brickman; Photography, Reynaldo Villalobos, Bruce Surtees; Designer, William J. Cassidy; Music, Tangerine Dream; Associate Producer, James O'Fallon; Editor, Richard Chew; Assistant Directors, Jerry Grandey, Jane Siegel, Richard H. Prince; Costumes, Robert de Mora; A Geffen release in Dolby Stereo and Technicolor; Rated R; 98 minutes; August release

CAST

Joel	Tom Cruise
Lana	Rebecca De Mornay
Guido	Joe Pantoliano
Rutherford	Richard Masur
Barry	Bronson Pinchot
Miles	Curtis Armstrong
Joel's Father	Nicholas Pryor
Joel's Mother	Janet Carroll
Vicki	Shera Danese
Glenn	Raphael Sbarge
Jackie	Bruce A. Young
Chuck	Kevin C. Anderson
Kessler	Sarah Partridge
Business Teacher	Nathan Davis
Stan Licata	Scott Harlan
Nurse Bolik	Sheila Keenan
Glenn's Girlfriend	Lucy Harrington
Derelict	Jerry Tullos
Kessler's Father	Jerome Landfield
Detective	Ron Dean
Mechanic	Bruno Aclin
Service Manager	Robert Kurcz
Lab Teacher	Fern Persons
Test Teacher	Cynthia Baker
Russell Bitterman	Wayne C. Kneeland
Evonne Williams	Jade Gold
Hall Marshal	Karen Grossman
Howie Rifkin	Brett Baer

Top: Tom Cruise
© Warner Bros.

Rebecca De Mornay, Tom Cruise
Top: Tom Cruise, Rebecca De Mornay, Shera Danese

MR. MOM

(20th CENTURY-FOX) Producers, Lynn Loring, Lauren Shuler; Director, Stan Dragoti; Screenplay, John Hughes; Co-Producer, Harry Colomby; Executive Producer, Aaron Spelling; Photography, Victor J. Kemper; Designer, Alfred Sweeney; Music, Lee Holdridge; Editor, Patrick Kennedy; Associate Producers, Art Levinson, Bill Wilson; Assistant Directors, Jim Dyer, Dustin Bernard; Costumes, Nolan Miller; A Sherwood production in Metrocolor; Rated PG; 108 minutes; August release

CAST

Jack	Michael Keaton
Caroline	Teri Garr
Alex	Frederick Koehler
Kenny	Taliesin Jaffe
Megan	Courtney White/Brittany White
Ron	Martin Mull
Joan	Ann Jillian
Jinx	Jeffrey Tambor
Larry	Christopher Lloyd
Stan	Tom Leopold
Humphries	Graham Jarvis
Eve	Carolyn Seymour
Bert	Michael Alaimo
Doris	Valri Bromfield
Phil	Charles Woolf
Annette	Mirriam Flynn

and Derek McGrath, Michael Ensign, Ken Olfson, Frank Birney, Hilary Beane, Edie McClurg, Patti Deutsch, Estelle Omens, Patty Dworkin, Bernadette Birkett, James Gallery, Tom Rayhall, Danny Mora, Maurice Sneed, Phil Simms; Bruce French, Henry Flores, Roger Menache, Dennis Landry, Lisa Freeman, Marley Simms, Kay Dingle, Robert Lussier, Jacque Lynn Colton, Mandy Ingber

© *Sherwood Productions*

Teri Garr, Martin Mull, Michael Keaton
Top Left: Teri Garr, Michael Keaton

Michael Keaton
Top: Ann Jillian

Michael Keaton
Top: Teri Garr

THE BIG CHILL

(COLUMBIA) Producer, Michael Shamberg; Director, Lawrence Kasdan; Screenplay, Lawrence Kasdan, Barbara Benedek; Executive Producers, Marcia Nasatir, Lawrence Kasdan; Photography, John Bailey; Design, Ida Random; Editor, Carol Littleton; Associate Producer, Barrie M. Osborne; Assistant Directors, Michael Grillo, Stephen Dunn, Dan Heffner; A Carson Productions Group Ltd. production in Metrocolor; Soundtrack available on Motown Records; Rated R; 104 minutes; September release

CAST

Sam	Tom Berenger
Sarah	Glenn Close
Michael	Jeff Goldblum
Nick	William Hurt
Harold	Kevin Kline
Meg	Mary Kay Place
Chloe	Meg Tilly
Karen	JoBeth Williams
Richard	Don Galloway
Minister	James Gillis
Peter the cop	Ken Place
Harold and Sarah's Son	Jon Kasdan
Running Dog Driver	Ira Stiltner
Autograph Seeker	Jacob Kasdan
Alex's Mother	Muriel Moore
Airline Hostess	Meg Kasdan
Annie	Patricia Gaul

Top: JoBeth Williams, Kevin Kline, William Hurt, Glenn Close
© *Columbia Pictures*

JoBeth Williams, Tom Berenger

Kevin Kline, Glenn Close
Top: Kevin Kline, Meg Tilly, Jeff Goldblum

William Hurt, Kevin Kline
Top: Mary Kay Place, William Hurt

CROSS CREEK

UNIVERSAL) Producer, Robert B. Radnitz; Director, Martin Ritt; Screenplay, Dalene Young; Based on Marjorie Kinnan Rawlings' memoirs of same title; Photography, John A. Alonzo; Designer, Walter Scott Herndon; Editor/Second Unit Director, Sidney Levin; Music, Leonard Rosenman; Costumes, Joe I. Tompkins; Co-Producer, Terry Nelson; Assistant Directors, Don Heitzer, Kenneth Collins; In Panavision and Technicolor; Rated PG; 127 minutes; September release

CAST

Marjorie Kinnan Rawlings	Mary Steenburgen
Marsh Turner	Rip Thorn
Norton Baskin	Peter Coyote
Ellie Turner	Dana Hill
Geechee	Alfre Woodard
Mrs. Turner	Joanna Miles
Paul	Ike Eisenmann
Floyd Turner	Gary Guffey
Tim's Wife	Toni Hudson
Leroy	Bo Rucker
Charles Rawlings	Jay O. Sanders
Tim	John Hammond
Postal Clerk	Tommy Alford
Preston Turner	Keith Michel
Store Keeper	Terrence Gehr
Mary Turner	Nora Rogers
Minister	Kenneth Vickery
Sheriff	C. T. Wakefield
Max Perkins	Malcolm McDowell

Left: Peter Coyote, Mary Steenburgen
Below: Dana Hill
© *Universal City Studios*

Alfre Woodard, Mary Steenburgen

Rip Torn, Mary Steenburgen
Above: Rip Torn, Dana Hill

Mary Steenburgen, Dana Hill, Rip Torn
Above: Mary Steenburgen, Peter Coyote

Alfre Woodard Top: Dana Hill, Mary
Steenburgen, Peter Coyote, Rip Torn

NEVER CRY WOLF

(BUENA VISTA) Producers, Lewis Allen, Jack Couffer, Joseph Strick; Director, Carroll Ballard; Executive Producer, Ron Miller; Screenplay, Curtis Hanson, Sam Hamm, Richard Kletter; Based on book by Farley Mowat; Narration written by C. M. Smith, Eugene Corr, Christina Luescher; Music, Mark Isham; Photography, Hiro Narita; Art Director, Graeme Murray; Associate Producer, Walker Stuart; Editors, Peter Parasheles, Michael Chandler; Assistant Directors, John Houston, Scott Maitland, Anthony Cookson, Colin Michael Kitchens; Special Effects, John Thomas; An Amarok production presented by Walt Disney Pictures; In Dolby Stereo and color; Rated PG; 105 minutes; September release

CAST

Tyler	Charles Martin Smith
Rosie	Brian Dennehy
Ootek	Zachary Ittimangnaq
Mike	Samson Jorah
Drunk	Hugh Webster
Woman	Martha Ittimangnaq
Hunters	Tom Dahlgren, Walker Stuart

Top: Charles Martin Smith, Brian Dennehy
© *Walt Disney Productions*

Charles Martin Smith

Charles Martin Smith

BRAINSTORM

(MGM/UA) Producer-Director, Douglas Trumbull; Screenplay, Robert Stitzel, Philip Frank Messina; Story, Bruce Joel Rubin; Executive Producer, Joel L. Freedman; Associate Producer-Photography, Richard Yuricich; Music, James Horner; Costumes, Donfeld; Editors, Edward Warschilka, Freeman Davies; Designer, John Vallone; Assistant Directors, David McGiffert, Brian Frankish, Robert Jeffords, Eugene Mazzola, Patrick Cosgrove; Art Director, David L. Snyder; Set Designer, Marjorie Stone; In Panavision and Metrocolor; Rated PG; 106 minutes; September release

CAST

Michael Brace	Christopher Walken
Karen Brace	Natalie Wood
Lillian Reynolds	Louise Fletcher
Alex Terson	Cliff Robertson
Gordy Forbes	Jordan Christopher
Landon Marks	Donald Hotton
Robert Jenkins	Alan Fudge
Hal Abramson	Joe Dorsey
James Zimbach	Bill Morey
Chris Brace	Jason Lively
Security Technician	Darrell Larson
Wendy Abramson	Georgianne Walken
Chef	Lou Walker
Andrea	Stacey Kuhne-Adams
Animal Lab Technician	John Hugh
Barry	David Wood
Dr. Ted Harris	Keith Colbert
Dr. Janet Bock	Jerry Bennett
Realtor	Mary-Fran Lyman
Colonel Howe	Jim Boyd
Colonel Easterbrook	Charlie Briggs

and Jack Harmon, Nina Axelrod, Kelly W. Brown, Desiree Ayres, Debbie Porter, Allen G. Butler, Robert Bloodworth, Ann Lincoln, Robert Terry Young, Bill Willens, Jim Burk, Jimmy Casino, Robert Hippard, John Gladstein, Herbert Hirschman, John Vidor, Bill Couch, Robert Gooden, Wallace Merck, Glen Lee, Ernie Robinson, Roger Black, Tommy Huff, May Raymond Boss, Clay Boss, Peter Harrell, Susan Kampe

Left: Christopher Walken, Louise Fletcher
Top: Walken, Joe Dorsey, Fletcher,
Cliff Robertson, Natalie Wood
© *MGM/UA Entertainment Co.*

Jason Lively, Christopher Walken

Christopher Walken, Natalie Wood

ROMANTIC COMEDY

(MGM/UA) Producers, Walter Mirisch, Morton Gottlieb; Director, Arthur Hiller; Screenplay, Bernard Slade from his play of same title; Executive Producer, Marvin Mirisch; Music, Marvin Hamlisch; Associate Producer, David Silver; Photography, David M. Walsh; Designer, Alfred Sweeney; Editor, John C. Howard; Costumes, Joe I. Tompkins; Assistant Directors, Joe Roe, Alan B. Rutiss; In Metrocolor; Rated PG; 103 minutes; October release

CAST

Jason	Dudley Moore
Phoebe	Mary Steenburgen
Blanche	Frances Sternhagen
Allison	Janet Eilber
Kate	Robyn Douglass
Leo	Ron Leibman
Maid	Rozsika Halmos
Minister	Alexander Lockwood
Young Woman	Erica Hiller
Timmy	Sean Patrick Guerin
TV Reporter	Dick Wieand
Bartender	Brass Adams
Maitre d'	Stephen Roberts
Bus Boy	Santos Morales
Passerby	Tom Kubjak
Doctors	Fran Bennett, George Tyne
Actors	Karen Raskind, Allan Kolman, Carole Hemingway, Stanley Ralph Ross, June Sanders, Darrah Meley, Rochelle Robertson

Top: Mary Steenburgen, Dudley Moore
© *United Artists*

Frances Sternhagen

Tom Cruise, Lea Thompson, also top
with Paige Price, Christopher Penn

ALL THE RIGHT MOVES

(20th CENTURY-FOX) Producer, Stephen Deutsch; Director, Michael Chapman; Screenplay, Michael Kane; Executive Producer, Gary Morton; Co-Producer, Phillip Goldfarb; Photography, Jan DeBont; Art Director, Mary Ann Biddle; Editor, David Garfield; Music, David Campbell; Assistant Directors, Jerry Grandey, Emmitt-Leon O'Neill; In DeLuxe Color; Soundtrack on Casablanca Records; Rated R; 113 minutes; October release

CAST

Stef Djordjevic	Tom Cruise
Nickerson	Craig T. Nelson
Lisa	Lea Thompson
Pop	Charles Cioffi
Greg	Gary Graham
Salvucci	Paul Carafores
Brian	Christopher Penn
Suzie	Sandy Faison
Bosko	James A. Baffico
Jess Covington	Mel Winkler
Rifleman	Walter Briggs
Tank	George Betor
Shadow	Leon Robinson
Mouse	Jonas C. Miller
Fox	Keith Ford
Tracy	Paige Price
Charlotte	Debra Varnardo
Coach	Donald A. Yanessa
Sherman Williams	Kyle Scott Jackson
Freeman Smith	Terrance O'Quinn
Henry the bartender	Victor Arnold
Teacher in auditorium	Dick Miller
Drunk in bar	Clayton S. Beaujon
Kirowki	William L. Stibich
Angela	Emma Floria Chapman
Principal	Donald B. Irwin
Civics Teacher	Darlene Dudukovich
Gina	Valerie Zabala

Top: Paige Price, Christopher Penn, Lea Thompson,
Tom Cruise, Leon Robinson, Debra Varnardo,
Paul Carafotes Below: Tom Cruise, Craig T. Nelson
Left: Cruise, Penn, Robinson
© 20th Century-Fox

72

RICHARD PRYOR HERE AND NOW

(COLUMBIA) Executive Producer, Jim Brown; Direction and Screenplay, Richard Pryor; Producers, Bob Parkinson, Andy Friendly; Assistant Directors, Linda Howard, Bernard Basley; Designers, Anthony Sabatino, William Harris; Technical Director, Terry Donahue; Editor, Raymond M. Bush; Associate Producer, Linda Howard; Art Director, Tom Meleck; In Metrocolor; Rated R; 94 minutes; October release

CAST
Richard Pryor

Right: Richard Pryor
© *Columbia Pictures*

Richard Pryor

THE RIGHT STUFF

(WARNER BROS.) Producers, Irwin Winkler, Robert Chartoff; Direction and Screenplay, Philip Kaufman; Based on book by Tom Wolfe; Photography, Caleb Deschanel; Designer, Geoffrey Kirkland; Special Visual Creations, Jordan Belson; Editors, Glen Farr, Lisa Fruchtman, Stephen A. Rotter, Tom Rolf, Douglas Stewart; Music, Bill Conti; Executive Producer, James D. Brubaker; Assistant Directors, Charles A. Myers, L. Dean Jones, Jr., Sharon Mann, Michael Looney; Art Directors, Richard J. Lawrence, W. Stewart Campbell, Peter Romero; Set Designers, Craig Edgar, Joel David Lawrence, Nicanor Navarro; In Technicolor and Dolby Stereo; Rated PG; 192 minutes; October release

CAST

Chuck Yeager	Sam Shepard
Alan Shepard	Scott Glenn
John Glenn	Ed Harris
Gordon Cooper	Dennis Quaid
Gus Grissom	Fred Ward
Glennis Yeager	Barbara Hershey
Bancho Barnes	Kim Stanley
Betty Grissom	Veronica Cartwright
Trudy Cooper	Pamela Reed
Deke Slayton	Scott Paulin
Scott Carpenter	Charles Frank
Wally Schirra	Lance Henriksen
Lyndon B. Johnson	Donald Moffat
Jack Ridley	Levon Helm
Annie Glenn	Mary Jo Deschanel
Scott Crossfield	Scott Wilson
Louise Shepard	Kathy Baker
Marge Slayton	Mickey Crocker
Rene Carpenter	Susan Kase
Jo Shirra	Mittie Smith
Minister	Royal Dano
Liaison Man	David Clennon
Air Force Major	Jim Haynie
Recruiters	Jeff Goldblum, Harry Shearer
Chief Scientist	Scott Beach
Nurse Murch	Jane Dornacker
Gonzales	Anthony Munoz
Head of Program	John P. Ryan
Life Reporter	Darryl Henriques,
Eric Sevareid	Himself
Slick Goodin	William Russ
Grand Designer	Edward Anhalt
Woman Reporter	Mary Apick
Dwight D. Eisenhower	Robert Beer
Eddie Hodges	Erik Bergmann
Waitress	Maureen Coyne
Sally Rand	Peggy David
Henry Luce	John Dehner
Review Board President	Robert ElRoss
Game Show M.C.	Robert J. Geary
Aborigine	David Gulpilil
Australian Driver	Anthony Wallace
Young Widow	Kaaren Lee
Fred	General Chuck Yeager

Top Left: Sam Shepard, Barbara Hershey
Below: Kim Stanley
Top next page: (front) Scott Glenn, Fred Ward,
Lance Henriksen, (back) Ed Harris, Charles
Frank, Scott Paulin, Dennis Quaid
© The Ladd Co.

1983 Academy Awards for Film Editing, Original Score, Sound, Sound Effects Editing

Sam Shepard, Gen. Chuck Yeager

Ed Harris, Kathy Walker, Donald Moffat

THE DEAD ZONE

(PARAMOUNT) Producer, Debra Hill; Director, David Cronenberg; Screenplay, Jeffrey Boam; Based on novel by Stephen King; Music, Michael Kamen; Photography, Mark Irwin; Editor, Ronald Sanders; Presented by Dino DeLaurentiis; In color; Rated R; 103 minutes; October release

CAST

Johnny Smith	Christopher Walken
Sarah Bracknell	Brooke Adams
Sheriff Bannerman	Tom Skerrit
Dr. Sam Welzak	Herbert Lom
Roger Stuart	Anthony Zerbe
Henrietta Dodd	Colleen Dewhurst
Greg Stillson	Martin Sheen
Frank Dodd	Nicholas Campbell
Herb Smith	Sean Sullivan
Vera Smith	Jackie Burroughs
Sonny Elliman	Geza Kovacs
Christopher Stuart	Simon Craig
Walter Bracknell	Barry Flatman

Left: Tom Skerritt, Christopher Walken
© *Dino De Laurentiis Corp.*

Christopher Walken, Brooke Adams

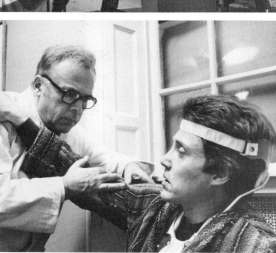

Herbert Lom, Christopher Walken
Above: Adams, Martin Sheen, Geza Kovacs
Top: Christopher Walken

Martin Sheen
Top: Colleen Dewhurst

DEAL OF THE CENTURY

(WARNER BROS.) Producer, Bud Yorkin; Director, William Friedkin; Screenplay, Paul Brickman; Executive Producers, Jon Avnet, Steve Tisch, Paul Brickman; Photography, Richard H. Kline; Designer, Bill Malley; Editors, Bud Smith, Ned Humphreys, Jere Huggins; Associate Producer, David Salven; Music, Arthur B. Rubinstein; Costumes, Rita Riggs; Assistant Directors, Terrence A. Donnelly, James Freitag; In Technicolor and Dolby Stereo; Rated PG; 98 minutes; November release

CAST

Eddie Muntz	Chevy Chase
Mrs. DeVoto	Sigourney Weaver
Ray Kasternak	Gregory Hines
Frank Stryker	Vince Edwards
General Cordosa	William Marquez
Colonel Salgado	Eduardo Ricard
Lyle	Richard Herd
Babers	Graham Jarvis
Harold DeVoto	Wallace Shawn
Ms. Della Rosa	Randi Brooks
Bob	Ebbe Roe Smith
Masaggi	Richard Libertini
Will	J. W. Smith
Woman Singer	Carmen Moreno
Dr. Rechtin	Charles Levin
Vardis	Pepe Serna
Rojas	Wilfredo Hernandez
Pilot on screen	John Davey
Molino	Miguel Pinero
Frenchman	Maurice Marsac
Russian Translator	Joe Ross
Gaylord	Jonathan Terry
Huddleston	Robert Cornthwaite
Rev. Borman	Gwil Richards
Newscaster	Kelly Lange
Senator Bryce	Ken Letner

and Jomarie Payton, Tony Plana, Betty Coe, John Hancock, Helen Martin, Eddie Hice, David Haskell, Ray Manzarek, David Hall, Alex Colon, John Reilly, James Staley, Stephen Keep, Louis Giambalvo, Robert Alan Browne, Brad English, Jim Ishida, Michael Yama, Judy Baldwin, Jan McGill, Frank Lugo, Loyda Ramos, Wendy Solomon, John Stinson, Janet Louise Smith, Jesus Carmona

Right: Chevy Chase, Gregory Hines, Sigourney Weaver
Top: Chevy Chase, Gregory Hines
© *Warner Bros.*

William Marquez, Sigourney Weaver, Chevy Chase

Vince Edwards

STREAMERS

(United Artists Classics) Producers, Robert Altman, Nick J. Mileti; Director, Robert Altman; Screenplay, David Rabe from his play of same title; Associate Producer, Scott Bushnell; Editor, Norman Smith; Photography, Pierre Mignot; Designer, Wolf Kroeger; Art Director, Steve Altman; Costumes, Scott Bushnell; Assistant Directors, Allan Nicholls, Ned Dowd; In color; Rated R; 118 minutes; November release

CAST

Billy	Matthew Modine
Carlyle	Michael Wright
Richie	Mitchell Lichtenstein
Roger	David Alan Grier
Rooney	Guy Boyd
Cokes	George Dzundza
Martin	Albert Macklin
Pfc. Bush	B. J. Cleveland
Lt. Townsend	Bill Allen
MP Lieutenant	Paul Lazar
MP Sgt. Kilick	Phil Ward
Orderly	Terry McIlvain
MP Sgt. Savio	Todd Savell
Dr. Banes	Mark Fickert
Staff Sergeant	Dustye Winniford
MP	Robert S. Reed

Top: Matthew Modine, Guy Boyd, David Alan Grier
Below: Mitchell Lichtenstein, Michael Wright
Top Right: Matthew Modine
© United Artists

Michael Wright (c)

YENTL

MGM/UA) Producer-Director, Barbra Streisand; Screenplay, Jack Rosenthal, Barbra Streisand; Based on "Yentl, the Yeshiva Boy" by Isaac Bashevis Singer; Co-Producer, Rusty Lemorande; Executive Producer, Larry DeWaay; Music, Michel Legrand; Lyrics, Alan Bergman, Marilyn Bergman; Photography, David Watkin; Designer, Roy Walker; Editor, Terry Rawlings; Costumes, Judy Moorcroft; Choreography, Gillian Lynne; Assistant Directors, Steve Lanning, Peter Waller, Steve Harding; Art Director, Leslie Tomkins; Soundtrack on Columbia Records; In Technicolor and Dolby Stereo; A Barwood Film; Rated PG; 134 minutes; November release

CAST

Yentl	Barbra Streisand
Avigdor	Mandy Patinkin
Hadass	Amy Irving
Papa	Nehemiah Persoff
Reb Alter Vishkower	Steven Hill
Shimmele	Allan Corduner
Esther Rachel	Ruth Goring
Rabbi Zalman	David DeKeyser
Tailor	Bernard Spear
Mrs. Shaemen	Doreen Mantle
Peshe	Lynda Barron
Bookseller	Jack Lynn
Mrs. Kovner	Anna Tzelniker
Sarah	Miriam Margolyes
Mrs. Jacobs	Mary Henry
Tailor's Assistant	Robbie Barnett
David	Ian Sears
Mrs. Shaemen's Daughter	Renata Buser
Students	Frank Baker, Anthony Rubes, Kerry Shale, Gary Brown, Peter Whitman, Danny Brainin, Jonathan Tafler, Teddy Kempner

Left: Barbra Streisand
© *Ladbroke Entertainments Ltd.*

1983 Academy Award for Best Original Song Score

Nehemiah Persoff, Barbra Streisand

Mandy Patinkin, Barbra Streisand

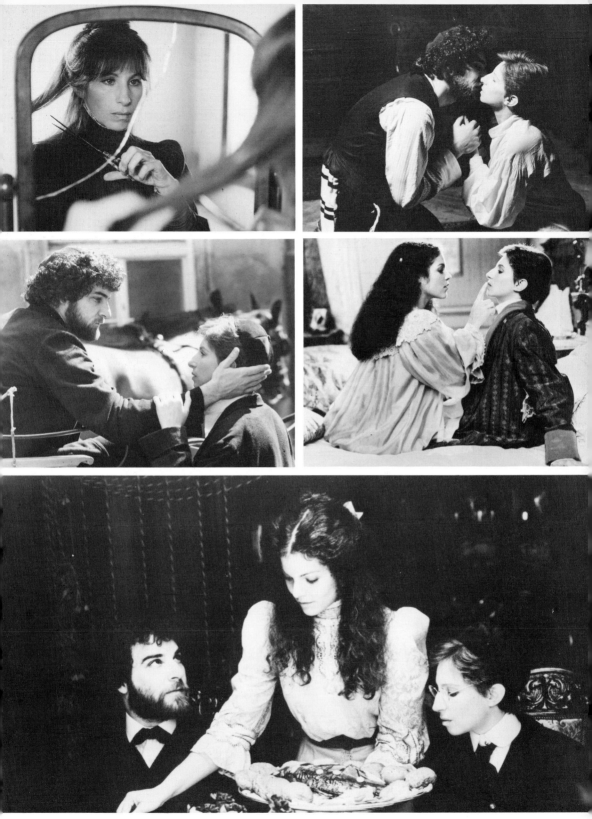

Mandy Patinkin, Amy Irving, Barbra Streisand Top: Barbra Streisand, Mandy Patinkin
Right Center: Amy Irving, Barbra Streisand

STAR 80

(WARNER BROS.) Producers, Wolfgang Glattes, Kenneth Utt; Direction and Screenplay, Bob Fosse; Based in part on "Death of a Playmate" by Teresa Carpenter; Photography, Sven Nykvist; Music, Ralph Burns; Art Directors, Jack G. Taylor, Jr., Michael Bolton; Editor, Alan Heim; Costumes, Albert Wolsky; Associate Producer, Grace Blake; Assistant Directors, David W. Rose, Glen Sanford; A Ladd Co. release in Technicolor; Rated R; 104 minutes; November release

CAST

Dorothy	Mariel Hemingway
Paul	Eric Roberts
Hugh Hefner	Cliff Robertson
Dorothy's Mother	Carroll Baker
Aram Nicholas	Roger Rees
Geb	David Clennon
Private Detective	Josh Mostel
Eileen	Lisa Gordon
Nightclub Owner	Sidney Miller
Photographer	Keith Hefner
Bobo Weller	Tina Willson
Betty	Shelly Ingram
Exotic Dancer	Sheila Anderson
Meg Davis	Cis Rundle
Robin	Kathryn Witt
Peter Rose	Jordan Christopher
Roy	James Luisi
Playboy Executive	Neva Patterson
Director	Robert Fields
Comic	Keenen Ivory Wayans
Woman M.C.	Sandy Wolshin
Actor	Robert Perault
Gunseller	James Blendick
Nightclub Dancer	Jacqueline Coleman
Bartender	Don Granbery
Vince Roberts	Stuart Damon
Phil Wass	Ernest Thompson
M.C.	Budd Friedman
Billie	Deborah Geffner

and Norman Browning, Hagen Beggs, Bobby Bass, Gilbert B. Combs, Terence Kelly, Tabitha Herrington, Dean Hajum, Dan Zaleski, Paul Ryan, Michael Joel Shapiro, Fred Pierce, John Horn, David W. Rose, Stanley Kamel, Liz Sheridan, John Sala, Robert Picardo, Erica Yohn, Marilyn Madderom

Left: Mariel Hemingway
© *The Ladd Co.*

Mariel Hemingway, Eric Roberts

Dean Hajum, Mariel Hemingway,
Lisa Gordon, Carroll Baker

Mariel Hemingway, Eric Roberts, Stuart Damon
Above: David Clennon Top: Tina
Wilson, Eric Roberts

Mariel Hemingway, Roger Rees Above: Cliff
Robertson Top: Carroll Baker, Eric Roberts

TESTAMENT

(PARAMOUNT) Producers, Jonathan Bernstein, Lynne Littman; Director, Lynne Littman; Screenplay John Sacret Young; Based on "The Last Testament" by Carol Amen; Music, James Horner; Photography, Steven Foster; Editor, Suzanne Pettit; Designer, David Nichols; Costumes, Julie Weiss; Associate Producer, Andrea Asimow; Assistant Directors, William Hassell, Peter Bogart, Ralph Singleton, Richard Graves; Art Director, Linda Pearl; In CFI Color; Rated PG; 90 minutes; November release

CAST

Carol Wetherly	Jane Alexander
Tom Wetherly	William Devane
Brad Wetherly	Ross Harris
Mary Liz Wetherly	Roxana Zal
Scottie Wetherly	Lukas Haas
Hollis	Philip Anglim
Fania	Lilia Skala
Henry Abhart	Leon Ames
Rosemary Abhart	Lurene Tuttle
Cathy Pitkin	Rebecca DeMornay
Phil Pitkin	Kevin Costner
Mike	Mako
Larry	Mico Olmos
Hiroshi	Gerry Murillo
Billdocker	J. Brennan Smith
Lady Mayor	Lesley Woods
Police Chief	Wayne Heffley
Pharmacist	William Schilling
Worried Man	David Nichols
Angry Man	Gary Bayer
Dr. Jenson	Martin Rudy
Boy Mayor	Jamie Abbott
Pied Piper	Rocky Krakoff
Nancy	Rachel Gudmundson
Lisa	Keri Houlihan
Woman	Pauline Lomas
Newscaster	Clete Roberts
Man in line	Jesse Wayne

Left: William Devane (top), Ross Harris,
Roxana Zal, Jane Alexander, Lukas Haas
© *Paramount Pictures*

Ross Harris, William Devane

Roxana Zal, Jane Alexander

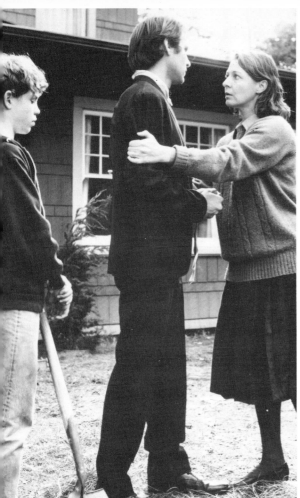

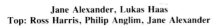

Jane Alexander, Lukas Haas
Top: Ross Harris, Philip Anglim, Jane Alexander

Ross Harris, Jane Alexander
Above: with Gerry Murillo (L)

SUDDEN IMPACT

(WARNER BROS.) Producer-Director, Clint Eastwood; Executive Producer, Fritz Manes; Screenplay, Joseph C. Stinson; Story, Earl E. Smith, Charles B. Pierce; Based on characters created by Harry Julian Fink, R. M. Fink; Photography, Bruce Surtees; Editor, Joel Cox; Music, Lalo Schifrin; Designer, Edward Carfagno; Associate Producer, Steve Perry; Assistant Director, David Valdes; In Technicolor and Panavision; Rated R; 117 minutes; December release

CAST

Harry Callahan	Clint Eastwood
Jennifer Spencer	Sondra Locke
Chief Jannings	Pat Hingle
Captain Briggs	Bradford Dillman
Mick	Paul Drake
Ray Parkins	Audrie J. Neenan
Kruger	Jack Thibeau
Lt. Donnelly	Michael Currie
Horace King	Albert Popwell
Officer Bennett	Mark Keyloun
Hawkins	Kevyn Major Howard
Leah	Bette Ford
Mrs. Kruger	Nancy Parsons

Top: Clint Eastwood
© *Warner Bros.*

Pat Hingle

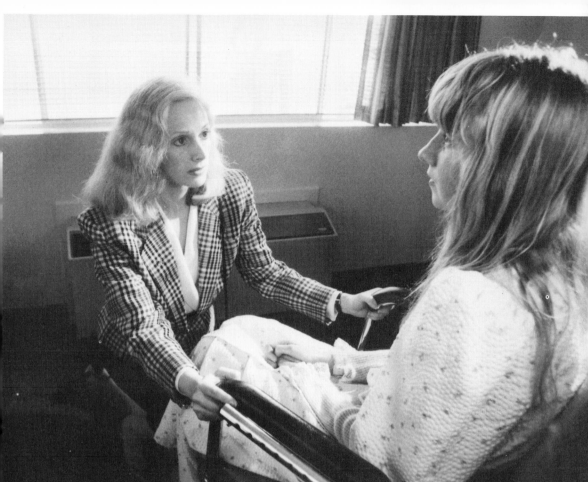

Paul Drake
Top: Sondra Locke,(L)

Clint Eastwood

REUBEN, REUBEN

(20th CENTURY-FOX) Producer, Walter Shenson; Co-Producer, Julius J. Epstein; Director, Robert Ellis Miller; Screenplay, Julius J. Epstein; Based on novel by Peter DeVries; Photography, Peter Stein; Editor, Skip Lusk; Designer, Peter Larkin; Music, Billy Goldenberg; Costumes, John Boxer; Associate Producers, Philip B. Epstein, Dan Allingham; A Taft Entertainment production in color; Rated R; 101 minutes; December release

CAST

Gowan McGland	Tom Conti
Geneva Spofford	Kelly McGillis
Frank Spofford	Roberts Blossom
Bobby Springer	Cynthia Harris
Lucille Haxby	E. Katherine Kerr
Dr. Haxby	Joel Fabiani
Edith McGland	Kara Wilson
Mare Spofford	Lois Smith
Dr. Ormsby	Ed Grady
Tad Springer	Damon Douglas

Left: Tom Conti
© *20th Century-Fox*

E. Katherine Kerr, Tom Conti

Kelly McGillis, Tom Conti
Top: Roberts Blossom, Tom Conti

GORKY PARK

(ORION) Producers, Gene Kirkwood, Howard W. Koch, Jr.; Director, Michael Apted; Executive Producer, Bob Larson; Screenplay, Dennis Potter; Based on novel of same title by Martin Cruz Smith; Music, James Horner; Associate Producers, Efrem Harkham, Uri Harkham; Photography, Ralf D. Bode; Designer, Paul Sylbert; Editor, Dennis Virkler; Assistant Director, Dan Kolsrud; Costumes, Richard Bruno; Assistant Directors, Dan Kolsrud, Peter Waller, Lauri Torhonen, Anders Hedin; In Technicolor; Rated R; 130 minutes; December release

CAST

Arkady Renko	William Hurt
Jack Osborne	Lee Marvin
William Kirwill	Brian Dennehy
Iamskoy	Ian Bannen
Irina	Joanna Pacula
Pasha	Michael Elphick
Anton	Richard Griffiths
Pribluda	Rikki Fulton
General	Alexander Knox
Golodkin	Alexei Sayle
Professor Andreev	Ian McDiarmid
KGB Agent Rurik	Niall O'Brien
Levin	Henry Woolf
Natasha	Tusse Silberg
Fet	Patrick Field
James Kirwill	Jukka Hirvikangas
Valerya Davidova	Marjatta Nissinen
Kostia Borodin	Hekki Leppanen
Director	Lauri Torhonen
Babuska	Elsa Salamaa
KGB Agent Nicky	Anatoly Davydov
Shadowers	Lasse Lindberg, Jussi Parvianen
Russian Tea Band	Black Pearls
Rock & Roll Band	Bad Sign

Right: Lee Marvin, William Hurt, Ian Bannen
Top: Brian Dennehy, William Hurt
© *Orion Pictures*

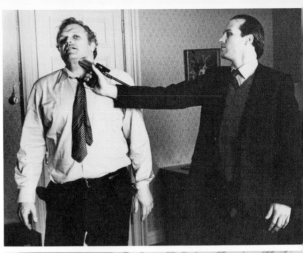

William Hurt, Joanna Pacula

William Hurt, Joanna Pacula

THE MAN WHO LOVED WOMEN

(COLUMBIA) Producers, Blake Edwards, Tony Adams; Director, Blake Edwards; Screenplay, Blake Edwards, Milton Wexler, Geoffrey Edwards; Based on Francois Truffaut's 1977 French comedy; Photography, Haskell Wexler; Designer, Roger Maus; Editor, Ralph E. Winters; Executive Producer, Jonathan D. Krane; Associate Producer, Gerald T. Nutting; Costumes, Ann Roth; Music, Henry Mancini; Theme Song, Mr. Mancini, Alan Bergman and Marilyn Bergman; Sung by Helen Reddy; Assistant Directors, Mickey McCardle, Joseph Paul Moore, Kevin A. Finnegan; Art Director, Jack Senter; Set Designers, Dianne I. Wager, Jacques Valin; In Metrocolor; Rated R; 118 minutes; December release

CAST

David	Burt Reynolds
Marianna	Julie Andrews
Louise	Kim Basinger
Agnes	Marilu Henner
Courtney	Cynthia Sikes
Nancy	Jennifer Edwards
Janet	Sela Ward
Svetlana	Ellen Bauer
Enid	Denise Crosby
Legs	Tracy Vaccaro
Roy	Barry Corbin
Al	Ben Powers
Sue	Jill Carroll
Doctor	Schweitzer Tanney
Himself	Regis Philbin
Dr. Simon Abrams	Joseph Bernard
Henry	John J. Flynn, Jr.
Carl	Jim Knaub
Lt. Cranzano	Jim Lewis
Sgt. Stone	Roger Rose
David's Mother	Jennifer Ashley
David at 16	Tony Brown
David at 12	Philip Alexander
David at 8	Jonathan Rogal
Aerobics Instructor	Margie Denecke
Man at barbeque	Jerry Martin
Nurses	Sharon Hughes, Nanci Rogers
Darla	Cindi Dietrich

Kai J. Wong, Walter Soo Hoo, Marilyn Child, Arnie Moore, Lisa Blake Richards, Noni White, Lynn Webb, Jason Ross, Alisa Lee, Los Angeles Ballet

Right: Burt Reynolds, Kim Basinger
Top: Julie Andrews, Burt Reynolds
© Columbia Pictures

Marilu Henner, Burt Reynolds

Cynthia Sykes, Burt Reynolds

SCARFACE

(UNIVERSAL) Producer, Martin Bregman; Director, Brian DePalma; Executive Producer, Louis A. Stroller; Screenplay, Oliver Stone; Based on 1932 film written by Ben Hecht; Photography, John A. Alonzo; Art Director, Ed Richardson; Editors, Jerry Greenberg, David Ray; Music, Giorgio Moroder; Co-Producer, Peter Saphier; Assistant Directors, Jerry Ziesmer, Joe Napolitano, Chris Soldo; Set Designers, Blake Russell, Steve Schwartz, Geoff Hubbard; Costumes, Patricia Norris; Soundtrack available on MCA Records; In Technicolor and Panavision; Rated R; 170 minutes; December release

CAST

Tony Montana	Al Pacino
Manny Ray	Steven Bauer
Elvira	Michelle Pfeiffer
Gina	Mary Elizabeth Mastrantonio
Frank Lopez	Robert Loggia
Mama Montana	Miriam Colon
Omar	F. Murray Abraham
Alejandro Sosa	Paul Shenar
Bernstein	Harris Yulin
Chi Chi	Angel Salazar
Ernie	Arnaldo Santana
Angel	Pepe Serna
Nick the Pig	Michael P. Moran
Hector the Toad	Al Israel
Banker	Dennis Holahan
Shadow	Mark Margolis
Sheffield	Michael Alldredge
Seidelbaum	Ted Beniades
M.C. at Babylon Club	Richard Belzer
Luis	Paul Espel
Immigration Officers	John Brandon, Tony Perez, Garnett Smith
Dr. Munoz	Loren Almaguer
Cuban Refugee	Gil Barreto
Gutierrez Child	Heather Benna
Miriam	Dawnell Bowers

and Tina Leigh Cameron, Victor Campos, Robert Hammer Cannerday, Rene Carrasco, Albert Carrier, John Carter, Richard Caselnova, Gary Cervantes, Carlos Cestero, John Contardo, Roberto Contreras, Caesar Cordova, Gregory N. Cruz, Dante D'Andre, Richard Delmonte, Wayne Doba, Michel Francois, Ben Frommer, Edward R. Frommer, John Gamble, Troy Isaacs, Ronald Joseph, Mario Machado, Joe Marmo, Ray Martel, John McCann, Richard Mendez, Victor Millan, Santos Morales

Mary Elizabeth Mastrantonio, Michelle Pfeiffer, Al Pacino, Steven Bauer
Top Left: Al Pacino, Miriam Colon, Mary Elizabeth Mastrantonio
Center: Harris Yulin, Al Pacino, Steven Bauer © *Universal City Studios*

F. Murray Abraham Above: Al Pacino,
Robert Loggia Top: Pacino, Al Israel

Al Pacino, and above with Michelle Pfeiffer,
Top with Paul Shenar

93

UNCOMMON VALOR

(PARAMOUNT) Producers, John Milius, Buzz Feitshans; Director, Ted Kotcheff; Screenplay, Joe Gayton; Photography, Steven Burum, Ric Waite; Editor, Mark Melnick; Music, James Horner; Associate Producers, Burton Elias, Wings Hauser; Designer, James Schoppe; Art Director, Jack G. Taylor, Jr.; Assistant Director, Craig Huston; In Movielab Color; Rated R; 105 minutes; December release

CAST

Colonel Rhodes	Gene Hackman
MacGregor	Roger Stack
Wilkes	Fred Ward
Blaster	Reb Brown
Sailor	Randall "Tex" Cobb
Scott	Patrick Swayze
Johnson	Harold Sylvester
Charts	Tim Thomerson
Lai Fun	Alice Lau
Jiang	Kwan Hi Lim
Mrs. Rhodes	Gail Strickland

Left: Gene Hackman, Gail Strickland
© *Paramount Pictures*

Randall "Tex" Cobb, Patrick Swayze, Fred Ward, Reb Brown, Gene Hackman, Tim Thomerson, Harold Sylvester Center (L) Sylvester, Robert Stack, Thomerson, Hackman (R) Reb Brown, Fred Ward, Tim Thomerson, Harold Sylvester

CHRISTINE

(COLUMBIA) Producer, Richard Kobritz; Director, John Carpenter; Co-Producer-Assistant Director, Larry Franco; Executive Producers, Kirby McCauley, Mark Tarlov; Screenplay, Bill Phillips; Based on novel by Stephen King; Photography, Donald M. Morgan; Editor, Marion Rothman; Music, John Carpenter with Alan Howarth; Design, Daniel Lomino; Set Design, William Joseph Durrell, Jr.; Special Effects, Roy Arbogast; Associate Producer, Barry Bernardi; In Metrocolor, Panavision and Dolby Stereo; Rated R; 116 minutes; December release

CAST

Arnie Cunningham	Keith Gordon
Dennis Guilder	John Stockwell
Leigh Cabot	Alexandra Paul
Will Darnell	Robert Prosky
Rudolph Junkins	Harry Dean Stanton
Regina Cunningham	Christine Belford
George LeBay	Roberts Blossom
Buddy	William Ostrander
Mr. Casey	David Spielberg
Moochie	Malcolm Danare
Rich	Steven Tash
Vandenberg	Stuart Charno
Roseanne	Kelly Preston
Chuck	Marc Poppel
Michael Cunningham	Robert Barnell

Keith Gordon, Alexandra Paul,
John Stockwell

Top: (L) Alexandra Paul, John Stockwell
(R) Keith Gordon, Stockwell, Robert Prosky
Center: (L) Gordon, Stockwell, Roberts Blossom
(R) Alexandra Paul, Keith Gordon
© Columbia Pictures

SILKWOOD

(20th CENTURY-FOX) Producers, Mike Nichols, Michael Hausman; Director, Mike Nichols; Screenplay, Nora Ephron, Alice Arlen; Music, Georges Delerue; Executive Producers, Buzz Hirsch, Larry Cano; Editor, Sam O'Steen; Photography, Miroslav Ondricek; Art Director, Richard James; Designer, Patrizia von Brandenstein; Costumes, Ann Roth; Associate Producers, Joel Tuber, Tom Stovall; Assistant Directors, Michael Hausman, Joel Tuber; In Technicolor; Rated R; 131 minutes; December release

CAST

Karen Silkwood	Meryl Streep
Drew Stephens	Kurt Russell
Dolly Pelliker	Cher
Winston	Craig T. Nelson
Angela	Diana Scarwid
Morgan	Fred Ward
Paul Stone	Ron Silver
Earl Lapin	Charles Hallahan
Max Richter	Josef Sommer
Thelma	Sudie Bond
Quincy Bissell	Henderson Forsythe
Gilda Schultz	E. Katherine Kerr
Mace Hurley	David Straithairn
Curtis Schultz	J. C. Quinn
Carl	Kent Broadhurst
Georgie	Richard Hamilton
Jimmy	Les Lannom
Walt Yarborough	M. Emmet Walsh
Union Meeting Doctor	Graham Jarvis
Pete Dawson	Ray Baker
Man in lunchroom	Bill Cobbs
Zachary	Norm Colvin
Ham	Haskell Kraver
Stewardess	Kathie Dean
Randy Fox	Gary Grubbs
Karen's Children	Susan McDaniel, Tana Hensley, Anthony Fernandez
May Bissell	Betty Harper
Linda Dawson	Tess Harper
2nd Union Meeting Doctor	Anthony Heald
Nurses	Nancy Hopton, Betty King
Man at fence	Dan Lindsey
Man with flashlight	John Martin
Joe	Will Patton
Bill Charlton	Vern Porter
Buddy	Christopher Saylors
Man in moonsuit	Don Slaton
Los Alamos Doctors	James Rebhorn, Michael Bond, Tom Stovall

© *ABC Motion Pictures*

Meryl Streep
(also above)

Cher Top Left: Kurt Russell, Meryl Streep

Meryl Streep, Cher Top: Meryl Streep, Kurt Russell, Cher

Anne Bancroft, Mel Brooks

TO BE OR NOT TO BE

(20th CENTURY-FOX) Producer, Mel Brooks; Director, Alan Johnson; Screenplay, Thomas Meehan, Ronny Graham; Executive Producer, Howard Jeffrey; Associate Producer, Irene Walzer; Photography, Gerald Hirschfeld; Designer, Terence Marsh; Music, John Morris; Editor, Alan Balsam; Based on 1942 film of same title; Assistant Directors, Ross G. Brown, Pamela Eilerson; Art Director, J. Dennis Washington; Set Designers, Craig Edgar, Joseph E. Hubbard; Costumes, Albert Wolsky; Choreography, Charlene Painter; In DeLuxe Color and Dolby Stereo; Rated PG; 108 minutes; December release

CAST

Frederick Bronski	Mel Brooks
Anna Bronski	Anne Bancroft
Lt. Andre Sobinski	Tim Matheson
Col. Erhardt	Charles Durning
Prof. Siletski	Jose Ferrer
Capt. Schultz	Christopher Lloyd
Sasha and Mutki	James Haake and Scamp
Ravitch	George Gaynes
Ratkowski	George Wyner
Dobish	Jack Riley
Lupinski	Lewis J. Stadlen
Sondheim	Ronny Graham
Gruba	Estelle Reiner
Bieler	Zale Kessler
Dr. Boyarski	Earl Boen
Gen. Hobbs	Ivor Barry
Maj. Cunningham	William Glover
British Intelligence Aide	John Francis
R.A.F. Flight Sergeant	Raymond Skipp
Rifka	Marley Sims
Her Husband	Larry Rosenberg
Her Son	Max Brooks
Gestapo Officer	Henry Kaiser
Nazi Officer	Henry Brandon
Gestapo Soldier	Milt Jamin
Gestapo Guard	George Caldwell
Desk Sergeant	Wolf Muser
Second Nazi Officer	Lee E. Stevens
Hitler	Roy Goldman
Hitler Adjutant	Robert Goldberg

and John McKinney, Eda Reiss Merin, Manny Kleinmuntz, Phil Adams, Curt Lowens, Dieter Curt, Howard Goodwin, Robin Haynes, Ron Kuhlman, John Otrin, Blane Savage, Joey Sheck, Gillian Eaton, Paddi Edwards, Terence Marsh, Winnie McCarthy, Paul Ratliff, Scott Beach, Sandra Gray, Lainie Manning, Antonette Yuskis, Clare Culhane, Leeyan Granger, Stephanie Wingate, Ian Bruce, John Frayer, Edward J. Heim, Spencer Henderson, George Jayne, Bill K. Richards, Neil J. Schwartz, Tucker Smith, Ted Sprague

Left: George Gaynes, Mel Brooks, Zale Kessler,
Lewis J. Stadlen, Jack Riley, George Wyner
Above: Jose Ferrer, Mel Brooks
© *Brooksfilms Ltd.*

Anne Bancroft, Mel Brooks,
Tim Matheson

(center) Mel Brooks, Anne Bancroft

Joan Harvey, Mike Olszanski
in "America-From Hitler to MX"
© *Parallel Films*

Gil Scott-Heron
in "Black Wax"

AMERICA–FROM HITLER TO M–X (Parallel Films) Created and directed by Joan Harvey; Producers, Albee Gordon, Ralph Klein, Saul Newton; Sound, Albee Gordon; Editors, Joan Harvey, Ken Eluto, Trudy Bagdon; Song "The Banks" by John Amato and performed by The Fourth Wall; Photography, John Hazard, Jeff Wayman, Mark Benjamin, Michael Camerini, Andy Ferullo, John Krauss, Stuart Math, Peter Schnall, Jeffrey Victor; In color; Not rated; 90 minutes; January release. An anti-war feature documentary.

STUCK ON YOU (Troma) Producers, Lloyd Kaufman, Michael Herz; Directors, Michael Herz, Samuel Weil; Executive Producers, William E. Kirksey, Spencer Tandy, Joseph L. Butt, Maverick Group; Editors, Darren Kloomok, Richard Haines, Ralph Rosenblum; Choreography, Jacques D'Amboise; Screenplay, Stuart Strutin, Warren Leight, Don Perman, Darren Kloomok, Melanie Mintz, Anthony Gittleson, Duffy Ceaser Magesis, Michael Herz, Lloyd Kaufman, Jeff Delman; Photography, Lloyd Kaufman; Art Director, Barry Shapiro; Costumes, Rosa Alfaro, Walter Steihl; Associate Producer, Stuart Strutin; Production Executive, Eileen Nad Castaldi; Assistant Directors, Kate Eisemann, Susan Dember, Claudia Gutworth, Lynne Christiansen; Title Design and Animation, John Paratore; Color By Guffanti; Optical Effects, Videart; Rated R; 88 minutes; January release. CAST: Irwin Corey (Judge), Virginia Penta (Carol), Mark Mikulski (Bill), Albert Pia (Artie), Norma Pratt (Bill's mother), Daniel Herris (Napoleon), Denise Silbert (Cavewoman), Eddie Brill (Caveman), June Martin (Eve), John Bigham (Adam), Robin Burroughs (Isabella), Carl Sturmer (Columbus), Julie Newdow (Pocahontas), Pat Tallman (Guenevere), Mr. Kent (King Arthur), Barbie Kielian (Josephine), Louis Homyak (Lance), Ben Kellman (Indian Chief).

BLOODSUCKING FREAKS (Troma) Produced and directed by Joel Reed; In color and Ghoul-O-Vision; Rated R; 87 minutes; January release. CAST: Lynette Sheldon, Karen Fraser, Michelle Craig, Seamus O'Brien, The Caged Sexoids

BLACK WAX (Mug-Shot) Producer-Director-Editor, Robert Mugge; Words-Music, Gil Scott-Heron; Photography, Lawrence McConkey; Audio, William Barth; In color; Not Rated; 79 minutes; January release. CAST: Gil Scott-Heron and the Midnight Band

SAY AMEN, SOMEBODY (United Artists Classics) Producer-Director, George Nierenberg; Producer, Karen Nierenberg; Editor, Paul Barnes; Photography, Ed Lachman, Don Lenzer; A GTN Production in color; Rated G; 100 minutes; January release. CAST: Willie May Ford Smith, Thomas A. Dorsey, Sallie Martin, DeLois Barrett Cambell, Billie Barrett Greenbey, Rhodessa Barrett Porter, Edward O'Neal, Edgar O'Neal, Zella Jackson Price, Michael Keith Smith, Billy Smith, Jackie Jackson, Bertha Smith

SPRING FEVER (COMWORLD) Producer, John F. Bassett; Director, Joseph L. Scanlan; Associate Producer, Donald Wilder; Executive Producers, Lawrence S. Nesis, John F. Bassett; Screenplay, Fred Stefan, Stuart Gillard; Music, Fred Molin; Editors, Kirk Jones, Tony Lower; Assistant Directors, Tony Lucibello, David MacLeod, Elizabeth Halko, Heidi Meitzler; Photography, Robert New, Paul Mitchnick, Christophe Bonniere; Wardrobe, Gina Kiellerman; Art Directors, Bruno Rubeo, Carmi Gallo; Set Designer, Richard D. Allen; Presented by Amulet Pictures; In color; Rated PG; 94 minutes; January release. CAST: Susan Anton (Stevie), Frank Converse (Lewis), Jessica Walter (Celia), Stephen Young (Neal), David Mall (Beechman), Lisa Brady (Rhoda), Barbara Cook (Chris), Maria Hontzas (Bunny), Alan Fawcett (Roger), Derrick Jones (Scotty), Lisa Foster (Lena), Brian Crabb (Ralph), Martin Schecter (Umpire), Stephen Shellin (Andy), Shawn Foltz (Melissa), Sheldon Rybowski (Mike), and Carling Bassett (K.C.), Tina Basle, Stacey Schefflin, Katie Lawrence, Heidi Bassett, Ed Montgomery, Dale Houlihan, Briane Nasimok, Ray Bouchard, Diana Goad, Ron Jackson, Joe Rujas, Danielle Bollettieri, Cayce Connell, John Maschino, Gaston Forest, Bill Ciaccia, Michael Doby, Earl Summerline, Craig Thomas, Don Fontana, Michael Lara, Doug Manley, Al Orzechowski, David Richardson, Michael Allen Willis

Willie May Ford Smith ("Mother Smith")
in "Say Amen, Somebody"
© *United Artists*

Frank Converse, Susan Anton
in "Spring Fever"

Dick Shawn (left)
in "Goodbye Cruel World"

Richard Alfieri, Mercedes McCambridge
in "Echoes"

WACKO (Jensen Farley) Producer-Director, Greydon Clark; Executive Producer, Michael R. Starita; Screenplay, Dana Olsen, Michael Spound, M. James Kauf, Jr., David Greenwalt; Photography, Nicholas von Sternberg; Editors, Earl Watson, Curtis Burch; Music, Arthur Kempel; In color; Rated PG; 84 minutes; January release. CAST: Joe Don Baker (Harbinger), Stella Stevens (Marg Graves), George Kennedy (Dr. Graves), Julia Duffy (Mary Graves), Scott McGinnis (Norman), Andrew Clay (Tony), Elizabeth Daily (Bambi), Michele Tobin (Rosie), Anthony James (Zeke), David Drucker (Looney), Sonny Davis (Weirdo), Victor Brandt (Dr. Moreau), Jeff Altman (Harry), Charles Napier (Patrick), Wil Albert (Dr. Denton), Michael Lee Gogin (Damien)

STARK RAVING MAD (Independent Artists) Producers, Tiger Warren, Don Gronquist; Executive Producers, Robert Warren, Swigert Warren; Director, George F. Hood; Screenplay, uncredited; Photography, J. Wilder; Editor, George F. Hood; Art Director, W. S. Warren; In color; Rated PG; 88 minutes; January release. CAST: Russell Fast (Richard), Marcie Severson (Laura), B. Joe Medley (Francis), Mike Walter (David), Janet Galen (Barbara), Don Beekman (Norman), Mildred Card (Dorothy), Marjorie Hall (Maid), Don Finley (Lucius)

KILL AND GO HIDE (New American Films) released in 1977 as "The Child."

GOODBYE CRUEL WORLD (Sharp Features) Producers, Louis Sardonis, Leopold Zahn; Director, David Irving; Screenplay, Nicholas Niciphor, Dick Shawn; Executive Producer, Stephen L. Newman; Photography, Jerry Hartleben; In color; Rated R; 90 minutes; January release. CAST: Dick Shawn, Cynthia Sikes, Chuck Mitchell

DOUBLE EXPOSURE (Crown International) Producers, Michael Callan, Von Deming, William Byron Hillman; Direction and Screenplay, William Byron Hillman; Music, Jack Goga; Photography, R. Michael Stringer; Executive Producer, Frank Silverman; In color; Rated R; 95 minutes; January release. CAST: Michael Callan

(Adrian), Joanna Pettet (Mindy), James Stacy (B. J.), Pamela Hensley (Sgt. Fontain), Cleavon Little (Police Chief), Seymour Cassel (Dr. Curtis), Robert Tessier (Bartender), David Young (Sgt. Buckhold), Don Potter (Lewis), Misty Rowe (Bambi), Frances Bay (Old Woman), Alfred Mazza (Charlie), Jeana Tomasino (Renee), Sally Kirkland (Hooker), Debbie Zipp (Toni), Teressa Macky (April)

MIDNIGHT (Independent-International) Executive Producers, Samuel Sherman, Daniel Kennis; Producer, Donald Redinger; Director, John A. Russo; Screenplay, John Russo from his novel; Photography-Editing, Paul McCollough; Music, The Sand Castle; Songs, One Man's Family; In Eastmancolor; Rated R; 91 minutes; January release. CAST: Lawrence Tierney (Bert), Melanie Verliin (Nancy), John Hall (Tom), Charles Jackson (Hank), Doris Hackney (Harriet), John Amplas (Abraham), Robin Walsh (Cynthia), David Marchick (Cyrus), Greg Besnak (Luke)

ONE DARK NIGHT (ComWorld) Producer, Michael Schroeder; Director, Tom McLoughlin; Screenplay, Tom McLoughlin, Michael Hawes; Executive Producer, Thomas P. Johnson; Photography, Hal Trussel; Designer, Craig Stearns; Editors, Charles Tetoni, Michael Spence; Music, Bob Summers; Assistant Directors, Dennis White, Nancy King; Art Directors, Craig Stearns, Randy Moore; Costumes, Linda Bass; In Movielab Color; Rated PG; 94 minutes; February release. CAST: Meg Tilly (Julie), Melissa Newman (Olivia), Robin Evans (Carol), Leslie Speights (Kitty), Donald Hotton (Dockstader), Elizabeth Daily (Leslie), David Mason Daniels (Steve), Adam West (Allan), Leo Gorcey, Jr. (Barlow), Rhio H. Blair (Coroner), Larry Carroll (TV Reporter), Katee McLure (Reporter), Kevin Peter Hall (Eddie), Ted Lehman (Drunk), Nancy Mott (Lucy), Martin Nosseck (Caretaker), Albert Cirimele (Reporter), Shandor (Russian Minister), Julie Chase, Peaches Johnson (Stand-ins)

"One Dark Night"

Richard Alfieri, Nathalie Nell
in "Echoes"

Barbara Hershey in "The Entity"
© *Pelleport Investors*

Ron Silver, Barbara Hershey
in "The Entity" © *Pelleport Investors*

SORCERESS (New World Pictures) Producer, Jack Hill; Director, Brian Stuart; Screenplay, Jim Wynorski; Photography, Alex Phillips, Jr.; Editors, Larry Bock, Barry Zetlin; Assistant Director, Mark Conway; Designer, Charles Grodin; Costumes, Kleomenes Stamatiades; In DeLuxe Color; Rated R; 81 minutes; February release. CAST: Leigh Harris (Mira), Lynette Harris (Mara), Bob Helson (Erlick), David Millbern (Pando), Bruno Rey (Baldar), Ana DeSade (Dellisia), Robert Ballesteros (Traigon), Douglas Sanders (Hunnu), Tony Stevens (Khrakannon), Martin LaSalle (Krona), Silvia Masters (Kanti), William Arnold (Dargon), Teresa Conway (Amaya), Lucy Jensen (Dancer), Michael Fountain (Player), Peter Farmer (Armorer), Charles Rogers (Servant), Phillip Garrigan (Soldier), Mark Arevan (Gambler), Gloria Meister (Nursemaid), Randy Rothman (Peasant), Marla Hill (Rich Lady), Ginger Baum (Sister), Gerald Hood (Executioner)

ECHOES (Continental) Producers, George R. Nice, Valerie Y. Belsky; Director, Arthur Allan Seidelman; Screenplay, Richard J. Anthony; Executive Producer, Barry E. Rosenthal; Photography, Hanania Baer; Editor, Dan Perry; Music, Stephen Schwartz; Additional Music, Gerard Bernard Cohen; Choreography, Dennis Wayne; In color; Rated R; 89 minutes; February release. CAST: Richard Alfieri (Michael Durant/Dream Michael), Nathalie Nell (Christine), Ruth Roman (Michael's mother), Gale Sondergaard (Mrs. Edmunds), Mercedes McCambridge (Lillian Gerben), Mike Kellin (Sid Berman), John Spencer (Stephen), Barbara Monte-Britton (Dream Woman), Duncan Quinn (Dream Man), Leonard Crofoot (Danny), Paul Joynt (Ed), Julie Burger (Susan), Sheila Coonan (Rose), Robin Karfo (Sheila), Ron Asher, Barry Eric (Stage Managers), Leib Lensky (Backstage Doorman), Raaf Baldwin (Theatre Doorman), Damian Akhan (Damian), David M. Brezniak (Art Student), James Dunne (Dancer Backstage), Dennis Wayne (Christine's Partner), John Teitsort (Robert), Jan Winetsky (Girl in red dress), Joe Zaloom (Truck Driver)

THE ENTITY (20th Century-Fox) Producer, Harold Schneider; Director, Sidney J. Furie; Screenplay, Frank DeFelitta; Based on his novel; Executive Producers, Michael Leone, Andrew D. T. Pfeffer; Photography, Stephen H. Burum; Designer, Charles Rosen; Editor, Frank J. Urioste; Music, Charles Bernstein; Assistant Directors, Tommy Thompson, William Cosentino; In DeLuxe Color and Panavision; Rated R; 125 minutes; February release. CAST: Barbara Hershey (Carla Moran), Ron Silver (Phil), David Labiosa (Billy), George Coe (Weber), Margaret Blye (Cindy), Jacqueline Brookes (Dr. Cooley), Richard Brestoff (Gene), Michael Alldredge (George), Raymond Singer (Joe), Allan Rich (Dr. Walcott), Natasha Ryan (Julie), Melanie Gaffin (Kim), Alex Rocco (Jerry), Sussy Boyar (Reisz), Tom Stern (Woody), Curt Lowens (Dr. Wilkes), Paula Victor (Dr. Chevalier), Lee Wilkof (Dr. Hase), Deborah Stevenson, Mark Weiner (Interns), Lisa Gurley (Receptionist), Chris Howell (Guard), Renee Neimark (Nurse), John Branagan, Daniel Furie, Amy Kirkpatric, Todd Kutches (Students)

LOVESICK (Warner Bros.) Producer, Charles Okun; Direction and Screenplay, Marshall Brickman; Photography, Gerry Fisher; Designer, Philip Rosenberg; Costumes, Kristi Zea; Editor, Nina Feinberg; Music, Philippe Sarde; Assistant Directors, Thomas Reilly, Lewis Gould; A Ladd Company release in Technicolor; Rated PG; 96 minutes; February release. CAST: Dudley Moore (Saul Benjamin), Elizabeth McGovern (Chloe Allen), Alec Guinness (Sigmund Freud), Christine Baranski (Nymphomaniac), Gene Saks (Frantic), Renee Taylor (Mrs. Mondragon), Kent Broadhurst (Gay), Lester Rawlins (Silent Patient), Wallace Shawn (Jaffe), Suzanne Barrie (His Wife), Anne Kerry (Katie), Lotte Palfi Andor, Paul Andor, Anna Berger, Sol Frieder, Merwin Goldsmith, Fred Kareman, Mohindra Nath Kawlra, E. Katherine Kerr, Arthur Klein, Fred Melamed, Benjamin Rayson, Jonathan Reynolds, Stewart Steinberg (Analysts), Ron Silver (Ted), Ann Gillespie (Actress), John Tillinger (Director), Jeff Natter (Stage Manager), Peggy LeRoy Johnson (Actress), Larry Rivers (Applezweig), Richard B. Shull (Dr. Fessner), David Strathairn (Zuckerman), Yanni Sfinias (Vendor), Jack Sevier, Raynor Scheine (In shelter), Mark Blum (Intern), Isabelle Monk (Nurse), Anne DeSalvo (Interviewer), Ray Ramirez (Menendez), Ellen Whyte (Waitress), Armalie Collier (Maid), John Huston (Dr. Geller), Kaylan Pickford (Anna), Alan King (Dr. Gross), Selma Diamond (Dr. Singer), Stefan Schnabel (Dr. Bergsen), Otto Bettman (Dr. Waxman)

Dudley Moore, Elizabeth McGovern
in "Lovesick" © *The Ladd Co.*

Dudley Moore, Alec Guinness
in "Lovesick" © *The Ladd Co.*

Jimmy McNichol, Julia Duffy
in "Night Warning"

"Before the Nickelodeon"

NIGHT WARNING (ComWorld) Producer, Stephen Breimer; Director, William Asher; Screenplay, Stephen Breimer, Alan Jay Glueckman, Boom Collins; Story, Messrs Glueckman and Boom Collins; Co-Producer, Eugene Mazzola; Executive Producers, Dennis D. Hennessy, Richard Carrothers; Song, Joyce Bulifant; Assistant Directors, Don Yorkshire, James Charleston; Editor, Rebecca Navert; In C.F.I. Color; Rated R; 97 minutes; February release. CAST: Bo Svenson (Carlson), Jimmy McNichol (Billy), Susan Tyrrell (Cheryl), Marcia Lewis (Margie), Julia Duffy (Julie), Steve Easton (Coach), Caskey Swaim (Phil), Brett Leach (Sgt. Cook), Cooper Neal (Frank), William Paxton (Eddie), Kay Kimler (Ann), Gary Baxley (Bill, Sr.), Vickie Oleson (Police Officer), Clemente Anchondo (Arrestee), Alex Baker (Officer Wescott), Randy Norton (Tony), Kelly Kapp (Student), Steve DeFrance (Lab Man), Bill Keene (Announcer), Riley Morgan (Chuck).

THE HOUSE ON SORORITY ROW (Film Ventures International) Producers, Mark Rosman, John G. Clark; Direction and Screenplay, Mark Rosman; Executive Producers, John Ponchock, W. Thomas McMahon; Music, Richard H. Band; Presented by Edward L. Montoro and Artists Releasing Corporation; In color; Rated R; 91 minutes; February release. CAST: Kathryn McNeil, Eileen Davidson

BEFORE THE NICKELODEON (First Run Features) Executive Producer, Steve Brier; Director, Charles Musser; Screenplay, Warren D. Leight, Charles Musser; Photography, Rob Issen; Editor, Charles Musser; Not rated; 60 minutes; February release. CAST: Voices of Jay Leyda, Robert Skier, R ob Issen, Robert Rosen, Mitchell Kriegman, Peter Davis, D. A. Pennebaker, Milow Forman, Warren D. Leight, Rick King, Tony Potter, Louis Malle, Robert Altman, Jim Walton, Michael Peyser, Grahame Weinbren, Steve Brier, Blanche Sweet.

SECOND THOUGHTS (Universal) Producers, Lawrence Turman, David Foster; Director, Lawrence Turman; Screenplay, Steve Brown; Story, Steve Brown, Terry Louise Fisher; Photography, King Baggot; Editor, Neil Travis; Music, Henry Mancini; Design, Paul Peters, Robert Goldstein; Costumes, Julie Weiss; Assistant Director, Jerry Grandey; In Technicolor; Rated PG; 98 minutes; February release. CAST: Lucie Arnaz (Amy), Craig Wasson (Will),

Ken Howard (John), Anne Schedeen (Janis), Arthur Rosenberg (Dr. Eastman), Peggy McCay (Dr. Carpenter), Tammy Taylor (Sharon), Alan Stock (Hondo), James O'Connell (Chief Staab), Louis Giambalvo (Sgt. Cabrillo), Alex Kubik (Behncke), Charles Lampkin (Judge)

HOLLYWOOD OUT-TAKES & RARE FOOTAGE (Manhattan Movietime) Producer, Ronald Blackman; Compilation directed by Ronald Blackman, Bruce Goldstein; Editor, Doug Rossini; In black and white and color; Not rated; 81 minutes; March release. A compilation of footage from other films.

VALLEY GIRL (Atlantic) Produced and Written by Wayne Crawford, Andrew Lane; Director, Martha Coolidge; Executive Producers, Thomas Coleman, Michael Rosenblatt; Photography, Frederick Elmes; Editor, Eva Gordos; Design, Mary Delia Javier; Assistant Directors, Nancy Isral, Michael Hacker; In color; Rated R; 95 minutes; February release. CAST: Nicolas Cage (Randy), Deborah Foreman (Julie), Elizabeth Daily (Loryn), Michael Bowen (Tommy), Cameron Dye (Fred), Heidi Holicker (Stacey), Michelle Meyrink (Suzie), Tina Theberge (Samantha), Lee Purcell (Beth), Colleen Camp (Sarah), Frederic Forrest (Steve)

ONE MORE CHANCE (Cannon) Producer, David Womark; Executive Producers, Menahem Golan, Yoram Globus; Direction-Screenplay, Sam Firstenberg; Photography, Jonathan Braun; Editor, K. V. Hoenig; Art Director, Lourdes Guiang; Music, David Powell; In color; Not rated; 90 minutes; February release. CAST: John LaMotta, Michael Pataki, Logan Clarke, Kirstie Aley, Jefferson Wales, Marvin Flint

BABY, IT'S YOU (Paramount) Producers, Griffin Dunne, Amy Robinson; Direction and Screenplay, John Sayles; Based on story by Amy Robinson; Photography, Michael Ballhaus; Designer, Jeffrey Townsend; Editor, Sonya Polonsky; Associate Producer, Robert F. Colesberry; Costumes, Franne Lee; Assistant Directors, Raymond L. Greenfield, Ira Halberstadt; In Movielab Color; Rated R; 105 minutes; March release. CAST: Rosanna Arquette (Jill), Vincent Spano (Sheik), Joanna Merlin (Mrs. Rosen), Jack Davidson (Dr. Rosen), Nick Ferrari (Capadilupo), Dolores Messina (Mrs. Capadilupo), Leora Dana (Miss Vernon), William Joseph Raymond (Ripeppi), Sam McMurray (McManus), Liane Curtis (Jody),

"The House on Sorority Row"
© *Artists Releasing Corp.*

"One More Chance"

Vincent Spano, Rosanna Arquette
in "Baby, It's You" © *Paramount*

"Joy Sticks"

Claudia Sherman (Beth), Marta Kober (Debra), Tracy Pollan (Leslie), Rachel Dretzin (Shelly), Susan Derendorf (Chris), Frank Vincent (Vinnie), Robin Johnson (Joann), Gary McCleery (Rat), Matthew Modine (Steve), John Ferraro (Plasky), Phil Brock (Biff), Merel Poloway (Miss Katz), Don Kehr (Barry), Michael Knight (Philip), Robert Downey, Jr. (Stewart), Brian Wry (Georgie), Richard Kantor (Curtis), Stephanie Keyser (Laura), Julie Philips (Karen), Frank Anthony Zagarino (Lew), Art Halperin (Band Leader), Caroline Aaron (Waitress), Jonathan Gero (Jack), Fisher Stevens (Stage Manager), Robin Geller (Tripper), Susan Busset, Steven Reed, Stephen Donato (Prom Singers)

SPRING BREAK (Columbia) Producer-Director, Sean S. Cunningham; Screenplay, David Smilow; Photography, Stephen Poster; Executive Producers, Mitch Leigh, Milton Herson; Music, Harry Manfredini; Designer, Virginia Field; Associate Producer, Barbara DeFina; Editor, Susan Cunningham; Assistant Directors, Brian Frankish, Dustin Bernard; Art Director, Nicholas Romanac; Choreographer, Roger Minami; Costumes, Susan Denison, Sara Denning; In color; Rated R; 101 minutes; March release. CAST: David Knell (Nelson), Perry Lang (Adam), Paul Land (Stu), Steve Bassett (O.T.), Jayne Modean (Susie), Corinne Alphen (Joan), Donald Symington (Dalby), Mimi Cozzens (May Dalby), Jessica James (Geri), Richard B. Shull (Eddie), Daniel Faraldo (Eesh), John Archie, Robert Small (Henchmen), Fred Buch (Ames), Mark Pellicori (Biker), Bobbi Fritz, Rhonda Flynn (Girls in Corvette), Bert Sheldon (Detective), Alex Panas (Dope Dealer), Barry Hober (Man in elevator), Ronn Carroll (Arresting Officer), Roger Minami (Dancing Officer), Paul Lorenzo (Candy Store M.C.), John Terry (Button M.C.)

JOE'S BED-STUY BARBERSHOP: WE CUT HEADS (First Run Features) No credits submitted; Not rated; 60 minutes; March release. CAST: Monty Ross (Zachariah), Donna Bailey (Ruth), Stuart Smith (Teapot), Tommie Hicks (Nicholas), Horace Long (Joe), LeVerne Summer (Esquire), Africanus Rocius (Spinks), Robert Delbert (Fletcher), Alphonzo Lewis (Deacon), Christine Campbell (Hanna), William Badgett (Silas), Herbert Burks (True God), Vanita Taylor, Lynn Dummett (Jehovah's Witnesses), Loretta Craggett (Model), Curtis Brown (Photographer), Ahmad Carson (Squeeze), Carolyn Laws (Ms. Maxwell), Eric Wilkins (Man by elevator)

MY TUTOR (Crown International) Producer, Marilyn J. Tenser; Co-Producer, Michael D. Castle; Director, George Bowers; Screenplay, Joe Roberts; Editor, Sidney Wolinsky; Music, Webster Lewis; Assistant Directors, Steven Eshelman, Robin Jones; Art Director, Linda Pearl; Costumes, Kristin Nelson; Executive Producer, Mark Tenser; Original Story, Mark Tenser; A Marimark Production in DeLuxe Color; Rated R; 97 minutes; March release. CAST: Caren Kaye (Terry), Matt Lattanzi (Bobby), Kevin McCarthy (Chrystal), Clark Brandon (Billy), Bruce Bauer (Don), Arlene Golonka (Mrs. Chrystal), Crispin Glover (Jack), Amber Denyse Austin (Bonnie), John Vargas (Manuel), Maria Melendez (Maria), Graem McGavin (Sylvia), Rex Ryon (Biker), Kathleen Shea (Mud Wrestler), Brioni Farrel (Mrs. Fontana), Shelley Taylor Morgan (Louisa), Kitten Natividad (Ana Maria), Jewel Shepard (Girl in phone booth), Michael Yama (Russell), Robin Honeywell (SueAnn), Mora Gray (Ramona), Jim Kester (Parking Attendant), Derek Partridge (Waiter), Gene Patton (Workman), Eric Lantis (Weight Lifter), Lyle Kanouse (Biker), Marilyn Tokuda (Aerobics Instructor), Jacqueline Jacobs (Bootsie)

JOYSTICKS (Jensen Farley) Producer-Director, Greydon Clark; Screenplay, Al Gomez, Mickey Epps; Associate Producers, Curtis Burch, Daryl Kass, George W. Perkins; Music, John Caper, Jr.; Photography, Nicholas von Sternberg; Editor, Larry Bock; In color; Rated R; 88 minutes; March release. CAST: Joe Don Baker (Mr. Rutter), Leif Green (Eugene), Jim Greenleaf (Jonathan Andrew McDorfus), Scott McGinnis (Jefferson), Jonathan Gries (King), Corinne Bohrer (Patsy), John Diehl (Arnie), John Voldstad (Max), Reid Cruickshanks (Coach), Morgan Lofting (Mrs. Rutter), Kym Malin (Lola), Kim G. Michel (Alva), Jacqulin Cole (Alexis), Logan Ramsey (Mayor)

A TASTE OF SIN (Ambassador) Executive Producers, Gary Gillingham, Tim Nielsen, James Honore; Producer-Director, Ulli Lommel; Screenplay, Ulli Lommel, John P. Marsh, Ron Norman; Photography, Ulli Lommel, Jochen Breitenstein, Jon Kranhouse, Dave Sperling, Jorg Walther; Editor/Co-Producer/Assistant Director, Terrell Tannen; Music, Joel Goldsmith; In color; Rated R; 84 minutes; March release. CAST: Suzanna Love (Olivia), Robert Walker (Michael), Jeff Winchester (Richard), Bibbe Hansen (Mother), Amy Robinson (Olivia at 6), Nicholas Love (G.I.), Ulli Lommel (Detective)

Horace Long, Monty Ross
in "Joe's Bed-Stuy Barbershop"

Vincent Spano, Rosanna Arquette
in "Baby, It's You" © *Paramount*

Jason Robards, Marsha Mason, Matthew
Broderick in "Max Dugan Returns"
© 20th Century-Fox

Jeff Bridges, Belinda Bauer
in "Success"

MAX DUGAN RETURNS (20th Century-Fox) Producers, Neil Simon, Herbert Ross; Director, Herbert Ross; Screenplay, Neil Simon; Executive Producer, Roger M. Rothstein; Photography, David M. Walsh; Design, Albert Brenner; Editor, Richard Marks; Music, David Shire; Costumes, Bob Mackie; Assistant Directors, Jack Roe, Alan B. Curtiss; Art Director, David Haber; Set Designer, Kandy Stern; In DeLuxe Color; Rated PG; 98 minutes; March release. CAST: Marsha Mason (Nora), Jason Robards (Max Dugan), Donald Sutherland (Brian), Matthew Broderick (Michael), Dody Goodman (Mrs. Litke), Sal Viscuso (Coach), Panchito Gomez (Luis), Charley Lau (Himself), Mari Gorman (Pat), Brian Part (Kevin), Billie Bird (Older Woman), Tessa Richarde (Blonde in shoe store), James Staahl (Man in shoe store), Duke Stroud, Sondra Blake (Teachers), David Morse (Shoe Store Cop), Santos Morales (Grocer), Irene Olga Lopez (His Wife), Tom Rosales, Jr.(Robber), Tommy Fridley (Steve), Kiefer Sutherland (Bill), Bill Aylesworth (Chris), Lydia Nicole (Celia), Elisa Dolenko (Maria), Marc Jefferson (Wendall), Tom Spratley (Truck Washer), Ray Girardin (Umpire), Joey Coleman (3rd Baseman), Pop Attmore (Baseball Player), Grace Woodard (Maitre d'), Ken Neumeyer (Waiter), Robert D'Arcy (Cabbie), Shelley Morrison (Mother), Frank D'Annibale (Bear's Coach), John Corvello (Basketball Coach), Howard Himelstein (Shoe Store Cop), Carmen Silveroli, Sr. (Shoe Store Manager)

VIGILANTE (Film Ventures International) Original title "Street Gang"; Producers, Andrew Garroni, William Lustig; Director, William Lustig: Screenplay, Richard Vetere; Executive Producers, John Packard, Jerry Masacci, Kenneth Pavia; Photography, James Lemmo; Editor, Lorenzo Marinelli; Music, Jay Chattaway; Associate Producer, Randy Jurgensen; An Artists Releasing Corp. production; In color; Rated R; 90 minutes; March release. CAST: Robert Forster (Eddie), Fred Williamson (Nick), Richard Bright (Burke), Rutanya Alda (Vickie), Don Blakely (Prago), Joseph Carberry (Ramon), Willie Colon (Rico), Joe Spinell (Eisenberg), Carol Lynley (D.A. Fletcher), Woody Strode (Rake), Vincent Beck (Judge), Bo Rucker (Horace), Peter Savage (Mr. T)

THE HEADLESS EYES (J.E.R. Pictures) Executive Producers, Chandler Warren, David Bowman; Producer, Ronald Sullivan; Direction-Screenplay, Kent Bateman; Associate Producer, Bayard Stevens; In color; Rated R; 79 minutes; March release. CAST: Bo Brundin, Gordon Ramon, Kelley Swartz, Mary Jane Early

AXE (New American Films) Executive Producer, Irwin Friedlander; Producer, J. G. Patterson, Jr.; Direction-Screenplay, Frederick R. Friedel; Photography, Austin McKinney; Editors, Frederick Friedel, J. G. Patterson, Jr.; Music, George Newman Shaw, John Wilhelm; In color; Rated R; 67 minutes; March release. CAST: Leslie Lee (Lisa), Jack Canon (Steele), Ray Green (Lomax), Frederick R. Friedel (Billy), Douglas Powers (Grandfather), Frank Jones (Aubrey)

SUCCESS (Invisible Studies) Released previously as "American Success" and "American Success Company."

SAVAGE WEEKEND (Cannon) Executive Producer, John Mason Kirby; Producers, John Mason Kirby, David Paulsen; Direction-Screenplay, David Paulsen; Photography, Zoli Vidor; Editors, Zion Avrahamian, Jonathan Day; Music, Dov Seltzer; Assistant Director, Peter Kean; In Technicolor; Rated R; 83 minutes; March release. CAST: Christopher Allpert (Nicky), James Doerr (Robert), Marilyn Hamlin (Marie), Kathleen Heaney (Shirley), David Gale (Mac), Devin Goldenberg (Jay), Jeffrey David Pomerantz (Greg), William Sanderson (Otis)

EDDIE MACON'S RUN (Universal) Producer, Louis J. Stroller; Direction–Screenplay, Jeff Kanew; Based on book by James McLendon; Executive Producer, Peter Saphler; Photography, James A. Contner; Designer, Bill Kenney; Music, Norton Buffalo; Assistant Directors, Michael R. Haley, Ellen Rauch; Editor, Jeff Kanew; In Technicolor; Rated PG; 95 minutes; April release. CAST: Kirk Douglas (Marzack), John Schneider (Eddie), Lee Purcell (Jilly), Leah Ayres (Chris), Lisa Dunsheath (Kay), Ton Noonan (Daryl), J. C. Quinn (Shorter), Gil Rogers (Logan), Jay O. Sanders (Rudy), Dan Anglin (Weigh Station), Nesbitt Blaisdell (Sheriff), Susan Bongard (Newscaster), Matthew Cowles (Ray), Bill DeWeese (Officer), Kenneth Allan Edgar, Vic Polizos (Desk Clerks), Dann Florek, J. T. Walsh (Men in bar), Buddy Gilbert (Tucker), John Goodman (Hebert), Jim Gough (Judge), Nik Hagler (Partner), Lou Hancock (Woman), Loyd David Hart (Bartender), Ron Jackson (Police Partner), Matthew Kimbrough (Charlie), Billy Lynch (Announcer), Jerry McKnight (Billy Bob), Mark Margolis (Bar Owner), John L. Martin (Homer), Glenn H. Matthews, Matthew Meece, Ricardo Montemayor, Harry Murphy, Donald B. Nunley, Cynthia Piton, Gilbert Rendon, Brick Tripp, Woody Watson, Fernando E. Guttierrez, Javier A. Gutierrez

Robert Forster, Fred Williamson
in "Vigilante"

John Schneider, Kirk Douglas
in "Eddie Macon's Run"
© Universal City Studios

"Evil Dead"
© *Renaissance Pictures Ltd.*

Raphael Sbarge, Richard Ryder
in "Abuse"

THE EVIL DEAD (New Line Cinema) Executive Producers, Robert G. Tapert, Bruce Campbell, Samuel M. Raimi; Producer, Robert G. Tapert; Direction and Screenplay, Samuel M. Raimi; Editor, Edna Ruth Paul; Music, Joe LoDuca; Photography, Tim Philo, Joshua M. Becker; Assistant Producer, George Holt; In color; Not rated; 90 minutes; April release. CAST: Bruce Campbell (Ash), Ellen Sandweiss (Cheryl), Betsy Baker (Linda), Hal Delrich (Scott), Sarah York (Shelly)

1990: THE BRONX WARRIORS (UFD) Producer, Fabrizio DeAngelis; Director, Enzo G. Castellari; Screenplay, Dardano Sacchetti, Elisa Livia Briganti, Enzo G. Castellari; Story, Dardano Sacchetti; Photography, Sergio Salvati; Design and Costumes, Massimo Lentini; Editor, Gianfranco Amicucci; Music, Walter Rizzati; In color; Rated R; 86 minutes; April release. CAST: Vic Morrow (Hammer), Christopher Connelly (Hot Dog), Fred Williamson (Ogre), Mark Gregory (Trash), Stefania Girolami (Anne), John Sinclair (Ice), Enio Girolami, Betty Dessy, Rocco Lerro, Massimo Vanni, Angelo Ragusa, Enzo Girolami

ABUSE (Cinevista) Executive Producer, Frederick R. Schminke; Director-Writer-Editor, Arthur J. Bressan, Jr.; Music, Shawn Phillips; Photography, Douglas Dickinson, Carl Teitelbaum, Gary Farley; In black and white; Not rated; 94 minutes; April release. CAST: Richard Ryder (Larry), Raphael Sbarge (Thomas Carroll), Steve W. James (Dr. Bennett), Kathy Garber (Kathy), Jack Halton (Prof. Rappaport), Mickey Clark (Laura), Maurice Massaro (Mr. Carroll), Susan Schneider (Mrs. Carroll), Luba Gregus (Sara), Kathy Giotta (Elaine), Tracy Vivat (Amy), Aron (Billy), Paul Peterson (David), David Schachter (Mark), Jean Garrett (Dean), Pam Poitier (Samantha), Jeff Olmsted (Richard), Jim O'Connor (Frankie), Carol Siskind (Telephone Operator), Ralph Penner (Gym Teacher), Max Schmid (Engineer), Keith Michl (Detective), Dennis Baines (Waiter), J. J. Davis (Woman in restaurant), John Kartovsky (Man in restaurant), Murray Rosenthal (Man in rest room), Jennifer Begansky (Shelter Switchboard)

LONE WOLF McQUADE (Orion) Producers, Yoram Ben-Ami, Steve Carver; Director, Steve Carver; Screenplay, B. J. Nelson; Story, H. Kaye Dyal, B. J. Nelson; Photography, Roger Shearman; Editor, Anthony Redman; Music, Francesco DeMasi; In color; Rated PG; 107 minutes; April release. CAST: Chuck Norris (J. J. McQuade), David Carradine (Rawley Wilkes), Barbara Carrera

(Lola), Leon Isaac Kennedy (Jackson), Robert Beltran (Kayo), L. Q. Jones (Dakota), Dana Kimmell (Sally), R. G. Armstrong (Tyler), Jorge Cervera, Jr. (Jefe), Sharon Farrell (Molly), Daniel Frishman (Falcon), William Sanderson (Snow), John Anderson (Burnside)

FEELIN' UP (Troma) Producer, Joseph Asaro; Direction and Screenplay, David Secter; Music, Tony Camillo; A Total Impact production in Movielab Color; Rated R; 85 minutes; April release. CAST: Malcolm Groome, Kathleen Seward, Rhonda Hansome, Tony Collado, Charles Douglass, Helga Kopperl

DUEL (Universal) Producer, George Eckstein; Director, Steven Spielberg; Screenplay, Richard Matheson from his story; Music, Billy Goldenberg; Photography, Jack A. Marta; Art Director, Robert S. Smith; Editor, Frank Morriss; Assistant Director, Jim Fargo; In color; Rated PG; 90 minutes; April release. CAST: Dennis Weaver (David Mann), Eddie Firestone (Cafe Owner), Gene Dynarski (Man in cafe), Tim Herbert (Gas Station Attendant), Charles Seel (Old Man), Alexander Lockwood (Old Man in car), Amy Douglass (Old Woman in car), Shirley O'Hara (Waitress), Lucille Benson (Lady at Snakerama), Cary Loftin (Truck Driver), Dale Van Sickle (Car Driver)

EXPOSED (MGM/UA) Produced, Directed and Written by James Toback; Executive Producer, Serge Silberman; Photography, Henri Decae; Designer, Brian Eatwell; Editor, Robert Lawrence; Music, Georges Delerue; Associate Producer, Brian Hamill; Assistant Directors, William Hassell, Bill Eustace; In Metrocolor; Rated R; 100 minutes; April release. CAST: Nastassja Kinski (Elizabeth), Rudolf Nureyev (Daniel), Harvey Keitel (Rivas), Ian McShane (Greg), Bibi Andersson (Margaret), Ron Randell (Curt), Pierre Clementi (Vic), Dov Gottesfeld (Marcel), James Russo (Nick), Marion Varella (Bridgit), Murray Moston (Hotel Manager), Stephanie Farrow (Waitress), Daisy Carrington (Daisy), Carl Lee (Duke), Mariana Magnasco (Maya), Miguel Pinero, Jeff Silverman, Ray Sawhill, Michel Delahaye (Men in street), Brian Hamill (Store Manager), Tony Sirico, Jr. (Thief), Geoffrey Carey, Dennis McGovern (Waiters), Patrick Baker (Skip), Emil Tchakarov (Conductor), Madeleine DeBlonay (Katia), Jacques Preyer, Vincent Lascoumes (French Cabbies), Jurgen Straub (Hans), Irving Buchman (Makeup Man), Anthony Cortino (Hairdresser), Marcela Moore (Hostess), James Toback (Leo Boscovitch)

Chuck Norris, Barbara Carrera, David
Carradine in "Lone Wolf McQuade"
© *Orion Pictures*

Rudolf Nureyev, Nastassja Kinski
in "Exposed" © *United Artists*

105

James Victor, Shelley Long
in "Losin' It" © *Embassy*

LOSIN' IT (Embassy) Producers, Bryan Gindoff, Hannah Hempstead; Director, Curtis Hanson; Story, B. W. L. Norton, Bryan Gindoff; Screenplay, B. W. L. Norton; Executive Producers, Joel B. Michaels, Garth H. Drabinsky; Photography, Gil Taylor; Editor, Richard Halsey; Music, Ken Wannberg; Designer, Robb Wilson King; Assistant Directors, Patrick Crowley, Dan Lupovitz; Art Director, Vance Lorenzini; Title Song, J. Alan, T. Shenale; Performed by Jeff Alan Band; In Deluxe Color; Rated R; 98 minutes; April release. CAST: Tom Cruise (Woody), Jackie Earle Haley (Dave), John Stockwell (Spider), Shelley Long (Kathy), John P. Navin, Jr. (Wendell), Henry Darrow (El Jefe), James Victor (Lawyer), Hector Elias (Chuey), Daniel Faraldo, Enrique Castillo (Cab Drivers), Mario Marcelino (Pablo), Rick Rossovitch (Marine), Kale Browne (Larry), John Valby (M.C.), Cornelio Hernandez, Hector Morales, Santos Morales, Laura James, Rita Rogers, Victoria Wells, Irma Garcia, Sosimo Hernandez, Jesse Aragon, Margarita Garcia, Joe Spinell, Susan Saldivar, Bell Hernandez, Rick Powell, Dean R. Miller, Jack M. Nietzsche, Jr., Timothy Brown, Amando Ogaz, Steve Gonzales

LIQUID SKY (Cinevista) Executive Producer, Robert Field; Associate Producer, Nina V. Kerova; Producer-Director, Slava Tsukerman; Screenplay, Slava Tsukerman, Anne Carlisle, Nina V. Kerova; Photography, Yuri Neyman; Production and Costume Design, Marina Levikova; Editor, Sharyn Leslie Ross; Music, Slava Tsukerman, Clive Smith; Lyrics, Slava Tsukerman; In color; Rated R; 112 minutes; April release. CAST: Anne Carlisle (Margaret/Jimmy), Paula E. Sheppard (Adrian), Susan Doukas (Sylvia), Otto von Wernherr (Johann), Bob Brady (Owen), Elaine C. Grove (Katherine), Stanley Knap (Paul), Jack Adalist (Vincent), Lloyd Ziff (Lester), Harry Lum (Deliveryman), Roy MacArthur (Jack), Sara Carlisle (Nellie), Nina V. Kerova (Designer), Alan Preston (Photographer), Christine Hatfull (Hairstylist), Calvin Haugen (Makeup Artist), Deborah Jacobs, Inansi, Tom Cote, Michael Drechsler, Jose Preval, David Ilku, Neke Carson, Jenifer, Chang, Vincent Pandoliano, Benjamin Liu, Angelo, Lucille, Jerre Edmunds, Marcel Fieve, Mariann Marlow, Perry Iannaconi, Rodger Martencen

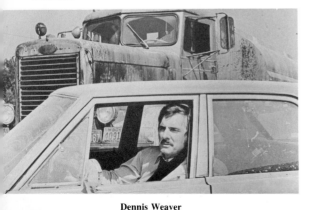

Dennis Weaver
in "Duel" © *Universal City Studios*

LOVE LETTERS (New World) also released as "My Love Letters"; Executive Producers, Mel Pearl, Don Levin; Producer, Roger Corman; Direction-Screenplay, Amy Jones; Associate Producer, Charles Skouras III; Photography, Alec Hirschfeld; Music, Ralph Jones; Editor, Wendy Greene; Art Director, Jeannine Oppewall; In color; Rated R; 98 minutes; April release. CAST: Jamie Lee Curtis (Anna), James Keach (Oliver), Amy Madigan (Wendy), Bud Cort (Danny), Matt Clark (Winter), Bonnie Bartlett (Mrs. Winter), Phil Coccioletti (Ralph), Shelby Leverington (Edith), Rance Howard (Chesley), Betsy Toll (Marcia), Sally Kirkland (Sally)

GEEK MAGGOT BINGO (Weirdo Films) Executive Producer, Donna Death; Producer-Director-Screenplay, Nick Zedd; Story, Robert Kirkpatrick, Nick Zedd; Photography-Editing-Design, Nick Zedd; In color; Not rated; 73 minutes; April release. CAST: Robert Andrews (Dr. Frankenberry), Brenda Bergman (Buffy), Richard Hell (Rawhide), Donna Death (Scumbalina), Zacherle (Host), Bruno Zeus (Geeko), Gumby Sangler (Flavian), Jim Giacama (Dean), Robert Martin (Street Hawker), Bob Elkin (Victim)

THE MGM THREE STOOGES FESTIVAL (United Artists Classics) Directed by Jack Cummings; In color/black and white; Not rated; 95 minutes; April release. A compilation of MGM productions.

THE DEADLY SPAWN (21st Century) Producer, Ted Bohus; Direction-Screenplay, Douglas McKeown; Story by McKeown, Bohus, John Dods; Additional Dialogue, Tim Sullivan; Photography, Harvey Birnbaum; Music, Michael Perilstein, Ken Walker, Paul Cornell; Special Effects-Associate Producer, John Dods; In color; Rated R; 78 minutes; April release. CAST: Charles George Hildebrandt (Charles), Tom DeFranco (Tom), Richard Lee Porter (Frankie), Jean Tafler (Ellen), Karen Tighe (Kathy), Ethel Michelson (Aunt Millie), John Schmerling (Uncle Herb), James Brewster (Sam), Elissa Neil (Barbara)

MODERN DAY HOUDINI (Mid America Promotions) Producers, Ron Hostetler, Eddie Beverly, Jr.; Executive Producer, Bill Shirk; Director, Eddie Beverly, Jr.; Screenplay, Steven Meyers; Photography, Steve Posey; Editor, Ron Hostetler; Music, Jeffrey Boze; In color; Rated PG; 90 minutes; April release. CAST: Bill Shirk (Shirk), Milbourne Christopher (Weiss), Peter Lupus (Sharky), Dick the Bruiser (The Bruiser), Gary Todd (Doug), Terry Mann (Polly), Cynthia Johns (Stormy), Elizabeth Bechtel (Sylvia), Sam Graves (Mike), Robert James Poorman, Jr. (Hardin), Dave Dugan (Butch), Larry Battson (Bubba)

REVENGE SQUAD (ComWorld) Executive Producers, Mitchell Cannold, Andy Meyer; Producer-Director, Chuck Braverman; Screenplay, Don Enright; Based on novel "$80 to Stamford" by Lucille Fletcher; Music, Brad Fiedel; In color; rated PG; April release. CAST: Paul Perri, Claudia Cron, Will Lee

DOCTOR DETROIT (Universal) Producer, Robert K. Weiss; Executive Producer, Bernie Brillstein; Director, Michael Pressman; Screenplay, Carl Gottlieb, Robert Boris, Bruce Jay Friedman; Story, Bruce Jay Friedman; Associate Producer, Peter V. Herald; Photography, King Baggot; Design, Lawrence G. Paull; Editor, Christopher Greenbury; Music, Lalo Schifrin; Title Song, Devo; Assistant Directors, Gary Daigler, Deborah A. Dell'Amico; Costumes, Betsy Cox; Choreographer, Carlton Johnson; Original soundtrack on Backstreet Records and tapes; In Technicolor; Rated R; 91 minutes; May release. CAST: Dan Aykroyd (Clifford Skridlow), Howard Hesseman (Smooth Walker), Donna Dixon (Monica), Lydia Lei (Jasmine), T. K. Carter (Diavolo), Lynn Whitfield (Thelma), Franc Drescher (Karen), Kate Murtagh (Mom), George Furth (Arthur), Nan Martin (Margaret), Andrew Duggan (Harmon), Glenne Headly (Miss Debbylike), Robert Cornthwaite (Prof. Blount), Parley Baer (Judge), John A. Moloney (Commodore), Pershing P. Anderson (Stretch), William Munchow (Prof. Ariel), Edward Meekin (Prof. Durant), Hank Salas (Johnny), Rudolf Kovar (Carson), Peter Elbling, Peter Aykroyd, Annabel Armour, Thomas Erhart Jr., Oliver Clark, Ben Kronen, Linace Kinsey, Lynda Aldon, Carla Barbour, Sue Bowser, Tamara Clarrett, Deidre Cowden, Deborah Koppel, Deanna Joy, Toni Naples, Roni Michelle, Laurie Senit, Robert Swan, Frank G. Rice, Michael Hagerty, Eugene Pressman, Victoria Brown, Ben Frommer, John Kapelos, James Spinks, James

Anne Carlisle in dual roles
in "Liquid Sky" © Z-Films

Stan Shaw, Warren Oates, Dennis Quaid
in "Tough Enough"
© Pelleport Investors

Brown, Clyde Barrett, Brad Barrios, Derrick Brice, Patricia Ann Douglas, Sonja Haney, Bruce Heath, Carlton Johnson, Ercelle Johnson, Keny Long, Sioux Marcelli, Ade Small, Dona Davis-Steckling, Blackie Dammett, Vincent J. Isaac, Steven Williams, Cheryl Carter, Diane Robin, Manny Weltman

SCREWBALLS (New World) Producer, Maurice Smith; Director, Rafal Zielinski; Screenplay, Linda Shayne, Jim Wynorski; Photography, Miklos Lente; Editor, Brian Ravok; Music, Tim McCauley; In color; Rated R; 80 minutes; May release. CAST: Peter Keleghan (Rick), Linda Shayne (Bootsie), Alan Daveau (Howie), Kent Deuters (Brent), Jason Warren (Melvin), Lynda Speciale (Purity)

ALL BY MYSELF (Blackwood) Produced, Directed and Photographed by Christian Blackwood; Editor, Susan Ardo Berger; Associate Producer, David Schmerler; Not rated; 85 minutes; May release. A documentary profile of singer-actress Eartha Kitt

REACHING OUT (Par Films) Produced, Directed and Written by Patricia Russell; Photography, David Sperling; Editor Jim McCreading; Music, Elizabeth Swados; In color; Rated R; 90 minutes; May release. CAST: Toni Craig (John), Frank McCarthy (Frank), Betty Andrews (Mrs. Stuart), Douglas Stark (Mr. Stuart), Pat Russell (Pat), Tyre Alls (Florence), Ralph Carlson (Agent), Marketa Kimbrel (Acting Teacher), Victor Truro (Psychiatrist), Ron Max (Drunk), Mary Milne (Girl with apartment), Ric Wynn (Waiter)

BILL COSBY . . . HIMSELF (20th Century-Fox Classics) Direction and Written by Bill Cosby; Photography, Joseph M. Wilcots; Editors, Ken Johnson, Steve Livingston; Produced by Jemmin Inc.; In color; Rated PG; 105 minutes; May release. A concert film recording highlights of four performances given by Bill Cosby.

CHICKEN RANCH (First Run Features) Producer, Nick Broomfield; Directors, Nick Broomfield, Sandi Sissel; Photography, Sandi Sissel; Editor, Julian Ware; In color; Not rated; 84 minutes; May release. CAST: People of the Chicken Ranch, a legalized brothel in Nevada.

THE GORDIMER STORIES (TeleCulture) "Country Lovers" with screenplay by Nadine Gordimer and directed by Manie Van Rensburg; "Six Feet of Country" with screenplay by Barney Simon and directed by Lynton Stephenson; "Nadine Gordimer Interview" with Joachim Braun as narrator; Not rated; 110 minutes; May release; No other credits available.

TOUGH ENOUGH (20th Century-Fox) Producer, William F. Gilmore; Director, Richard O. Fleischer; Screenplay, John Leone; Executive Producers, Michael Leone, Andrew D. T. Pfeffer; Music, Michael Lloyd, Steve Wax; Photography, James A. Contner; Design, Bill Kenney; Editor, Dann Cahn; Assistant Directors, Peter Bogart, Richard Graves; Associate Producer, Mark Fleischer; Costumes, Clifford Capone; In Technicolor; Rated PG; 107 minutes; May release. CAST: Dennis Quaid (Art), Carlene Watkins (Caroline), Stan Shaw (P.T.), Pam Grier (Myra), Warren Oates (James), Bruce McGill (Tony), Wilford Brimley (Bill), Fran Ryan (Gert), Christopher Norris (Christopher), Terra Perry (Wet T-Shirt Girl), Big John Hamilton (Big John), Steve Ward, Susann Benn, Mark Edson, Steve "Monk" Miller, Jimmy Nickerson, Rod Kieschnick, Preston Salisbury, Darryl Poafpybitty, Tino Zaragoza, Pat Reilly, John Hyden, Charles Griffin, Cindy Judy, Susanne Hasty, Kathy Lynch, Cloryce Miller, Ernest Lee Smith, Eli Cummins, Murray Sutherland, Tody Smith, Bennie Moore, Doug Lord, Bob Watson, Jackie Kallen, Michael Brown, Darlene O'Hara, Domenico Seminara, John McKee

SPACEHUNTER: ADVENTURES IN THE FORBIDDEN ZONE (Columbia) Producers, Don Carmody, Andre Link, John Dunning; Associate Producer, Stewart Harding; Executive Producer, Ivan Reitman; Screenplay, Edith Rey, David Preston, Dan Goldberg, Len Blum; Story, Stewart Harding, Jean Lafleur; Music, Elmer Bernstein; Photography, Frank Tidy; Designer, Jackson DeGovia; Editor, Scott Conrad; Special Makeup, Thomas R. Burman; Costumes, Julie Weiss; Assistant Directors, Tony Lucibello, Elizabeth Halko, Erika Zborowsky; Art Directors, John R. Jenson, Brent Swift, Michael Nemirsky; Art Director, Michael Minor; In Metrocolor and Dolby Stereo; Rated PG; 90 minutes; May release. CAST: Peter Strauss (Wolff), Molly Ringwald (Niki), Ernie Hudson (Washington), Andrea Marcovicci (Chalmers), Michael Ironside (Overdog), Beeson Carroll (Grandman Patterson), Hrant Alianak (Chemist), Deborah Pratt (Meagan), Aleisa Shirley (Reena), Cali Timmins (Nova), Paul Boretski (Jarrett), Patrick Rowe (Duster), Reggie Bennett (Barracuda Leader)

Nan Martin, George Furth, Dan Aykroyd
in "Doctor Detroit"
© Universal City Studios

Peter Strauss, Molly Ringwald in "Spacehunter:
Adventures in the Forbidden Zone"
© Columbia Pictures

107

Tommy Chong, Mariette Bout, Cheech Marin
in "Still Smokin' " © *Cheeck and Chong's
Film Festival*

Lewis Smith, Darryl Hannah
in "The Final Terror" © *ComWorld*

STILL SMOKIN' (Paramount) Producer, Peter MacGregor-Scott; Director, Thomas Chong; Screenplay, Thomas Chong, Cheech Marin; Photography, Harvey Harrison; Editor, David Ramirez, James Coblentz; Music, George S. Clinton; In color; Rated R; 91 minutes; May release. CAST: Cheech Marin (Cheech), Tommy Chong (Chong), Hans Van IntVeld (Promoter), Carol VanHerwilen (Hotel Manager), Shireen Strooker (Assistant Manager), Susan Hahn (Maid), Arjan Ederveen, Kees Prins (Bellboys), Mariette Bout (Waitress), Fabiola (Barge Lady), Carla Van Amstel (Queen Beatrix)

THE GOLDEN SEAL (Samuel Goldwyn) Producer, Samuel Goldwyn, Jr.; Director, Frank Zuniga; Screenplay, John Groves; Associate Producer, Russell Thacher; Assistant Director, Joe Canutt; Photography, Eric Saarinen; Based on novel "A River Ran Out of Eden" by James Vance Marshall; Music, Dana Kaproff; Designer, Douglas Higgins; Editor, Robert Q. Lovett; In color; Rated PG; 95 minutes; May release. CAST: Steve Railsback (Jim), Michael Beck (Crawford), Penelope Milford (Tania), Torquil Campbell (Eric), Seth Sekai (Semeyon), Richard Narita (Alexei), Sandra Seacat (Gladys), Peter Anderson (Tom), Terence Kelly (Mongo), Tom Heaton (Stutterer)

CHAINED HEAT (Jensen Farley) Executive Producers, Ernst Von Theumer, Lou Paciocco; Producer, Billy Fine; Associate Producer, Gerhard Scheurich; Director, Paul Nicolas; Screenplay, Vincent Mongol, Paul Nicolas; Photography, Mac Ahlberg; In color; Rated R; 95 minutes; May release. CAST: Linda Blair (Carol), John Vernon (Warden Backman), Sybil Danning (Ericka), Tamara Dobson (Dutchess), Stella Stevens (Capt. Taylor), Sharon Hughes (Val), Henry Silva (Lester), Edy Williams, Nita Talbot, Michael Callan, Louisa Moritz

THE GORE GORE GIRLS (New American) Director, Hershel Gordon Lewis; In color; May release. CAST: Frank Kress, Heda Lubin, Henny Youngman

MAUSOLEUM (Motion Picture Marketing) Producers, Robert Barich, Robert Madero; Executive Producers, Jerry Zimmerman, Michael Franzese; Director, Michael Dugan; Screenplay, Robert Barich, Robert Madero from an original screenplay and story by Katherine Rosenwink; Photography, Robert Barich; Editor, Richard C. Bock; Music, Jaime Mendoza-Nava; Assistant Director,

Charles Norton; Art Director, Robert Burns; Special Effects, Roter George; In color; Rated R; 96 minutes; May release. CAST: Marjoe Gortner (Oliver), Bobbie Bresee (Susan), Norman Burton (Dr. Andrews), Maurice Sherbanee (Ben), Laura Hippe (Aunt Cora), LaWanda Page (Elsie), Sheri Mann (Dr. Logan), Julie Christy Murray (Susan at 10)

THE FINAL TERROR (ComWorld) Executive Producer, Samuel Z. Arkoff; Producer, Joe Roth; Director, Andrew Davis; Screenplay, Ronald Shusett; Assistant Directors, Luca Kouimelis, Anthony J. Ridio; Editors, Paul Rubell, Erica Flaum, Hannah Washonig; Art Director, Aleka Corwin; Photography, Randy Robinson; Costumes, Sue Miller; In color; May release. CAST: John Friedrich (Zorich), Rachel Ward (Margaret), Adrian Zmed (Cerone), Darryl Hannah (Windy), Joe Pantoliano (Eggar), Ernest Harden, Jr. (Hines), Mark Metcalf (Mike), Lewis Smith (Boone), Cindy Harrell (Melanie), Akosua Busia (Vanessa), Irene Sanders (Sammie), Richard Jacobs (Morgan), Donna Pinder (Mrs. Morgan)

PORKY'S II: THE NEXT DAY (20th Century-Fox) Producers, Don Carmody, Bob Clark; Director, Bob Clark; Screenplay, Roger E. Swaybill, Alan Ormsby, Bob Clark; Executive Producers, Melvin Simon, Harold Greenberg, Alan Landsburg; Photography, Reginald H. Morris; Art Director, Fred Price; Editor, Stan Cole; Music, Carl Zittrer; Costumes, Mary E. McLeod; Associate Producers, Gary Goch, Ken Heeley-Ray; Assistant Directors, Ken Goch, Don Moody, Udanne Uditis; In DeLuxe Color; Rated R; 97 minutes; June release. CAST: Dan Monahan (PeeWee), Wyatt Knight (Tommy), Mark Herrier (Billy), Roger Wilson (Mickey), Cyril O'Reilly (Tim), Tony Ganios (Meat), Kaki Hunter (Wendy), Scott Colomby (Brian), Nancy Parsons (Balbricker), Joseph Running Fox (John Henry), Eric Christmas (Carter), Bill Wiley (Rev. Flavel), Edward Winter (Gebhardt), Cisse Cameron (Sandy), Else Earl (Mrs. Morris), Art Hindle (Ted), Anthony Penya (Bill), Rod Ball (Steve), Russell Bates (Mike), Jack Mulcahy (Frank), Chuck Wahl (Stemrick), Pete Conrad, Tom Tully, William Fuller, Will Knickerbocker, Mal Jones, Richard Liberty, Fred Buch, Brian Smith, Melanie Grefe, William Hindman, Bill Wohrman, Joe Friedman, Blaine Grose, Baby Jane, Joel Goss, Rooney Kerwin, Robin Paradise, Roger Swaybill, Howard Neu, Daniel Fitzgerald, Tracy Durphy, Carlo Fittanto, Francine Joyce, Wendy Becker, Adrienne Hampton, Madeline Kern, Betty Mae Jumper, Vernon Tiger, Mark Madrid

Linda Blair (R)
in "Chained Heat" © *Jensen Farley*

Nancy Parsons, Rod Ball, Wyatt Knight,
Tony Ganios, Mark Herrier, Roger Wilson,
Jack Mulcahy in "Porky's II" © *Simon Films*

Anthony Perkins
in "Psycho II"
© Universal City Studios

Ned Beatty, Burt Reynolds, Loni Anderson,
Jim Nabors in "Stroker Ace"
© Universal Studios/Warner Bros.

PSYCHO II (Universal-Oak) Producer, Hilton A. Green; Director, Richard Franklin; Screenplay, Tom Holland; Executive Producer, Bernard Schwartz; Photography, Dean Cundey; Designer, John W. Corso; Editor, Andrew London; Music, Jerry Goldsmith; Assistant Directors, Don Zepfel, Lisa Marmon; Based on characters created by Robert Bloch; Original soundtrack album on MCA Records; In Dolby Stereo and Technicolor; Rated R; 115 minutes; June release. CAST: Anthony Perkins (Norman Bates), Vera Miles (Lila), Meg Tilly (Mary), Robert Loggia (Dr. Raymond), Dennis Franz (Toomey), Hugh Gillin (Sheriff), Claudia Bryar (Mrs. Spool), Robert Alan Browne (Statler), Ben Hartigan (Judge), Lee Garlington (Myrna), Tim Maier (Josh), Jill Carroll (Kim), Chris Hendrie (Deputy Pool), Tom Holland (Deputy Norris), Michael Lomazow (D.A.), Robert Destri (Public Defender), Osgood Perkins (Young Norman), Ben Frommer (Sexton), Gene Whittington (Diver), Robert Traynor (Desk Clerk), George Dickerson (County Sheriff), Thaddeus Smith (Deputy Sheriff), Sheila K. Adams (Deputy Woman), Victoria Brown (Deputy Clerk)

STROKER ACE (Universal/Warner Bros.) Producer, Hank Moonjean; Director, Hal Needham; Screenplay, Hugh Wilson, Hal Needham; Based on novel "Stand On It" by William Neely, Robert K. Ottum; Photography, Nick McLean; Art Director, Paul Peters; Editors, Carl Kress, William Gordean; Music, Al Capps; Costumes, Norman Salling; Assistant Directors, Tom Connors, James Van Wyck, Jan DeWitt; Associate Producer, Kathy Shea; Soundtrack available on MCA Records; In Technicolor; Rated PG; 96 minutes; June release. CAST: Burt Reynolds (Stroker), Ned Beatty (Clyde), Jim Nabors (Lugs), Parker Stevenson (Aubrey), Loni Anderson (Pembrook), John Byner (Doc Seegle), Frank O. Hill (Dad Seegle), Cassandra Peterson (Girl with lugs), Bubba Smith (Arnold), Warren Stevens (Jim), Alfie Wise (Charlie), Jim Lewis (Chrew Chief), Jonathan Williams, Donna Fowler, Hunter Bruce, Cary Guffey, Victor Langdon, Phil Mattingly, Linda Vaughn, Debbie Casperson, Valerie Mitchell, Madonna Christian, Terri Ann Bantle, B. J. France, Chip Kaye

PRIVATE SCHOOL (Universal) Producers, R. Ben Efraim, Don Enright; Director, Noel Black, Screenplay, Dan Greenburg, Suzanne O'Malley; Editor, Fred Chulack; Photography, Walter Lasally; Designer, Ivo Cristante; Assistant Directors, Ric Rondell, Stephen Lofaro, L. Dean Jones, Jr.; Assistant Producer, Lane Maloney; Choreography, Paula Abdul; In Metrocolor; Rated R; 97 minutes; June release. CAST: Phoebe Cates (Christine), Betsy Russell (Jordan), Matthew Modine (Jim), Michael Zorek (Bubba), Fran Ryan (Miss Dutchbok), Kathleen Wilhoite (Betsy), Ray Walston (Chauncey), Sylvia Kristel (Ms. Copuletta), Jonathan Prince (Roy), Kari Lizer (Rita), Richard Stahl (Flugel), Julie Payne (Coach Whelan), Frank Aletter (Leigh-Jensen), Frances Bay (Birdie), Bill Wray (Bandleader), Karen Chase (Bambi), Burke Byrnes (Ramsay), Zale Kessler (Desk Clerk), Steve Levitt (Bellboy), Robert Ackerman (Maitre d'), Gayle Goldin (Arcade Voice), Lynda Wiesmeier, Christy Curtis, Nadine Van Der Velde, Lori Plager, Joni Lynn Ward, Chris McDermott, Zetta Whitlow, Vernon Scott, Douglas Warhit, Randy Chance Graham, Robert Parker.

A TIME TO DIE (Almi) Formerly "Seven Graves for Rogan"; Producer, Charles Lee; Director, Matt Cimber; Screenplay, John Goff, Matt Cimber, William Russell; Story, Mario Puzo; Music, Robert O. Ragland, Ennio Morricone; Photography, Eddy van der Enden, Tom Denove; Editors, Byron Brandt, Fred Chulack; Assistant Director, Peter Carpenter; Art Directors, Frank Rosen, John Thompson; In CFI Color; Rated R; 91 minutes; June release. CAST: Edward Albert, Jr. (Michael Rogan), Rod Taylor (Bailey), Rex Harrison (Von Osten), Linn Stokke (Dora), Raf Vallone (Genco Bari), Cor Van Rijn (Vrost), Lucie Visser (Mrs. Rogan)

THE SURVIVORS (Columbia) Producer, William Sackheim; Director, Michael Ritchie; Screenplay, Michael Leeson; Photography, Billy Williams; Designer, Gene Callahan; Editor, Richard A. Harris; Costumes, Ann Roth; Music, Paul Chihara; Executive Producer, Howard Pine; Assistant Directors, Tom Mack, Joseph Reidy, Bill M. Elvin, Louis Race, Peter Norman; Art Director, Jay Moore; A Rastar production in Metrocolor; Rated R; 102 minutes; June release. CAST: Walter Matthau (Sonny Paluso), Robin Williams (Donald Quinelle), Jerry Reed (Jack), James Wainwright (Wes), Kristen Vigard (Candice), Annie McEnroe (Doreen), Anne Pitoniak (Betty), Bernard Barrow (TV Manager), Marian Hailey (Jack's Wife), Joseph Carberry (Det. Burke), Skipp Lynch (Wiley), Marilyn Cooper (Waitress), Meg Mundy (Mace Lover), Sanford Seeger (Old Man), Yudie Bank (Old Lady), Michael Moran (Salesman), Norma Pratt, John DeBallo, Del Hinkley, Morgan Upton, John Goodman, Regina David, Francisco Prado, J. B. Waters, Indira Manjrekar, Riffany Clark, Marc Stevens

Matthew Modine, Phoebe Cates
in "Private School"
© Unity Pictures/Universal City Studios

Jerry Reed, Walter Matthau, Robin Williams
in "The Survivors" © Columbia Pictures

Madeline Kahn, David Bowie
in "Yellowbeard" © *Orion Pictures*

YELLOWBEARD (Orion) Producer, Carter DeHaven; Director, Mel Damski; Executive Producer, John Daly; Screenplay, Graham Chapman, Peter Cook, Bernard McKenna; Photography, Gerry Fisher; Music, John Morris; Designer, Joseph R. Jennings; Editor, William Reynolds; Costumes, T. Stephen Miles, Gilly Hebden; Assistant Directors, Richard L. Espinoza, Samuel M. Epstein, Clive Reed, Ted Morley, Mario Cisneros, A Seagoat production in DeLuxe Color; Rated PG; 101 minutes; June release. CAST: Graham Chapman (Yellowbeard), Peter Boyle (Moon), Richard Cheech Marin (El Segundo), Tommy Chong (El Nebuloso), Peter Cook (Lord Lambourn), Marty Feldman (Gilbert), Martin Hewitt (Dan), Michael Hordern (Dr. Gilpin), Eric Idle (Cmdr. Clement), Madeline Kahn (Betty), James Mason (Capt. Hughes), John Cleese (Blind Pew), Kenneth Mars (Crisp/Verdugo), Spike Milligan (Flunkie), Stacey Nelkin (Triola), Nigel Planer (Mansell), Susannah York (Lady Churchill), Beryl Reid (Lady Lambourn), Ferdinand Mayne (Beamish), John Francis (Chaplain), Peter Bull (Queen Anne), Bernard Fox (Tarbuck), Ronald Lacey, Greta Blackburn, Nigel Stock, Kenneth Danziger, Monte Landis, Gillian Eaton, Bernard McKenna, John Diar, Carlos Romano, Alvaro Carcano, Leopoldo Frances, Ava Harela, Garry O'Neill

LUGGAGE OF THE GODS (General Pictures) Producer-Assistant Director, Jeff Folmsbee; Director, David Kendall; Photography, Steven Ross; Editor, Jack Haigis; Music, Cengiz Yaltkaya; Art Director, Joshua Harrison; Costumes, Dawn Johnson; Special Effects, Glenn Van Fleet; In color; Not rated; 74 minutes; June release. CAST: Mark Stolzenberg (Yuk), Gabriel Barre (Tull), Gwen Ellison (Hubba), Martin Haber (Zoot), Rochelle Robins (Kono), Lou Leccese (Flon), Dog Thomas (Gurn), John Tarrant (Whittaker), Conrad Bergschneider (Lionel)

DON'T CHANGE MY WORLD (Enfield) Producer, George P. Macrenaris; Written, Directed and Edited by Robert Rector; In color; Rated G; June release. CAST: Roy Tatum (Eric), Ben Jones (Jake), George Macrenaris (Mike), Edie Kramer

ASSAULT WITH A DEADLY WEAPON (Aquarius) Director, Walter Gaines; Screenplay, William Dyer; Music, Paul Fox; In color; Not rated; June release. CAST: Richard Holliday, Sandra Foley, Lamont Jackson, Rinaldo Rincon

Frederic Forrest
in "Hammett" © *Zoetrope Studios*

THE SALAMANDER (ITC Films International) Producer, Paul Maslansky; Director, Peter Zinner; Screenplay, Robert Katz from novel by Morris West; Photography, Marcello Gatti; Editor, Claudio Cutry; Music, Jerry Goldsmith; In color; Not rated; 107 minutes; June release. CAST: Anthony Quinn (Bruno), Franco Nero (Dante), Martin Balsam (Stefanelli), Sybil Danning (Lili), Christopher Lee (Director), Cleavon Little (Malinowsky), Paul Smith (Surgeon), Claudia Cardinale (Elena), Eli Wallach (Leporello), John Steiner (Roditi), Renzo Palmer (Giorgione)

HAMMETT (Orion/Warner Bros.) Producers, Fred Roos, Ronald Colby, Don Guest; Director, Wim Wenders; Screenplay, Ross Thomas, Dennis O'Flaherty; Adaptation, Thomas Pope; Based on book by Joe Gores; Photography, Philip Lathrop, Joseph Biroc; Editors, Barry Malkin, Marc Laub, Robert Q. Lovett, Randy Roberts; Presented by Francis Ford Coppola; In color; 100 minutes; Rated PG; June release. CAST: Frederic Forrest (Hammett), Peter Boyle (Jimmy Ryan), Marilu Henner (Kit Conger/Sue Alabama), Roy Kinnear (Eddie Hagedorn), Elisha Cook (Eli), Lydia Lei (Crystal Ling), R. G. Armstrong (Lt. O'Mara), Richard Bradford (Det. Bradford), Michael Chow (Fong), David Patrick Kelly (Punk), Sylvia Sidney (Donaldina), Jack Nance (Gary), Elmer L. Kline (Doc Fallon), Royal Dano (Pops)

PINK MOTEL (New Image) Executive Producer, Don McCormack; Producers, M. James Kouf, Jr., Ed Elbert; Director, Mike MacFarland; Screenplay, M. James Kouf, Jr.; Photography, Nicholas von Sternberg; Editor, Earl Watson; Music, Larry K. Smith; Assistant Director, George W. Perkins; Associate Producer, Bren Plaistowe; In Movielab Color; Rated R; 88 minutes; June release. CAST: Terri Berland, Brad Cowgill, Cathryn Hartt, Andrea Howard, Tony Longo, Squire Fridel, Heidi Holicher, John Maccia, Christopher Nelson, Phyllis Diller, Slim Pickens

STACY'S KNIGHTS (Crown International) Executive Producers, Jim Wilson, David L. Peterson; Producers, JoAnn Locktov, Freddy Sweet; Director, Jim Wilson; Screenplay, Michael Blake; Editor, Bonnie Koehler; Music, Norton Buffalo; Photography, Raoul Lomas; Assistant Directors, Jacqueline Zambrano, Lisa Blok; Art Director, Florence Fellman; Costumes, Jill Ohannison; An American Twist Film in DeLuxe Color; Rated PG; 100 minutes; June release. CAST: Andra Millian (Stacy), Kevin Costner (Will), Eve Lilith (Jean), Mike Reynolds (Shecky), Ed Semenza (Kid), Don Hackstaff (Lawyer), Gary Tilles (Rudy), Garth Howard (Mr. C), Cheryl Ferris (Marion), Roge Roush (Rollin'), John Brevick (Floor Boss), Shawshanee Hall, Bobby Condor, Frederick Hughes, Peter Farnum, Steve Noonan, Robin Landis, David Brevick, Steve Kopanke, Jim Kosub, Ray Whittey, Roy Reeves, Teresa Knox, JoAnn Lisosky, Theresa Thompson, Mark Conrad, Pete Borsz, Dennis Pflederer, Jay Conder

SPACESHIP (Almi) Producer, Mark Haggard; Direction and Screenplay, Bruce Kimmel; Executive Producers, Michael S. Landes, Albert Schwartz; Music, David Spear; Associate Producers, Alain Silver, Patrick Regan; In color; Rated PG; 80 minutes; July release. CAST: Cindy Williams (Anne), Leslie Nielsen (Cmdr. Jameson), Patrick MacNee (Scientist), Gerrit Graham (Rodzinski), Bruce Kimmel (John)

EASY MONEY (Orion) Producer, John Nicolella; Director, James Signorelli; Executive Producer, Estelle Endler; Screenplay, Rodney Dangerfield, Michael Endler, P. J. O'Rourke, Dennis Blair; Photography, Fred Schuler; Music, Laurence Rosenthal; Title Song, Billy Joel; Editor, Ronald Roose; Designer, Eugene Lee; Costumes, Joe Aulisi; Assistant Directors, Robert Girolani, Henry Bronchtein; Soundtrack available on CBS Records; In Technicolor; Rated R; 100 minutes; July release. CAST: Rodney Dangerfield (Monty), Joe Pesci (Nicky), Geraldine Fitzgerald (Mrs. Monahan), Candy Azzara (Rose), Val Avery (Louie), Tom Noonan (Paddy), Taylor Negron (Julio), Lili Haydn (Belinda), Jeffrey Jones (Clive), Tom Ewell (Scrappleton), Jennifer Jason Leigh (Allison), Jeffrey Altman (Bill), David Vasquez (Hector), Kimberly McArthur (Ginger), Frank Simpson (Fr. McIntyre), Arch Johnson (Vendor), Dennis Blair (Critic), Steve Szucs (Barfly), Jennifer Dana Giangrasso (Birthday Girl), Mary Pat Gleason, Angela Pietropinto (Party Mothers), Carmen Bonifant (Julio's Mother), Pedro Ocampo (Julio's Father), Taylor Reed (Fat Guy), Peter Laurelli (Fat Anthony), Fiddle Viracola, John Scoletti, Filomena Spagnuolo, Peter D'Arcy, Polly Magaro, Rafael Cruz, Alfred De La Fuente, Harsh Nayyar, Sid Raymond, Jeff Gillen, Eric Van Valkenburg, Richard Van Valkenburg, John Delph, Walt Gorney, Jessica James, B. Constance Barry, Mary Wilshire, Gregor Roy, Milton Seaman, Wade Barnes, James Cahill, Ian Sullivan, Lisa McMillan, Andrea Coles, Jade Bari, McKenzie Allen, Richard Dow, Margot Avery

Dennis Quaid, Simon MacCorkindale, Bess Armstrong,
Louis Gossett, Jr. in "Jaws 3-D"
© *Universal City Studios*

Dennis Quaid, Lisa Maurer, Bess Armstrong,
Louis Gossett, Jr. in "Jaws 3-D"
© *Universal City Studios*

JAWS 3-D (Universal) Producer, Rupert Hitzig; Director, Joe Alves; Screenplay, Richard Matheson, Carl Gottlieb; Story, Guerdon Trueblood; Suggested by novel "Jaws" by Peter Benchley; Executive Producers, Alan Landsburg, Howard Lipstone; Photography, James A. Contner; Designer, Woods Macintosh; Editor, Randy Roberts; Associate Producer, David Kappes; Shark Theme, John Williams; Music, Alan Parker; Art Directors, Chris Horner, Paul Eads; Assistant Directors, Scott Maitland, J. Alan Hopkins, David Sosna, Deborah Love; Soundtrack available on MCA Records; In Technicolor, Arrivision 3-D, Stereovision, and Dolby Stereo; 98 minutes; July release. CAST: Dennis Quaid (Mike), Bess Armstrong (Kathryn), Simon MacCorkindale (Philip), Louis Gossett, Jr. (Calvin), John Putch (Sean), Lea Thompson (Kelly Ann), P. H. Moriarty (Jack), Dan Blasko (Dan), Liz Morris (Liz), Lisa Maurer (Ethel), Harry Grant (Shelby), Andy Hansen (Silver Bullet), P. T. Horn (Guide), John Edson, Jr. (Bob), Kay Stevens (Mrs. Kallender), Archie Valliere (Leonard), Alonzo Ward (Fred), Cathy Cervenka (Sherrie), Steve Mellor (Announcer), Ray Meunich (Paramedic), Les Alford, Gary Anstaett (Reporters), Muffett Baker (Guide), William Bramley, Scott Christoffel, Debbie Connoyer, Mary David Duncan, Barbara Eden, John Floren, John Gaffey, Joe Gilbert, Will Knickerbocker, Jackie Kuntarich, Edward Laurie, Holly Lisker, M. J. Lloyd, Carl Mazzocone, Brendan Murray, Kim Nordstrom, Ken Olson, Ronnie Parks, Al Pipkin

BLUE SKIES AGAIN (Warner Bros.) Producers, Alex Winitsky, Arlene Sellers; Director, Richard Michaels; Screenplay, Kevin Sellers; Photography, Don McAlpine; Art Director, Don Ivey; Editor, Danford B. Greene; Music, John Kander; Assistant Directors, Michael Daves, Robert Doherty, Jeffrey Stacey; In Technicolor and Dolby Stereo; Rated PG; 110 minutes; July release. CAST: Harry Hamlin (Sandy Mendenhall), Mimi Rogers (Liz), Kenneth McMillan (Dirk), Dana Elcar (Lou), Robyn Barto (Paula), Marcos Gonzales (Brushback), Cilk Cozart (Wallstreet), Joey Gian (Calvin), Doug Moeller (Carroll), Tommy Lane (Roy), Ray Negron (Jerry), Joel Goodman (Andy), Rooney Kerwin (Mike), Julian Byrd (Coach Lindburne), Jeff Rosenberg (Pitcher), Bill Hindman (Blues' Manager), Julio Oscar Mechosa (Blues' Translator), Frank Schuller (Umpire), Susan Hatfield (National Anthem Singer), Jeff Gillen, Jan Oniki (Couple in stands), Will Knickerbocker (Redneck in stands), Florence McGee (Elderly Lady in stands), Bernie Knee (Frand),

Frank Umont (2nd Base Umpire), Fred Buch, Toni Crabtree, Bobby Gale (Reporters), Ralph Weintraub (Vendor), Robyn Peterson (Crystal), Phil Philbin (Policeman), Brody Howell, Tommy Barone (Intercoastal Duck Players), Earl Houston Bullock (Publicity Man), Carol Nadell (Motel Desk Clerk), Patrick Marie (Maitre d'), Gregg Gilbert (Bellhop)

THE FIRST TIME (New Line) Producer, Sam Irvin; Director, Charlie Loventhal; Screenplay, Mr. Loventhal, Susan Weiser-Finley, W. Franklin Finley; Story, Mr. Loventhal; Photography, Steve Fierberg; Editor, Stanley Vogel; Music, Lanny Meyers; In color; Rated R; 95 minutes; July release. CAST: Tim Choate (Charlie), Krista Errickson (Dana), Marshall Efron (Rand), Wendy Fulton (Wendy), Raymond Patterson (Ron), Wallace Shawn (Goldfarb), Wendle Jo Sperber (Eileen), Cathryn Damon (Gloria), Jane Badler (Karen), Bradley Bliss (Melanie), Eva Charney (Polly), Bill Randolph (Rick), Rex Robbins (Leon), Robert Trebor

HEARTBREAKER (Monorex) Producers, Chris D. Nebe, Chris Anders; Director, Frank Zuniga; Screenplay, Vicente Gutierrez; Photography, Michael Lonzo; Editor, Larry Bock; Music, Rob Walsh; In color; Rated R; 90 minutes; July release. CAST: Fernando Allende (Beto), Dawn Dunlap (Kim), Peter Gonzales Falcon (Hector), Miguel Ferrer (Angel), Michael D. Roberts (Hopper), Robert Dryer (Wings), Pepe Serna (Loco), Rafael Campos (Alfonso), Carmen Martinez (Minnie), Carlo Allen (Gato)

DEADLY FORCE (Embassy) Producer, Sandy Howard; Director, Paul Aaron; Screenplay, Ken Barnett, Barry Schneider, Robert Vincent O'Neil; Story, Mr. Barnett; Photography, Norman Leigh, David Myers; Editor, Roy Watts; Music, Gary Scott; In color; Rated R; 95 minutes; July release. CAST: Wings Hauser (Stoney), Joyce Ingalls (Eddie), Paul Shenar (Joshua), Al Ruscio (Sam), Arlen Dean Snyder (Ashley), Lincoln Kilpatrick (Otto), Bud Ekins (Harvey), J. Victor Lopez (Diego), Hector Elias (Lopez), Ramon Franco (Jesus), Gina Gallego (Maria)

NOW AND FOREVER (Inter Planetary) Producers, Treisha Ghent, Carnegie Fieldhouse; Director, Adrian Carr; Screenplay, Richard Cassidy; Based on novel by Danielle Steel; Photography, Don McAlpine; Music, Graham Russell; In color; Rated R; 93 minutes; July release. CAST: Cheryl Ladd (Jessie Clark), Robert Coleby (Ian Clark), Carmen Duncan (Astrid Bonner), Christine Amor (Margaret Burton)

Joe Pesci, Rodney Dangerfield
in "Easy Money" © *Orion Pictures*

Harry Hamlin, Mimi Rogers
in "Blue Skies Again"
© *Warner Bros.*

111

Cliff Robertson, Rob Lowe, Andrew
McCarthy in "Class"
© Orion Pictures

CLASS (Orion) Producer, Martin Ransohoff; Director, Lewis John Carlino; Executive Producer, Cathleen Summers; Screenplay, Jim Kouf, David Greenwalt; Music, Elmer Bernstein; Photography, Ric Waite; Editor, Stuart Pappe; Art Director, Jack Poplin; Assistant Directors, L. Andrew Stone, Scott Maitland, Katterli Fraudenfelder; Associate Producers, Jim Kouf, David Greenwalt; Jill Chadwick; Editor, Dennis Dolan; Ms. Bisset's costumes, Donfeld; Additional Music, Tom Scott; In DeLuxe Color; Rated R; 100 minutes; July release. CAST: Jacqueline Bisset (Ellen), Rob Lowe (Skip), Andrew McCarthy (Jonathan), Cliff Robertson (Burroughs), Stuart Margolin (Balaban), John Cusack (Roscoe), Alan Ruck (Roger), Rodney Pearson (Allen), Remak Ramsay (Kennedy), Virginia Madsen (Lisa), Deborah Thalberg (Susan), Fern Persons (Headmistress), Casey Siemaszko (Doug), Aaron Douglas (Barry), Anna Maria Horsford (Maggie), Hal Frank (Schneider), Dick Cusack (Chaplain). William Visteen (Dr. Kreiger), James O'Reilly (Bernhardt), Caitlin Hart, Virginia Morris, Stewart Figa, Paula Clarendon, Gita Tanner, Joan Cusack, John Kapelos, George Womack, Maria Ricossa, Candace Collins, Marty Britton, Bruce Norris, Kevin Swerdlow, Wayne Kneeland, J. Todd Shaughnessy, Carole Arterbery, Nancy Serlin, Bruno Aclin

LOVELY BUT DEADLY (Juniper) Executive Producer, V. Paul Hreljanovic; Producers, Doro Vlado Hreljanovic, David Sheldon; Director, David Sheldon; Screenplay, David Sheldon, Patricia Joyce; From story by Lawrence D. Foldes; Photography, Robert Roth; Editor, Richard Brummer; Music, Robert O. Ragland; Assistant Director, John Cummins; In color; Rated R; 93 minutes; July release. CAST: Lucinda Dooling (Lovely), John Randolph (Franklin), Richard Herd (Honest Charlie), Susan Mechsner (Martial Arts Teacher), Mel Novak, Marie Windsor, Mark Holden, Rick Moser, Mary McDonough, Pamela Bryant, Irwin Keyes, Judd Omen, Linda Shayne, Vincent Roberts, Wendell Wright, Jeana Tomasino

ANGEL OF H.E.A.T. (Studios Pan Imago) Executive Producer, Hal Kant; Producer-Director, Myrl A. Schreibman; Screenplay, Helen Sanford; Photography, Jacques Haitkin; Editor, Barry Zetlin; Music, Guy Sobell; Assistant Director, Mary Lou MacLaury; In DeLuxe Color; Rated R; 93 minutes; July release. CAST: Marilyn Chambers (Angel), Stephen Johnson (Mark), Mary Woronov (Samantha), Milt Kogan (Harry), Remy O'Neill (Andrea), Dan Jesse (Albert), Harry Townes (Peter), Gerald Okamura (Hans), Andy Abrams (Mean), Jerry Riley (Rady)

SPACE RAIDERS (New World) Title changed to "Star Child"; Producer, Roger Corman; Direction and Screenplay, Howard R. Cohen; Photography, Alec Hirschfeld; Editor, Robert Kizer; Assistant Directors, Gordon Booz, Nancy Nuttall; Art Director, Wayne Springfield; In color; Rated PG; 85 minutes; July release. CAST: Vince Edwards (Hawk), David Mendenhall (Peter), Drew Snyder (Aldebaran), Patsy Pease (Amanda), Luca Bercovici (Ace), Thom Christopher (Flightplan), Ray Stewart (Zariatin), George Dickerson (Tracton), Virginia Kiser (Janeris), Don Washburn (Jessup), Michael Miller (Lou), Bill Boyett (Taggert), Howard Dayton (Elmer), Elizabeth Charlton (Cookie), Dick Miller (Crazy Mel)

OFF THE WALL (Jensen Farley) Executive Producer, Lisa Barsamian; Producer, Frank Mancuso, Jr.; Director, Rick Friedberg; Screenplay, Ron Kurz, Dick Chudnow, Rick Friedberg; Photography, Donald R. Morgan; Editor, George Hively; Music, Dennis McCarthy; Assistant Director, Steve Perry; Design, Richard Sawyer; In Movielab Color; Rated R; 85 minutes; July release. CAST: Paul Sorvino (Warden), Rosanna Arquette (Governor's Daughter), Patrick Cassidy (Randy), Billy Hufsey (Rico), Ralph Wilcox (Johnny), Dick Chudnow (Miskewicz), Monte Markham (Governor), Brianne Leary (Jennifer), Mickey Gilley, Gary Goodrow, Biff Manard, Stu Gilliam, Jenny Neumann, Lewis Arquette, Jeana Tomasino, Roselyn Royce

HYSTERICAL (Embassy) Producer, Gene Levy; Executive Producer, William Immerman; Director, Chris Bearde; Screenplay, William, Mark and Brett Hudson, Trace Johnston; Photography, Donald Morgan; Editor, Stanley Frazen; In DeLuxe Color; Rated PG; 87 minutes; July release. CAST: William Hudson (Frederick), Mark Hudson (Paul), Brett Hudson (Fritz), Cindy Pickett (Kate), Richard Kiel (Capt. Howdy), Julie Newmar (Venetia), Bud Cort (Dr. John), Robert Donner (Ralph), Murray Hamilton (Mayor), Clint Walker (Sheriff), Franklin Ajaye (Leroy), Charlie Callas (Dracula), Keenan Wynn (Fisherman), Gary Owens (TV Announcer)

THE INSTRUCTOR (American Eagle) Executive Producer, Richard F. Lombardi; Written, Produced, Directed by Don Bendell; Photography, Ron Hughes; Editor, Shirley Bendell; Art Director, Joyce Edwards; Music, Marti Lunn; Not rated; 91 minutes; July release. CAST: Bob Chaney (The Instructor), Bob Saal (Bud), Lynda Scharnott (Dee), Bruce Bendell (Fender), Tony Blanchard (Ben), Don Bendell (Thumper), Jack Holderbaum (Shank), Hank Gordon (Grasshopper), Denise Blankenship (Choo-Choo), Bob Huey (Alex), Bradley Norfolk (Roach), Denise Phillips (Karen), Bob Dorman (Rick), Steve Boergadien (Al)

DAFFY DUCK'S MOVIE: FANTASTIC ISLAND (Warner Bros.) Producer-Director, Friz Freleng; Executive Producer, Jean H. MacGurdy; Screenplay, John Dunn, David Detiege, Friz Freleng; Editor, Jim Champin; Associate Producer, Hal Geer; Design and Layout, Bob Givens, Michael Mitchell; In color; Rated G; 78 minutes; July release. A full-length cartoon with the voices of Mel Blanc, June R. Foray, Les Tremayne

HERCULES (Cannon) Producers, Menahem Golan, Yoram Globus; Executive Producer, John Thompson; Direction and Screenplay, Lewis Coates; Photography, Alberto Spagnoli; Music, Pino Donnaggio; Art Director, Antonello Geleng; Costumes, Adriana Spadaro; Editor, Sergio Montanari; Assistant Director, Giancarlo Santi; Optical Effects, Armando Valcauda, Gerard Olivier; In color; Rated PG; 101 minutes; August release. CAST: Lou Ferrigno (Hercules), Mirella D'Angelo (Circe), Sybil Danning (Arianna), Ingrid Anderson (Cassiopea), William Berger (King Minos), Brad Harris (King Augeius), Claudio Cassinelli (Zeus), Rossana Podesta (Hera), Delia Boccardo (Athena), Yehuda Efroni (Dorcon), Gianni Garko (Valcheus), Bobby Rhodes (King Xeno-

Vince Edwards, David Mendenhall
in "Spaceraiders" © New World

Mirella D'Angelo, Lou Ferrigno
in "Hercules" © Cannon Films

Danny Pintauro, Dee Wallace, Daniel
Hugh-Kelly in "Cujo"
© Warner Bros.

Tim Thomerson, Jeffrey Byron
in "Metalstorm"
© Universal City Studios

dan), Franco Garofolo (Thief), Stellio Candelli (Tegeus), Gabriella Giorgielli (Chio), Alessandro Ardenti (Young Hercules), Raffaele Baldassare (Sostratus), Sergio Bruzzichinini (Melite)

THE MAN WHO WASN'T THERE (Paramount) Producer, Frank Mancuso, Jr.; Director, Bruce Malmuth; Screenplay, Stanford Sherman; Photography, Frederick Moore; Editor, Harry Keller; Music, Miles Goodman; In color and 3-D; Rated R; 111 minutes; August release. CAST: Steve Guttenberg (Sam), Lisa Langlois (Cindy), Jeffrey Tambor (Boris), Art Hindel (Ted)

CUJO (Warner Bros.) Producers, Daniel H. Blatt, Robert Singer; Director, Lewis Teague; Screenplay, Don Carlos Dunaway, Lauren Currier; From novel "Cujo" by Stephen King; Photography, Jan DeBont; Editor, Neil Travis; Music, Charles Bernstein; In color; Rated R; 97 minutes; August release. CAST: Dee Wallace (Donna), Danny Pintauro (Tad), Daniel Hugh-Kelly (Vic), Christopher Stone (Steve), Ed Lauter (Joe), Kaiulani Lee (Charity), Billy Jacoby (Brett), Mills Watson (Gary), Sandy Ward (Bannerman), Jerry Hardin (Masen)

GETTING IT ON! (ComWorld) Formerly "American Voyeur"; Producers, Jan Thompson, William Olsen; Direction and Screenplay, William Olsen; Executive Producer, Michael Rothschild; Music, Ricky Keller; Art Director, James Eric; Photography, Austin McKinney; Costumes, Bonnie Jones; In color; Rated R; 96 minutes; August release. CAST: Martin Yost (Alex), Heather Kennedy (Sally), Jeff Edmond (Nicholas), Kathy Brickmeier (Marilyn), Mark Alan Ferri (Richard), Charles King Bibby (White), Sue Satoris (Mrs. White), Terry Loughlin (Carson), Caroline McDonald (Mrs. Carson), Kim Saunders (Prostitute), Dan Thompson (Chuck), Peggy Van Dyke (Hostess), Steve Howard (Harris), Ralph Conner, Jr. (Coach), Steve Smith, Paul Assion, Art Gerard, Steve Robinson, Todd Gorelick, The Late Bronze Age, Robert McMillan, Bryan Elsom, Amrita Bost, Tim Bost, Steve Boles, Mark Rose, John Rudy, Fred Stevenson, Aaron Lewis, Bill Biggs, Gina Sain, Fran Taylor, Jevon Morris, John Tucker

METALSTORM: THE DESTRUCTION OF JARED-SYN (Universal) Producers, Charles Band, Alan J. Adler; Executive Producers, Albert Band, Arthur H. Maslansky; Director, Charles Band; Screenplay, Alan J. Adler; Music, Richard Band; Associate Producer, Gordon W. Gregory; Editor, Brad Arensman; Photography, Mac Ahlberg; Art Director, Pamela B. Warner; Costumes, Kathie

Clark; Designer, Douglas J. White; Assistant Directors, Thomas Calabrese, Matia Karrell, Debbie Pinthus, Stephen Buck; Special Effects, Joe Quinlan, Gregory Van Der Veer; In 3-D and MovieLab Color; Rated PG; 84 minutes; August release. CAST: Jeffrey Byron (Dogen), Mike Preston (Jared-Syn), Tim Thomerson (Rhodes), Kelly Preston (Dhyana), Richard Moll (Hurok), R. David Smith (Baal), Larry Pennell (Alx), Marty Zagon (Zax), Mickey Fox (Poker Annie), J. Bill Jones (Baal's Lt.), Winston Jones (Chimera), Mike Jones, Mike Walter, Rick Militi, Speed Stearns, Lou Joseph, Rush Adams

STRANGE BREW (MGM/UA) Producer, Louis M. Silverstein; Directors, Dave Thomas, Rick Moranis; Executive Producer, Jack Grossberg; Screenplay, Rick Moranis, Dave Thomas, Steven DeJarnatt; Music, Charles Fox; Photography, Steven Poster; Designer, David L. Snyder; Editor, Patrick McMahon; Associate Producer, Brian Frankish; Assistant Directors, Brian Frankish, David A. MacLeod, Edwina Follows, Larry Pall; Art Directors, Suzanna Smith, Debra Gjendem; Costumes, Larry Wells; Title Song, Ian Thomas; Soundtrack on PolyGram Records; In Metrocolor; Rated PG; 90 minutes; August release. CAST: Dave Thomas (Doug), Rick Moranis (Bob), Max von Sydow (Brewmeister Smith), Paul Dooley (Claude), Lynne Griffin (Pam), Angus MacInnes (Jean), Tom Harvey (Inspector), Douglas Campbell (Henry), Brian McConnachie (Ted), Len Doncheff (Jack), Jill Frappier (Gertrude), David Beard (Judge), Thick Wilson (Prosecutor), Robert Windsor (Bailiff), Sid Lynas, Ron James, Dora Dainton, David Clement, Paddy Sampson, Roger Dunn, Diane Douglass, Eric House, J. Winston Carroll, James Conroy, Glenn Beck, Desh Bandhu

BRAINWAVES (Motion Picture Marketing) Executive Producers, Charles Aperia, Gary Gillingham, Tim Nielsen; Producer-Director-Screenplay, Ulli Lommel; Additional Dialogue, Buz Alexander, Suzanna Love; Photography, Jon Kranhouse, Ulli Lommel; Editor, Richard Brummer; Music, Robert O. Ragland; Assistant Director, Bruce Starr; Art Director, Stephen E. Graff; Associate Producer, David DuBay; In Getty Color; Rated PG; 81 minutes; August release. CAST: Keir Dullea (Julian Bedford), Suzanna Love (Kaylie), Vera Miles (Marian), Percy Rodrigues (Dr. Tobinson), Tony Curtis (Dr. Clavius), Paul Wilson (Dr. Schroder), Ryan Seitz (Danny), Nicholas Love (Willy), Corinne Alphen (Lelia), Eve Brent Ashe (Miss Simpson)

Sandy Ward, Bill Sanderson,
Daniel Hugh-Kelly in "Cujo"
© Universal City Studios

Rick Moranis, Dave Thomas
in "Strange Brew"
© MGM/UA Entertainment Co.

113

Emilio Estevez in "Nightmares"
© Universal City Studios

Robert Carradine, Keenan Wynn
in "Wavelength"
© New World

DREAMLAND (First-Run Features) Executive Producer, Richard Lourie; Producer, Jonathan Stathakis; Directors, Oz Scott, Nancy Baker, Joel Schulman; Screenplay, Nancy Baker, Richard Lourie; Photography, Joe Mangine, Don Lenzer; Music, Butler; Editors, Nancy Baker, Jay Freund; In color; Not rated; 83 minutes; August release. A documentary on gospel and jazz music.

NIGHTMARES (Universal) Producer, Christopher Crowe; Director, Joseph Sargent; Screenplay, Christopher Crowe, Jeffrey Bloom; Photography, Mario DiLeo, Gerald Perry Finnerman; Art Director, Jack Taylor; Designer, Dean Edward Mitzner; Editors, Rod Stephens, Michael Brown; Executive Producers, Andrew Mirisch, Alex Beaton; Associate Producer, Alan Barnette; Music, Craig Safan; Assistant Directors, Kevin Cremin, Doug Metzger; In Panavision and Technicolor; Rated PG; 99 minutes; September release. CAST: "Terror in Topanga": Cristina Raines (Wife), Joe Lambie (Husband), Anthony James (Clerk), Clare Nono (Newswoman), Raleigh Bond (Neighbor), Robert Phelps (Newsman), Dixie Lynn Royce (Little Girl), Lee James Jude (Glazier), "Bishop of Battle": Emilio Estevez (J.J.), Mariclare Costello (Mrs. Cooney), Louis Giambalvo (Cooney), Moon Zappa (Pamela), Billy Jacoby (Zock), Joshua Grenrock (Willie), Gary Cervantes (Mazenza), C. Stewart Burns (Root), Andre Diaz (Pedro), Rachel Goslins (Phyllis), Joel Holman (Z-Man), Christopher Bubetz (Jeffrey), Rudy Negretl (Emiliano), James Tolkan (Bishop's Voice), "The Benediction": Lance Henriksen (MacLeod), Tony Plana (Del Amo), Timothy Scott (Sheriff), Robin Gammell (Bishop), Rose Marie Campos (Mother), "Night of the Rat": Richard Masur (Steven), Veronica Cartwright (Claire), Bridgette Andersen (Brooke), Albert Hague (Mel), Howard F. Flynn (Announcer)

MORTUARY (Film Ventures) Produced and Written by Howard Avedis, Marlene Schmidt; Director, Howard Avedis; Music, John Cacavas; Photography, Gary Graver; Editor, Stanford C. Allen; Assistant Director, Herman Grigsby; Art Director, Randy Ser; In color; Rated R; 91 minutes; September release. CAST: Mary McDonough (Christie), David Wallace (Greg), Lynda Day George (Eve), Christopher George (Dr. Andrews), Bill Paxton (Paul)

SMOKEY AND THE BANDIT PART 3 (Universal) Producer, Mort Engelberg; Director, Dick Lowry; Screenplay, Stuart Birnbaum, David Dashev; Based on characters created by Hal Needham, Robert L. Levy; Photography, James Pergola; Art Director, Ron Hobbs; Editors, Byron Buzz Brandt, David Blewitt, Christopher Greenbury; Music, Larry Cansler; Assistant Directors, Ron Bozman, Richard Graves; Costumes, Andre Lavery, Linda Benedict; Soundtrack available on MCA Records; In Panavision and Technicolor; Rated PG; 86 minutes; September release. CAST: Jackie Gleason (Buford T. Justice), Jerry Reed (Cletus/Bandit), Paul Williams (Little Enos), Pat McCormick (Big Enos), Mike Henry (Junior), Colleen Camp (Dusty Trails), Faith Minton (Tina), Burt Reynolds (The Real Bandit), Sharon Anderson (Policewoman), Silvia Arana (Latin Woman), Alan Berger (Hippie), Ray Bouchard (Purvis Beethoven), Connie Brighton (Girl), Earl Houston Bullock (Flagman), Ava Cadell (Blond), Cathy Cahill (Mother Trucker), Dave Cass (Tough Guy), Leon Cheatom (Guide), Candace Collins (Maid), Peter Conrad (Midget), Janis Cummins (Nudist Female), Jackie Davis, DeeDee Deering, Al De Luca, Ray Forchion, Veronica Gamba, Jorge Gil, Marilyn Gleason, Charles P. Harris, Timothy Hawkins, Craig Horwich, Pirty Lee Jackson, Austin Kelly, William L. Kingsley, Will Knickerbocker, Kim Kondziola, Dick Lowry, Sandy Mielke, Toni Moon, Alejandro Moreno, Gloria Nichols, Mel Pape, Dan Rambo, Richard Walsh, Curry Worsham

GET CRAZY (Embassy) Producer, Hunt Lowry; Director, Allan Arkush; Screenplay, Danny Opatoshu, Henry Rosenbaum, David Taylor; Editors, Kent Beyda, Michael Jablow; Music, Michael Boddicker; A Herbert Solow production in color; Rated R; 92 minutes; September release. CAST: Malcolm McDowell (Reggie), Allen Goorwitz (Max), Daniel Stern (Neil), Gaij Edwards (Willy), Miles Chapin (Sammy), Ed Begley, Jr. (Colin), Stacey Nelkin (Susie), Bill Henderson (King Blues), Lou Reed (Auden), Howard Kaylan (Capt. Cloud)

WAVELENGTH (New World) Executive Producer, Maurice Rosenfield; Producer, James Rosenfield; Direction-Screenplay, Mike Gray; Music, Tangerine Dream; Photography, Paul Goldsmith; Editors, Mark Goldblatt, Robert Leighton; Assistant Directors, Nick Marck, Bradley Gross; Art Director, Linda Pearl; In color; Rated PG; 87 minutes; September release. CAST: Robert Carradine (Bobby), Cherie Currie (Iris), Keenan Wynn (Dan), Cal Bowman (Gen. Ward), James Hess (Col. MacGruder), Terry Burns (Capt. Hinsdale), Eric Morris (Dr. Cottrell), Bob McLean (Dr. Stern), Eric Heath (Dr. Sidey), Robert Glaudini (Dr. Wolf), George O. Petrie (Savianno), George Skaff (Gen. Hunt), Milt Kogan (Pathologist), Dov Young (Gamma), Joshua Oreck (Beta)

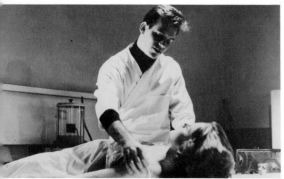

"Mortuary"
© Artists Releasing Corp.

Colleen Camp, Jerry Reed
in "Smokey and the Bandit III"
© Universal City Studios

Jackie Gleason, Faith Minton
in "Smokey and the Bandit Part 3"
© Universal City Studios

Sho Kosugi, Kane Kosugi
in "Revenge of the Ninja"
© MGM/UA Entertainment Co.

EDDIE AND THE CRUISERS (Embassy) Producers, Joseph Brooks, Robert K. Lifton; Director, Martin Davidson; Screenplay, Mr. Davidson, Arlene Davidson; Based on novel by P. F. Kluge; Photography, Fred Murphy; Editor, Priscilla Nedd; Music, John Cafferty; In color; Rated PG; 94 minutes; September release. CAST: Tom Berenger (Frank), Michael Pare (Eddie), Joe Pantoliano (Doc), Matthew Laurance (Sal), Helen Schneider (Joann), David Wilson (Kenny), Michael (Tunes), Antunes (Wendell), Ellen Barkin (Maggie), Kenny Vance (Lew), John Stockwell (Keith), Joe Cates (Lois), Barry Sand (Barry), Vebe Borge (Gerry)

CITY NEWS & NEWS BRIEFS (Cinecom International) Produced, Directed, Written and Edited by David Fishelson, Zoe Zinman; Photography, Jonathan Sinaiko; Music, Saheb Sarbib, Jules Baptiste, Peter Gordon, Monty Waters, Duke Ellington, the Normal; In color; Not rated; 81 minutes; Shown with two shorts, "Too Much Oregano" and "Ballet Robotique"; September release. CAST: Elliot Crown (Tom), Nancy Cohen (Daphne), Thomas Trivier (Frenchy), Richard Schlesinger (Lou), Valerie Felitto (DeeDee), Tony Mangis (Tony), Gail Gibney (Gail), David Fishelson (Punch), Zoe Zinman (Judy)

THE LONELY LADY (Universal) Producer, Robert R. Weston; Director, Peter Sasdy; Screenplay, John Kershaw, Shawn Randall; Based on novel by Harold Robbins; Adaptation, Ellen Shepard; Associate Producer, Tino Barzie; Photography, Brian West; Music, Charles Calello; Editor, Keith Palmer; Designer, Giorgio Desideri; Assistant Directors, Gerald Morin, Gil Rossellini, Jacques de Longeville; Art Directors, Adriana Bellone, Luciano Spadoni; Costumes, Giorgio Armani, Annamode; Title song by Charles Calello, Roger Voudouris; Performed by Larry Graham; In Technicolor; Rated R; 92 minutes; September release. CAST: Pia Zadora (Jerilee), Lloyd Bochner (Walter), Bibi Besch (Veronica), Joseph Cali (Vincent), Anthony Holland (Guy), Jared Martin (George), Ray Liotta (Joe), Carla Romanelli (Carla), Olivier Pierre (George), Kendal Kaldwell (Joanne), Lou Hirsch (Bernie), Kerry Shale (Walt, Jr.), Sandra Dickinson (Nancy), Shane Rimmer (Adolph), Nancy Wood (Janie), Ed Bishop (Dr. Baker), Giovanni Rizzo (Gino), Mickey Knox (Tom), Kenneth Nelson (Bud), Jay Benedict (Dr. Sloan), Robyn Mandell (Kim), Cecily Browne Laird (Mrs. Stone), Billy J. Mitchell (Gross), Glory Annen (Marion), Harrison Muller, Jr. (Martin), Mary D'Antin (Margaret), Carolynn DeFonseca (Joanna), Cyrus Elias (Nick), Kieran Canter (Gary)

REVENGE OF THE NINJA (MGM/UA) Producers, Menahem Golan, Yoram Globus; Associate Producer, David Womark; Director, Sam Firstenberg; Screenplay, James R. Silke; Photography, David Gurfinkel; Music, Rob Walsh; Choreographer, Sho Kosugi; Editors, Mark Helfrich, Michael J. Duthie; Special Effects, Joe Quinlivan; Assistant Directors, Michael Schroeder, Dennis White, Linda Kiffe; Art Director, Paul Staheli; Additional Music, W. Michael Lewis, Laurin Rinder; A Cannon Group Film in TVC Lab Color; Rated R; 90 minutes; September release. CAST: Sho Kosugi (Cho), Keith Vitali (Dave), Virgil Frye (Lt. Dime), Arthur Roberts (Braden), Mario Gallo (Caifano), Grace Oshita (Grandmother), Ashley Ferrare (Cathy), Kane Kosugi (Kane), John LaMotta (Joe), Melvin C. Hampton (Det. Rios), Oscar Rowland (One-eyed Informant), Toru Tanaka (Sumo Servant), Dan Shanks (Chief), Joe Pagliuso (Alberto) Ladd Anderson, Cyrus Theibeault (Thieves), Steve Ketcher (Big Thug), Don ReSimpson (Shooting Thug), Steven Lambert (Cowboy Thug), Jogi Hollands (Thug), Al Lai (Tatooed Torturer), Alan Amiel (Red Ninja Leader), Eddie Tse (Masked Ninja), David Barth (Donny), George Sullivan, Tim Eisenhart, Dan Rogers, Jerry North, Jack North, Jack Turner, Ken McConnell, Jody Asbury, Frank Bare

THE LAST FIGHT (Best Film & Video) Producers, Fred Williamson, Jerry Masucci; Direction and Screenplay, Fred Williamson; Photography, James Limmo; In color; Rated R; 89 minutes; September release. CAST: Fred Williamson (Jesse), Willie Colon (Joaquin), Ruben Blades (Andy), Nereida Mercado (Nancy), Darianne Fluegel (Sally), Nick Corello (Pedro), Sal Corolio (Papa), Izzy Sanabria (Slim)

THE LAST AMERICAN VIRGIN (Cannon) Producers, Menahem Golan, Yoram Globus; Direction and Screenplay, Boaz Davidson; Photography, Adam Greenberg; Editor, Bruria Davidson; In color; Rated R; 90 minutes; September release. CAST: Lawrence Monoson (Gary), Diane Franklin (Karen), Steve Antin (Rick), Joe Rubbo (David), Luisa Moritz (Carmelia)

KOYAANISQATSI (New Cinema) Producer-Director, Godfrey Reggio; Photography, Ron Fricke; Editors, Ron Fricke, Alton Walpole; Music, Philip Glass; In color; Not rated; 87 minutes; September release. An essay in images and sound on the state of American civilization.

Pia Zadora, Carla Romanelli
in "The Lonely Lady"
© KGA Industries

Pia Zadora, Joseph Cali
in "The Lonely Lady"
© KGA Industries

Paul LeMat, Nancy Allen
in "Strange Invaders" © *Orion*

Kenneth Tobey, Diana Scarwid, Lulu Sylbert,
Paul LeMat in "Strange Invaders"
© *Orion*

STRANGE INVADERS (Orion) Producer, Walter Coblenz; Director, Michael Laughlin; Screenplay, William Condon, Michael Laughlin; Photography, Louis Norvath; Music, John Addison; Editor, John W. Wheeler; Production and Costume Design, Susanna Moore; Associate Producers, Richard Moore, Joel Cohen; Assistant Directors, David Shepherd, David MacLeod, Edwina Follows; Visual Effects Design, John Muto, Robert Skotak; Art Director, Emad Helmy; In Panavision and DeLuxe Color; Rated PG; 100 minutes; September release. CAST: Paul LeMat (Charles), Nancy Allen (Betty), Diana Scarwid (Margaret), Michael Lerner (Willie), Louise Fletcher (Mrs. Benjamin), Wallace Shawn (Earl), Fiona Lewis (Waitress/Avon Lady), Kenneth Tobey (Arthur), June Lockhart (Mrs. Bigelow), Charles Lane (Prof. Hollister), Lulu Sylbert (Elizabeth), Joel Cohen (Tim), Dan Shor, Dey Young, Jack Kehler, Mark Goddard, Thomas Kopache, Bobby Pickett, Connie Kellers, Nancy Johnson, Betsy Pickering, Jonathan Ulmer, Ron Gillham, Al Roberts, Edwina Follows, Patti Medwid

LAST PLANE OUT (New World) Producers, Jack Cox, David Nelson; Director, David Nelson; Screenplay, Ernest Tidyman; Photography, Jacques Haitkin; In color; Rated PG; 92 minutes; September release. CAST: Jan-Michael Vincent (Jack), Julie Carmen (Maria), Mary Crosby (Liz), David Huffman (Jim), William Windom (James), Lloyd Battista (Anastasio), Yeg Wilson (Harry), Anthony Feijo (Ramon), Ronnie Gonzalez (Luis)

SWEET SIXTEEN (CIF) Executive Producers, Martin Perfit, June Perfit; Producer-Director, Jim Sotos; Screenplay, Erwin Goldman; Photography, James L. Carter; Editor, Drake Silliman; Music, Tommy Vig; Assistant Director, Tony Loree; Associate Producer, Sandy Charles; In color; Rated R; 90 minutes; September release. CAST: Bo Hopkins (Dan), Susan Strasberg (Joanne), Don Stroud (Billy), Dana Kimmell (Marci), Aleisa Shirley (Melissa), Don Shanks (Jason), Steve Antin (Hank), Logan Clarke (Jimmy), Michael Pataki (George), Patrick Macnee (John), Larry Storch (Earl), Henry Wilcoxon (Greyfeather), Sharon Farrell (Kathy)

FRIGHTMARE (Saturn International) Executive Producer, Henry Gellis; Producers, Patrick Wright and Tallie Wright; Direction-Screenplay, Norman Thaddeus Vane; Photography, Joel King; Editor, Doug Jackson; Music, Jerry Moseley; Assistant Director, Sam Baldoni; Art Director, Anne Welch; Associate Producers, Hedayat Javid, Harold D. Young; In color; Rated R; 86 minutes; September

release. CAST: Ferdinand Mayne (Conrad), Luca Bercovici (Saint), Nita Talbot (Mrs. Rohmer), Leon Askin (Wolfgang), Jennifer Starrett (Meg), Barbara Pilavin (Etta), Carlene Olson (Eve), Scott Thomson (Bobo), Donna McDaniel (Donna), Jeffrey Combs (Stu), Peter Kastner (Director), Chuck Mitchell (Detective), Jesse Ehrlich (Professor)

THE TWO WORLDS OF ANGELITA (First Run Features) Producer-Director, Jane Morrison; Screenplay, Jose Manuel Torres Santiago, Rose Rosenblatt, Jane Morrison; Associate Producer, Lianne Halfon; Photography, Affonso Beato; Editor, Suzanne Fenn; Design, Randy Barcelo; Music, Dom Salvador; Based on novel "Angelita" by Wendy Kesselman; Assistant Directors, Michael Waxman, Yvette Frankel; In Du-Art Color; Not rated; 73 minutes; October release. CAST: Marien Perez Riera (Angelita), Rosalba Rolon (Fela), Angel Domenech Soto (Chuito), Delia Esther Quinones (Dona Angela), Roberto Rivera Negron (Don Curro), Pedro Juan Texidor (Manolo), Idalia Perez Garay (Fortuna), Bimbo Rivas (Goyin), Geisha Otero (Rosa), Malik Mandes (Littleman), Sandra Rodriguez (Linda), Leonard Golubchick (Principal), Gary Samuels (Shore), Tawny Thomas (Lisa), Lewanne Jones (Blondie), Ben Lanco (Mateo), Tony Arroyo (Rivera), Iluminada Cartagena (Mrs. Perez) Alvan Colon (Johnny), Sandy Rivas (Tammy), Miguel Garcia (Hoodlum), Francisco Rodriguez (Jam)

HEARTLAND REGGAE (Libra) Producer, John W. Mitchell; Director, Jim Lewis; Photography, Jim Lewis, Jim Swaby, Tony Marsh; Editor Jim Lewis, Randal Torno, John Mayes; In color; Not rated; 90 minutes; October release. CAST: Bob Marley and the Wailers, Peter Tosh, Jacob Miller and Inner Circle Band, Little Junior Tucker, Althea and Donna, Judy Mowatt and the Light of Love, U-Roy, Dennis Brown, Lloyd Parkes and We the People Band, Ras Lee Morris, Natty Garfield

HELLS ANGELS FOREVER (Marvin Films) Producers, Richard Chase, Sandy Alexander, Leon Gast; Directors, Richard Chase, Kevin Keating, Leon Gast; Screenplay, Peterson Tooke, Richard Chase; Photography, Kevin Keating; In color; Rated R; 92 minutes; October release. CAST: Hells Angels, Willie Nelson, Jerry Garcia, Johnny Paycheck, Bo Diddley

THE BALLAD OF GREGORIO CORTEZ (Embassy) Producers, Moctesuma Esparza, Michael Hausman; Director, Robert M. Young; Screenplay, Victor Villasenor; Screenplay, Mr. Young from

David Carradine, Barbara Hershey
in "Americana" © *Crown International*

Matt Dillon, Mickey Rourke
in "Rumble Fish"
© *Hot Weather Films/Universal Studios*

"Dark Circle"
© *New Yorker*

Nick Nolte, Joanna Cassidy
in "Under Fire"
© *Orion Pictures*

the book "With His Pistol in His Hand" by Americo Paredes; Photography, Ray Villalobos; Editors, Arthur Coburn, John Bertucci; Music, W. Michael Lewis, Edward James Olmos; In color; Rated PG; 104 minutes; October release. CAST: Edward James Olmos (Gregorio Cortez), James Gammon (Frank Fly), Tom Bower (Boone Choate), Bruce McGill (Reporter Blakly), Brion James (Capt. Rogers), Alan Vint (Mike), Timothy Scott (Sheriff), Pepe Serna (Romaldo), Michael McGuire (Sheriff Glover), William Sanderson (Cowboy)

DARK CIRCLE (New Yorker) Producer, Ruth Landy; Written, Directed, Photographed, and Edited by Chris Beaver, Judy Irving; Co-Produced and Narrated by Judy Irving; Associate Producer, Judith Lit; Music, Gary S. Remal, Bernard L. Krause; In color; Not rated; 82 minutes; October release. A feature length documentary about the nuclear industry.

AMERICANA (Crown International) Producer-Director, David Carradine; Story and Screenplay, Richard Carr; Based on "The Perfect Round" by Henry Morton Robinson; Photography, Michael Stringer; Music, Craig Hundley; Editors, David Carradine, David Kern; Design, Rick Van Ness; Assistant Director, Larry Bischoff; Costumes, Pat Greene; Art Director, Bliem Kern; In Metrocolor; Rated PG; 91 minutes; October release. CAST: David Carradine (U.S. Soldier), Barbara Hershey (Jess's Daughter), Michael Greene (Mike the garage man), Arnold Herzstein (Old Storekeeper), Sandy Ignon (Sandy), John Barrymore III (John), Greg Walker (Greg), Bruce Carradine (Cop), Glenna Walters (Old Lady), Fran Ryan (Colonel), Claire Townsend (Lt.), David Kern (Wrecking Yard Man), Dan Haggarty (Jake), Buz Storch (New Storekeeper), James Kelly Durgin (Bartender), Rick Van Ness

IN OUR HANDS (Almi) Producers, Robert Richter, Stanley Warnow; Associate Producer, Jacqueline Leopold; Editors, Stanley Warnow, Sharon Sachs, Anthony Forma, Donald Blank; Executive Producer, Leon Falk; Photography, Robert Achs, Pedro Bonilla, Gary Corrigan, Gerald Cotts, Joseph Dell'olio, Steve Sierberg, Dick Fisher, Morris Flam, Anthony Forma, Robert Giraldini, Steve Harris, Douglas Hart, Terry Hopkins, Tom Hurwitz, Mike Jackson, Jeep Johnson, Allen Kinsberg, Ed Lachmad, Hal Landen, Robert Leacock, Don Lenzer, Rick Liss, Vic Losick, William Markle, Neil Marshad, Stuart Math, Robert Nickson, Phil Parmet, Peter Pearce, Hart Perry, Sidney Reichman, Peter Schnall, Jim Scurti, Gene

Searchinger, Nessya Shapiro, Thomas Sigel, Jonathan Smith, Buddy Squires, Burleigh Wartes, Alicia Weber, Jeff Weinstock, Brad Weiss, Oliver Wood; In color; Not rated; 90 minutes; October release. A documentary covering the massive protest in New York's Central Park against the nuclear arms race.

UNDER FIRE (Orion) Executive Producer, Edward Teets; Producer, Jonathan Taplin; Director, Roger Spottiswoode; Screenplay, Ron Shelton, Clayton Frohman; Story, Clayton Frohman; Photography, John Alcott; Art Directors, Augustin Ytuarte, Toby Rafelson; Editor, Mark Conte; Associate Producer, Anna Roth; Music, Jerry Goldsmith; Assistant Directors, Patrick Crowley, Jesus Marin; Soundtrack available on Warner Bros. Records; In Technicolor; Rated R; 108 minutes; October release. CAST: Nick Nolte (Russel), Ed Harris (Oates), Gene Hackman (Alex), Joanna Cassidy (Claire), Alma Martinez (Isela), Holly Palance (Journalist), Ella Laboriel (Singer), Richard Masur (Hub), Jean-Louis Trintignant (Jazy), Fernando Elizondo (Businessman), Hamilton Camp (Regis), Jorge Santoyo, Lucina Rojas (Guerrilla Leaders), Raul Garcia (Waiter), Andaluz Russel (Journalist), Enrique Lucero (Priest), Enrique Beraza (Officer), Jenny Gago (Miss Panama), Eloy Phil Casados (Pedro), Rene Enriquez (Somoza), Jose Campos, Jr. (Soldier)

RUMBLE FISH (Universal) Producers, Fred Roos, Doug Claybourne; Executive Producer, Francis Coppola; Director, Francis Ford Coppola; Screenplay, S. E. Hinton, Francis Coppola; From novel of same title by S. E. Hinton; Photography, Stephen H. Burum; Designer, Dean Tavoularis; Editor, Barry Malkin; Music, Stewart Copeland; Associate Producers, Gian-Carlo Coppola, Roman Coppola; Assistant Directors, David Valdes, Mark Radcliffe; Choreography, Michael Smuin; Costumes, Marge Bowers; From Zoetrope Studios; Soundtrack on A & M Records; In Technicolor; Rated R; 105 minutes; October release. CAST: Matt Dillon (Rusty-James), Mickey Rourke (Motorcycle Boy), Dennis Hopper (Father), Diane Lane (Patty), Vincent Spano (Steve), Nicholas Cage (Smokey), Christopher Penn (B. J.), Larry Fishburne (Midget), William Smith (Patterson), Michael Higgins (Harrigan), Glenn Withrow (Biff), Tom Waits (Benny), Herb Rice, Maybelle Wallace, Nona Manning, Domino, Gio, S. E. Hinton, Emmett Brown, Tracey Walter, Lance Guecia, Bob Maras, J. T. Turner, Keeva Clayton, Kirsten Hayden, Karen Parker, Sussannah Darcy, Kristi Somers

"In Our Hands"
© *Almi Distribution Corp.*

Matt Dillon, Diane Lane
in "Rumble Fish"
© *Hot Weather Films/Universal Studios* **117**

Steve Railsback, Olivia Hussey
in "Escape 2000"
© New World

Ernie Hudson, John Candy
in "Going Berserk"
© Universal City Studios

ESCAPE 2000 (New World) Executive Producer, David Hemmings; Producers, Anthony I. Giannane, William Fayman; Director, Brian Trenchard-Smith; Associate Producer, Brian W. Cook; Screenplay, Jon George, Neill Hicks; Based on story by George Schenck, Robert Williams, David Lawrence; Photography, John McClean; Designer, Bernard Hides; Music, Brian May; Editor, Alan Lake; Costumes, Aphrodite Kondos; A Filmco production in color; Rated R; 80 minutes; October release. CAST: Steve Railsback (Paul), Olivia Hussey (Chris), Noel Ferrier (Mallory), Carmen Duncan (Jennifer), Lynda Stoner (Rita), Michael Craig (Thatcher), Roger Ward (Ritter), Michael Petrovich (Tito), Gus Mercurio (Red), Steve Rackmann (Alph), John Ley (Dodge), Marina Finaly (Melinda), John Godden (Andy), Bill Young (Griff)

TOUCHED (Lorimar) Producers, Dirk Petersmann, Barclay Lottimer; Director, John Flynn; Screenplay, Lyle Kessler; Photography, Fred Murphy; Editor, Harry Keramidas; Design, Patricia von Brandenstein; Music, Shirley Walker; In color; Not rated; 93 minutes; October release. CAST: Robert Hays (Daniel), Kathleen Beller (Jennifer), Ned Beatty (Herbie), Gilbert Lewis (Ernie), Lyle Kessler (Timothy), Farnham Scott (Thomas)

TWICE UPON A TIME (Warner Bros.) Producer, Bill Couturie; Directors, John Korty, Charles Swenson; Executive Producer, George Lucas; Screenplay, John Korty, Charles Swenson, Suella Kennedy, Bill Couturie; Technical Director, John Baker; Supervising Animator, Brian Narell; Editor, Jennifer Gallagher; Art Director, Harley Jessup; A Ladd Co. release in color; Rated PG; 75 minutes; October release. An animated film with the voices of Lorenzo Music (Ralph), Judith Kaham Kampmann (Fairy Godmother), Marshall Efron (Synonamess), James Cranna (Scuzzbopper), Julie Payne (Flora Fauna), Hamilton Camp (Greensleeves), Paul Frees (Narrator).

THE DEVONSVILLE TERROR (MPM) Executive Producers, Jochen Breitenstein, David Dubay; Producer-Director, Ulli Lommel; Screenplay, Ulli Lommel, George T. Lindsey, Suzanna Love; Photography, Ulli Lommel; Editor, Richard Brummer; Music, Ray Colcord, Ed Hill; Assistant Director, Bruce Starr; Design, Priscilla van Gorder; Co-Producer, Charles Aperia; Associate Producers, Tim Nielsen, Bill Rebane; In Pacific Color; Not rated; 82 minutes; October release. CAST: Suzanna Love (Jenny), Robert Walker (Matthew), Donald Pleasence (Dr. Warley), Paul Willson (Walter)

GOING BERSERK (Universal) Executive Producer, Pierre David; Producer, Claude Heroux; Director, David Steinberg; Screenplay, Dana Olsen, David Steinberg; Photography, Bobby Byrne; Designer, Peter Lansdown Smith; Editor, Donn Cambern; Music, Tom Scott; Executive Producer, Pierre David; Associate Producer, Denise DiNovi; Assistant Directors, Dan Kolsrud, Patrick Cosgrove; Costumes, Harry Curtis; In technicolor; Rated R; 85 minutes; October release. CAST: John Candy (John), Joe Flaherty (Chick), Eugene Levy (Sal), Alley Mills (Nancy), Pat Hingle (Ed), Ann Bronston (Patti), Eve Brent Ashe (Mrs. Reese), Elizabeth Kerr (Grandmother Reese), Richard Libertini (Sun Yi), Dixie Carter (Angela), Paul Dooley (Dr. Ted), Ronald E. House (Bruno), Kurtwood Smith (Clarence), Ernie Hudson (Muhammed), Gloria Gifford (Francine), Frantz Turner (Wallace), Murphy Dunne (Public Defender), Dan Barrows (Minister), Julius Harris (Judge), Elinor Donahue (Margaret), Bill Saluga (Skipper), Kathy Bendet (Reporter), Brenda Currin (Sal's Secretary), Hope Haves (Princess), Natasha Ryan (Kitten), Mark Bringelson (Mom Jr.), John Paragon (Rooster)

SEPARATE WAYS (Crown International) Formerly "Valentine"; Executive Producer, Marlene Schmidt; Producer-Director, Howard Avedis; Screenplay, Leah Appet; Photography, Dean Cundey; Editor, John Wright; Music, John Cavacas; Associate Producer, Bill Kawata; In DeLuxe Color; Rated R; 92 minutes; October release. CAST: Karen Black (Valentine), Tony Lo Bianco (Ken), Arlene Golonka (Annie), David Naughton (Jerry), Sharon Farrell (Karen), Jack Carter (Burney), William Windom (Huey), Robert Fuller (Woody), Noah Hathaway (Jason), Walter Brooke, Jordan Charney, Sybil Danning, Angus Duncan, Monte Markham, Bob Hastings, Katherine Justice

RETURN ENGAGEMENT (Island Alive) Producer, Carolyn Pfeiffer; Associate Producer, Barbara Leary; Director, Alan Rudolph; Photography, Jan Kiesser; Editor, Tom Walls; Music, Adrian Belew; In color; Not rated; 90 minutes; November release. A documentary with G. Gordon Liddy and Timothy Leary, with Carole Hemmingway as moderator for debate.

HILARY'S BLUES (Golden Union) Producer, Mack Gilbert; Director, Peter Jensen; Screenplay, Elmer Kline; Editor, Stan Rapjohn; Music, Bill Marx; Lyrics, Marilyn Lovell; In color; Rated R; 80 minutes; November release. CAST: Melinda Marx (Hilary), Diane Berghoff (Helen), Sean Berti (Harvey), Alan Mann (Leader), Alan Dumont (Photographer), Bill Wegney (Detective)

"Escape 2000"
© New World

Ann Bronston, Alley Mills, Dan Barrows,
John Candy in "Going Berserk"
© Universal City Studios

<table>
</table>

Robert Macnaughton, Cynthia Nixon
in "I Am the Cheese"
© *I Am the Cheese Co.*

Burt Lancaster
in "The Osterman Weekend"
© *Osterman Weekend Associates*

BORN IN FLAMES (First Run Features) Produced, Directed and Edited by Lizzie Borden; Photography, Ed Bowes, Al Santana; Story Consultant, Ed Bowes; Music, The Bloods, Ibis, The Red Crayola; In color; Not rated; 90 minutes; November release. CAST: Honey (Honey), Adele Bertei (Isabel), Jeanne Satterfield (Adelaide), Flo Kennedy (Zella), Pat Murphy, Kathryn Bigelow, Becky Johnston (Editors), Ron Vawter, John Coplans (FBI Agents), Hillary Hurst, Sheila McLaughlin, Marty Pottenger (Army Women), John Rudolph, Valerie Smaldone, Warner Schreiner (Newscasters)

THE BIG SCORE (Almi) Producers, Michael S. Landes, Albert Schwartz; Director, Fred Williamson; Executive Producers, Harry Hurwitz, David Forbes; Associate Producer, Irving Schwartz; Screenplay, Gail Morgan Hickman; Editor, Dan Lowenthal; Photography, Joao Fernandes; In color; Rated R; 85 minutes; November release. CAST: Fred Williamson (Hooks), Nancy Wilson (Angi), John Saxon (Davis), Richard Roundtree (Gordon), Ed Lauter (Parks), D'Urville Martin (Easy), Michael Dante (Goldy), Bruce Glover (Koslo), Joe Spinell (Mayfield), Frank Pesce (J.C.), Tony King (Jumbo), James Spinks (Cheech), Chelcie Ross (Hoffa), Stack Pierce (New), Jerome Landfield (Chief Detective), Frank Rice (Pete), Karl Theodore (Huge), Ron Dean (Kowalski), Katherine Wallach (Prostitute), Ernest Perry Jr. (Allen), Greg Noonan (Martin), The Ramsey Lewis Trio, Grand Slam

I AM THE CHEESE (Almi) Producer, David Lange; Director, Robert Jiras; Executive Producers, Jack Schwartzman, Albert Schwartz, Michael S. Landes; Screenplay, David Lange, Robert Jiras; From novel of same title by Robert Cormier; Associate Producer, David Forbes; Music, Jonathan Tunick; Editor, Nicholas Smith; Photography, David Quaid; In color; Rated PG; 100 minutes; November release. CAST: Robert Macnaughton (Adam), Hope Lange (Betty), Don Murray (David), Robert Wagner (Dr. Brint), Cynthia Nixon (Amy), Frank McGurran (Young Adam), Russell Goslant (Gardener), Robert Cormier (Hertz), Dorothea Macnaughton (Produce Lady), Milford Keene (Harvester), Lee Richardson (Grey), Joey Jerome (Whipper), Ronnie Bradbury (Corn), Robert Dutil (Jed), Jeff Rumney (Counterman), David Lange (Montgomery), Christopher Murray (Eric), Sudie Bond (Edna), John Fielder (Arnold), John Bernek (Store Owner), Paul Romero (Coke)

D. C. CAB (Universal) Producer, Topper Carew; Director, Screenplay, Joel Schumacher; Co-Producer, Cassius Vernon Weathersby;

Executive Producers, Peter Guber, Jon Peters; Story, Topper Carew, Joel Schumacher; Photography, Dean Cundey; Designer, John J. Lloyd; Editor, David Blewitt; Associate Producer, Peter V. Herald; Music, Giorgio Moroder; Costumes, Roberta Weiner; Assistant Directors, Newton D. Arnold, Russ Harling; Choreography, Jeffrey Hornaday; Art Director, Bernie Cutler; In Technicolor; Rated R; 104 minutes; November release. CAST: Adam Baldwin (Albert), Charlie Barnett (Tyrone), Irene Cara (Herself), Anne DeSalvo (Myrna), Max Gail (Harold), Gloria Gifford (Miss Floyd), DeWayne Jessie (Bongo), Bill Maher (Baba), Whitman Mayo (Mr. Rhythm), Mr. T (Samson), Jose Perez (Bravo), Paul Rodriguez (Xavier), David Barbarian (Buzzy), Peter Barbarian (Buddy), Marsha Warfield (Ophelia), Gary Busey (Dell), Bob Zmuda (Cubby), Jim Moody (Arnie), Denise Gordy (Denise), Alfredine P. Brown (Matty), Scott Nemes, Senta Moses (Ambassador's son and daughter), Jill Schoelen (Claudette), Diana Bellamy (Maudie), John Diehl, Bonnie Keith, J. W. Smith (Kidnappers), Moriah Shannon (Waitress), Newton D. Arnold (FBI Chief), Michael Elliott Hill, Dennis Stewart, Paula Earlette Davis, Jacki Clark, Don Jacob, Ann Guilford-Grey, Timothy Rice, Patricia Duff, Martha Jane Urann, Michael DeSanto, Dale Stephenson, Esther Lee, Scott Perry, Marti Soyoa, Anthony Thompkins

THE OSTERMAN WEEKEND (20th Century-Fox) Producers, Peter S. Davis, William N. Panzer; Director, Sam Peckinpah; Screenplay, Alan Sharp; Adaptation, Ian Masters; Based on book by Robert Ludlum; Executive Producers, Michael T. Murphy, Larry Jones, Marc W. Zavat; Associate Producers, Don Guest, E. C. Monell; Editors, Edward Abroms, David Rawlins; Music, Lalo Schifrin; Photography, John Coquillon; Assistant Directors, Win Phelps, Robert Rooy; Art Director, Robb Wilson King; In DeLuxe Color; Rated R; 102 minutes; November release. CAST: Rutger Hauer (Tanner), John Hurt (Fassett), Craig T. Nelson (Osterman), Dennis Hopper (Tremayne), Chris Sarandon (Cardone), Burt Lancaster (Danforth), Meg Foster (Ali), Helen Shaver (Virginia), Cassie Yates (Betty), Sandy McPeak (Stennings), Christopher Starr (Steve), Cheryl Carter (Marcia), John Bryson, Anne Haney (Honeymoon Couple), Kristen Peckinpah (Secretary), Jan Triska (Mikalovich), Hansford Rowe (Gen. Keever), Merete Van Kamp (Zuna), Bruce Block (Manager), Buddy Joe Hooker (Kidnapper), Tim Thomerson, Deborah Chiaramonte, Walter Kelley, Brick Tilley, Eddy Donno, Den Surles

Adam Baldwin, Mr. T, Charlie Barnett
in "D. C. Cab"
© *Universal City Studios*

Rutger Hauer, Craig T. Nelson
in "The Osterman Weekend"
© *Osterman Weekend Associates*

Juliana, Princess Teegra
in "Fire and Ice"
© Polyc International

Christopher Atkins, Lesley Ann Warren
in "A Night in Heaven"
© 20th Century-Fox

FIRE AND ICE (20th Century-Fox) Producers, Ralph Bakshi, Frank Frazetta; Director, Ralph Bakshi; Screenplay, Roy Thomas, Gerry Conway; Characters created by Ralph Bakshi, Frank Frazetta; Executive Producers, John W. Hyde, Richard R. St. Johns; Associate Producer, Lynne Betner; Music, William Kraft; Editor, A. David Marshall; Animation Production Supervisor, Michael Svayko; In DeLuxe Color and Dolby Stereo; Rated PG; 82 minutes; November release. CAST: Randy Norton (Larn), Cynthia Leake (Teegra), Steve Sandor (Darkwolf), Sean Hannon (Nekron), Leo Gordon (Jarol), William Ostrander (Taro), Elleen O'Neill (Juliana), Elizabeth Lloyd Shaw (Roleil), Mickey Morton (Otwa), Tamarah Park (Tutor), Big Yank (Monga), Greg Elam (Pako), Holly Frazetta (Subhuman Priestess), Subhumans: James Bridges, Shane Callan, Archie Hamilton, Michael Kelloff, Dale Park, Douglas Payton, with additional voices of Susan Tyrrell (Juliana), Maggie Roswell (Teegra), William Ostrander (Larn), Stephen Mendel (Nekron), Alan Koss (Envoy), Clare Nono (Tutor), Hans Howes (Defender Captain)

THE FIRST TURN-ON! (Troma) Producers, Lloyd Kaufman, Michael Herz; Executive Producers, William E. Kirksey, Spencer A. Tandy; Directors, Michael Herz, Samuel Weil; Screenplay, Stuart Strutin; Additional Material, Mark Torgl, Georgia Harrell, Lloyd Kaufman, Michael Herz; Photography, Lloyd Kaufman; Editors, Richard Haines, Adam Fredericks, Richard King; Special Effects, Les Larrain; Art Director, Ellen Christiansen; Costumes, Danielle Brunon; Associate Producer, Stuart Strutin; Assistant Director, Ilan Cohen; In color; Rated R; 90 minutes; November release. CAST: Georgia Harrell (Michelle), Michael Sanville (Mitch), Googy Gress (Henry), John Flood (Danny), Heidi Miller (Annie), Al Pia (Alfred), Betty Pia (Mrs. Anderson), Gilda Gumbo (Mme. Gumbo) Lara Grills (Lucy), Kristina Marie Wetzel (Barbara), Frank Trent Saladino (Jeff), David Berardi (Johnny), Ted Henning (Ted), Donna Winter (Mona), Sheila Kennedy (Dreamgirl), Mark Torgl (Dwayne), Donna Barnes (Jane), Sioban Fergus (Cathy), Steve Hollander (Stinky), Vincent D'Onofrio (Lobotomy), Russel Matthews (Pissing Johnnie), Mitchell Whitfield (Micky), Nick Pannone (Bozo), Michael Schoffel (Melvin), Randy Matthews (Snake), Gretchen Weiner (Mrs. Richards), Ebb Miller (Richards), William Kirksey (Announcer)

A CHRISTMAS STORY (MGM/UA) Producers, Rene Dupont, Bob Clark; Director, Bob Clark; Screenplay, Jean Shepherd, Leigh Brown, Bob Clark; Based on novel "In God We Trust, All Others Pay Cash" by Jean Shepherd; Photography, Reginald H. Morris; Designer, Reuben Freed; Editor, Stan Cole; Music, Carl Ziffrer, Paul Zaza; Costumes, Mary E. McLeod; Associate Producer, Gary Goch; Assistant Director, Ken Goch; Art Director, Gavin Mitchell; In color; Rated PG; 98 minutes; November release. CAST: Melinda Dillon (Mother), Darren McGavin (Old Man), Peter Billingsley (Ralphie), Ian Petrella (Randy), Scott Schwartz (Flick), R. D. Robb (Schwartz), Tedde Moore (Miss Shields), Yano Anaya (Grover), Zack Ward (Scot), Jeff Gillen (Santa Claus), Colin Fox (Ming), Paul Hubbard (Flash Gordon), Les Carlson (Tree Man), Jim Hunter (Freight Man), Patty Johnson (Head Elf), Drew Hocevar (Male Elf), David Svoboda (Goggles), Dwayne McLean (Black Bart), Helen E. Kaider (Wicked Witch), John Wong (Chinese Father), Rocco Bellusci (Street Kid), Tommy Wallace (Boy in school), Waiters: Johan Sebastian Wong, Fred Lee, Dan Ma

A NIGHT IN HEAVEN (20th Century-Fox) Producers, Gene Kirkwood, Howard W. Koch, Jr.; Director, John G. Avildsen; Screenplay, Joan Tewkesbury; Score, Jan Hammer; Photography, David Quaid; Designer, William Cassidy; Editor, John G. Avildsen; Associate Producer, Barry Rosenbush; Designer, Anna Hill Johnstone; Assistant Directors, Alan Hopkins, Robert E. Warren; Choreography, Deney Terrio; Soundtrack on A & M Records; In DeLuxe Color; Rated R; 83 minutes; November release. CAST: Christopher Atkins (Rick), Lesley Ann Warren (Faye), Robert Logan (Whitney), Deborah Rush (Patsy), Deney Terrio (Tony), Sandra Beall (Slick), Alix Elias (Shirley), Carrie Snodgress (Mrs. Johnson), Amy Levine (Eve), Fred Buch (Jack), Karen Margret Cole (Louise), Don Cox (Revere), Veronica Gamba (Tammy), Joey Gian (Pete), Bill Hindman (Russel), Linda Lee (Ivy), Rosemary McVeigh (Alison), Gail Merrill (Grace), Cindy Perlman (Linda), Brian Smith (Osgood), Scott Stone (Lee), Andy Garcia (T. J.), Craig Nedrow (Man Mountain Dean), Anthony Avildsen (Scooter), Harold Bergman (Sladkus), Spatz Donovan (Heaven M.C.), Dan Fitzgerald (Guard), Butch Warren (Orshan), Robert Goodman (Disick), John Archie (Raymer), Will Knickerbocker (Larry), Sherry Moreland, Robbie Wolf, Tiffany Myles, Sally Ricca, Pam Tindal, Judy Arman, Mary Teahan

YOUNG WARRIORS (Cannon Group) Producer, Victoria Paige Meyerink; Director, Lawrence D. Foldes; Co-Producers, Screenplay, Lawrence D. Foldes, Russell W. Colgin; Music, Rob Walsh;

Tom Reilly, Ed DeStefane, James Van Patten,
Mike Norris in "Young Warriors"
© Cannon Films/Star Cinema

Melinda Dillon, Darren McGavin, Ian Petrella,
Peter Billingsley in "A Christmas Story"
© MGM/UA Entertainment Co.

Tommy Lee Jones, Michael O'Keefe, Jenny
Seagrove in "Nate and Hayes"
© *Paramount Pictures*

Tony Roberts, Robert Joy
in "Amityville 3-D"
© *Orion Pictures*

Photography, Mac Ahlberg; Editor, Ted Nicolaou; Art Director, Richard S. Bylin; Designer, Karl Pogany; Associate Producers, Joseph R. Milligan, Adam Slater; Costumes, Laura Cogin; Assistant Directors, Michael Sourapas, Carol Lewis; A Star Cinema production in color; Rated R; 105 minutes; November release. CAST: Ernest Borgnine (Lt. Bob Carrigan), Richard Roundtree (Sgt. John Austin), Lynda Day George (Beverly), James Van Patten (Kevin), Anne Lockhart (Lucy), Tom Reilly (Scott), Ed DeStefane (Stan), Mike Norris (Fred), Dick Shawn (Prof. Hoover), Linnea Quigley (Ginger), John Alden (Jorge), Britt Helfer (Heather), Don Hepner (Animation Instructor), April Dawn (Tiffany), Nels Van Patten (Roger), Rick Easton (Bartender), Paul Tanashian (Dicter), Jimmy Patterson, Bernard Bloomer, Darlene D'Angelo, George O'Mara Mason, Gregory Bennett, Michelle Rossi, Randy Woltz

NATE AND HAYES (Paramount) Originally "Savage Islands"; Producers, Lloyd Phillips, Rob Whitehouse; Director, Ferdinand Fairfax; Screenplay, John Hughes, David Odell; from screen story by Mr. Odell; Story, Lloyd Phillips; Music, Trevor Jones; Editor, John Shirley; Designer, Maurice Cain; Costumes, Norma Moriceau; Photography, Tony Imi; Assistant Directors, Bert Batt, Terry Pearce, Chris Short, Tim Coddington; Art Directors, Jo Ford, Dan Hennah, Rick Kofoed; In color and Dolby Stereo; Rated PG; 100 minutes; November release. CAST: Tommy Lee Jones (Capt. Bully Hayes), Michael O'Keefe (Nate Williamson), Max Phipps (Ben), Jenny Seagrove (Sophie), Grant Tilly (Count von Rittenberg), Peter Rowley (Louis), Bill Johnson (Rev. Williamson), Kate Harcourt (Mrs. Williamson), Reg Ruka (Moaka), Roy Billing (Auctioneer), Bruce Allpress (Blake), David Letch (Ratbag), Prince Tui Teka (King of Ponape), Pudji Waseso (Fong), Peter Vere Jones (Gunboat Captain), Tom Vanderlaan (Lt.), Mark Hadlow (Gun Operator), Philip Gordon (Timmy), Norman Fairley (Pegleg), Warwick Simmons (Pug), Crewmen: Paul Farrell, Frank Taurua, Norman Kessing, Robert Bruce, Timothy Lee, Peter Bell, Peter Diamond, John Rush, Grant Price, Karl Bradley

PURPLE HAZE (Triumph) Producer, Thomas Anthony Fucci; Director, David Burton Morris; Executive Producer, Screenplay, Victoria Wozniak; Story, Tom Kelsey, Victoria Wozniak, David Burton Morris; Assistant Director, Kelly Van Horn; Photography, Richard Gibb; Editor, Dusty Nabili; Art Director, James Johnson; Fight Choreography, Peter Thoemke; In color; Rated R; 97 minutes; No-

vember release. CAST: Peter Nelson (Matt), Chuck McQuary (Jeff), Bernard Baldan (Derek), Susanna Lack (Kitty), Bob Breuler (Walter), Joanne Bauman (Margaret), Katy Horsch (Phoebe), Heidi Helmen (Angela), Tomy O'Brien (Marcus), Dan Jones (Snitch), Don Bakke, James Craven (NCOs), John Speckhardt (Oath Officer), Jean Ashley (Mrs. Maley), Sara Hennessy (Lori), Michael Bailey (Ed), Peter Thoemke (Bill), Hayden Saunier, Donna Moen (Waitresses), Spare Change (Country Club Band), Don Westling, Steve Gjerde (Campus Cops), Jake Braziel (Bus Driver), Ky Michaelson (Cop), Jane Rogers (Cara), Norie Helm (Penny), Mary Bea Arman (Stacey)

AMITYVILLE 3-D (Orion) Producer, Stephen F. Kesten; Director, Richard Fleischer; Screenplay, William Wales; Photography, Fred Schuler; Music, Howard Blake; Editor, Frank J. Urioste; Art Director, Giorgio Postiglione; Costumes, Clifford Capone; Assistant Director, Joe Reidy; In ArriVision 3-D and color; Rated R; 105 minutes; November release. CAST: Tony Roberts (John Baxter), Tess Harper (Nancy Baxter), Robert Joy (Elliott), Candy Clark (Melanie), John Beal (Harold), Leora Dana (Emma), John Harkins (Clifford), Lori Loughlin (Susan), Meg Ryan (Lisa), Neill Barry (Jeff), Pete Kowanko (Roger), Rikke Borge (Elliot's Assistant), Carlos Romano (David), Josephina Echanove (Dolores), Jorge Zepeda (Van Driver), Raquel Pankowsky (Sensory Woman), Paco Pharres (Maintenance Man)

SLEEPAWAY CAMP (United Film Distribution Co.) Executive Producer, Screenplay, Director, Robert Hiltzik; Producers, Michele Tatosian, Jerry Silva; Photography, Benjamin Davis; Editors, Ron Kalish, Sharyn L. Ross; Music, Edward Bilous; Assistant Director, Richard Feury; Design, William Billowit; In Technicolor; Rated R; 84 minutes; November release. CAST: Mike Kellin (Mel), Felissa Rose (Angela), Jonathan Tierston (Ricky), Karen Fields (Judy), Christopher Collet (Paul), Paul DeAngelo (Ron), Robert Earl Jones (Ben), Katherine Kamhi (Meg), John E. Dunn (Kenny)

THE BEING (BFV) Producer, William Osco; Director-Screenplay, Jackie Kong; Photography, Robert Ebinger; Editor, David Newhouse; Music, Don Preston; Art Director, Alexia Corwin; Associate Producer, Kent Perkins; In color; Rated R; 79 minutes; November release. CAST: Martin Landau (Garson), Jose Ferrer (Mayor), Dorothy Malone (Marge), Ruth Buzzi (Mayor's Wife), Rexx Coltrane (Mortimer), Marianne Gordon Rogers (Laurie), Kent Perkins (Dudley)

Susanna Lack, Peter Nelson
in "Purple Haze"
© *Columbia Pictures*

Christopher Collet, Karen Fields
in "Sleepaway Camp"
© *American Eagle Films*

Michael Margotta, Karen Black, Michael
Emil in "Can She Bake a Cherry Pie?"

MY BREAKFAST WITH BLASSIE (Artist Endeavors International) Conceived, Produced, Directed by Johnny Legend, Linda Lautrec; Editors, Johnny Legend, Linda Lautrec, Lynne Margulies; Music, Linda Mitchell; In color; 60 minutes; November release. CAST: Andy Kaufman, Freddie Blassie, Lynne Elaine, Laura Burdick, Linda Burdick, Linda Hirsch, Bob Zmuda

CHRISTMAS EVIL (Edward R. Pressman) Formerly "You Better Watch Out"; Producer, Burt Kleiner, Peter Kameron; Associate Producer, Michael Levine; Direction-Screenplay, Lewis Jackson; Editors, Corky O'Hara, Linda Leeds; Photography, Ricardo Aronovich; Costumes, Diedre Williams; Designer, Lorenzo Jodie Harris; In color; Not rated; 100 minutes; November release. CAST: Brandon Maggart (Harry), Dianne Hull (Jackie), Scott McKay (Fletcher), Joe Jamrog (Frank), Peter Friedman (Grosch), Ray Barry (Gleason), Bobby Lesser (Gottleib), Sam Gray (Grilla), Ellen McElduff (Harry's Mother), Patty Richardson (Moss' Mother)

SIMPLY IRRESISTIBLE (Essex) Producer, Summer Brown; Director, Edwin Brown; Screenplay, Sandra Winters; Edwin Brown; Executive Producer, Joe Steinman; Music, Geoffrey Pekofsky; Photography, Teru Hyashi; Editor, Terrance O'Reilly; In color; Rated R; 100 minutes; November release. CAST: Richard Pacheco (Walter), Samantha Fox (Arlene), Gayle Sterling (Juliet), Star Wood (Cleopatra), Gina Gianetti (Sunshine), Nicole Black (Mata Hari), Dorothy Lemay (Hitchhiker), Misha Garr (Miracle), Mai Lin, Lynn Francis, C. Garr, Shu Garr

SEVEN DOORS OF DEATH (Aquarius) Producer, Terry Levene; Director, Louis Fuller; Screenplay, Roy Corchoran; Music, Mitch Yuspeh and Ira Yuspeh; Photography, Glenn Kimbell; Executive Producer, Ron Harvey; In color; Rated R; November release. CAST: Katherine MacColl, David Warbeck, Sarah Keller, Tony Saint John, Veronica Lazar

THE SMURFS AND THE MAGIC FLUTE (Atlantic) Created by Peyo; Adapted by Peyo, Yuan Delporte; Music, Michel Legrand; Presented by First Performance Pictures in association with Stuart R. Ross; In color; Rated G; 89 minutes; November release.

VIDEO VIXENS (Troma) Producer, Roland S. Smither; Director, Ronald Sullivan; Screenplay, Joel Gross; Music, Jacques Urbont; Photography, Arthur D. Marks; In Movielab Color; Rated R; 75 minutes; December release. CAST: Robyn Hilton, Sandy Dempsey, Cheryl Smith

Olivia Newton-John, John Travolta
in "Two of a Kind"
© *20th Century-Fox*

CAN SHE BAKE A CHERRY PIE? (Frank Moreno) Producer, M. H. Simonsons; Writer-Director, Henry Jaglom; Executive Producer, Michael Jaglom; Photography, Bob Fiore; Music, written and sung by Karen Black; An International Rainbow Picture in color; A World Wide Classics release; Rated R; 90 minutes; December release. CAST: Karen Black (Zee), Michael Emil (Eli), Michael Margotta (Larry), Frances Fisher (Louise), Martin Harvey Friedberg (Mort), Robert Hallak, Anna Raviv (Young Couple in cafe), Paul Williams (Zee's Husband), Ariela Nicole (Eli's Daughter), Larry David (Philosopher), The Lost Wandering Band, Eddie the Pigeon

VOICE OVER (Welsh Arts) Directed, Written and Edited by Chris Monger; Producers, Mr. Monger, Laurie McFadden, Welsh Arts Council; Photography, Roland Denning; Music, Schubert/Edward Klak; Not rated; 105 minutes; December release. CAST: Ian McNeice (Ed "Fats" Bannerman), Bish Nethercote (Bitch/Elizabeth), John Cassady (F. X. Jones), Sarah Martin (Celia), David Pearce (Frank), Stuart Hutton (Doctor), Eira Moore (PAP Boss), Paul Chandler (RDOV Boss), Carol Owen (Bitch's Friend), Jon Groome (Capt. Thompson)

GOSPEL (Aquarius) Produced and Directed by David Leivick, Frederick A. Ritzenberg; Photography, David Myers; Music, Miles Goodman; Editor, Glenn Farr; In color; Rated G; 92 minutes; December release. A concert film featuring James Cleveland and the Southern California Community Choir, Walkter Hawkins and the Hawkins Family, The Love Center Choir, Mighty Clouds of Joy, Shirley Caesar, Twinkie Clark, the Clark Sisters

DEAR MR. WONDERFUL (Lilienthal) Producer, Joachim von Vietinghoff; Director, Peter Lilienthal; Screenplay, Sam Koperwas; Photography, Michael Ballhaus; Songs, Joe Pesci, Larry Fallon; In color; Not rated; 100 minutes; December release. CAST: Joe Pesci (Ruby Dennis), Karen Ludwig (Paula), Evan Handler (Ray), Ivy Ray Browning (Sharon), Frank Vincent (Louie), Paul Herman (Hesh), Tony Martin (Guest)

TWO OF A KIND (20th Century-Fox) Producers, Roger M. Rothstein, Joe Wizan; Direction and Screenplay, John Herzfeld; Photography, Fred Koenekamp; Designer, Thomas Bronson; Music, Patrick Williams; Associate Producers, Michele Panelli, Joan Edwards, Kate Edwards; Assistant Directors, Fredric Blankfein, Joseph Moore, John Moio; Art Director, Spencer Deverell; Set Designers, Kandy Stern, Diane Wager; Soundtrack available on MCA Records; In Panavision and DeLuxe Color; Rated PG; 90 minutes; December release. CAST: John Travolta (Zack), Olivia Newton-John (Debbie), Charles Durning (Charlie), Beatrice Straight (Ruth), Scatman Crothers (Earl), Castulo Guerra (Gonzales), Oliver Reed (Beazley), Richard Bright (Stuart), Vincent Bufano (Oscar), Toni Kalem (Terri), James Stevens (Ron), Jack Kehoe (Chotiner), Ernie Hudson (Det. Staggs), Warren Robertson (Himself), Deborah Dalton (Angie), Tony Crupi (Det. Bruno), Bobby Costanzo (Capt. Cinzari), Kurek Ashley (SoHo Cop), Jill Andre (Gladys), Ann Travolta (Bank Teller), Kathy Bates (Furniture Man's Wife), John Hudkins (Guard), Sheila Frazier (Reporter), Tony Munafo, Steven Hirsch, Pam Bowman, Jacque Foti, Ted Grossman, Joe Cirillo, Christopher Loomis, Michael Prince

SCALPS (21st Century) Producer, T. L. Lankford; Direction-Screenplay, Fred Olen Ray; Photography, Brett Webster, Larry van Loon; Editor, John Barr; Music, Drew Neumann, Eric Rasmussen; Assistant Director, Jeff Vernon; In color; Rated R; December release. CAST: Kirk Alyn (Dr. Machen), Carroll Borland (Dr. Reynolds), Jo Ann Robinson (D.J.), Richard Hench (Randy), Roger Maycock (Kershaw), Barbara Magnusson (Ellen), Frank McDonald (Ben), Carol Sue Flockhart (Louise), George Randall (Billy Iron Wing), Forrest J. Ackerman (Prof. Treatwood)

THE FOREST (Fury Films) Executive Producer, Frank Evans; Producer-Director, Don Jones; Screenplay, Evan Jones; Photography, Stuart Asbjorsen; Music, Richard Hieronymus, Alan Oldfield; Art Director, Sandra Saunders; In color; Rated R; 85 minutes; December release. CAST: Dean Russell (Steve), Michael Brody (John), Elaine Warner (Sharon), John Batis (Charley), Ann Wilkinson (Teddi), Jeanette Kelly (Mother), Corky Pigeon (John, Jr.), Becki Burke (Jennifer), Don Jones (Forest Ranger), Tony Gee, Stafford Morgan, Marilyn Anderson

IN LOVE (Platinum) Producer-Director, Chuck Vincent; Screenplay, Rick Marx, Chuck Vincent; Story, Henri Pachard; Music, Ian Shaw; Photography, Larry Revene; Editor, James Macreading; In color; Rated R; 100 minutes; December release. CAST: Kelly Nichols (Jill), Jerry Butler (Andy), Tish Ambrose (Janet), Joanna Storm (April), Samantha Fox (Elaine), Jack Wrangler (Dick), Michael Knight (Kip), Susan Nero (Hooker), Beth Alison Broderick (Ella), Veronica Hart (Belinda)

PROMISING NEW ACTORS OF 1983

STEVEN BAUER

JENNIFER BEALS

DIANE LANE

MATTHEW BRODERICK

TOM CRUISE

CYNTHIA NIXON

AMANDA PLUMMER

GREGORY HINES

MICHAEL KEATON

CYNTHIA RHODES

ALFRE WOODARD

VINCENT SPANO

125

ACADEMY AWARDS OF 1983

(Presented Monday, April 9, 1984)

BEST PICTURE OF 1983

TERMS OF ENDEARMENT

(PARAMOUNT) Produced, Directed and Written by James Brooks; Co-Producers, Penney Finkelman, Martin Jurow; Photography, Andrzej Bartkowiak; Designer, Polly Platt; Editor, Richard Marks; Music, Michael Gore; Based on novel of same title by Larry McMurtry; In color; Rated PG; 129 minutes; November release

CAST

Emma Horton	Debra Winger
Aurora Greenway	Shirley MacLaine
Garrett Breedlove	Jack Nicholson
Vernon Dahlart	Danny DeVito
Flap Horton	Jeff Daniels
Sam Burns	John Lithgow
Rosie	Betty King
Patsy Clark	Lisa Hart Carroll
Teddy	Huckleberry Fox
Melanie	Megan Morris
Tommy	Troy Bishop
Young Tommy Horton	Shane Serwin
Young Emma Greenway	Jennifer Josey

Left: Shirley MacLaine, Debra Winger
© *Paramount Pictures*

1983 Academy Awards for Best Picture,
Best Actress (Shirley MacLaine),
Supporting Actor (Jack Nicholson),
Director, Screenplay Adaptation

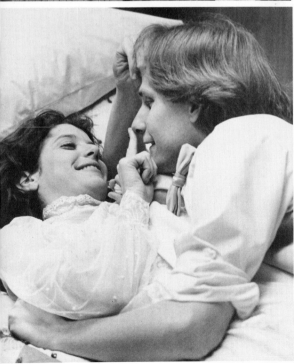

Debra Winger, Jeff Daniels

Shirley MacLaine, Jack Nicholson
Above: Lisa Hart Carroll, Debra Winger

Debra Winger, Shirley MacLaine
Above: Debra Winger, John Lithgow
Top: Norman Bennett, Shirley MacLaine, Danny DeVito
Below: Jack Nicholson, Shirley MacLaine

Jack Nicholson, Shirley MacLaine, also above
Top: Jeff Daniels, Shirley MacLaine

ROBERT DUVALL
in "Tender Mercies"
© *Universal City Studios*

1983 ACADEMY AWARD FOR BEST ACTOR

SHIRLEY MacLAINE
in "Terms of Endearment"
© *Paramount Pictures*

1983 ACADEMY AWARD FOR BEST ACTRESS

JACK NICHOLSON
in "Terms of Endearment"
© *Paramount Pictures*

1983 ACADEMY AWARD FOR BEST SUPPORTING ACTOR

LINDA HUNT
in "The Year of Living Dangerously"
© MGM/UA Entertainment Co.

1983 ACADEMY AWARD FOR BEST SUPPORTING ACTRESS

FANNY AND ALEXANDER

(EMBASSY) Executive Producer, Jorn Donner; Direction and Screenplay, Ingmar Bergman; Assistant Director, Peter Schildt; Photography, Sven Nykvist; Editor, Sylvia Ingemarsson; Music, Daniel Bell, Benjamin Britten, Frans Helmerson, Robert Schumsnn, Marianne Jacobs; Art Director, Anna Asp; Designer, Jacob Tigerskiold; Costumes, Marik Vos; A Swedish-French Co-Production in color; Rated R; 190 minutes; June release

CAST

Fanny Ekdahl (8 years) .... Pernilla Allwin
Alexander Ekdahl (10 years) .... Bertil Guve
Carl Ekdahl ....Borje Ahlstedt
Justina .... Harriet Andersson
Aron.. Mats Bergman
Filip Landahl....................................... Gunnar Bjornstrand
Oscar Ekdahl...Allan Edwall
Ismael.. Stina Ekblad
Emilie Ekdahl .... Ewa Froling
Isak Jacobi.. Erland Josephson
Gustav Adolf Ekdahl .... Jarl Kulle
Aunt Emma... Kabi Laretei
Alma Ekdahl .... Mona Malm
Bishop Edward Vergerus .... Jan Malmsjo
Lydia Ekdahl...Christina Schollin
Helena Ekdahl...Gunn Wallgren

Left: Pernilla Allwin, Bertil Guve
© *Svenska Filminstitutet*

1983 Academy Awards for Best Foreign Language Film, Best Cinematography, Art Direction, Costume Design

Erland Josephson, Gunn Wallgren

1983 ACADEMY AWARD FOR BEST FOREIGN LANGUAGE FILM

Ewa Froling, Mona Malm Top: (L) Jan Malmsjo, Ewa Froling, (R) Bertil Guve, Pernilla Allwin

HE MAKES ME FEEL LIKE DANCIN'

(EDGAR J. SCHERICK) Executive Producers, Edgar J. Scherick, Scott Rudin; Producer-Director, Emile Ardolino; Co-Producer, Judy Kinberg; Editors, Thomas Haneke, Charlotte Grossman, Jean Standish, Neil Wenger; Photography, Francis Kenny, Don Lenzer, John Lindley, Phil Parmet, Carl Teitelbaum, Jim McCalmont, Scott Sorenson; Production Executive, Susan Pollock; Associate Producer/Production Manager, Mel Howard; Assistant Directors, Joan Feinstein, Nina Steiner; Production Assistant, Diana McNally; Music Composed, Conducted and Arranged by Lee Norris; Additional Music, George Balanchine, Martin Charnin, Christopher d'Amboise, Arthur Schwartz; In color; Not rated; 60 minutes; November release. With Jacques d'Amboise, Judy Collins (Hostess), and over 1000 children from the National Dance Institute.

Carolyn George Photos

Left: Jacques d'Amboise

Jacques d'Ambois (c)

1983 ACADEMY AWARD FOR BEST FEATURE DOCUMENTARY

Jacques d'Ambois (center) and class of police

Jose Ferrer	Greer Garson	Laurence Olivier	Katharine Hepburn	James Stewart	Gale Sondergaard

PREVIOUS ACADEMY AWARD WINNERS

(1) Best Picture, (2) Actor, (3) Actress, (4) Supporting Actor,
(5) Supporting Actress, (6) Director, (7) Special Award, (8) Best Foreign Language Film

1927–28: (1) "Wings," (2) Emil Jannings in "The Way of All Flesh," (3) Janet Gaynor in "Seventh Heaven," (6) Frank Borzage for "Seventh Heaven," (7) Charles Chaplin.

1928–29: (1) "Broadway Melody," (2) Warner Baxter in "Old Arizona," (3) Mary Pickford in "Coquette," (6) Frank Lloyd for "The Divine Lady."

1929–30: (1) "All Quiet on the Western Front," (2) George Arliss in "Disraeli," (3) Norma Shearer in "The Divorcee," (6) Lewis Milestone for "All Quiet on the Western Front."

1930–31: (1) "Cimarron," (2) Lionel Barrymore in "A Free Soul," (3) Marie Dressler in "Min and Bill," (6) Norman Taurog for "Skippy."

1931–32: (1) "Grand Hotel," (2) Fredric March in "Dr. Jekyll and Mr. Hyde" tied with Wallace Beery in "The Champ," (3) Helen Hayes in "The Sin of Madelon Claudet," (6) Frank Borzage for "Bad Girl."

1932–33: (1) "Cavalcade," (2) Charles Laughton in "The Private Life of Henry VIII," (3) Katharine Hepburn in "Morning Glory," (6) Frank Lloyd for "Cavalcade."

1934: (1) "It Happened One Night," (2) Clark Gable in "It Happened One Night," (3) Claudette Colbert in "It Happened One Night," (6) Frank Capra for "It Happened One Night," (7) Shirley Temple.

1935: (1) "Mutiny on the Bounty," (2) Victor McLaglen in "The Informer," (3) Bette Davis in "Dangerous," (6) John Ford for "The Informer," (7) D. W. Griffith.

1936: (1) "The Great Ziegfeld," (2) Paul Muni in "The Story of Louis Pasteur," (3) Luise Rainer in "The Great Ziegfeld," (4) Walter Brennan in "Come and Get It," (5) Gale Sondergaard in "Anthony Adverse," (6) Frank Capra for "Mr. Deeds Goes to Town."

1937: (1) "The Life of Emile Zola," (2) Spencer Tracy in "Captains Courageous," (3) Luise Rainer in "The Good Earth," (4) Joseph Schildkraut in "The Life of Emile Zola," (5) Alice Brady in "In Old Chicago," (6) Leo McCarey for "The Awful Truth," (7) Mack Sennett, Edgar Bergen.

1938: (1) "You Can't Take It with You," (2) Spencer Tracy in "Boys' Town," (3) Bette Davis in "Jezebel," (4) Walter Brennan in "Kentucky," (5) Fay Bainter in "Jezebel," (6) Frank Capra for "You Can't Take It with You," (7) Deanna Durbin, Mickey Rooney, Harry M. Warner, Walt Disney.

1939: (1) "Gone with the Wind," (2) Robert Donat in "Goodbye, Mr. Chips," (3) Vivien Leigh in "Gone with the Wind," (4) Thomas Mitchell in "Stagecoach," (5) Hattie McDaniel in "Gone with the Wind," (6) Victor Fleming for "Gone with the Wind," (7) Douglas Fairbanks, Judy Garland.

1940: (1) "Rebecca," (2) James Stewart in "The Philadelphia Story," (3) Ginger Rogers in "Kitty Foyle," (4) Walter Brennan in "The Westerner," (5) Jane Darwell in "The Grapes of Wrath," (6) John Ford for "The Grapes of Wrath," (7) Bob Hope.

1941: (1) "How Green Was My Valley," (2) Gary Cooper in "Sergeant York," (3) Joan Fontaine in "Suspicion," (4) Donald Crisp in "How Green Was My Valley," (5) Mary Astor in "The Great Lie," (6) John Ford for "How Green Was My Valley," (7) Leopold Stokowski, Walt Disney.

1942: (1) "Mrs. Miniver," (2) James Cagney in "Yankee Doodle Dandy," (3) Greer Garson in "Mrs. Miniver," (4) Van Heflin in "Johnny Eager," (5) Teresa Wright in "Mrs. Miniver," (6) William Wyler for "Mrs. Miniver," (7) Charles Boyer, Noel Coward.

1943: (1) "Casablanca," (2) Paul Lukas in "Watch on the Rhine," (3) Jennifer Jones in "The Song of Bernadette," (4) Charles Coburn in "The More the Merrier," (5) Katina Paxinou in "For Whom the Bell Tolls," (6) Michael Curtiz for "Casablanca."

1944: (1) "Going My Way," (2) Bing Crosby in "Going My Way," (3) Ingrid Bergman in "Gaslight," (4) Barry Fitzgerald in "Going My Way," (5) Ethel Barrymore in "None but the Lonely Heart," (6) Leo McCarey for "Going My Way," (7) Margaret O'Brien, Bob Hope.

1945: (1) "The Lost Weekend," (2) Ray Milland in "The Lost Weekend," (3) Joan Crawford in "Mildred Pierce," (4) James Dunn in "A Tree Grows in Brooklyn," (5) Anne Revere in "National Velvet," (6) Billy Wilder for "The Lost Weekend," (7) Walter Wanger, Peggy Ann Garner.

1946: (1) "The Best Years of Our Lives," (2) Fredric March in "The Best Years of Our Lives," (3) Olivia de Havilland in "To Each His Own," (4) Harold Russell in "The Best Years of Our Lives," (5) Anne Baxter in "The Razor's Edge," (6) William Wyler for "The Best Years of Our Lives," (7) Laurence Olivier, Harold Russell, Ernst Lubitsch, Claude Jarman, Jr.

1947: (1) "Gentleman's Agreement," (2) Ronald Colman in "A Double Life," (3) Loretta Young in "The Farmer's Daughter," (4) Edmund Gwenn in "Miracle On 34th Street," (5) Celeste Holm in "Gentleman's Agreement," (6) Elia Kazan for "Gentleman's Agreement," (7) James Baskette, (8) "Shoe Shine."

1948: (1) "Hamlet," (2) Laurence Olivier in "Hamlet," (3) Jane Wyman in "Johnny Belinda," (4) Walter Huston in "The Treasure of the Sierra Madre," (5) Claire Trevor in "Key Largo," (6) John Huston for "The Treasure of the Sierra Madre," (7) Ivan Jandl, Sid Grauman, Adolph Zukor, Walter Wanger, (8) "Monsieur Vincent."

1949: (1) "All the King's Men," (2) Broderick Crawford in "All the King's Men," (3) Olivia de Havilland in "The Heiress," (4) Dean Jagger in "Twelve O'Clock High," (5) Mercedes McCambridge in "All the King's Men," (6) Joseph L. Mankiewicz for "A Letter to Three Wives," (7) Bobby Driscoll, Fred Astaire, Cecil B. DeMille, Jean Hersholt, (8) "The Bicycle Thief."

1950: "All about Eve," (2) Jose Ferrer in "Cyrano de Bergerac," (3) Judy Holliday in "Born Yesterday," (4) George Sanders in "All about Eve," (5) Josephine Hull in "Harvey," (6) Joseph L. Mankiewicz for "All about Eve," (7) George Murphy, Louis B. Mayer, (8) "The Walls of Malapaga."

1951: (1) "An American in Paris," (2) Humphrey Bogart in "The African Queen," (3) Vivien Leigh in "A Streetcar Named Desire," (4) Karl Malden in "A Streetcar Named Desire," (5) Kim Hunter in "A Streetcar Named Desire," (6) George Stevens for "A Place in the Sun," (7) Gene Kelly, (8) "Rashomon."

1952: (1) "The Greatest Show on Earth," (2) Gary Cooper in "High Noon," (3) Shirley Booth in "Come Back, Little Sheba," (4) Anthony Quinn in "Viva Zapata," (5) Gloria Grahame in "The Bad and the Beautiful," (6) John Ford for "The Quiet Man," (7) Joseph M. Schenck, Merian C. Cooper, Harold Lloyd, Bob Hope, George Alfred Mitchell, (8) "Forbidden Games."

1953: (1) "From Here to Eternity," (2) William Holden in "Stalag 17," (3) Audrey Hepburn in "Roman Holiday," (4) Frank Sinatra in "From Here to Eternity," (5) Donna Reed in "From Here to Eternity," (6) Fred Zinnemann for "From Here to Eternity," (7) Pete Smith, Joseph Breen.

1954: (1) "On the Waterfront," (2) Marlon Brando in "On the Waterfront," (3) Grace Kelly in "The Country Girl," (4) Edmond O'Brien in "The Barefoot Contessa," (5) Eva Marie Saint in "On the Waterfront," (6) Elia Kazan for "On the Waterfront," (7) Greta Garbo, Danny Kaye, Jon Whitely, Vincent Winter, (8) "Gate of Hell."

1955: (1) "Marty," (2) Ernest Borgnine in "Marty," (3) Anna Magnani in "The Rose Tattoo," (4) Jack Lemmon in "Mister Roberts," (5) Jo Van Fleet in "East of Eden," (6) Delbert Mann for "Marty," (8) "Samurai."

1956: (1) "Around the World in 80 Days," (2) Yul Brynner in "The King and I," (3) Ingrid Bergman in "Anastasia," (4) Anthony Quinn in "Lust for Life," (5) Dorothy Malone in "Written on the Wind," (6) George Stevens for "Giant," (7) Eddie Cantor, (8) "La Strada."

1957: (1) "The Bridge on the River Kwai," (2) Alec Guinness in "The Bridge on the River Kwai," (3) Joanne Woodward in "The Three Faces of Eve," (4) Red Buttons in "Sayonara," (5) Miyoshi Umeki in "Sayonara," (6) David Lean for "The Bridge on the River Kwai," (7) Charles Brackett, B. B. Kahane, Gilbert M. (Bronco Billy) Anderson, (8) "The Nights of Cabiria."

1958: (1) "Gigi," (2) David Niven in "Separate Tables," (3) Susan Hayward in "I Want to Live," (4) Burl Ives in "The Big Country," (5) Wendy Hiller in "Separate Tables," (6) Vincente Minnelli for "Gigi," (7) Maurice Chevalier, (8) "My Uncle."

1959: (1) "Ben-Hur," (2) Charlton Heston in "Ben-Hur," (3) Simone Signoret in "Room at the Top," (4) Hugh Griffith in "Ben-Hur," (5) Shelley Winters in "The Diary of Anne Frank," (6) William Wyler for "Ben-Hur," (7) Lee de Forest, Buster Keaton, (8) "Black Orpheus."

1960: (1) "The Apartment," (2) Burt Lancaster in "Elmer Gantry," (3) Elizabeth Taylor in "Butterfield 8," (4) Peter Ustinov in "Spartacus," (5) Shirley Jones in "Elmer Gantry," (6) Billy Wilder for "The Apartment," (7) Gary Cooper, Stan Laurel, Hayley Mills, (8) "The Virgin Spring."

1961: (1) "West Side Story," (2) Maximilian Schell in "Judgment at Nuremberg," (3) Sophia Loren in "Two Women," (4) George Chakiris in "West Side Story," (5) Rita Moreno in "West Side Story," (6) Robert Wise for "West Side Story," (7) Jerome Robbins, Fred L. Metzler, (8) "Through a Glass Darkly."

1962: (1) "Lawrence of Arabia," (2) Gregory Peck in "To Kill a Mockingbird," (3) Anne Bancroft in "The Miracle Worker," (4) Ed Begley in "Sweet Bird of Youth," (5) Patty Duke in "The Miracle Worker," (6) David Lean for "Lawrence of Arabia," (8) "Sundays and Cybele."

1963: (1) "Tom Jones," (2) Sidney Poitier in "Lilies of the Field," (3) Patricia Neal in "Hud," (4) Melvyn Douglas in "Hud," (5) Margaret Rutherford in "The V.I.P.'s," (6) Tony Richardson for "Tom Jones," (8) "8½."

1964: (1) "My Fair Lady," (2) Rex Harrison in "My Fair Lady," (3) Julie Andrews in "Mary Poppins," (4) Peter Ustinov in "Topkapi," (5) Lila Kedrova in "Zorba the Greek," (6) George Cukor for "My Fair Lady," (7) William Tuttle, (8) "Yesterday, Today and Tomorrow."

1965: (1) "The Sound of Music," (2) Lee Marvin in "Cat Ballou," (3) Julie Christie in "Darling," (4) Martin Balsam in "A Thousand Clowns," (5) Shelley Winters in "A Patch of Blue," (6) Robert Wise for "The Sound of Music," (7) Bob Hope, (8) "The Shop on Main Street."

1966: (1) "A Man for All Seasons," (2) Paul Scofield in "A Man for All Seasons," (3) Elizabeth Taylor in "Who's Afraid of Virginia Woolf?," (4) Walter Matthau in "The Fortune Cookie," (5) Sandy Dennis in "Who's Afraid of Virginia Woolf?," (6) Fred Zinnemann for "A Man for All Seasons," (8) "A Man and A Woman."

1967: (1) "In the Heat of the Night," (2) Rod Steiger in "In the Heat of the Night," (3) Katharine Hepburn in "Guess Who's Coming to Dinner," (4) George Kennedy in "Cool Hand Luke," (5) Estelle Parsons in "Bonnie and Clyde," (6) Mike Nichols for "The Graduate," (8) "Closely Watched Trains."

1968: (1) "Oliver!," (2) Cliff Robertson in "Charly," (3) Katharine Hepburn in "The Lion in Winter" tied with Barbra Streisand in "Funny Girl," (4) Jack Albertson in "The Subject Was Roses," (5) Ruth Gordon in "Rosemary's Baby," (6) Carol Reed for "Oliver!," (7) Onna White for "Oliver!" choreography, John Chambers for "Planet of the Apes" make-up, (8) "War and Peace."

1969: (1) "Midnight Cowboy," (2) John Wayne in "True Grit," (3) Maggie Smith in "The Prime of Miss Jean Brodie," (4) Gig Young in "They Shoot Horses, Don't They?," (5) Goldie Hawn in "Cactus Flower," (6) John Schlesinger for "Midnight Cowboy," (7) Cary Grant, (8) "Z."

1970: (1) "Patton," (2) George C. Scott in "Patton," (3) Glenda Jackson in "Women in Love," (4) John Mills in "Ryan's Daughter," (5) Helen Hayes in "Airport," (6) Franklin J. Schaffner for "Patton," (7) Lillian Gish, Orson Welles, (8) "Investigation of a Citizen above Suspicion."

1971: (1) "The French Connection," (2) Gene Hackman in "The French Connection," (3) Jane Fonda in "Klute," (4) Ben Johnson in "The Last Picture Show," (5) Cloris Leachman in "The Last Picture Show," (6) William Friedkin for "The French Connection," (7) Charles Chaplin, (8) "The Garden of the Finzi-Continis."

1972: (1) "The Godfather," (2) Marlon Brando in "The Godfather," (3) Liza Minnelli in "Cabaret," (4) Joel Grey in "Cabaret," (5) Eileen Heckart in "Butterflies Are Free," (6) Bob Fosse for "Cabaret," (7) Edward G. Robinson, (8) "The Discreet Charm of the Bourgeoisie."

1973: (1) "The Sting," (2) Jack Lemmon in "Save the Tiger," (3) Glenda Jackson in "A Touch of Class," (4) John Houseman in "The Paper Chase," (5) Tatum O'Neal in "Paper Moon," (6) George Roy Hill for "The Sting," (8) "Day for Night."

1974: (1) "The Godfather Part II," (2) Art Carney in "Harry and Tonto," (3) Ellen Burstyn in "Alice Doesn't Live Here Anymore," (4) Robert DeNiro in "The Godfather Part II," (5) Ingrid Bergman in "Murder on the Orient Express," (6) Francis Ford Coppola for "The Godfather Part II," (7) Howard Hawks, Jean Renoir, (8) "Amarcord."

1975: (1) "One Flew over the Cuckoo's Nest," (2) Jack Nicholson in "One Flew over the Cuckoo's Nest," (3) Louise Fletcher in "One Flew over the Cuckoo's Nest," (4) George Burns in "The Sunshine Boys," (5) Lee Grant in "Shampoo," (6) Milos Forman for "One Flew over the Cuckoo's Nest," (7) Mary Pickford, (8) "Dersu Uzala."

1976: (1) "Rocky," (2) Peter Finch in "Network," (3) Faye Dunaway in "Network," (4) Jason Robards in "All the President's Men," (5) Beatrice Straight in "Network," (6) John G. Avildsen for "Rocky," (8) "Black and White in Color."

1977: (1) "Annie Hall," (2) Richard Dreyfuss in "The Goodbye Girl," (3) Diane Keaton in "Annie Hall," (4) Jason Robards in "Julia," (5) Vanessa Redgrave in "Julia," (6) Woody Allen for "Annie Hall," (7) Maggie Booth (film editor), (8) "Madame Rosa."

1978: (1) "The Deer Hunter," (2) Jon Voight in "Coming Home," (3) Jane Fonda in "Coming Home," (4) Christopher Walken in "The Deer Hunter," (5) Maggie Smith in "California Suite," (6) Michael Cimino for "The Deer Hunter," (7) Laurence Olivier, King Vidor, (8) "Get Out Your Handkerchiefs."

1979: (1) "Kramer vs. Kramer," (2) Dustin Hoffman in "Kramer vs. Kramer," (3) Sally Field in "Norma Rae," (4) Melvyn Douglas in "Being There," (5) Meryl Streep in "Kramer vs. Kramer," (6) Robert Benton for "Kramer vs. Kramer," (7) Robert S. Benjamin, Hal Elias, Alec Guinness, (8) "The Tin Drum."

1980: (1) "Ordinary People," (2) Robert DeNiro in "Raging Bull," (3) Sissy Spacek in "Coal Miner's Daughter," (4) Timothy Hutton in "Ordinary People," (5) Mary Steenburgen in "Melvin and Howard," (6) Robert Redford for "Ordinary People," (7) Henry Fonda, (8) "Moscow Does Not Believe in Tears."

1981: (1) "Chariots of Fire," (2) Henry Fonda in "On Golden Pond," (3) Katharine Hepburn in "On Golden Pond," (4) John Gielgud in "Arthur," (5) Maureen Stapleton in "Reds," (6) Warren Beatty for "Reds," (7) Fuji Photo Film Co., Barbara Stanwyck, (8) "Mephisto"

1982: (1) "Gandhi," (2) Ben Kingsley in "Gandhi," (3) Meryl Streep in "Sophie's Choice," (4) Louis Gossett, Jr. in "An Officer and a Gentleman," (5) Jessica Lange in "Tootsie," (6) Richard Attenborough for "Gandhi," (7) Mickey Rooney, (8) "Volver a Empezar" (To Begin Again)

FOREIGN FILMS RELEASED IN 1983

THE MAN FROM SNOWY RIVER

(20th CENTURY-FOX) Producer, Geoff Burrowes; Executive Producers, Michael Edgley, Simon Wincer; Director, George Miller; Screenplay, John Dixon from a script by Fred Cul Cullen; Based on poem by A. B. (Banjo) Paterson; Music, Bruce Rowland; Editor, Adrian Carr; Art Director, Leslie Binns; Photography, Keith Wagstaff; Production Supervisor, Michael Lake; Assistant Directors, Murray Newey, Stewart Wright, Jan Elliot; Costumes, Robin Hall; Makeup, Vivien Mephan; In Panavision and Dolby Stereo; Rated R; 105 minutes; January release

CAST

Spur	Kirk Douglas
Clancy	Jack Thompson
Jim Craig	Tom Burlinson
Henry Craig	Terence Donovan
Mountain Man	Tommy Dysart
Harrison	Kirk Douglas
Man in the street	Bruce Kerr
Banjo Paterson	David Bradshaw
Jessica	Sigrid Thornton
Kane	Tony Bonner
Mrs. Bailey	June Jago
Curly	Chris Haywood
Moss	Kristopher Steele
Frew	Gus Mercurio
Short Man	Howard Eynon
Rosemary	Lorraine Bayly
Tall Man	John Nash

© *Snowy River Investments*

Tom Burlinson, Kirk Douglas
Top Left: Sigrid Thornton, Tom Burlinson

Tom Burlinson, Sigrid Thornton

LA TRAVIATA

(UNIVERSAL CLASSICS) Producer, Tarak Ben Ammar; Written, Designed and Directed by Franco Zeffirelli; Original Music, Giuseppe Verdi; Conductor/Music Director, James Levine; Associate Producer, Carlo Lastricati; Art Director, Gianni Quaranta; Set, Bruno Carlino; Photography, Ennio Guarnieri; Costumes, Piero Tosi; Choreographer, Alberto Testa; Editors, Peter Taylor, Franca Sylvi; Opera Lyrics, Francesco Maria Piave; Presented by Accent Films and Producers Sales Organization; In color; Rated G; 112 minutes; January release

CAST

Violetta	Teresa Stratas
Alfredo	Placido Domingo
Germont	Cornell MacNeil
Baron	Alan Monk
Flora	Axelle Gall
Annina	Pina Cei
Gastone	Maurizio Barbacini
Doctor	Robert Sommer
Marquis	Ricardo Oneto
Giuseppe	Luciano Brizi
Messenger	Tony Ammirati

and Russell Christopher, Charles Antony, Geraldine Decker, Michael Best, Ferruccio Furlanetto, Ariel Bybee, Richard Vernon, Ekaterina Maksimova, Vladimir Vassiljev

Top: Placido Domingo, Teresa Stratas
© *Universal City Studios*

Teresa Stratas

Teresa Stratas   Placido Domingo (also above)

THE YEAR OF LIVING DANGEROUSLY

(MGM/UA) Producer, James McElroy; Director, Peter Weir; Screenplay, David Williamson, Peter Weir, C. J. Koch; From novel by C. J. Koch; Original Music, Maurice Jarre; Photography, Russell Boyd; Design Coordinator, Wendy Weir; Art Director, Herbert Pinter; Editor, Bill Anderson; Associate Editors, Jeanine Chialvo, Lee Smith; Assistant Editors, Karen Foster, Peter Erskine; Assistant Directors, Chris Webb, Michael Bourchier; Costumes, Terry Ryan; Makeup, Judy Lovell; In Panavision and Metrocolor; Rated PG; 115 minutes; January release

CAST

Guy Hamilton	Mel Gibson
Jill Bryant	Sigourney Weaver
Billy Kwan	Linda Hunt
Pete Curtis	Michael Murphy
Kumar	Bembol Roco
Hortono	Domingo Landicho
Immigration Officer	Hermono De Guzman
Wally O'Sullivan	Noel Ferrier
Kevin Condon	Paul Sonkkila
Ali	Ali Nur
Betjak Man	Dominador Robridillo
Palace Guard	Joel Agona
Sukarno	Mike Emperio
Dwarf	Bernardo Nacilla
Colonel Henderson	Bill Kerr
Tiger Lily	Kuh Ledesma
Pool Waiter	Coco Marantha
Ibu	Norma Uatuhan
Udin	Lito Tolentino
Moira	Cecily Polson
Hadji	David Oyang
Embassy Aide	Mark Egerton
Naval Officer	Joonee Gamboa
Officer in cafe	Pudji Waseso
Doctor	Jabo Djohansjan
Roadblock Soldier	Agus Widjaja
Airport Official	Chris Quivak
Security Men	Joel Lamangan, Mario Layco

Top: Mel Gibson, Michael Murphy
© MGM/UA Entertainment Co.

***1983 Academy Award for Best Supporting Actress
(Linda Hunt)***

Linda Hunt (with camera),
Mel Gibson (in car)

Mel Gibson (R) and above
with Sigourney Weaver
Top: Norma Uatuhan, Linda Hunt

Sigourney Weaver, and above
with Mel Gibson

PARSIFAL

(TRIUMPH FILMS) Associate Producers, Henry Nap, Annie Nap-Oleon; Director, Hans-Jurgen Syberberg; Architect, Werner Achmann; Costumes, Veronicka Dorn, Hella Wolter; Musical Director, Armin Jordan; Photography, Igor Luther; Editors, Jutta Brandstaedter, Marianne Fehrenberg; Music, Richard Wagner; A Gaumont-T.M.S. Coproduction; Presented by Francis Ford Coppola; In color; Not rated; 255 minutes; January release

CAST

Amfortas	Armin Jordan
	sung by Wolfgang Schone
Titurel	Martin Sperr
	sung by Hans Tschammer
Gurnemanz	Robert Lloyd
	sung by Robert Lloyd
Parsifal 1	Michael Kutter
Parsifal 2	Karen Krick
	sung by Reiner Goldberg
Kliingsor	Aage Haugland
	sung by Aage Haugland
Kundry	Edith Clever
	sung by Yvonne Minton
Knights of the Grail	Rudolph Gabler, Urban von Klebelsberg, Bruno Romani-Versteeg
	sung by Gilles Cachemaille, Paul Frey
Squires	Monika Gaertner, Thomas Fink, David Meyer, Judith Schmidt
	sung by Christer Bladin, Tamara Herz, Michael Roider, Hanna Schaer
Bearer of the Grail	Amelie Syberberg
The Young Parsifal	David Luther
	sung by Gertrude Oertel

Flowermaidens .... Anahita Farroschad, Miriam Feldmann, Johanna Fink, Alexandra Grunsberg, Vivian Kintisch, Martina Lanzinger, Antonia Preser, Catharina Preser, Claudia Schmann, Bettina Stiller, Anya Toelle, Annette Woll, Stephanie Corler, Eva Kessler, Catharina Klemm, Judith Klemm, Sabine Kuckelmann, Isabelle Malbrun, Caroline Riollot, Guillemette Riollot, Sofia Romani, Ina Schroter, Balthasar Thomass, Sophie von Uslar, sung by Britt-Marie Aruhn, Jocelyne Chamonin, Tamara Herz, Gertrude Oertel, Eva Saurova, Hanna Schaer

Michael Kutter

Michael Kutter

THE STATIONMASTER'S WIFE

(TELECULTURE) Director, Rainer Werner Fassbinder; Screenplay, Mr. Fassbinder from the novel by Oskar Maria Graf; Photography, Michael Ballhaus; Editors, Ila von Hasperg, Franz Walsh, Juliane Lorenz; Music, Peer Raben; Set, Kurt Raab, Nico Kehrhan; In color; Not rated; 112 minutes; January release

CAST

Bolwieser	Kurt Raab
Hanni Bolwieser	Elisabeth Trissenaar
Neidhart	Hustal Bayrhammer
Franz Merkl	Bernard Helfrich
Schafftaller	Udo Kier
Windegger	Karl-Heinz von Hassel

Right: Elisabeth Trissenaar, Kurt Raab
© *Teleculture*

Bernard Helfrich, Elisabeth Trissenaar

Elisabeth Trissenaar

ENIGMA

(EMBASSY PICTURES) Producers, Peter Shaw, Ben Arbeid, Andre Pergament; Director, Jeannot Szwarc; Screenplay, John Briley; Based on novel by Michael Barak; Assistant Directors, Michel Cheyko, Christopher Carreras; Photography, Jean-Louis Picavet; Art Directors, Francois Comtet, Marc Frederix; Editors, Peter Weatherley, Peter Culverwell; Presented by Filmcrest International; In color; Rated PG; 101 minutes; January release

CAST

Alex Holbeck	Martin Sheen
Dimitri Vasilkov	Sam Neill
Karen	Brigitte Fossey
Kurt Limmer	Derek Jacobi
Bodley	Michel Lonsdale
Canarsky	Frank Finlay
Melton	David Baxt
Bruno	Kevin McNally
Hirsch	Michael Williams
Konstantin	Warren Clarke

Right: Brigitte Fossey

Sam Neill, Derek Jacobi
Above: Martin Sheen, Sam Neill

Brigitte Fossey, Martin Sheen
Above: Sam Neill

LA NUIT DE VARENNES

(TRIUMPH FILMS) Producer, Renzo Rossellini; Director, Ettore Scola; Screenplay, Sergio Amidei, Ettore Scola; Photography, Armando Nannuzzi; Music, Armando Trovajoli; Art Director, Dante Ferretti; Costumes, Gabriella Pescucci; Editor, Raimondo Crociani; Assistant Director, Paola Scola; Associate Producers, Lise Fayolle, Georgio Silvagni; Original soundtrack on Polydor record; In color; A Gaumont/Columbia production; Rated R; 135 minutes; February release

CAST

Casanova	Marcello Mastroianni
Nicolas Edme Restif	Jean-Louis Barrault
Countess Sophie de la Borde	Hanna Schygulla
Thomas Paine	Harvey Keitel
Monsieur Jacob	Jean-Claude Brialy
De Wendel	Daniel Gelin
Monsieur Sauce	Jean-Louis Trintignant
King Louis XVI	Michel Piccoli
Queen Marie-Antoinette	Eleonore Hirt
Mme. Adelaide Gagnon	Andrea Ferreol
De Florange	Michel Vitold
Virginia Capacelli	Laura Betti
Italian Barker	Enzo Jannacci
Emile Delage	Pierre Malet
Jean-Louis Romeuf	Hugues Quester
Nanette Precy	Dora Doll
Mme. Faustine	Caterina Boratto
Mme. Sauce	Didi Perego
Agnes Restif	Evelyne Dress
Marie-Madeleine	Aline Messe
National Guard Commander	Patrick Osmond
Outrider	Jacques Peyrac
Drouet	Yves Collignon
Hubertine	Agnes Nobecourt

and Claude LeGros, Vernon Dobtcheff, Ugo Fangareggi, Roger Trapp, Annie Bell, Fausto di Bella, Jacques Zanetti, Antonella Cancellieri, Robert Nobaret, Bruno DuLouvat, Noelle Mesny, Jeanne Carre, Jeanne Tatu, Albert Michel, Enrico Bergier

Left: Hanna Schygulla, Marcello Mastroianni, Andrea Ferreol, Harvey Keitel, Jean-Louis Barrault, Pierre Malet Top: Jean-Claude Brialy, Marcello Mastroianni
© *Columbia Pictures*

Hanna Schygulla

Hanna Schygulla, Laura Betti, Andrea Ferreol

THRESHOLD

(20th CENTURY-FOX INTERNATIONAL CLASSICS) Producers, Jon Slan, Michael Burns; Director, Richard Pearce; Screenplay, James Salter; Photography, Michel Brault; Music, Micky Erbe, Maribeth Solomon; Editor, Susan Martin; Designer, Anne Pritchard; Assistant Directors, Jim Kaufman, Pedro Gandol, Jerome McCann; Art Director, Jackie Field; Wardrobe, Sharon Purdy; In color; Rated PG; 97 minutes; February release

CAST

Dr. Thomas Vrain	Donald Sutherland
Dr. Aldo Gehring	Jeff Goldblum
Dr. Basil Rents	Allan Nicholls
Tilla Vrain	Sharon Acker
Sally Vrain	Jana Stinson
Tracy Vrain	Jessica Steen
Usher	Mavor Moore
Carol Severance	Mare Winningham
Anita	Lally Cadeau
Edgar Fine	John Marley
Henry DeVici	Michael Lerner
Vivian	Marilyn Gardner
Rex	Bob Warner
David Art	Robert Joy
Wanda	Barbara Gordon
Pleatman	Jonathan Welsh
Simone	Ray Stancer
Diamond	Jan Muzynski
Marcia	Marcia Brunne
Roger	Dr. Darrell Walsh
Motercyclists	Bob Hannah, Steve Ballantine
Cutter	Richard Blackburn
Bonnie	Maureen McRae
Fallaci	Paul Hecht
Cathy	Carol Berry

and Valeria Elia (Announcer), Michael C. Gwynne (Jay), Murray Westgate (Host), Robert Goodier (Elegant Man), Elza Pickthorne (His Wife), Ara Hovan (Arab), Kate Trotter (Ms. Anderson), Ken James (Severance), Deborah Turnbull (Mrs. Severance), Margaret Edgar (Secretary), Stan Lesk (Attendant), Jack Messinger, Barry Flatman (Newsmen), Harvey Chao (Cameraman), Dennis Hayes (Keene), Ian Orr (Willimer), Gordon Jocelyn (Shack), Harry Gulkin (Jawit), James Loxley (Headwaiter), Kenny Wells (Engineer)

Top: Donald Sutherland, and right
with Jeff Goldblum, and right center
with Mare Winningham
© *20th Century-Fox*

Jeff Goldblum

KAMIKAZE '89

(TELECULTURE) Producer, Regina Ziegler; Director, Wolf Gremm; Screenplay, Robert Katz, Wolf Gremm; From Novel "Murder on the 31st Floor" by Per Wahloo; Photography, Xaver Schwarzenberger; Music, Edgar Froese; Editor, Thorsten Nater; Costumes and Makeup, Barbara Naujok; In color; Not rated; 106 minutes; February release

CAST

Police Lieutenant Jansen	Rainer Werner Fassbinder
Anton	Gunther Kaufmann
Blue Panther	Boy Gobert
Police Chief	Arnold Marquis
Nephew	Richy Muller
Barbara	Nicole Heesters
Personnel Director	Brigitte Mira
Vice-President	Jorg Holm
Zerling	Hans Wyprachtiger
Elena Farr	Petra Jokisch
Police Doctor	Ute Fitz-Koska
Gangster	Frank Ripploh
Policeman	Hans-Eckardt Eckardt
Plainclothesman	Christoph Baumann
Nurse	Juliane Lorenz
Policewoman	Christel Harthaus
Weiss	Franco Nero

Top: Gunther Kaufmann, Rainer Werner Fassbinder Below: Franco Nero (L)
© *TeleCulture Inc.*

Rainer Werner Fassbinder, Petra Jokisch Top: Rainer Werner Fassbinder

PRIVATE LIFE

(IFEX) Director, Yuli Raisman; Screenplay, Anatoly Grebnev, Yuli Raisman; Photography, Nikolai Olonovsky; A Mosfilm production in color; Russian with English subtitles; Not rated; 103 minutes; February release

CAST

Sergei Abrikosov ....Mikhail Ulyanov and Iya Savvina, Irina Gubanova, Evgeni Lazarev, Alexei Blokhin, Tatiana Dogileva

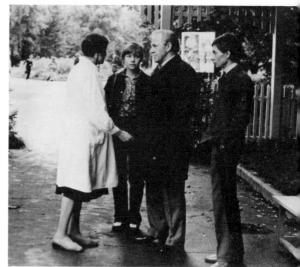

BETRAYAL

(20th CENTURY-FOX INTERNATIONAL CLASSICS) Producer, Sam Spiegel; Director, David Jones; Screenplay, Harold Pinter from his play of same title; Associate Producer, Eric Rattray; Designer, Eileen Diss; Editor, John Bloom; Music, Dominic Muldowney; Photography, Mike Fash; In color; Rated R; 95 minutes; February release

CAST
Robert ....Ben Kingsley
Jerry ....Jeremy Irons
Emma.. Patricia Hodge

Left: Ben Kingsley, Patricia Hodge
© *Horizon/20th Century-Fox*

Jeremy Irons, Ben Kingsley

Jeremy Irons, Patricia Hodge
Top: Patricia Hodge, Ben Kingsley

THE GIFT

(SAMUEL GOLDWYN CO.) Producer, Gilbert de Goldschmidt; Direction and Screenplay, Michel Lang; Based on play "Bankers Also Have Souls" by Valme and Terzolli; Music, Michel LeGrand; Executive Producer, Michel Zemer; Photography, Daniel Gaudry; Assistant Directors, Jean-Patrick Costantini, Victor Tourjansky; Decorator, Jean-Claude Gallouin; Costumes, Tanine Autre; In color; Rated R; 105 minutes; February release

CAST

Gregoire	Pierre Mondy
Antonella	Claudia Cardinale
Barbara	Clio Goldsmith
Loriol	Jacques Francois
Charlotte	Cecile Magnet
Emir Faycal	Renzo Montagnani
Laurent	Remi Laurent
Sandrine	Leila Frechet
Andre	Henri Guybet
Jennifer	Yolande Gilot
Umberto	Diulio Del Prete

Right: Pierre Mondy, Claudia Cardinale

Pierre Mondy, Clio Goldsmith

154

MONTY PYTHON'S THE MEANING OF LIFE

(UNIVERSAL) Producer, John Goldstone; Director, Terry Jones; Animation Director, Terry Gilliam; Screenplay, Graham Chapman, John Cleese, Terry Gilliam, Eric Idle, Terry Jones, Michael Palin; Photography, Peter Hannan; Editor, Julian Doyle; Designer, Harry Lange; Costumes, Jim Acheson; Choreography, Arlene Phillips; Art Director, Richard Dawking; Assistant Director, Ray Corbett; Music, Eric Idle, John du Prez; In Technicolor; Rated R; 107 minutes; March release

CAST

Graham Chapman
John Cleese
Terry Gilliam
Eric Idle
Terry Jones
Michael Palin
and Carol Cleveland, Judy Loe, Simon Jones, Andrew MacLachlan, Valerie Whittington, Mark Holmes, Patricia Quinn, Jennifer Franks, Peter Lovstrom, Imogen Bickford-Smith, Victoria Plum, George Silver, Angela Mann, Anne Rosenfeld

INVITATION AU VOYAGE

(TRIUMPH FILMS) Producer, Claude Nedjar; Director, Peter Del Monte; Screenplay, Peter Del Norte, Franco Ferrini; Based on novel "Moi, Ma Soeur" by Jean Bany; Photography, Bruno Muytten; Designer, Ghislain Uhry; Editor, Agnes Giullemot; Music, Gabriel Yared; Songs by Nina Scott and Law Less Ness (band), Christophe Rambault and Rambo (band); French with English subtitles; In color; Rated R; 93 minutes; April release

CAST

Lucien	Laurent Malet
Woman on the turnpike	Aurore Clement
Timour, the Turk	Mario Adorf
Jeanne	Nina Scott
Old Man	Raymond Bussieres

Left: Nina Scott, Laurent Malet
Below: (L) Mario Adorf, (R) Laurent Malet
© *Columbia Pictures*

Nina Scott, Laurent Malet

FLIGHT OF THE EAGLE

(SUMMIT FEATURE DISTRIBUTORS) Director-Photographer-Editor, Jan Troell; Screenplay, Georg Oddner, Ian Rakoff, Klaus Rifbjerg, Jan Troell; Based on novel by Per Olof Sundman; Art Director, Ulf Axen; Music, Hans Erik Philip; Executive Producer, Goran Setterberg; In Swedish with English subtitles; In color; Not rated; 141 minutes; April release

CAST

Salomon August Andree	Max von Sydow
Nils Strindberg	Goran Stangertz
Knut Fraenkel	Sveree Anker Ousdal
Lachambre	Clement Harari
Guril Linder	Eva von Hanno
Anna Charlier	Lotta Larsson
Nils Ekholm	Jon-Olof Strandberg
GVE Svendenborg	Henric Holmberg
Mina Andree	Mimi Pollak
Lundstrom	Cornelis Vreswijk
Andree's Sister	Ulla Sjoblem
Alfred Nobel	Ingvar Kjellson
Oscar II	Brunno Serwing
The Captain	Ake Whilney
Nansen	Knut Husebo

Top: Max von Sydow, also below, and
right with Sveree Anker Ousdal, Goran Stangertz

Sveree Anker Ousdal, Max von Sydow,
Goran Stangertz

QUERELLE

(TRIUMPH) Producer, Dieter Schidor; Direction and Screenplay, Rainer Werner Fassbinder; From novel "Querelle de Brest" by Jean Genet; Photography, Xaver Schwarzenberger; Sets, Rolf Zehetbauer; Costumes, Barbara Baum; Music and Songs, Peer Raben; Editor, Juliane Lorenz; In color; Rated R; 106 minutes; April release

CAST

Querelle	Brad Davis
Lt. Seblon	Franco Nero
Lysiane	Jeanne Moreau
Roger	Laurent Malet
Paulette	Nadja Brunkhorst
Robert/Gil	Hanno Poschl
Nono	Gunther Kaufmann
Mario	Burkhard Driest
Vic	Dieter Schidor
Marcellin	Roger Fritz
Matrose	Michael McLernon
Theo	Neil Bell
Armenier	Harry Baer

Right: Brad Davis
© *Columbia Pictures*

Franco Nero, Jeanne Moreau, Brad Davis

THE WHITE ROSE

(TELECULTURE) Director, Michael Verhoeven; Screenplay, Michael Verhoeven, Mario Krebs; Photography, Axel DeRoche; Photography, Horst Chlupka, Rodger Hinrichs; Editor, Barbara Hennings; Music, Konstantin Wecker; Costumes, Anastasia Kurz; German with English subtitles; In color; Not rated; 108 minutes; May release

CAST

Sophie Scholl	Lena Stolze
Hans Scholl	Wulf Kessler
Alex Schmorell	Oliver Siebert
Willi Graf	Ulrich Tuker
Christoph Probst	Werner Stocker
Prof. Huber	Martin Benrath
Traute Lafrenz	Anja Kruse
Fritz	Ulf-Jurgen Wagner
Gisela Schertling	Mechthild Reinders
Falk Harnack	Peter Kortenbach
Mr. Scholl	Gerhard Friedrich
Mrs. Scholl	Sabine Kretzschmar
Werner Scholl	Heinz Keller
Inge Scholl	Susanne Seuffert
Elizabeth Scholl	Christine Schwartz
Herta Probst	Beate Himmerlstoss
Clara Huber	Monika Madras
Nazi Student Leader	Hans-Jurgen Schatz
Dr. Wust	Werner Schnitzer
Gauleiter Giesler	Reinhold K. Olszewski
Lubjanka	Agnes Csere

Right: Lena Stolze, Ulf-Jurgen Wagner
© *TeleCulture Inc.*

Wulf Kessler, Lena Stolze

LA BOUM

(TRIUMPH FILMS) Producer, Alain Poire; Director, Claude Pinoteau; Screenplay, Daniele Thompson, Claude Pinoteau; Photography, Edmond Sechan; Music, Vladimir Cosma; Editor, Marie-Joseph Yoyotte; Art Director, Jacques Bufnoir; French with English subtitles; In color; Rated PG; 108 minutes; May release

CAST

Francois	Claude Brasseur
Francoise	Brigitte Fossey
Vic	Sophie Marceau
Poupette	Denise Grey
Vanessa	Dominique Lavanant
Eric	Bernard Giraudeau

Left: Sophie Marceau, Denise Gray
Below: Brigitte Fossey, Claude Brasseur
© *Columbia Pictures*

Sophie Marceau

Sophie Marceau

ALSINO AND THE CONDOR

(LIBRA-CINEMA 5) Executive Producer, Hernan Littin; Director, Miguel Littin; Screenplay, Miguel Littin, Isidora Aguirre, Tomas Perez Turrent; Photography, Jorge Herrera, Pablo Martinez; Art Director, Elly Menz; Editor, Miriam Talavera; Music, Leo Brower; Spanish with English subtitles; In color; Not rated; 89 minutes; May release

CAST

Frank	Dean Stockwell
Alsino	Alan Esquivel
Alsino's Grandmother	Carmen Bunster
The Major	Alejandro Parodi
Rosario	Delia Casanova
Lucia	Marta Lorena Perez
Don Nazario, the birdman	Reinaldo Miravalle
Lucia's Grandfather	Marcelo Gaete
Dutch Adviser	Jan Kees De Roy

Left: Alan Esquivel
© *Almi Distribution Corp.*

Dean Stockwell, Alan Esquivel

THE RETURN OF MARTIN GUERRE

(EUROPEAN INTERNATIONAL) Director, Daniel Vigne; Screenplay, Daniel Vigne, Jean-Claude Carriere; Photography, Andre Neau; Editor, Denise de Casablanca; Music, Michel Portal; French with English subtitles; In color; Not rated; 111 minutes; June release

CAST

Martin Guerre	Gerard Depardieu/Bernard Pierre Donnadieu
Bertrand de Rois	Nathalie Baye
Jean de Coras	Roger Planchon
Judge Rieux	Maurice Jacquemont
Catherine Boere	Isabelle Sadoyan
Raimonde de Rois	Rose Thiery
Pierre Guerre	Maurice Barrier
Young Martin	Stephane Pean
Young Bertrande	Sylvie Meda
Jeanne	Chantal Deruaz
Guillemette	Valerie Chassigneux
Augustin	Tcheky Karyo
Antoine	Dominique Pinon
Sanxi	Adrien Duquesne
The Cure	Andre Chaumeau
Jacques	Philippe Babin

Right: Gerard Depardieu

Gerard Depardieu (also above),
Nathalie Baye

Nathalie Baye, Gerard Depardieu

L'ETOILE DU NORD

(UNITED ARTISTS CLASSICS) Producer, Alain Sarde; Director, Pierre Granier-Deferre; Screenplay, Jean Aurenche, Michel Grisolia, Pierre Granier-Deferre; From "La Locataire" by George Simenon; Photography, Pierre William Glenn; Assistant Directors, Olivier Horlait, Frederic Blum; Designer, Dominique Andre; Costumes, Catherine Letterier; A Sara Films production in color; Rated PG; June release

CAST

Madame Baron	Simone Signoret
Edouard	Philippe Noiret
Sylvie	Fanny Cottencon
Antoinette	Julie Jezequel
Monsieur Baron	Jean Rougerie
Moise	Jean-Pierre Klein
Valesco	Jean-Yves Chatelais
Domb	Michel Koniencny
Engineer	Jean Dautremay
Arlette	Patricia Malvoisin
Nemrod	Gamil Ratib
Jasmina	Liliana Gerace
Albert	Pierre Forget

Right: Simone Signoret (c)
© *United Artists*

Simone Signoret, Philippe Noiret
Above: Fanny Cottencon, Philippe Noiret

Philippe Noiret, Simone Signoret

OCTOPUSSY

(MGM/UA) Producer, Albert R. Broccoli; Director, John Glen; Story and Screenplay, George MacDonald Fraser, Richard Maibaum, Michael G. Wilson; Photography, Alan Hume; Editors, Peter Davies, Henry Richardson; Music, John Barry; In color; Rated PG; 130 minutes; June release

CAST

James Bond	Roger Moore
Octopussy	Maud Adams
Kamal	Louis Jourdan
Magda	Kristina Wayborn
Gobinda	Kabir Bedi
Orlov	Steven Berkoff
Twin One	David Meyer
Twin Two	Tony Meyer
Vilay	Vilay Amritral
Q	Desmond Llewelyn
M	Robert Brown
Gogol	Walter Gotell
Minister of Defense	Geoffrey Keen
Gwendoline	Suzanne Jerome

Left: Roger Moore
© *Danjaq, S.A.*

Maud Adams

Kristina Wayborn, Louis Jourdan
Above: Vijay Amritraj, Roger Moore,
Desmond Llewelyn

Roger Moore, Maud Adams
Top: Maud Adams, Kristina Wayborn

Roger Moore
Above: Kabir Bedi

THE DRAUGHTSMAN'S CONTRACT

(UNITED ARTISTS CLASSICS) Direction and Screenplay, Peter Greenaway; Photography, Curtis Clark; Art Director, Bob Ringwood; Costumes, Sue Blane; Editor, John Wilson; Music, Michael Nyman; Producer, David Payne; In color; Rated R; 107 minutes; June release

CAST

Mr. Neville	Anthony Higgins
Mrs. Herbert	Janet Suzman
Mrs. Talmann	Anne Louise Lambert
Mr. Talmann	Hugh Fraser
Mr. Noyles	Neil Cunningham
Mr. Herbert	Dave Hill
Mr. Seymour	David Gant
The Poulencs	David Meyer, Tony Meyer
Mr. Parkes	Nicholas Amer
Mrs. Pierpont	Suzan Crowley
Mrs. Clement	Lynda Marchal
The Statue	Michael Feast
Philip	Alastair Cummings
Mr. Van Hoyton	Steve Ubels
Augustus	Ben Kirby
Governess	Sylvia Rotter
Maid	Kate Doherty
Mr. Porringer	Joss Buckley
Mr. Clark	Mike Carter
Laundress	Vivienne Chandler
Mr. Hammond	Geoffrey Larder
Servants	Harry Avn Engel, George Miller

Left: Anthony Higgins
© *United Artists*

Anthony Higgins, Janet Suzman

Janet Suzman, Anthony Higgins
Top: Hugh Fraser, Anne Louise Lambert

PAULINE AT THE BEACH

(ORION) Producer, Margaret Menegoz; Director, Eric Rohmer; Photography, Nestor Almendros; Editor, Cecile Decugis; Music, Jean-Louis Valero; In color; Rated R; 94 minutes; July release

CAST

Pauline	Amanda Langlet
Marion	Arielle Dombasle
Pierre	Pascal Greggory
Henry	Feodor Atkine
Sylvain	Simon De La Brosse
Louisette	Rosette

Left: Amanda Langlet, Simon De La Brosse
© *Orion Classics*

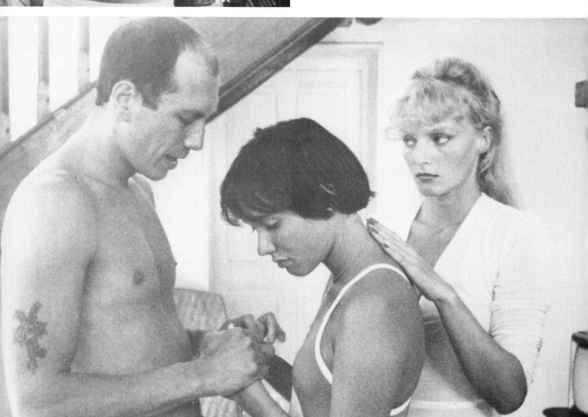

Feodor Atkine, Amanda Langlet, Arielle Dombasle

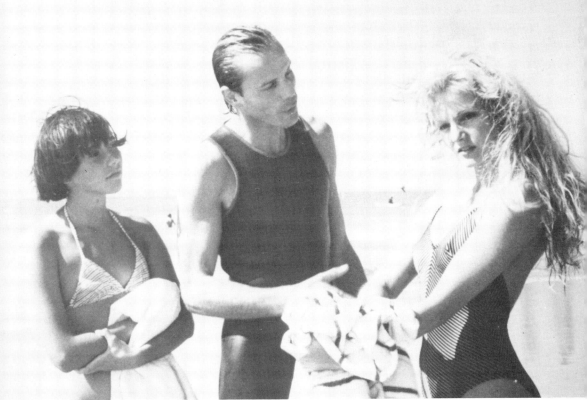

Amanda Langlet, Feodor Atkine, Arielle Dombasle
Top: Rosette, Pascal Greggory

THE GREY FOX

(UNITED ARTISTS CLASSICS) Producer, Peter O'Brian; Co-Producers, Phillip Borsos, Barry Healey; Executive Producer, David H. Brady; Director, Phillip Borsos; Screenplay, John Hunter; Photography, Frank Tidy; Design, Bill Brodie; Music, Michael Conway Baker; Traditional Irish Music, The Chieftans; Editor, Frank Irvine; Associate Producer-Assistant Director, John Board; Costumes, Christopher Ryan; In color; Rated PG; 92 minutes; July release

CAST

Bill Miner	Richard Farnsworth
Kate Flynn	Jackie Burroughs
Shorty	Wayne Robson
Jack Budd	Ken Pogue
Fernie	Timothy Webber
Detective Seavey	Gary Reineke
Louis Colquhoun	David Petersen
Al Sims	Don MacKay
Jenny	Samantha Langevin
Tom	Tom Heaton
Accomplices	James McLarty, George Dawson
Gunsmith	Ray Michal
Danny Young	Stephan E. Miller
Oregon Engineer	David L. Crowley
Shopkeeper	Jack Leaf
Town Boy	Isaac Hislop
Newspaper Editor	Sean Sullivan
Mission Engineer	Bill Murdock
Firemen	David McCulley, Jack Ackroyd, David Raines
Mail Clerks	Gary Chalk, Nicolas Rice
Hotel Clerk	Frank Turner
Ducks Engineer	Bill Meilen
Conductor	Paul Jolicoeur
Baggage Clerk	Mel Tuck
Sgt. Wilson	Peter Jobin
Judge	Anthony Holland
Prison Guard	Jon York
Farm Girl	Lisa Westman
Piano Player	John Owen

Jackie Burroughs, Richard Farnsworth (also above)
© *United Artists*

WAYS IN THE NIGHT

(TELECULTURE) Producer, Hartwig Schmidt; Direction and Screenplay, Krzysztof Zanussi; Photography, Witold Sobocinski; Editor, Liesgret Schmitt-Klink; Music, Wojciech Kilar; Designers, Tadeusz Wybult, Wolfgang Schunke, Maciej Putowski; Costumes, Anna Biedrzycka, Delia Fredrich; In color; Not rated; German with English subtitles; 98 minutes; July release

CAST

Friedrich	Mathieu Carriere
Countess Elzbieta	Maja Komorowska
Hans Albert	Horst Frank
Mattei Amidei	Zbigniew Zapasiewicz
Friedrich's Mother	Imgard Forst
Charlotte	Diane Korner
Police Officer	Wolfgang Gronebaum
Schultz	Claus Enskat
Harpsichord Tuner	Hans-Karl Friedrich
Farm Manager	Edward Dziewonski
Gertrud	Lilly Towska
Officers	Peter Drescher, Andrzej von Schoenaich, Peter Kuiper

Right: Maja Komorowska, Mathieu Carriere

Horst Frank, Mathieu Carriere

MERRY CHRISTMAS, MR. LAWRENCE

(UNIVERSAL) Producer, Jeremy Thomas; Director, Nagisa Oshima; Screenplay, Nagisa Oshima, Paul Mayersberg; Based on "The Seed and the Sower" by Laurens Van Der Post; Executive Producers, Masato Hara, Eiko Oshima, Geoffrey Nethercott, Terry Glinwood; Associate Producer, Joyce Herlihy; Photography, Toichiro Narushima; Music, Ryuichiro Sakamoto; Designer, Shigemasa Toda; Directors, Lee Tamahori, Roger Pulvers; Editor, Tomoyo Oshima; Art Director, Andrew Sanders; In Technicolor and Dolby Stereo; Rated R; 124 minutes; August release

CAST

Celliers	David Bowie
Colonel John Lawrence	Tom Conti
Captain Yonoi	Ryuichi Sakamoto
Sergeant Hara	Takeshi
Hicksley-Ellis	Jack Thompson
Kanemoto	Johnny Okura
DeJong	Alistair Browning
Celliers' Brother	James Malcolm
Celliers at age 12	Chris Broun

Top: Takeshi,(R) David Bowie, James
Malcolm Center: (L) Jack Thompson,
(R) Takeshi, Tom Conti
© *Universal City Studios*

David Bowie, Ryuichi Sakamoto

BERLIN ALEXANDERPLATZ

(TELECULTURE) Producer, Peter Marthesheimer; Direction and Screenplay, Rainer Werner Fassbinder; From Alfred Doblin's novel of same title; Art Director, Harry Baer; Photography, Xaver Schwarzenberger; Editor, Juliane Lorenz; Music, Peer Raben; Set Designs, Helmut Gassner, Werner Achmann, Jurgen Henze; Costumes, Barbara Baum; Assistant Director, Renate Leiffer; German with English subtitles; Thirteen parts with an epilogue; In color; Not rated; 15 hours and 21 minutes; August release

CAST

Franz Biberkopf	Gunter Lamprecht
Nachum, the old Jew	Peter Kolleck
Eliser, Nachum's friend	Hans Zander
Paula, a prostitute	Mechthild Grossmann
Frau Bast	Brigitte Mira
Minna	Karin Baal
Ida	Barbara Valentin
Eva	Hanna Schygulla
Herbert Virchow	Roger Fritz
Meck	Franz Buchrieser
Max the barman	Claus Wirt
Lina	Elisabeth Trissenaar
Old Newspaper Vendor	Herbert Steinmetz
Handicapped Rightwing Man	Klaus Hohne
Sausage Vendor	Jurgen Draeger
Dreske, the Communist	Axel Bauer
Luders	Hark Bohm
Widow	Angela Schmid
Baumann	Gerhard Zwerenz
Bruno	Volker Spengler
Rudi	Vitus Zeplichal
Theo	Gunther Kauffman
Pums	Ivan Desny
Reinhold	Gottfried John
Franze	Helen Vita
Cilly	Annemarie Duringer
Trude	Irm Hermann
Bald Man	Peter Kuiper
Emmi	Traute Hoess
Willy	Franz Schediwy
Young Man in nightclub	Udo Kier
Mieze	Barbara Sukowa
Terah, an angel	Margit Carstensen
Sarug, an angel	Helmut Griem

Right: Gunter Lamprecht, Hanna Schygulla
Top: Gunter Lamprecht, Barbara Sukowa
© TeleCulture

LA PASSANTE

(LIBRA/CINEMA 5) Director, Jacques Ruffio; Screenplay, Jacques Ruffio, Jacques Kirsner; Photography, Jean-Jacques Cazoit; Music, Georges Delerue; In color; No rating; French with English subtitles; 106 minutes; August release

CAST

Elsa Weiner/Lina Baumstein	Romy Schneider
Max Baumstein	Michel Piccoli
Max as a child	Wendelin Werner
Michel Weiner	Helmut Griem
Maurice Bouillard	Gerard Klein
Charlotte	Dominique Labourier
Ruppert/Federico/Ambassador	Mathieu Carriere

Left: Romy Schneider, Wendelin Werner
© Libra Cinema 5

Wendelin Werner, Romy Schneider

Romy Schneider, Michel Piccoli
Above: Helmut Griem, Romy Schneider

I MARRIED A SHADOW

(INTERNATIONAL SPECTRAFILM) Producer, Alain Sarde; Director, Robin Davis; Screenplay, Patrick Laurent, Robin Davis; Based on novel "I Married a Dead Man" by William Irish; Photography, Bernard Zitzermann; Art Director, Ivan Maussion; Editor, Marie Castro Vasquez; Music, Philippe Sarde; In color; Rated PG; 110 minutes; August release

CAST

Helene/Patricia	Nathalie Baye
Pierre	Francis Huster
Frank	Richard Bohringer
Lena	Madeleine Robinson
Monsieur Meyrand	Guy Trejan
Fifo	Victoria Abril
Patricia	Veronique Genest
Notary	Maurice Jacquemont
Nelly	Solenn Jarniou
Bertrand	Humbert Balsan
Pessac	Marcel Roche
Midwife	Arlette Gilbert
Doctor	Andre Thorent
Nurse	Christine Paolini
Family Doctor	Jean-Henri Chambois
Folk Singer	Los Reyes

Top: Guy Trejan, Nathalie Baye,
Francis Huster
© *Spectrafilm*

Nathalie Baye, Francis Huster

VALENTINA

(FRANK MORENO) Producers, Javier Moro, Carlos Escobedo; Director, Antonio Jose Betancor; Screenplay, Lautano Murua, Mr. Betancor, Mr. Escobedo, Javier Moro; From novel "Days of Dawn" by Ramon J. Sender; Photography, Juan A. Ruiz Anchia; Music, Riz Ortolani; In color; Not rated; 85 minutes; August release

CAST

Mosen Joaquin	Anthony Quinn
Pepe	Jorge Sanz
Valentina	Paloma Gomez
Don Jose	Saturno Cerra
Dona Luisa	Conchita Leza
Don Arturo	Alfredo Luchetti
Dona Julia	Marisa de Leza

Left: Anthony Quinn, Jorge Sanz
© *Ofelia Films*

Jorge Sanz, Paloma Gomez

CURSE OF THE PINK PANTHER

(MGM/UA) Producers, Blake Edwards, Tony Adams; Director, Blake Edwards; Executive Producer, Jonathan D. Krane; Screenplay, Blake Edwards, Geoffrey Edwards; Music, Henry Mancini; Associate Producer, Gerald T. Nutting; Photography, Dick Bush; Designer, Peter Mullins; Editor, Ralph E. Winters; Costumes, Patricia Edwards; Art Directors, Tim Hutchinson, Alan Tomkins, John Siddall; Assistant Directors, Ray Corbett, Kieron Phipps, Peter Kohn; Editor, Bob Hathaway; In Technicolor and Panavision; Rated PG; 110 minutes; August release

CAST

Sir Charles Litton	David Niven
George Litton	Robert Wagner
Dreyfus	Herbert Lom
Chandra	Joanna Lumley
Lady Litton	Capucine
Bruno	Robert Loggia
Professor Balls	Harvey Korman
Clifton Sleigh	Ted Wass
Juleta Shane	Leslie Ash
Bored Waiter	Graham Stark
Francois	Andre Maranne
Colonel Bufoni	Peter Arne
Michelle Chauvin	Patricia Davis
Valencia Police Chief	Michael Elphick
Drunk	Steve Franken
Chong	Ed Parker
Bruno's Moll	Denise Crosby
Angry Hooker	Emma Walton
Lugash Secret Policeman	Sidi Bin Tanney

Top: Pat Corley, Ted Wass, (R) Herbert Lom
Below: (L) Capucine, David Niven, (R) Robert Wagner,
Ted Wass, Capucine, David Niven
© Titan Productions

Leslie Ash, Ted Wass

DANTON

(TRIUMPH) Executive Producer, Emmanuel Schlumberger; Director, Andrzej Wajda; Screenplay, Jean-Claude Carriere; Based on "L'Affaire Danton" by Stanislawa Przybyszewska; Photography, Igor Luther; Sets, Allan Starski, Gilles Vaster; Costumes, Yvonne Sassinot de Nesle; Music, Jean Prodromides; Editor, Halina Prugar-Ketling; Production Director, Alain Depardieu; Assistant Directors, Hugues de Laugardiere, Michel Lisowski; French with English subtitles; Rated PG; 136 minutes; In color; September release

CAST

Danton	Gerard Depardieu
Robespierre	Wojciech Pszoniak
Eleonore Duplay	Anne Alvaro
Lacroix	Roland Blanche
Camille Desmoulins	Patrice Chereau
Louison Danton	Emmanuelle Debever
Amar	Krzysztof Globisz
Herman	Ronald Guttman
Tallien	Gerard Hardy
Couthon	Tadeusz Huk
Panis	Stephane Jobert
Lindet	Marian Kociniak
Barere de Vieuzad	Marek Kondrat
Saint Just	Boguslaw Linda
Heron	Alain Mace
Legendre	Bernard Maitre
Fabre d'Eglantine	Lucien Melki
Philippeaux	Serge Merlin
Collot d'Herbois	Erwin Nowiaszack
Carnot	Leonard Pietraszak
Fouquier Tinville	Roger Planchon
Frere d'Eleonore	Angel Sedgwick
Bourdon	Andrzej Seweryn
David	Franciszek Starowieyski
Billaud-Varenne	Jerzy Trela
Chanteuse Boulangerie	Anne-Marie Vennel
Westermann	Jacques Villeret
Lucile Desmoulins	Angela Winkler
Herault de Sechelles	Jean-Loup Wolff
Vadier	Czeslaw Wollejko
Chef des Gardes	Wladimir Yordanoff
Servante des Duplay	Matgorzata Zajaczkowska
Lebas	Szymon Zaleski

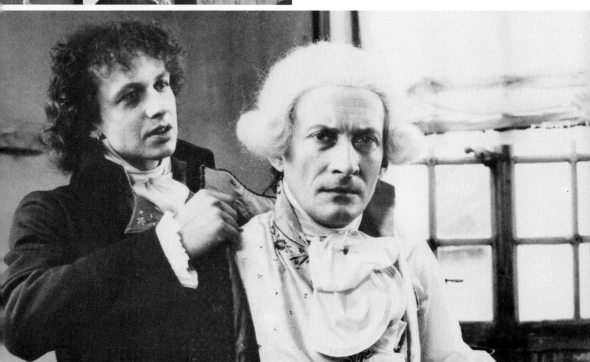

Boguslaw Linda, Wojciech Pszoniak Top Left and below: Gerard Depardieu
© *Columbia Pictures*

Gerard Depardieu Top: (L) Patrice Chereau, Angela Winkler, (R) Wojciech Pszoniak
Center: (L) Patrice Chereau, Gerard Depardieu, (R) Wojciech Pszoniak

HEAT AND DUST

(UNIVERSAL CLASSIC) Producer, Ismail Merchant; Director, James Ivory; Novel and Screenplay, Ruth Prawer Jhabvala; Music, Richard Robbins; Designer, Wilfred Shingleton; Costumes, Barbara Lane; Editor, Humphrey Dixon; Assistant Directors, Kevan Barker, David Nichols; Associate Producers, Rita Mangat, Connie Kaiserman; Art Directors, Maurice Fowler, Ram Yadekar; In color; Rated R; 130 minutes; September release

CAST

1920's in the Civil Lines at Satipur:
Douglas Rivers .... Christopher Cazenove
Olivia, his wife... Greta Scacchi
Crawford .... Julian Glover
Mrs. Crawford.......................................Susan Fleetwood
Dr. Saunders .... Patrick Godfrey
Mrs. Saunders .... Jennifer Kendal
At the Palace in Khatm:
The Nawab .... Shashi Kapoor
The Begum, his mother .... Madhur Jaffrey
Harry .... Nickolas Grace
Major Minnies.. Barry Foster
Lady Mackleworth .... Amanda Walker
Chief Princess ....Sudha Chopra
1980's in Satipur town:
Anne ....Julie Christie
Inder Lal ....Zakir Hussain
Rita, his wife.. Ratna Pathak
Inder Lal's Mother .... Tarla Mehta
Chid .... Charles McCaughan
Maji ....Parveen Paul
Dr. Gopal .... Jayut Kripilani
Dacoit Chief .... Sajid Khan
Leelavati... Leelabhai

Top: Greta Scacchi, Christopher Cazenove
Below: Julie Christie, Charles McCaughan
© *Universal City Studios*

Shashi Kapoor Top: Zakir Hussain, Julie
Christie Below: Nickolas Grace, Christie

BEYOND THE LIMIT

(**PARAMOUNT**) Producer, Norman Heyman; Director, John Mackenzie; Screenplay, Christopher Hampton; Based on novel "The Honorary Consul" by Graham Greene; Music, Stanley Myers; Additional Music, Richard Harvey; Theme, Paul McCartney; Associate Producer, Richard F. Dalton; Photography, Phil Meheux; Designer, Allan Cameron; Editor, Stuart Baird; Costumes, Barbara Lane; Art Director, Terry Pritchard; Assistant Directors, Simon Hinkly, Melvin Lind; In Movielab Color; Rated R; 103 minutes; September release

CAST

Charley Fortnum	Michael Caine
Dr. Plarr	Richard Gere
Col. Perez	Bob Hoskins
Clara	Elpidia Carrillo
Leon	Joaquim De Almeida
Aquino	A. Martinez
Marta	Stephanie Cotsirilos
Diego	Domingo Ambriz
Pablo	Eric Valdez
Miguel	Nicholas Jasso
British Ambassador	Geoffrey Palmer
Dr. Humphries	Leonard Maguire
Senor Escobar	Jorge Russek
Senora Escobar	Erika Carlsen
Senora Sanchez	Josefina Echanove
Henry Plarr	Ramon Alvarez
U.S. Ambassador	George Belanger
Gruber	Juan Antonio Llanez
Ana	Aline Davidoff
Maria	Zohra Segal
Teresa	Anais DeMelo
Youth	Arturo Rodriquez Doring
Officer	Alejandro Compean
Senior Official	Mario Valdez

© *Parsons & Whittemore Lyddon Ltd.*

Richard Gere, Elpidia Carrillo, Michael Caine Top: Elpidia Carrillo, Richard Gere
Center: Bob Hoskins, Richard Gere

EDUCATING RITA

(COLUMBIA) Producer-Director, Lewis Gilbert; Screenplay, Willy Russell; Co-Producer, William P. Cartlidge; Music, David Hentschel; Executive Producer, Herbert L. Oakes: Photography, Frank Watts; Art Director, Maurice Fowler; Editor, Garth Craven; Assistant Director, Michel Cheyko; In Technicolor; Rated PG; 110 minutes; September release

CAST

Dr. Frank Bryant	Michael Caine
Rita	Julie Walters
Brian	Michael Williams
Trish	Maureen Lipman
Julia	Jeananne Crowley
Denny	Malcolm Douglas
Rita's Father	Godfrey Quigley
Elaine	Dearbhla Molloy
Bursar	Pat Daly
Collins	Kim Fortune
Tiger	Philip Hurdwood
Lesley	Hilary Reynolds
Price	Jack Walsh
Professor	Christopher Casson
Denise	Rosamund Burton
Marcus	Marcus O'Higgins
Disco Manager	Mark Drew
Barbara	Gabrielle Reidy
Invigilator	Des Nealon
Customer in hairdresser's	Marie Conmee
Tutor	Oliver Maguire
Photographer	Derry Power
Bistro Manager	Alan Stanford
Security Officer	Gerry Sullivan
Rita's Mother	Patricia Jeffares
Sandra	Maeve Germaine
Sandra's Fiance	Liam Stack

Julie Walters, Michael Caine (also top left)
© *Columbia Pictures*

Malcolm Douglas, Gabrielle Reidy, Julie Walters
Top: Julie Walters, Michael Caine

LONELY HEARTS

(SAMUEL GOLDWYN CO.) Producer, John B. Murray; Executive Producer, Phillip Adams; Associate Producer, Erwin Rado; Assistant Producer, Fran Haarsma; Director, Paul Cox; Screenplay, Paul Cox, John Clarke; Photography, Yuri Sokol; Editor, Tim Lewis; Music, Norman Kaye; Art Director, Neil Angwin; Assistant Director, Bernard Eddy; Australia 1982; In color; Rated R; 95 minutes; September release

CAST

Patricia Curnov	Wendy Hughes
Peter Thompson	Norman Kaye
George, theatre director	Jon Finlayson
Pamela, Peter's sister	Julia Blake
Bruce, Pamela's husband	Jonathan Hardy
Patricia's Mother	Irene Inescort
Patricia's Father	Vic Gordon
Peter's Father	Ted Grove-Rogers
Wig Salesman	Ronald Falk
Detective	Chris Haywood
Sally Gordon	Diana Greentree
Psychiatrist	Margaret Steven
Rosemarie	Kris McQuade
Priest	Laurie Dobson
"Bye Bye Blackbird" Sisters	Myrtle Roberts, Irene Hewitt
Old Couple in park	Jean Campbell, Ernest Wilson
Martin	Tony Llewellyn-Jones
Flower Seller	Dawn Klingberg
Mrs. Eddy	Lola Russell
Bingo Caller	Jack Hill
Dorothy	Christine Calcutt
Man in toilet	Ernie Bourne
Pianist	Barry Chambers
Girl in bank	Sue Chapman
Bank Customer	Isobel Harley

Norman Kaye, Wendy Hughes

Norman Kaye, Wendy Hughes

HANNA K.

(UNIVERSAL) Producer-Director, Costa-Gavras; Executive Producer, Michele Ray-Gavras in association with Edward Lewis, Bob Cortes; Screenplay, Franco Solinas; Photography, Ricardo Aronovich; Editor, Francoise Bonnot; Music, Gabriel Yared; Design, Pierre Guffroy; Assistant Directors, Claire Denis, Louis Becker; Costumes, Edith Vesperini; In Panavision and Technicolor; Rated R; 111 minutes; September release

CAST

Hanna Kaufman	Jill Clayburgh
Victor Bonnet	Jean Yanne
Joshue Herzog	Gabriel Byrne
Selim Bakri	Muhamad Bakri
Amnon	David Clennon
Prof. Leventhal	Shimon Finkel
The Stranger	Oded Kotler
Russian Woman	Michael Bat-Adam
Dafna	Dafna Levy
Capt. Allenby Bridge	Dan Muggia
President - Court	Robert Sommer
Judge	Ronald Guttman
President - Court	Bruno Corazzari
Judge	Amnon Kapeliouk
Sergeant	Dalik Wolinitz
Young Lawyer	Luca Barbareschi
Lawyer - Court	Gideon Amir
German Journalist	William Berger
Interpreter - Jail	Murray Gronwall
Guard in jail parlor	Cyrus Elias
Tourist Guide	Izviad Arad
Ex-Soldier at airport	Jacques Cohen
Barman at airport	Uri Gavriel
Barman at beach	Manuel Cauchi
Airport Control	Sinay Peter
Huissier	Edward Betz
Ludmilla	Sarit Shatsky
Village Captain	Tal Ron
Village Sergeant	Zinedine Soualem
TWA Hostess	Esther Zewko

Top: Muhamad Bakri, Jill Clayburgh
Right Center: Muhamad Bakri
© *Universal City Studios*

Muhamad Bakri, Jill Clayburgh

Martin Halm (left)

ERNESTO

(SPECTRAFILM) Director, Salvatore Samperi; Screenplay, Barbara Alberti, Amedeo Pagani, Salvatore Samperi; Based on novel "Ernesto" by Umberto Saba; Executive Producer, Marco Tamburella; Photography, Camillo Bazzoni; Music, Carmelo Beraola; Editor, Sergio Montanari; Designer, Rzio Altieri; Costumes, Cristiana Lafayette; In color; Italian (1978) with English subtitles; Rated R; 95 minutes; September release

CAST

Ernesto .... Martin Halm
His Mother .... Virna Lisi
and Michele Placido, Turo Ferro, Lara Wendel, Gisela Hann, Francisco Marso, Stefano Madia, Miranda Nocelli, Conchita Velasco, Renato Salvatori

© *Spectrafilm*

PASSION

(UNITED ARTISTS CLASSICS) Producer, Alain Sarde; Direction and Screenplay, Jean-Luc Godard; Photography, Raoul Coutard; A French/Swiss Co-Production in color; French with English subtitles; Rated R; 87 minutes; October release

CAST

Isabelle Huppert
Hanna Schygulla
Michel Piccoli
Jerzy Radziwilowicz
Lazlo Szabo
Sophie Lucachevski
Patrick Bonnel
Myriem Russel
Magaly Campos

Top: (L) Michel Piccoli, Hanna Schygulla
Below: Jerzy Radiwilowicz, Hanna Schygulla
© *United Artists*

Hanna Schygulla, Isabelle Huppert

ENTRE NOUS

(UNITED ARTISTS CLASSICS) Producer, Ariel Zeitoun; Direction and Screenplay, Diane Kurys; Photography, Bernard Lutic; Editor, Joele Van Effenterre; Music, Luis Bacalov; French with English subtitles; Not rated; 110 minutes; October release

CAST

Madeleine	Miou Miou
Lena	Isabelle Huppert
Costa	Jean-Pierre Bacri
Michel	Guy Marchand
Raymond	Robin Renucci
Carlier	Patrick Bauchau
Monsieur Vernier	Jacques Airic
Madame Vernier	Jacqueline Doyen
Florence	Patricia Champane
Sophie	Saga Blanchard
Rene	Guillaume LeGuellec
Sarah	Christine Pascal

Left: Miou Miou
© *United Artists*

Isabelle Huppert, Miou Miou

Isabelle Huppert, Guy Marchand
Top: Isabelle Huppert, Miou Miou

NEVER SAY NEVER AGAIN

(WARNER BROS.) Producer, Jack Schwartzman; Director, Irvin Kershner; Screenplay, Lorenzo Semple, Jr.; Based on story by Kevin McClory Jack Whittingham, Ian Fleming; Executive Producer, Kevin McClory; Associate Producer, Michael Dryhurst; Photography, Douglas Slocombe; Designers, Philip Harrison, Stephen Grimes; Editor, Robert Lawrence; Music, Michel Legrand; Assistant Directors, Michael Moore, Ricou Browning, David Tomblin; Costumes, Charles Knode; Art Directors, Leslie Dilley, Michael White, Roy Stannard; Editor, Ian Crafford; In Dolby Stereo, Technicolor; Title Song by Michel Legrand, Alan Bergman and Marilyn Bergman; Sung by Lani Hall; Rated PG; 137 minutes; October release

CAST

James Bond	Sean Connery
Largo	Klaus Maria Brandauer
Blofeld	Max von Sydow
Fatima	Barbara Carrera
Domino	Kim Basinger
Leiter	Bernie Casey
Q/Algy	Alec McCowen
M	Edward Fox
Miss Moneypenny	Pamela Salem
Small-Fawcett	Rowan Atkinson
Lady in Bahamas	Valerie Leon
Kovacs	Milow Kirek
Lippe	Pat Roach
Lord Ambrose	Anthony Sharp
Patricia	Prunella Gee
Jack Petachi	Gavan O'Herlihy
Elliott	Ronald Pickup
Italian Ministers	Robert Rietty, Guido Adorni
Culpepper	Vincent Marzello
Number 5	Christopher Reich
Capt. Pederson	Billy J. Mitchell
General Miller	Manning Redwood
Kurt	Anthony Van Laast
Nicole	Saskie Cohen Tanui

and Sylvia Marriott, Dan Meaden, Michael Medwin, Lucy Hornak, Derek Deadman, Joanna Dickens, Tony Alleff, Paul Tucker, Brenda Kempner, Jill Meager, John Stephen Hill, Wendy Leach, Roy Bowe

Left: Bernie Casey, Sean Connery, Kim Basinger Top: Sean Connery
© Taliafilm

Barbara Carrera, Klaus Maria Brandauer

Sean Connery, Barbara Carrera

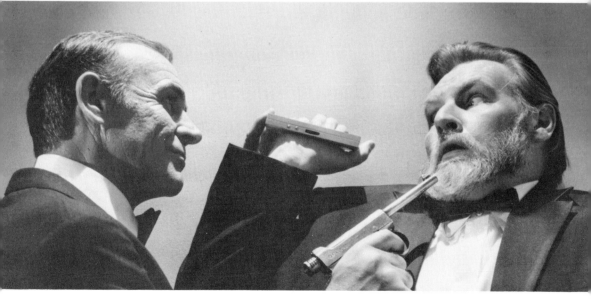

Sean Connery, Dan Meaden Top: (L) Sean Connery, Klaus Maria Brandauer, (R) Barbara
Carrera, Sean Connery, Center: (L) Kim Basinger, Connery, (R) Basinger, Carrera

CARMEN

(ORION CLASSICS) Producer, Emiliano Piedra; Director, Carlos Saura; Interpretation, Carlos Saura, Antonio Gades; Choreography, Carlos Saura, Antonio Gades; Photography, Teo Escamilla; Original Music, Paco De Lucia; Excerpts from Bizet's "Carmen" sung by Regina Resnik, Mario Del Monaco; Editor, Pedro Del Rey; Design, Felix Murcia; Costumes, Teresa Nieto; Assistant Directors, Julian Marcos, Carlos Saura, Jr.; In color; Rated R; 99 minutes; October release

CAST

Antonio	Antonio Gades
Carmen	Laura Del Sol
Paco	Paco De Lucia
Cristina	Cristina Hoyos
Juan y Madrido	Juan Antonio Jimenez
Escamillo	Sebastian Moreno
Pepe Giron	Jose Yepes
Featured Dancer	Pepa Flores

and singers, guitarists, dancers, and corps de ballet

Left: Laura del Sol, Antonio Gades
© *Orion Classics*

Cristina Hoyos, Laura del Sol

Antonio Gades, Laura del Sol
Top: Cristina Hoyes, Laura del Sol

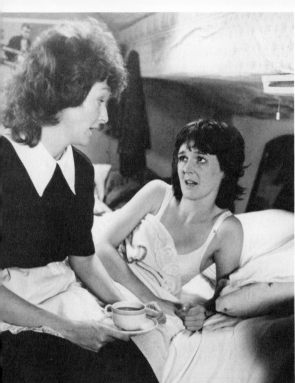

EXPERIENCE PREFERRED ... BUT NOT ESSENTIAL

(SAMUEL GOLDWYN CO.) Producer, Chris Griffen; Executive Producer, David Puttnam; Director, Peter Duffell; Screenplay, June Roberts; Photography, Phil Meheux; Associate Producer, David Bill; Editor, John Shirley; Music, John Scott; Art Director, Jane Martin; Assistant Directors, Dominic Fulford, Andrew Montgomery, Russell Lodge; Costumes, Tudor George; In color; Rated PG; 80 minutes; November release

CAST

Annie	Elizabeth Edmonds
Mavis	Sue Wallace
Doreen	Geraldine Griffith
Paula	Karen Meagher
Arlene	Maggie Wilkinson
Mike	Ron Bain
Hywel	Alun Lewis
Ivan	Robert Blythe
Wally	Roy Heather
Dai	Peter Doran
Helen	Arwen Holm
Nin	Sion Tudor Owen
Gareth	Robert Gwilym
Now	Mostyn Evans
Howard	Paul Haley
Mrs. Howard	Margo Jenkins
M.C.	Jerry Brooke

Left: Sue Wallace, Elizabeth Edmonds

Elizabeth Edmonds, Ron Bain

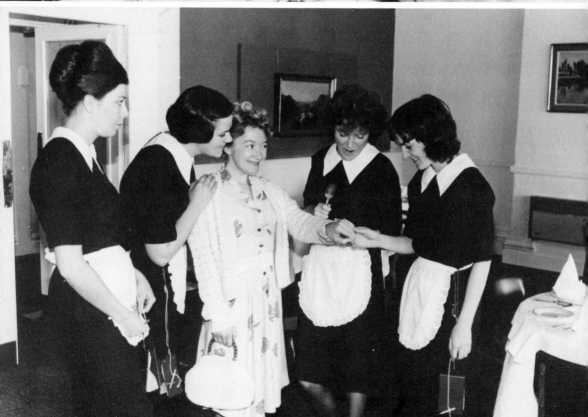

Karen Meagher, Geraldine Griffith, Maggie Wilkinson, Sue Wallace, Elizabeth Edmonds
Top: Elizabeth Edmonds (center)

BOAT PEOPLE

(INTERNATIONAL SPECTRAFILM) Executive Producer, Miranda Yang; Director, Ann Hui; Producer, Chui Po-Chu; Screenplay, K. C. Chiu; Photography, Chung Chi-Man; Editor, Wong Yee-Sun; Music, Law Wing-Fai; Costumes/Makeup, Lo Shui-Lien; In color; Chinese with English subtitles; Rated R; 106 minutes; November release

CAST

Akutagawa	Lam
The Madame	Cora Miao
Cam Nuong	Season Ma
To Minh	Andy Lau
Ah Thanh	Paul Chung
Inour	Wong Shau-Him
Officer Nguyen	Qi Mengshi
Comrade Le	Jia Meiying
Comrade Vu	Lin Shujin
Cam Nuong's Mother	Hao Jialin
Ah Nhac	Wu Shujun
Second Brother	Guo Junyi
Commander of Zone 16	Lin Tao
Doctor in Zone 15	Zhang Dongsheng
Second Officer in Zone 15	Cai Jianzhou
To Minh's Father	Wang Huangwen
Woman Neighbor	Meng Pingmei

© *Spectrafilm*

Lam and child
Top: Lam

VASSA

(INTERNATIONAL FILM EXCHANGE) Direction and Screenplay, Gleb Panfilov; Based on play by Maxim Gorky; Photography, Leonid Kalashnikov; Music, Vadim Bibergan; Russian with English subtitles; In color; Not rated; 106 minutes; November release

CAST

Vassa ....Inna Churikova
Anna, Vassa's secretary .... Valentina Telichkina
Rachel .... Valentina Yakunina
Vassa's Brother .... Vadim Medvedev

Right: Inna Churikova
© *International Film Exchange*

THE DRESSER

(COLUMBIA) Producer-Director, Peter Yates; Screenplay, Ronald Harwood from his play of same title; Photography, Kelvin Pike; Designer, Stephen Grimes; Editor, Ray Lovejoy; Music, James Horner; Associate Producer, Nigel Wooll; Art Director, Colin Grimes; Assistant Directors, Andy Armstrong, Christopher Figg, Tony Aherne; Costumes, Bermans and Nathans; A Goldcrest Films-World Film Services production in color; Rated PG; 118 minutes; November release

CAST

Sir	Albert Finney
Norman	Tom Courtenay
Oxenby	Edward Fox
Her Ladyship	Zena Walker
Madge	Eileen Atkins
Frank Carrington	Michael Gough
Irene	Cathryn Harrison
Violet Manning	Betty Marsden
Lydia Gibson	Sheila Reid
Geoffrey Thornton	Lockwood West
Mr. Godstone	Donald Eccles
Horace Brown	Llewellyn Rees
Benton	Guy Manning
Beryl	Anne Mannion
C. Rivers Lane	Kevin Stoney
Miss White	Ann Way
Mr. Bottomley	John Sharp
Bombazine Woman	Kathy Staff
Charles	Roger Avon
Evelyn, the Airman	Christopher Irvin
Evelyn's Friend	Stuart Richman
Actress on station	Sandra Gough
Arthur	Joe Belcher
Electrician	Johnny Maxfield
Stallkeeper	Paul Luty
Barmaid	Lori Wells
Train Guard	Alan Starkey

© *Columbia Pictures*

center: Tom Courtenay, Albert Finney surrounded by touring company
Top Left: Tom Courtenay, Albert Finney

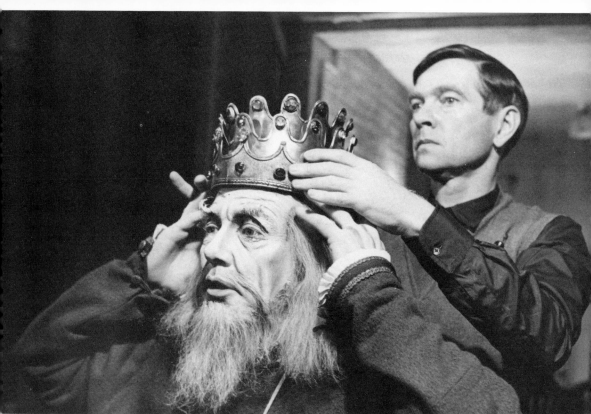

Tom Courtenay, Albert Finney, and at top

LA BALANCE

(SPECTRAFILM) Executive Producers, Georges Dancigers, Alexandre Mnouchkine; Director, Bob Swaim; Screenplay, Bob Swaim, M. Fabiani; Photography, Bernard Zitzermann; Art Director, Eric Moulard; Editor, Francoise Javet; Music, Roland Bocquet; Wardrobe, Catherine Meurisse; In color; Rated R; 102 minutes; November release

CAST

Nicole	Mathalie Baye
Dede	Philippe Leotard
Palouzi	Richard Berry
Tintin	Christophe Malavoy
Le Belge	Jean-Paul Connart
Le Capitaine	Bernard Freyd
Carlini	Albert Dray
Simoni	Florent Pagny
Arnaud	Jean-Daniel Laval
Picard	Luc-Antoine Diquero
Massina	Maurice Ronet
Petrovic	Tcheky Karyo
Sabrina	Anne-Claude Salimo
Guy	Michel Anphoux
Djerbi	Raouf Ben Yaghlane
Ayouche	Robert Atlan
Calemard	Guy Dhers
Inspector Mondaine	Francois Berleand
Paulo	Sam Karmann

Right: Nathalie Baye
© *Spectrafilm*

Nathalie Baye, Richard Berry
(also above)

Nathalie Baye, Philippe Leotard
(also above)

MALOU

(QUARTET) Direction and Screenplay, Jeanine Meerapfel; Executive Producer, Horst Burkhard; A Regina Zeigler production in color; Photography, Michael Ballhaus; Editor, Dagmar Hirtz; Music, Peer Raben; Designer, Rainer Schaper; Costumes, Anna Spaghetti; Not rated; 93 minutes; December release

CAST

Malou	Ingrid Caven
Hannah	Grischa Huber
Martin	Helmut Griem
Paul	Ivan Desny
Lotte	Marie Colbin
Albert	Peter Chatel
Lucia	Margarita Calahorra
Paul's Father	Lo Van Hensbergen
Paul's Mother	Liane Saalborn
Hannah at 12	Cordula Riedel
Uncle Max	Jim Kain

Right: Ingrid Caven, Ivan Desny
© *Quartet/Films Inc.*

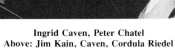

Ingrid Caven, Peter Chatel
Above: Jim Kain, Caven, Cordula Riedel

Ingrid Caven, Grischa Huber
Above: Helmut Griem, Grischa Huber

Rolf Zacher, Burkhard Driest
in "Slow Attack"

Renee Soutendijk as "The Girl
with the Red Hair" © *United Artists*

SLOW ATTACK (New Yorker Films) Executive Producers, Eberhard Junkersdorf, Dieter Schidor; Director, Reinhard Hauff; Screenplay, Burkhard Driest; Photography, Frank Bruhne; Editors, Peter Przygodda, Barbara von Weitershausen; Music, Irmin Schmidt; Art Direction, Toni and Heidi Ludi; Assistant Director, Ursula Kley; Costumes, Monika Altmann, Gerlind Gies; In color; 112 minutes; In German with English subtitles; January release. CAST: Burkhard Driest (Nik), Rolf Zacher (Henry), Katja Rupe (Eva), Carla Egerer (Leila), Kurt Raab (Beekenbrandt), Eckehard Ahrens (Donald), Jóey Buschmann (Janni), Hark Bohm (TV Moderator), Veit Relin, Werner Eichhorn, Hans Noever, Reinhold Olschewski, Michael Gspandl, David Hess, Gabriela Dossi, Irm Herrmann, Marquand Bohm, Peter Hick, Horst Hesslein, Hans, Fretz, Heinz Hurlander, Maya Speth, Peter Genee

THE CONCERT FOR KAMPUCHEA (Miramax Films) Executive Producer for EMI Films, Bob Mercer; Director, Keith McMillan; A Keefco Production; In color; 72 minutes; January release. CAST: The Who, Paul McCartney, Robert Plant, Pretenders, Elvis Costello, The Clash, Rockpile, The Specials, Ian Dury, Rockestra, Matumbi

TREASURE OF THE FOUR CROWNS (Cannon Group) Executive Producers, Menahem Golan, Yoram Globus; Associate Producer, Marshall Lupo; Music, Ennio Morricone; Producers, Tony Anthony, Gene Quintana; Director, Ferdinando Baldi; Screenplay, Lloyd Battista, Jim Bryce, Jerry Lazarus; Original Story, Tony Anthony, Gene Quintana; Photography, Marcello Masciocchi, Giuseppe Ruzzolini; Art Director, Luciano Spadoni; Costumes, Eugenia Escriba; Editor, Franco Fraticelli; Music, Ennio Morricone; In color and Dolby Stereo; Rated PG; 99 minutes; January release. CAST: Tony Anthony, (J. T. Striker), Ana Obregon (Liz), Gene Quintana (Edmund), Francisco Rabal (Socrates), Jerry Lazarus (Rick), Emiliano Redondo (Brother Jonas), Francisco Villena (Professor)

THE GIRL FROM LORRAINE (New Yorker) Producers, Yves Peyrot, Raymond Pousaz; Director, Claude Goretta; Screenplay, Goretta, Jacques Kirsner, Rosine Rochette; Photography, Philippe Rousselot, Dominique Bringuier; Music, Arie Dzierlatka; In color; French with English subtitles; 1980 film; Not rated; 107 minutes; January release. CAST: Nathalie Baye (Christine), Bruno Ganz (Remy), Angela Winkler (Claire), Patrick Chesnais (Pascal)

SWEE' PEA (Summit) Producer, Anna Marie Clementelli; Director, Peter Del Monte; Screenplay, Bernardino Zapponi, Peter Del Monte; Photography, Giuseppe Lanci; Editor, Sergio Montanari; Music, Fiorenzo Carpi; In color; Italian with English subtitles; Not rated; 105 minutes; January release. CAST: Luca Porro, Fabio Peraboni, Leopoldo Trieste, Valeria D'Obici, Alessandro Habel

THE GIRL WITH THE RED HAIR (United Artists Classics) Producers, Chris Brouwer, Haig Balian; Director, Ben Verbong; Screenplay, Ben Verbong, Pieter de Vos; Based on novel by Theun De Vries; Photography, Theo Van de Sande; Editor, Ton De Graaff; Music, Nicolai Piovani; Design, Jos Van der Linden; Costumes, Yan Tax; Assistant Director, Hans Kemna; In color; Dutch with English subtitles; Rated PG; 116 minutes; January release. CAST: Renee Soutendijk (Hannie), Peter Tuinman (Hugo), Loes Luca (An), Johan Leysen (Frans), Robert Delhez (Floor), Ada Bouwman (Tinka), Lineke Rijxman (Judith), Maria De Booy (Mother), Henk Rigters (Father), Adrian Brine (German Officer), Chris Lomme (Ms. DeRuyter), Lou Landre (Otto), Jan Retel (Professor), Elsje Scherjon (Carlien), Hennie Van Den Akker (Van Den Heuvel)

TIME FOR REVENGE (Televicine) Producers, Hector Olivera, Luis Osvaldo Repetto; Direction-Screenplay, Adolfo Aristarain; Photography, Horacio Maira; Editor, Eduardo Lopez; Assistant Director, Jorge Gundin; Costumes, Marta Albertinazzi; Sets, Abel Facello; Music, Enrique Kauderer; In color; Not rated; 112 minutes; January Release. CAST: Federico Luppi (Pedro), Haydee Padilla (Amanda), Julio de Grazia (Larsen), Ulises Dumont (Bruno), Rodolfo Ranni, Aldo Barbero, Enrique Liporace, Alberto Benegas, Arturo Maly, Jorge Hacker

HARRY TRACY (QFI/Quartet) Producer, Ronald I. Cohen: Associate Producer, Patricia Johnson; Co-Producer, Alan Simmonds; Executive Producers, Sid Krofft, Marty Krofft, Albert J. Tenzer; Screenplay, David Lee Henry; Photography, Allen Daviau; Designer, Karen Bromley; Editor, Ron Wisman; Music, Mickey Erbe, Maribeth Solomon; In color; Rated PG; 111 minutes; January release. CAST: Bruce Dern (Harry Tracy), Helen Shaver (Catherine), Michael C. Gwynne (Dave), Gordon Lightfoot (Morrie)

MURDER BY PHONE (New World) released in 1982 as "The Calling."

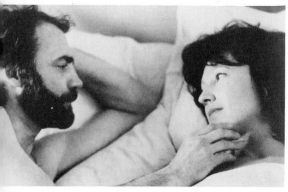

Bruno Ganz, Nathalie Baye
in "A Girl from Lorraine"

Helen Shaver, Bruce Dern
in "Harry Tracy"

Mirjana Karanovic, Marko Nikolic
in "Petria's Wreath"

"Menudo"

XTRO (New Line Cinema) Executive Producer, Robert Shaye; Producer, Mark Forstater; Director, Harry Bromley Davenport; Associate Producer, James M. Crawford; Screenplay, Robert Smith, Iain Cassie; Based on original screenplay by Harry Bromley Davenport, Michel Parry; Additional Dialogue, Jo Ann Kaplan; Editors, Nick Gaster, Jo Ann Kaplan; Assistant Directors, Jake Wright, Hugh O'Donnell, Michael Zimbrich; Art Directors, Andrew Mollo, Peter Body; In color; Rated R; 82 minutes; January release. CAST: Bernice Stegers (Rachel), Philip Sayer (Sam), Danny Brainin (Joe), Simon Nash (Tony), Maryam D'Abo (Analise), David Cardy (Michael), Anna Wing (Miss Goodman), Peter Mandell (Clown), Robert Fyfe (Doctor), Arthur Whybrow (Knight-Porter), Anna Mottram (Teacher), Katherine Best (Jane), Robert Pereno (Ben), Tik (Monster), Vanya Seager (Paula)

THE KILLING OF ANGEL STREET (Satori) Producer, Anthony Buckley; Director, Donald Crombie; Story, Michael Craig; Screenplay, Evan Jones, Michael Craig, Cecil Holmes; Photography, Peter James; Editor, Tim Wellburn; Art Director, Lindsay Hewson; Music, Brian May; In color; Rated PG; 101 minutes; January Release. CAST: Liz Alexander (Jessica), John Hargreaves (Elliot), Alexander Archdale (B. C.), Reg Lye (Riley), Gordon McDougall (Sir Arthur), David Downer (Alan), Ric Herbert (Ben), Brendon Lunney (Scott), Allen Bickford (Collins), John Stone (Benson)

TOO SHY TO TRY (Quartet) Producer, Albina Du Boisrouvray; Executive Producer, Georges Casati; Director, Pierre Richard; Screenplay, Pierre Richard, Jean-Jacques Annaud, Alain Godard; Photography, Claude Agostini; Music, Vladimir Cosma; Editor, Pierre Gillette,; In Eastmancolor; Rated PG; 91 minutes; January release. CAST: Pierre Richard, Mimi Coutelier, Catherine Lachens, Robert Castel, Aldo Maccione, Jacques Francois, Jacques Fabbri, Robert Dalban, Jean-Claude Massoulier

VIDEODROME (Universal) Producer, Claude Heroux; Direction and Screenplay, David Cronenberg; Executive Producers, Victor Solnicki, Pierre David; Associate Producer, Lawrence Nesis; Photography, Mark Irwin; Music, Howard Shore; Editor, Ronald Sanders; Art Director, Carol Spier; Special Makeup, Rick Baker; Assistant Directors, John Board, Libby Bowden, Rocco Gismondi; Costumes, Delphine White; Choreographer, Kirsteen Etherington; A Filmplan International Production in color; Rated R; 90 minutes; February release. CAST: James Woods (Max Renn), Sonja Smits

(Bianca), Deborah Harry (Nicki), Peter Dvorsky (Harlan), Les Carlson (Barry), Jack Creley (Brian), Lynne Gorman (Masha), Julie Khaner (Bridey), Reiner Schwarz (Moses), David Bolt (Raphael), Lally Cadeau (Rena), Henry Gomez (Brolley), Kay Hawtrey (Matron), Sam Malkin (Derelict), Bob Church (Newscaster), Jayne Eastwood (Caller), Franciszka Hedland (Bellydancer), Harvey Chao, David Tsubouchi (Salesmen)

PETRIA'S WREATH (New Yorker) Direction and Screenplay, Srdjan Karanovic; Based on novel by Dragoslav Mihajlovic; Photography, Tomislav Pinter; Music, Zoran Simjanovic; Editor, Branka Ceperac; Costumes, Sasha Kuljaca; Designer, Misha Miric; In Serbo-Croation with English subtitles; In color; Not rated; 100 minutes; February release. CAST: Mirjana Karanovic (Petria), Marko Nikolic (Dobrivoje), Pavle Vujisic (Ljubisha), Dragan Maksimovic (Misa), Ljiljana Krstic (Vela), Olivera Markovic (Vlajna), Mica Tomic (Photographer), Misha Zutic (Ing. Markovic), Veljko Mandic (Kamenche)

MENUDO (Embassy) Producer, Jorge Garcia; Director, Orestes A Trucco; Executive Producer, Jorge Fusaro: Associate Producer, Paquito Cordero; Photography, Hector Collodoro; Musical Director, A. Monroy, C. Villa; Artistic Director, Edgardo Diaz; In color; Not rated; 95 minutes; February release. CAST: Rickie, Xavier, Johnny, Charlie, Miguel and Alondra, Luis Lucio, Eduardo Trucco

WE OF THE NEVER NEVER (Triumph Films) Executive Producer, Phillip Adams; Producer, Greg Tepper; Co-Producer, John B. Murray: Director, Igor Auzins; Screenplay, Peter Schreck; Associate Producer, Brian Rosen; Music, Peter Best; Editor, Clifford Hayes; Photography, Gary Hansen; Assistant Directors, Tim Higgins, Brendan Lavelle, Ian Goddard, Jess Tapper; Design, Josephine Ford; In color; Rated G; 132 minutes; February release. CAST: Angela Punch McGregor (Jeannie), Arthur Dignam (Aenus Gunn), Tony Barry (Mac), Tommy Lewis (Jackeroo), Lewis Fitz-Gerald (Jack), Martin Vaughan (Dan), John Jarratt (Dandy), Tex Morton (Landlord), Donald Blitner (Goggle Eye), Kim Chiu Kok (Sam Lee), Mawuyul Yanthalawuy (Rose), Cecil Parkee (Cheon), Brian Granrott (Neaves), Danny Adcock (Brown), John Cameron (Jimmy), Sibina Willy (Bett), Jessie Roberts (Nellie), Christine Conway (Judy), Ray Pattison (Johnny Wakelin), George Jadarku (Charly), Sally McKenzie (Carrie), Sarah Craig (Liz), Fincina Hopgood (Dot), Lise Rodgers, Dayle Alison, Jenni Cunningham (Friends)

James Woods, Deborah Harry
in "Videodrome" © *Universal City Studios*

Angela Punch McGregor, Arthur Dignam
in "We of the Never Never"
© *Columbia Pictures*

Karl Malden, Jodi Thelen
in "Twilight Time"
© United Artists

WHEN JOSEPH RETURNS (New Yorker Films) Direction and Screenplay, Zsolt Kezdi-Kovacs; Photography, Janos Kende; Editor, Zoltan Farkas; Art Director, Luca Karall; Sets, Tamas Banovich; Costumes, Zsuzsa Vicze; Assistant Directors, Lilla Matis, Nora Kovats; In Hungarian with English subtitles; Not rated; In color; 92 minutes; February release. CAST: Lili Monori (Maria), Eva Ruttkai (Agnes), Gyorgy Pogany (Joseph), Gaboroncz (Laci), Maria Ronyecz (Chauffeur's Boss), Istvan Bujtor (Tibor), Ferenc Palancz (Karcsi), Tibor Molnar (David), Mark Zala (Zoltan), Sandor Halmagyi (Sanyi), Laszlo Czurka (Gray-haired man)

TALES OF ORDINARY MADNESS (Fred Baker) Producer, Jacqueline Ferreri; Director Marco Ferreri; Associate Producers, Jacqueline Ferreri, Sergio Galiano; Story, Sergio Amidei, Marco Ferreri; Based on short stories by Charles Bukowski; Screenplay, Marco Ferreri, Sergio Amidei, Anthony Foutz; Photography, Tonino delli Colli; Editor, Ruggero Mastroianni; Music, Philippe Sarde; Designer, Dante Ferretti; Costumes, Nicoletta Ercole, Rita Corradini; Assistant Director, Ludovico Gasparini; In Eastmancolor; Not rated; 107 minutes; February release. CAST: Ben Gazzara (Charles), Ornella Muti (Cass), Susan Tyrrell (Vera), Tanya Lopert (Vicky), Roy Brocksmith (Bartender), Katia Berger (Girl on beach), Hope Cameron (Landlady), Judith Drake (Fat Woman), Patrick Hughes (Pimp), Wendy Welles (Teenage Runaway), Jay Julien (Publisher)

THE STATE OF THINGS (Gray City) Producer, Chris Sievernich; Director, Wim Wenders; Screenplay, Robert Kramer, Wim Wenders; Photography, Henri Alekan, Fred Murphy; Editor, Barbara von Weitershausen; Music, Jurgen Knieper; Associate Producers, Paulo Branco, Pierre Cottrell; Not rated; In black and white; 120 minutes; February release. CAST: Isabelle Weingarten (Anna), Rebecca Pauly (Joan), Jeffrey Kime (Mark), Geoffrey Carey (Robert), Camilla Mora (Julia), Alexandra Auder (Jane), Patrick Bauchau (Director), Paul Getty III (Writer), Viva Auder (Scriptgirl), Sam Fuller (Cameraman), Artur Semedo (Production Manager), Francisco Baiao (Soundman), Robert Kramer (Camera Operator), Allen Goorwitz (Gordon), Roger Corman (Lawyer), Martine Getty (Secretary), Monty Bane (Herbert), Janet Rasak (Karen), Judy Mooradian (Waitress)

CAMERA BUFF (New Yorker) Director, Krzysztof Kieslowski; Screenplay, Krzysztof Kieslowski, Jerzy Stuhr; Photography, Jacek Petrycki; Editor, Halina Nawrocka; Music, Krzysztof Knittel; Designer, Rafal Waltenberger; Costumes, Gabriela Star-Tyszkiewicz; Not rated; In Polish with English subtitles; 112 minutes; February release. CAST: Jerzy Stuhr (Filip Mosz), Malgorzata Zabkowska (His Wife), Ewa Pokas (Anna), Stefan Czyzewski (Director), Jerzy Nowak (Osuch), Tadeusz Bradecki (Witek), Marek Litewka (Piotrek), Krzysztof Zanussi (Himself), Boguslaw Sobczuk, Andrzej Warchol (TV Directors)

TWILIGHT TIME (MGM/UA) Producer, Dan Tana; Director, Goran Paskaljevic; Screenplay, Goran Paskaljevic, Filip David, Dan Tana, Rowland Barber; Executive Producer, Milan Zmukic; Composer, Walter Scharf; Associate Producer, Andrew Wood: Assistant Directors, Zoran Andric, Jan-Aleksandar Koscalik; Choreography, Renato Pernic; Photography, Tomislav Pinter; Art Director, Niko Matul; Editor, Olga Skrigin; Costumes, Marija Danc; Title Song, Buck Ram, Morty Nevins, Al Nevins; In color; Rated PG; 112 minutes; February release. CAST: Karl Malden (Marko), Jodi Thelen (Lena), Damien Nash (Ivan), Mia Roth (Ana), Pavle Vujisic (Pashko), Dragan Maksimovic (Tony), Stole Arandjelovic (Matan), Petar Bozovic (Rocky), Milan Srdoc (Karlo), Peter Carsten (Gateman), Bora Todorovic (Nikola), Bozidar Pavicevic (Luka), Davor Antolic (Driver), Slobodanka Markovic (Kristina), Ethan Stone (Milan), Bojana Stankovic (Vera), Izabela Gavric (Helena), Predrag Dejanovic (Vlatko), Nenad Dejanovic (Vladimir), Branislav Ranisavljev (Aldo)

LET'S SPEND THE NIGHT TOGETHER (Embasay) Producer, Ronald L. Schwary; Director, Hal Ashby; Creative Associate, Pablo Ferro; Photography, Caleb Deschanel, Gerald Feil; Editor, Lisa Day; Associate Producer, Kenneth J. Ryan: Assistant Directors, Charles Myers, Mary Ellen Canniff, Patrick Burns; In Technicolor and Dolby Stereo; Rated PG; 95 minutes; February release. A filmed record of Mick Jagger and the Rolling Stones record-breaking U. S. tour in 1982.

LOBSTER FOR BREAKFAST (Quartet) Producer, Italian International Films; Director, Giorgio Capitani; Photography, Carlo Carlini; Music, Piero Umiliani; In color; Rated R; 93 minutes; February release. CAST: Enrico Montesano (Enrico), Claude Brasseur (Mario), Claudine Auger (Carla), Silvia Dionisio (Matilde), Janet Agren (Monique)

THE RETURN OF CAPTAIN INVINCIBLE (7 Keys Films) Producer, Andrew Gaty; Director, Philippe Mora; Screenplay, Steve de Souza, Andrew Gaty; Photography, Mike Molloy: Art Director, Owen Patterson; Editor, John Scott; Designer, David Copping; Score, William Motzing; Associate Producer, Brian Burgess; In color; Not rated; 90 minutes; February release. CAST: Alan Arkin (Capt. Invincible), Christopher Lee (Mr. Midnight), Kate Fitzpatrick (Patty), Bill Hunter (Tupper), Graham Kennedy (Prime Minister), Michael Pate (President), Hayes Gordon (Kirby), Max Phipps (Admiral), Noel Ferrier (General)

THE CONSTANT FACTOR (New Yorker) Direction and Screenplay, Krzysztof Zanussi; Photography, Slawomir Idziak; Editor, Urszula Sliwinska; Music, Wojciech Kilar; Designers, Tadeusz Wybult, Maciej Putowski; In Polish (1980) with English subtitles; Not rated; 96 minutes; March release. CAST: Tadeusz Bradecki (Witold), Zofia Mrozowska (His Mother), Malgorzata Zajaczkowska (Grazyna), Cezary Morawski (Stefan), Witold Myrkosz (Mariusz), Ewa Lejczak (Stefan's Wife), Jan Jurewicz (Zenek), Juliusz Machulski (Wladek), Marek Litewka (Wlodzimierz), Jacek Strzemazalski (Scientist)

Rebecca Pauley, Jeffrey Kime
in "The State of Things"
© Gray City Inc.

Claude Brasseur (left)
in "Lobster for Breakfaster"
© Quartet/Films Inc.

PROVINCIAL ACTORS (New Yorker) Director, Agnieszka Holland; Screenplay, Agnieszka Holland, Witold Zatorski; Photography, Jacek Petrycki; Music, Andrzej Zarycki; Art Director, Bogdan Solle; In Polish (1979) with English subtitles; Not rated; 121 minutes; March release. CAST: Tadeusz Huk (Krzysztof), Halina Labonarska (Anka), Tomasz Zygadlo (Director), Ewa Dalkowska (Krystyna)

ARIA FOR AN ATHLETE (New Yorker) Direction and Screenplay, Filip Bajon; Photography, Jerzy Zielinski; Design, Andrzej Kowalczyk; Music, Zdzislaw Szostak; In Polish (1980) with English subtitles; Not rated; 108 minutes; March release. CAST: Krzysztof Majchrzak, Pola Raksa, Roman Wilhelmi, Bogusz Bilewski, Wojciech Pszoniak, Ryszard Pietruski, Zdzislaw Wardejn

THE WIZARD OF BABYLON (New Yorker) Director, Dieter Schidor; Commentary, Wolf Wondratschek; Photography, Carl-Friedrich Koschnik, Rainer Lenuschny; Editor, Rice Renz; Artistic Collaborator, P. Michael McLernon; Narrator, Klaus Lowitsch; Music, Peer Raben; In color; Not rated; 83 minutes; March release. A documentary about Rainer Werner Fassbinder made during the shooting of his last film "Querelle." It includes interviews with Jeanne Moreau, Brad Davis, Franco Nero, Dieter Schidor, and Fassbinder only 10 hours before his death.

WILD STYLE (First Run Features) Produced, Directed and Written by Charlie Ahearn; Photography, Clive Davidson, John Foster; Editor, Steve Brown; Music, Chris Stein; Associate Producers, Frederick Brathwaite, Jane Dickson; Assistant Directors, Colen Fitzgibbon, Rex Piano; In color; Not rated; 85 minutes; March release. CAST: Lee George Quinones (Raymond), Frederick Brathwaite (Phade), Sandra Pink Fabara (Rose), Patti Astor (Virginia), Andrew Zephyr Witten (Zroc), Carlos Morales (Raymond's Brother), Alfredo Valez (Boy with broom), Niva Kislac (Patronness), Bill Rice (TV Producer), Glenn O'Brien (Curator), Dondi White (Zoro's Double), Joe Lewis (Organizer), Pookie Daniels (Gangster), Johnny Crash Matos, Chris Daze Ellis, Fred Caz Glover, Michael Iz Martin, Nathan Ingram, Lisa Lee, Henrietta Henry, Pamela Smith, Diane Parker, Lillian Cookie Brown, Lil Markey C, Lil Sput, Chief Rocker Busy Bee, DJ, Fantastic Five, Cold Crush Four, Double Trouble, Electric Force, Rock Steady Crew

HARLEQUIN (New Image) Producer, Antony I. Ginnane; Executive Producer, William Fayman; Associate Producer, Jane Scott; Director, Simon Wincer; Screenplay, Everett de Roche; Presented by F. G. Film Productions/Stanley R. Caidin, Eric J. Caidin; In color; Not rated; 95 minutes; March release. CAST: Robert Powell (Gregory Wolfe), David Hemmings (Senator Rast), Carmen Duncan (Sandra), Broderick Crawford (Doc Wheelan)

JEANNE DIELMAN, 23 QUAI DU COMMERCE, 1080 BRUXELLES (New Yorker) Direction and Screenplay, Chantal Akerman; Photography, Babette Mangolte; Belgium 1975; French with English subtitles; Not rated; 198 minutes; March release. CAST: Delphine Seyrig (Jeanne), Jan Decorte, Henri Storck, J. Doniol-Valcroze

NEXT YEAR IF ALL GOES WELL (New World) Producers, Serge Laski, Jean-Claude Fleury; Director, Jean-Loup Hubert; Screenplay, Jean-Loup Hubert, Josyane Balasko, Gerard Zingg; Photography, Robert Alazraki; Music, Vladimir Cosma; Title song sung by Sodie Kremen; Editor, Helene Viard; Costumes, Renee Renard; Assistant Director, Alain-Michael Blanc; Executive Producer, Pierre Gauchet; French with English subtitles; In color; Rated R; 95 minutes; March release. CAST: Isabelle Adjani (Isa-

Halina Labonarska, Tadeusz Huk
in "Provincial Actors"

belle), Thierry Lhermitte (Maxime), Marie-Anne Chazel (Huguette), Michel Dussarrat (Henry), Bernard Crommbe (Moinet), Fred Personne (Isabelle's Father), Antoinette Moya (Isabelle's Mother), Paul Vally (Grandpa), Louise Rioton (Grandma), Virginie Thevenet (Fan), Madeleine Bouchez (Tantine), Maiwenn Le Besco (Prune), Sebastien Demarigny (Barnaby)

VICTORY MARCH (Summit) Producer, Silvio Clementelli; Director, Marco Bellocchio; Screenplay, Marco Bellocchio, Sergio Bazzini; Photography, Franco Di Giacomo; Art Director, Amedeo Fago; Editor, Sergio Montanari; Music, Nicola Piovani; In Technicolor; Not rated; 118 minutes; March release. CAST: Franco Nero (Capt. Asciutto), Miou Miou (Rosanna), Michele Placido (Paolo), Patrick Dewaere (2nd Lt. Baio)

HERE ARE LADIES (Arthur Cantor) Executive Producer, Martin C. Schute; Producers, Marvin Liebman, Davis Fasken; Director, John Quested; Photography, Dudley Lovell; Editor, Mamoun Hassan; Music, David Fanshawe; Assistant Director, Redmond Morris; In color; Not rated; 60 minutes; March release. An Irish documentary with Siobhan McKenna, Niall Buggy, May Clusky, Paul Farrell, Sarah Gallagher, Maireni Ghrainne, Pat Layde, Patsy Madden, Bernadette McKenna, Owen McMahon, Brian Murray

ATOR (Comworld) Producer, Alex Sussamn; Direction and Screenplay, David Hills; Photography, Frederick Slonisco; Editor, David Framer; Art Director, John Gregory; Music, Maria Cordio; Assistant Director, Sam Stone; In color; Rated PG; 100 minutes; March release. CAST: Miles O'Keeffe, Sabrina Siani, Ritza Brown, Edmund Purdom, Laura Gemser

CHOICE OF ARMS (Summit) Producer, Alain Sarde; Director, Alain Corneau; Screenplay, Alain Corneau, Michel Grisolia; Photography, Pierre-William Glenn; Music, Philippe Sarde; Art Direction-Costumes, Jean-Pierre Kohut-Svelko; Editor, Thierry Derocles; French with English subtitles; In color; Not rated; 130 minutes; March release. CAST: Yves Montand (Noel), Gerard Depardieu (Mickey), Catherine Deneuve (Nicole), Michel Galabru (Monnardot), Gerard Lanvin (Sarlat), Jean-Claude Dauphin (Ricky), Richard Anconina (Dany)

Rainer Werner Fassbinder, Jeanne Moreau,
Brad Davis in "The Wizard of Babylon"

Krzysztof Majchrzak
in "Aria for an Athlete"

Richard Moir, Judy Davis
in "Heatwave" © *New Line Cinema*

John Vernon, Linda Thorson
in "Curtains" © *Jensen Farley*

POWERFORCE (Bedford Entertainment) Producer, George Mason; Director, Michael King; Executive Producers, Y. W. Cheung, Johnny Mak; Screenplay, Terry Chalmers, Dennis Thompsett; Photography, Bob Huke, Robert Hope; Music, Chris Babida; In color; Rated R; March release. CAST: Bruce Baron, Mandy Moore, James Barnett, Jovy Couldry, Frances Fong, Olivia Jeng, Randy Channel, Seon Blake, Sam Sorono, Bruce Li

HEATWAVE (New Line Cinema) Producer, Hilary Linstead; Director, Phillip Noyce; Co-Producer, Ross Matthews; Screenplay, Marc Rosenberg, Phillip Noyce; Based on original screenplay by Mark Stiles, Tim Gooding; Photography, Vincent Monton; Designer, Ross Major; Costumes, Terry Ryan; Editor, John Scott; Music, Cameron Allan; In color; Rated R; 92 minutes; April release. CAST: Judy Davis (Kate), Richard Moir (Steven), Chris Haywood (Peter), Bill Hunter (Robert), John Gregg (Phillip), Anna Jemison (Victoria), John Meillon (Freddy), Dennis Miller (Mick), Peter Hehir (Bodyguard), Carole Skinner (Mary), Gillian Jones (Barbie Lee), Frank Gallacher (Dick), Tui Bow (Annie), Don Crosby (Jim), Lynette Curran (Evonne)

WAITING FOR GAVRILOV (IFEX) Director, Pyotr Todorovsky; Screenplay, Sergei Bodrov; Photography, Yevgeny Guslinsky; Russian with English subtitles; A Mosfilm Production in color; Not rated; 80 minutes; April release. CAST: Ludmila Gurchenko (Rita), Sergei Shakurov (Gavrilov), Evgeny Evstegneev (Uncle), A. Vasilyev (Slava), Mikhail Svetin (Victor), Sbilowski (Pasha), S. Ponomareva (Tanya), Natalya Nazarova (Lucya), S. Sokolov (Victor)

PRIVILEGED (New Yorker) Producer, Richard Stevenson; Director, Michael Hoffman; Screenplay, Michael Hoffman, David Woolcombe, Rupert Walters; Music, Rachel Portman; Photography, Fiona Cunningham Reid; Editor, Derek Goldman; Assistant Director/Producer, Andrew Paterson; Art Director, Peter Schwabach; Art Designer, Jason Cooper; Assistant Director, Rupert Walters; Assistant Producer, Neil Mendoza; Background and party music, Kudos Points; Pianist, Titus Earle; In Technicolor; Not rated; 94 minutes; April release. CAST: Robert Woolley (Edward), Diana Katis (Anne), Hughie Grant (Lord Adrian), Victoria Studd (Lucy), James Wilby (Jamie), Simon Shackleton (Justin), Imogen Stubbs (Imogen), Mark Williams (Wilf), Jenny Waldman (Waitress), Ted Coleman (Barman), Stefan Bednarcyzk (Pianist), "Duchess of Malfi" cast: Neville Watchurst (Julian), Michael Hoffman (Alan),

Mark Saban (Geoff/Cardinal), Alex Wellesley-Wesley (Claire/Cariola), John Cullen (Martin/Delio), Alex Marengo (Simon/-Malateste), Charles Eliot, Peter Garrod, Richard Stevenson (Murderers), Jonathan Barrett (Young Prince), Anthea Platt (Young Princess)

CURTAINS (Jensen Farley) Producer, Peter R. Simpson; Director, Jonathan Stryker; Executive Producer, Richard Simpson; Screenplay, Robert Guza, Jr.; Photography, Robert Paynter, Fred Guthe; Music, Paul Zaza; Design, Roy Forge Smith; Editor, Michael MacLaverty; In color; Rated R; 90 minutes; April release. CAST: John Vernon (Jonathan), Samantha Eggar (Samantha), Linda Thorson (Brooke), Anne Ditchburn (Laurian), Lynne Griffin (Patti O'Connor), Sandra Warren (Tara), Lesleh Donaldson (Christie), Deborah Burgess (Amanda), Michael Wincott (Matthew), Maury Chaykin (Monty), Joann McIntyre (Secretary), Calvin Butler (Dr. Pendleton), Kate Lynch (Receptionist), Booth Savage, William Marshall, James Kidnie, Jeremy Jenson, Donald Adams, Diane Godwin, Janelle Hutchison, Virginia Laight, Kay Griffin, Bunty Webb, Daisy White, Vivian Reis, Sheila Currie, Frances Gunn, Suzanne Russell, Jenna Louise, Anna Migliarese, Elaine Crosley, Mary Durkin, Angela Carrol, Julie Massie, Pat Carroll Brown, Teresa Tova, Janie Nicholson, Alison Lawrence, Jo-Anne Hannah

DIRTY DISHES (Quartet) Producer, Vera Belmont; Direction-Screenplay, Joyce Bunuel; Music, Jean-Marie Senia; Editor, Jean-Bernard Bonis; Photography, Francois Protat; Presented by Robert A. McNeil; In color; French with English subtitles; 97 minutes; Rated R; April release. CAST: Carole Laure (Armelle), Pierre Santini (Husband), Liliane Roveyre (Friend), Liza Broconnier, Daniel Sarky, Bernard Haller

ONE-ARMED EXECUTIONER (Super-Pix) Executive Producers, Gene S. Suarez, Rey Q. Santos; Producer-Director, Bobby A. Suarez; Screenplay, Wray Hamilton; Photography, Juan Pereira; Editor, Joe Zucchero; Music, Gene Kavel; Associate Director, Pepito Diaz; Assistant Director, Butch Santos; Special Effects, Benny Macabale; In color; Rated R; 88 minutes; April release. CAST: Franco Guerrero, Jody Kay, Pete Cooper, Nigel Hogge, Mike Cohen, James Gaines, Brian Smith, Leopoldo Salcedo, Joe Zucchero, Joe Sison, Odeth Khan, Danny Rojo, Joe Cunanan, Nestie Mercado, Celso Lindaya

Robert Woolley, Victoria Studd
in "Privileged" © *New Yorker*

Natalya Nazarova (upper left, clockwise)
Stanislov Sokolov, S. Ponomareva, Evgyny
Evstegneev, Ludmila Gurchenko in "And They
Lived Happily Ever After . . ." © *IFEX*

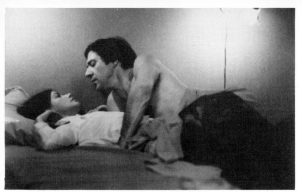

"Dirty Dishes"
© Quartet/Films Inc.

Fernanda Montenegro, Gianfrancesco Guarnieri
in "They Don't Wear Black Tie"

LIGHT YEARS AWAY (New Yorker) Producer, Pierre Heros; Direction-Screenplay, Alain Tanner; Based on novel "La Voie Sauvage" by Daniel Odier; Photography, Jean-Francois Robin; Editor, Brigitte Sousselier; Music, Arie Dzierlatka; In color; Not rated; 95 minutes; April release. CAST: Trevor Howard (Yoshka), Mick Ford (Jonas), Bernice Stegers (Betty), Henri Virlogeux (Lawyer), Odile Schmitt (Dancer), Louis Samier (Trucker), Joe Pilkington (Thomas), John Murphy (Man in bar), Mannix Flynn (Drunk Boy), Don Foley (Cafe Owner), Jerry O'Brien (Bar Owner), Vincent Smith (Cop), Gabrielle Keenan (Girl at village dance)

NANA (Cannon Group) Executive Producer, Alexander Hacohen; Producers, Menahem Golan, Yoram Globus; Director, Dan Wolman; Screenplay, Marc Behm; Photography, Armando Nannuzzi; Designer, Amadeo Mellone; Costumes, Ugo Pericoli; Music, Ennio Morricone; In color; Not rated; April release. CAST: Katya Berger (Nana), Jean-Pierre Aumont (Count Muffat), Mandy Rice-Davis (Countess Sabine), Debra Berger (Satin), Shirin Taylor (Zoe), Yehuda Efroni (Steiner), Paul Mueller (Xavier), Robert Bridges (Fontan), Massimo Serato (Faucherie), Marcus Beresford (Hector), Annier Belle (Renee), Tom Felleghy (Mellier)

THE SANDGLASS (Polish Corp.) Director, Wojciech J. Has; Based on story "The Sanatorium under the Sign of the Hourglass' by Bruno Schulz; Photography, Witold Sobocinski; Editor, Janina Niedzwiedzka; Music, Jerzy Maksymiuk; Polish with English subtitles; Not rated; 124 minutes; May release. CAST: Jan Nowicki (Joseph), Tadeusz Kondrat (Jacob), Halina Kowalska (Adela), Gustaw Holoubek (Dr. Gotard)

LIEBELEI (Elite Tonfilm) Director, Max Ophuls; Screenplay, Hans Wilhelm, Curt Alexander; From play by Arthur Schnitzler; Photography, Franz Planer; Editor, Friedel Buchott; Music, Theo Mackeben; Executive Producer, Fred Lissa; German with English subtitles; Not rated; 88 minutes; May release. CAST: Wolfgang Liebeneiner (Fritz), Magda Schneider (Christine), Luise Ullrich (Mitzi), Willy Eichberger (Theo), Paul Hoerbiger (Hans), Gustaf Gruendgans (Baron), Olga Tschechowa (Baroness)

THEY DON'T WEAR BLACK TIE (New Yorker) Director, Leon Hirszman; Story and Screenplay, Gian-Francesco Guarnieri, Leon Hirszman; Photography, Lauro Escorel; Costumes, Yurika Yamasaki; Editor, Eduardo Escorel; Music, Radames Gnatalli; Theme Music, Adoniram Barbosa; Executive Producer, Carlos Alberto Diniz; In color; Portuguese with English subtitles; 120 minutes; Not rated; May release. CAST: Fernanda Montenegro (Romana), Gianfrancesco Guarnieri (Otavio), Bete Mendes (Maria), Milton Goncalves (Braulio), Rafael de Carvalho (Maria's father), Anselmo Vasconcelos (Tiao's friend), Francisco Milani (Sartini), Fernando Ramos da Silva (Maria's brother), Lelia Abramo (Malvina)

NUDO DI DONNA or "Portrait of a Woman, Nude" (Horizon Films) Producer, Franco Committeri; Director, Nino Manfredi; Screenplay, Agenore Incrocci, Ruggero Maccari, Nino Manfredi, Furio Scarpelli, Silvana Buzzo; Story, Nino Manfredi, Paolo Levi; Photography, Danilo Desideri; Music, Maurizio Giammarco, Roberto Gatto; Editor, Sergio Montanari; Sets, Lorenzo Baraldi; In color; Italian with English subtitles; Rated PG; 112 minutes; May release. CAST: Nino Manfredi (Sandro), Eleonora Giorgi (Laura/-Riri), Jean-Pierre Cassel (Pireddu the photographer), George Wilson (Zanetto), Carlo Bagno (Giovanni)

EAGLE VS SILVER FOX (Almi) Director, Godfrey Ho; Rated R; 90 minutes; May release; No other credits. CAST: Wang Cheng Li, Mario Chan, Richard Kong, Wing Pui Shan, Wu Kam Bu

FIST OF GOLDEN MONKEY (Almi) Director, Godfrey Ho; Rated R; 91 minutes; May release. CAST: Elton Chong, Eagle Han, Si-Fu Wong

ROUTES OF EXILE: A MOROCCAN JEWISH ODYSSEY (First Run Features) Producer-Director, Eugene Rosow; Co-Producer, Howard Dratch; Associate Producer, Vivian Kleinman; Photography, Armand Marco, Affonso Beato, Jeri Sopanen; Editors, Eugene Rosow, Anne Stein; Screenplay, Linda Post; Narrator, Paul Frees; In color; Not rated; 90 minutes; May release. A documentary on the Moroccan Jews.

Katya Berger, Debra Berger
in "Nana" © Cannon

Eleonora Giorgi, Nino Manfredi
in "Nuda di Donna" © Horizon

Philippe Noiret, Michel Serrault
in "Heads or Tails"

HEADS OR TAILS (Castle Hill) Producer, Georges Cravenne; Director, Robert Enrico; Screenplay, Michel Audiard; Adapted by Marcel Julian, Robert Enrico, Michel Audiard from novel "Follow the Widower" by Alfred Harris; Photography, Didier Tarot; Editor, Patricia Neny; Music, Lino Leonardi; French with English subtitles; Presented by Julian and Beverly Schlossberg; Not rated; 100 minutes; May release. CAST: Philippe Noiret (Baroni), Michel Serrault (Edouard), Dorothee (Laurence), Pierre Arditi (Inspector), Jean Desailly (Chief Inspector), Andre Falcon (Senior Detective), Fred Personne (Det. Maupas), Gaelle Legrand (Zep), Guilhaine Dubos (Michele), Bernard LeCoq (Baroni's son-in-law), Jacques Maury (Swiss Lawyer), Jean Pierre Heibert (Dr. Lacazeaux)

THE GATES OF HELL (Motion Picture Marketing) previously released as "The Fear," "Fear in the City," "Living Dead," "City of the Living Dead" and "Twilight of the Dead." May release.

THE TERRY FOX STORY (20th Century-Fox) Producer, Robert Cooper; Executive Producers, Gursten Rosenfeld, Michael Levine; Associate Producer, John Eckert; Director, Ralph L. Thomas; Screenplay, Edward Hume; Story, John and Rose Kastner; Photography, Richard Ciupka; Art Director, Gavin Mitchell; Editor, Ron Wisman; Music, Bill Conti; In color; Not rated; 98 minutes; May release. CAST: Robert Duvall (Bill Vigars), Eric Fryer (Terry Fox), Michael Zeiniker (Alward), Chris Makepeace (Darrell Fox), Rosalind Chao (Rika), Elva Mai Hoover (Betty Fox), Frank Adamson (Rolly Fox), Marie McCann (Judith Fox), R. H. Thomson (Dr. Simon), Saul Rubinek (Dan), Gary Darycott (Gregg), Matt Craven (Bob), Chuck Shamata (Wilson), Patrick Watson (Peg Leg)

CLARETTA AND BEN (Aquarius) Producer, Carlo Ponti; Director, Gian Luigi Polidoro; Screenplay, Rafael Azcona, Leo Benvenuti; Photography, Mario Vulpiani; Music, Carlo Rusticchelli; In color; Not rated; 102 minutes; May release; Italy 1974. CAST: Ugo Tognazzi (Gino), Bernadette Lafont (Sandra), Franco Fabrizi, Lia Tanzi, Gigi Ballista, Quinto Parmeggiani, Ernesto Colli, Felice Andreasi, Rossana di Lorenzo

UNKNOWN CHAPLIN (Thames TV) Producers-Screenplay, Kevin Brownlow, David Gill; Consultant, Raymond Rohauer; Music, Charles Chaplin, Carl Davis; Editor, Trevor Waite; In color, black and white; Not rated; 156 minutes; May release. A documentary of Charlie Chaplin's outtakes from his two-reelers and feature films.

Bozidara Turronovova, George Kukura
in "The Divine Emma"
© United Artists

THE DIVINE EMMA (United Artists Classics) Director, Jiri Krejcik; Screenplay, Zdenek Mahler, Jiri Krejcik; Musical Directors, Frantisek Belfin, Josef Chaloupka; Photography, Miroslav Ondricek; In color; Rated PG; 107 minutes; June release. CAST: Bozidara Turronovova (Emma Destinn), George Kukura (Victor), Milos Kopecky (Samuel), Jiri Adamire (Colonel), Gabriela Benackova (Singing voice of Emma)

SHADOW OF ANGELS (Albatross/Artcofilm) Producers, Michael Fengler, Jordan Bojillov; Director, Daniel Schmid; Screenplay, Daniel Schmid, Rainer Werner Fassbinder; From Mr. Fassbinder's play; Photography, Renato Berta; Editor, Ila von Hasperg; Music, Peer Raben, Gottfried Hungsperg; German with English subtitles; In color; Not rated; 108 minutes; June release. CAST: Ingrid Caven (Lily), Rainer Werner Fassbinder (Raoul), Klaus Lowitsch (Real Estate Mogul), Annemarie Duringer (Frau Muller), Adrian Hoven (Muller), Bov Govert (Chief of Police), Ulli Lommel (Keliner), Jean-Claude Dreyfus (Zwerg), Irm Hermann (Emma), Debria Kalpataru (Marie-Antoinette), Hans Gratzer (Oscar), Peter Chafel (Mann Thomas), Ila Von Hasperg (Violet), Gail Curtis (Tau), Christine Jirku (Olga), Raul Gimenez (Jim), Alexander Allerson (Hans Von Gluck), Harry Baer (Hellfritz)

PRIX DE BEAUTE (Nicole Jouve Interama) Director, Augusto Genina; Screenplay, Mr. Genina, Rene Clair, Bernard Zimmer, Alessandro de Stefani; Photography, Rudolf Mate, Louis Nee; French with English subtitles (1920); In black and white; Not rated; 97 minutes; June release. CAST: Louise Brooks (Parisian Typist). Shown with a 1974 interview of Miss Brooks in her Rochester, NY apartment. Photography, Sandy Dannunzio; Director, Richard Leacock; 23 minutes.

IRRECONCILABLE MEMORIES (Goethe House) Directors, Klaus Volkenborn, Karl Siebig, Johann Feindt; German with English subtitles; Not rated; 87 minutes; June release. Interviews with Ludwig Stiller, a former bricklayer, and Henning Strumpell, a career officer. Shown with OF JUDGES AND OTHER SYMPATHIZERS in German with English subtitles; Director, Axel Engstfeldt; Not rated; 60 minutes. A documentary attempting to link Germany's past with its present.

FLIGHTS OF FANCY (IFEX) Director, Roman Balayan; Screenplay, Victor Merezhko; Photography, Vilen Kaliuta; Music, Vadim Khrapachov; Russian with English subtitles: In color; Not rated; 90 minutes; June release. CAST: Oleg Yankovsky (Sergei), Ludmila Gurchenko (Larisa), Oleg Tabakov (Nikolai), Ludmila Ivanova (Nina), Ludmila Zorina (Natasha), Elena Kostina (Alisa), Oleg Menshikov (Her Friend), Lubov Rudneva (Sveta), Alexander Adabashian (Sculptor), Nikita Mikhalkov (Director), Elena Chernyak (Trackwoman), Alyona Odinokova (Masha)

THE MISSION (New Film Group) Produced, Directed, Written and Edited by Parviz Sayyad; From story by Hesam Kowsar; Photography-Co-Producer, Reza Aria; Farsi with English subtitles; In color; Not rated; 108 minutes; June release. CAST: Hooshang Touzie (Agent), Parviz Sayyad (Colonel), Mary Apick (Maliheh), Mohammad B. Ghaffari (His Eminence), Hatam Anvar (Maziar), Hedyeh Anvar (Farzaneh), Kamran Nozad (Gaffar)

THE SPAWNING (Saturn International) Title changed to "Piranha II"; Executive Producer, Ovidio G. Assonitis; Producers, Chako van Leuwen, Jeff Schectman; Director, James Cameron; Screenplay, H. A. Milton; Photography, Roberto D'Ettore Piazzoli; Editor, Roberto Silvi; Music, Steve Powder; Assistant Director, Ruggero Salvadori; In color; Rated R; 95 minutes; June release. CAST: Tricia O'Neil (Anne), Steve Marachuk (Tyler), Lance Henriksen (Steve), Ricky G. Paul (Chris), Ted Richert (Raoul), Leslie Graves (Allison), Carole Davis, Connie Lynn Hadden, Arnie Ross, Tracy Berg, Albert Sanders, Anne Pollack

KUNG FU WARLORDS (World Northal) Producer, Sir Run Run Shaw; In color; Rated R; June release. CAST: Alexander Fu Sheng, Tien Niu, Li Hsiu-Hsein

UTILITIES (New World) Title changed to "Getting Even"; Producer, Robert Cooper; Executive Producers, Gurston Rosenfeld, Mike MacFarland; Director, Harvey Hart; Screenplay, David Greenwalt, M. James Kouf, Jr.; Photography, Richard Leiterman; Editor, John Kelly; Design, Bill Boeton; Music, John Erbe, Mickey Solomon; In color; Not rated; 91 minutes; June release. CAST: Robert Hays (Bob), Brooke Adams (Marion), John Marley (Roy), James Blendick (Kenneth), Ben Gordon (Eddie), Jane Mallet (Dr. Rogers), Toby Tarnow (Gilda), Helen Burns (Ruby), Lee Broker (Jack)

Geoff Rhoe, Nell Schofield
in "Puberty Blues"
© *Universal City Studios*

Reb Brown, Corinne Clery in "Yor.."
© *Columbia Pictures*

PUBERTY BLUES (Universal Classics) Producers, Joan Long, Margaret Kelly; Director, Bruce Beresford; Screenplay, Margaret Kelly; Photography, Don McAlpine; Assistant Directors, Mark Egerton, Sue Parker, Marshall Crosby; Editor, Bill Anderson; Art Director, David Copping; Musical Director, Les Gock; Based on novel by Kathy Lee, Gabrielle Carey; Theme Song written by Tim Finn; In color; Rated R; 90 minutes; July release. CAST: Nell Schofield (Debbie), Jad Capelja (Sue), Geoff Rhoe (Garry), Tony Hughes (Danny), Sandy Paul (Tracy), Leander Brett (Cheryl), Jay Hackett (Bruce), Ned Lander (Strach), Joanne Olsen (Vicki), Julie Medana (Kim), Michael Shearman (Glenn), Dean Dunstone (Seagull), Tina Robinson (Freda), Nerida Clark (Carol), Alan Cassell (Vickers), Kirrily Nolan (Mrs. Vickers), Rowena Wallace (Mrs. Knight), Charles Tingwell (Headmaster), Kate Shiel (Mrs. Yelland), Pamela Gibbons (Teacher), Lyn Murphy (Mrs. Hennessy), Andrew Martin (Berkhoff), Rob Thomas (Salesman), Brian Harrison (Little), Brian Anderson (Drive-In Attendant)

NEIGE (Papp/Public) Producers, Ken and Romaine Legarguant; Directors, Juliet Berto, Jean-Henri Roger; Screenplay, Marc Villard from idea by Miss Berto; Photography, William Lubtchansky; Editor, Yann Dedet; Music, Vernard Lavilliers, Francois Breant; In color; French with English subtitles; Not rated; 90 minutes; July release. CAST: Juliet Berto (Anita), Jean-Francois Stevenin (Willy), Robert Liensol (Jocko), Paul le Person (Bruno), Patrick Chenais, Jean Francois Balmer (Policemen), Res Paul Nephtali; Nini Crepon (Betty)

DRUGSTORE ROMANCE (Almi) Written, Directed and Edited by Paul Vecchiali; Photography, George Strouve; Music, Gabriel Faure, Ronald Vincent; In color; Not rated; 126 minutes; July release. CAST: Helene Surgere (Jeanne-Michele), Nicolas Silberg (Pierre), Beatrice Bruno (Emma), Myriam Mezieres (Melinda), Christine Murillo (Anna), Liza Branconnier (Marcelle), Emmanuel Lemoine (Pupuce), Louis Lyonnet (Louis), Sonia Saviange (Sonia), Madeleine Robinson (Mother)

THE FUNNY FARM (New World-Mutual) Producer, Claude Heroux; Direction-Screenplay, Ron Clark; Photography, Rene Verzier; Editor, Marcus Manton; Music, Pierre Brousseau; Art Director,

Carol Spier; In color; Not rated; 96 minutes; July release. CAST: Miles Chapin (Mark), Tracy Bregman (Amy), Eileen Brennan (Gail), Jack Carter (Philly), Peter Aykroyd (Stephen), Mike MacDonald (Bruce), Howie Manel (Larry), Jack Blum (Peter)

YOR, THE HUNTER FROM THE FUTURE (Columbia) Producer, Michele Marsala; Director, Anthony M. Dawson; Screenplay, Robert Bailey, Anthony M. Dawson; Based on novel "Yor" by Juan Zanotto and Ray Collins; Associate Producers, Sedat Akdemir, Ugur Terzioglu; Music, John Scott, Guido DeAngelis, Maurizio DeAngelis; Editor, Alberto Moriani; Photography, Marcello Masciocchi; Art Director, Walter Patriarca; Costumes; Enrico Luzzi; Special Effects, Edward Margheriti, Tony Margheriti; Assistant Director, Ignazio Dolce; A Diamont Film in Eastmancolor; Rated PG; 105 minutes; August release. CAST: Reb Brown (Yor), Corinne Clery (Ka-Laa), John Steiner (Overlord), Carole Andre (Ena), Alan Collins (Pag), Ayshe Gul (Roa), Aytekin Akkaya (Ukan), Marina Rocchi (Tarita), Sergio Nicolai (Kay)

THE MIRROR (Mosfilm) Producer, E. Waisberg; Director, Andrei Tarkovsky; Screenplay, Mr. Tarkovsky, Aleksandr Misharin; Photography, Georgy Rerberg; Editor, L. Feiginova; Music, Eduard Artemyev, J. S. Bach, Pergolese Purcell; In color, black and white; Russian with English subtitles (1974); Not rated; 106 minutes; August release. CAST: Margarita Terekhova (Natalia), Philip Yankovsky (Ignat at 5), Ignat Daniltsev (Ignat at 12), Oleg Yankovsky (Father), Alla Demidova (Lisa), Yuri Nazarov (Military Instructor), L. Tarkofskaya (Natalia as an old woman)

KITTY AND THE BAGMAN (Quartet) Producer, Anthony Buckley: Director, Donald Crombie; Screenplay, John Burney, Phillip Cornford; Photography, Dean Semmler; In color; Rated R; 95 minutes; August release. CAST: Liddy Clark (Kitty O'Rourke), Val Lehman (Lil), John Stanton (Bagman), Gerard McGuire (Cyril), Collette Mann (Doris), Reg Evans (Chicka), Kylie Foster (Sarah), Ted Hepple (Sam), David Adcock (Thomas), David Bradshaw (Larry), Anthony Hawkins (Simon), Paul Chubb (Slugger), John Ewart (Train Driver)

TIGER CLAWS (Almi) Director, Godfrey Ho; Starring Wong Cheng Li, Charles Han. No other credits.

Beatrice Bruno, Nicolas Silberg
in "Drugstore Romance"
© *Libra Cinema 5*

Liddy Clark (left)
in "Kitty and the Bagman"
© *Quartet/Films Inc.*

209

"Jom"
© New Yorker

COIL OF THE SNAKE (Ami) Director, Godfrey Ho; Starring Elton Chong, Eagle Han. No other credits.

C.O.D. (Lone Star) Executive Producer, Wolfgang von Schiber; Producer-Director, Chuck Vincent; Screenplay, Chuck Vincent, Rick Marx, Johnathan Hannah; Story, Wolfgang von Schiber; Photography, Larry Revene; Editor, James Macreading; Music, Johnathan Hannah; Assistant Director, Bill Slobodian; Design, Robert Pusilo; In color; Rated PG; 94 minutes; August release. CAST: Chris Lemmon (Albert), Olivia Pascal (Holly), Jennifer Richards (Lydia), Teresa Ganzel (Lisa), Corinne Alphen (Cheryl), Marilyn Joi (Debbie), Carol Davis (Countess), Dolly Dollar (Christina)

EL BRUTO (Plexus) Producer, Oscar Danciger; Director, Luis Bunuel; Screenplay, Luis Bunuel, Luis Alcoriza; Photography, Agustin Jimenez; Editor, Jorge Bustos; Music, Raul Lavista; Spanish with English subtitles; Mexico 1952; In black and white; Not rated; 83 minutes; September release. CAST: Katy Jurado (Paloma), Pedro Armendariz (Pedro), Andres Soler (Cabrera), Rosita Arenas (Meche), Roberto Meyer, Beatriz Ramos, Paco Martinez, Gloria Mestre

JOM (New Yorker) Director, Ababacar Samb; Story and Screenplay, Ababacar Samb, Babacar Sine; Photography, Peter Chappell, Orlando Lopez; Editor, Alix Regis; Music, Lamine Konte; In Wolof with English subtitles; In color; Not rated; 80 minutes; September release. CAST: Oumar Seck (Dieri), Oumar Gueye (Khaly), Amadou Lamine Camara (Madieumbe), Abou Camara (N'Dougoutte), Zator Sarr (M. Diop), Fatou Samb Fall (Mlle. Diop), N'Deye Ami Fall (Mlle. Sall), Dumi Sene (Koua Thiaw), Charly (Governor), Makhouredia Gueye (Canar Fall), M'Bayang Gaye (Madjeumbe's Wife), Aimee Diallo (Dieri's Wife), Isseu Niang (Dieri's Sister), Jacques Maillard (Officer), Madiodio Lam (Mlle. Sall's Friend), Kewe N'Diaye, Fatou Fall, Deba N'Diaye (Maids)

PIECES (Film Ventures) Producers, Dick Randall, Steve Manasian; Director, Juan Piquer Simon; Screenplay, Dick Randall, John Shadow; Music, Cam; Photography, John Marine; In color; Not rated; 91 minutes; September release. CAST: Christopher George (Lt. Bracken), Edmund Purdom (Dean), Lynda Day George (Mary), Paul Smith (Willard), Frank Brana (Sgt. Hoden), Ian Sera (Kendall), Jack Taylor (Prof. Brown), Gerard Tichy (Dr. Jennings)

SILVER DREAM RACER (Almi) Producer, Rene Dupont; Direction and Screenplay, David Wickes; Music, David Essex; Photography, Paul Beeson; Assistant Director, Ken Baker; Art Director, Malcolm Middleton; Costumes, Judy Moorcroft; Editor, Peter Hollywood; In color; Rated PG; 101 minutes; September release. CAST: David Essex (Nick), Beau Bridges (Bruce), Cristina Raines (Julie), Clarke Peters (Cider), Harry H. Corbett (Wiggins), Diane Keen (Tina), Lee Montague (Jack), Sheila White (Carol), David Baxt (Ben), Ed Bishop (Al), Nick Brimble (Jack Davis), Stephen Hoye (Clarke), T. P. McKenna (Bank Manager), Richard Parmentier (Journalist), Patrick Ryecart (Benson)

THE FINAL OPTION (MGM/UA) Executive Producer, Chris Chrisafis; Producer, Euan Lloyd; Director, Ian Sharp; Screenplay, Reginald Rose; Based on "The Tiptoe Boys" by George Markstein; Associate Producer, Raymond Menmuir; Photography, Phil Meheux; Designer, Syd Cain; Editor, John Grover; Assistant Director, Bill Westley; Art Director, Mo Cain; Choreographer, Anthony Van Laast; A Richmond Light Horse Production in color; Rated R; 125 minutes; September release. CAST: Lewis Collins (Capt. Skellen), Judy Davis (Frankie), Richard Widmark (Secretary of State), Robert Webber (Gen. Potter), Edward Woodward (Cmd. Powell), Tony Doyle (Col. Hadley), John Duttine (Rod), Kenneth Griffith (Bishop Crick), Rosalind Lloyd (Jenny), Ingrid Pitt (Helga), Norman Rodway (Ryan), Maurice Roeves (Maj. Steele), Patrick Allen (Police Commissioner), Bob Sherman (Capt. Hagen), Albert Fortell (Capt. Freund), Mark Ryan (Mac), Aharon Ipale (Malek), Paul Freeman (Sir Richard), Allan Mitchell (Harkness), Richard Coleman (Martin), Nigel Humphreys (Sgt. Pope), Stephen Bent (Neil), Martyn Jacobs (Policeman), Raymond Brody (Bank Manager), Andrew McLachlan (Immigration Officer), Peter Geddes (Butler), Jon Morrison (Dennis), Ziggy Byfield (Baker), Michael Forrest (Pickley), Don Fellows (Ambassador Franklin), Meg Davies (Mary)

STRYKER (New World) Producer-Director, Cirio H. Santiago; Screenplay, Howard R. Cohen; Story, Leonard Hermes; Associate Producers, Jose Buenaventura, Vincent Dayrit; Music, Ed Gatchlian; Photography, Dick Remias; Editor, Bas Santos; In Technicolor; Rated R; 84 minutes; September release. CAST: Steve Sandor (Stryker), Andria Savio (Delha), William Ostrander (Bandit), Michael Lane (Kardis), Julie Gray (Laurenz), Monique St. Pierre (Cerce), Ken Metcalfe (Trun), Jon Harris III (Oiric), Joe Zucchero (Bazil)

LUCIE SUR SEINE (Janus) Producer-Director, Jean-Louis Bertuccelli; Screenplay, S. Majerowitcz; Adapted by Mr. Bertuccelli; Photography, Jean-Francois Robin; Editor, Andre Gaultier; Music, Gabriel Yared; Assistant Director, Olivier Peray; In color; French with English subtitles; Not rated; 90 minutes; September release. CAST: Patrick Depeyrat (Louis), Sandra Montaigu (Lucie), Akim Oumaouche (Nonoeil), Maryline Even (Chantal)

"Pieces"
© Film Ventures

Richard Widmark (L), Judy Davis (R)
in "The Final Option"
© Richmond Light Horse Productions

Nastassja Kinski, Gerard Depardieu
in "Moon in the Gutter"
© *Columbia Pictures*

Robby Benson, Claudia Cron
in "Running Brave"
© *Englander Productions*

THE MOON IN THE GUTTER (Triumph) Executive Producer, Lise Fayolle; Direction and Screenplay, Jean-Jacques Beineix; Photography, Philippe Rousselot, Dominique Brenguier; Editors, Monique Prim, Yves Deschamps; Music, Gabriel Yared; Design, Hilton McConnico, Sandro dell'Orco, Angelo Santucci, Bernhard Vezat; Costumes, Claire Fraisse; In color; Rated R; French-Italian Co-Production; 137 minutes; September release. CAST: Gerard Depardieu (Gerard), Nastassja Kinski (Loretta), Victoria Abril (Bella), Vittorio Mezzogiorno (Newton), Dominique Pinon (Frank), Bertice Reading (Lola), Gabriel Monnet (Tom), Milena Vukotic (Frieda), Bernard Farcy (Jesus), Anne-Marie Coffinet (Dora)

BETTER LATE THAN NEVER (Warner Bros.) Producers, Jack Haley, Jr., David Niven, Jr.; Executive Producer, Raymond Chow; Direction-Screenplay, Bryan Forbes; Photography, Claude Lecomte; Music, Henry Mancini; Design, Peter Mullins; Editor, Philip Shaw; In color; Rated PG; 87 minutes; September release. CAST: David Niven (Nick), Art Carney (Charley), Maggie Smith (Anderson), Kimberley Partridge (Bridget), Catherine Hicks (Sable), Lionel Jeffries (Bertie), Melissa Prophet (Marlene)

THE WILD DUCK (Orion) Producer, Phillip Emanuel; Co-Producer, Basil Appleby; Director, Henri Safran; Screenplay, Henri Safran, Peter Smalley, John Lind; Based on play by Henrik Ibsen; Photography, Peter James; Design, Darrell Lass; Editor, Don Saunders; Music, Simon Walker; In color; Not rated; 96 minutes; September release. CAST: Liv Ullmann (Gina), Jeremy Irons (Harold), Lucinda Jones (Henrietta), John Meillon (Maj. Ackland), Arthur Dignam (Gregory), Michael Pate (George), Colin Croft (Mollison), Rhys McConnochie (Dr. Roland), Marion Edward (Bertha), Peter DeSalis (Peters), Jeff Truman (Johnson)

RUNNING BRAVE (Buena Vista) Producer, Ira Englander; Director, D. S. Everett (Donald Shebib); Screenplay, Henry Bean, Shirl Hendryx; Photography, Francois Protat; Editors, Tony Lower, Earl Herdan; Music, Mike Post; Art Director, Barbra Dunphy; Associate Producer, Maurice Wolf; Assistant Director, Martin Walters; In Medallion Color; Rated PG; 105 minutes; September release. CAST: Robby Benson (Billy Mills), Pat Hingle (Coach Easton), Claudia Cron (Pat Mills), Jeff McCraken (Dennis), August Schellenberg (Billy's Father), Denis Lacroix (Frank), Graham Greene (Eddie), Margo Kane (Catherine)

RUN, WAITER, RUN (IFEX) Director, Ladislav Smoljak; Story and Screenplay, Zdenek Sverak; Photography, Ivan Slapeta; Art Director, Jan Oliva; Music, Jaroslav Uhlir; In color; Not rated; 88 minutes; October release. CAST: Josef Abrham (Vrana), Libuse Safrankova (Vranova), Zdenek Sverak (Parizek), Eliska Balzerova (Vera), Dagmar Patrasova (Manuela), Jiri Kodet (Vyskocil), Karel Augusta (Ludva), Zuzana Fiserova (Douchova)

EAGLE'S WING (Samuel Goldwyn Co.) Executive Producer, Peter Shaw; Producer, Ben Arbeid; Director, Anthony Harvey; Screenplay, John Briley; Music, Marc Wilkinson; Photography, Billy Williams; Based on story by Michael Syson; Art Director, Agustin Ytuarte; In color; 1979 film; Not rated; 104 minutes; October release. CAST: Martin Sheen (Pike), Sam Waterston (White Bull), Harvey Keitel (Henry), Stephane Audran (Widow), Caroline Langrishe (Judith), John Castle (Priest), Claudio Brook (Sanchez), Jorge Luke (Red Sky), Jose Carlos Ruiz (Lame Wolf), Manuel Ojeda (Miguel), Jorge Russek (Gonzalo), Pedro Damieari (Jose), Farnesio De Bernal (Monk), Cecilia Camacho (Girl), Julio Lucena (Don Luis), Enrique Lucero (Shaman)

POSSESSION (Limelight International) Executive Producer, Marie-Laure Reyre; Director Special Effects, Carlo Rambaldi; Director, Andrzej Zulawski; Screenplay, Andrzej Zulawski, Frederic Tuten; Assistant Director, Eva Marie Schoneckler; Photography, Bruno Nuytten; Art Director, Holger Gross; Music, Art Phillips; French-West German Co-Production in English; In color; Rated R; 97 minutes; October release. CAST: Isabelle Adjani (Anna/Helen), Sam Neill (Marc), Heinz Bennent (Heinrich), Margit Carstensen (Margie), Michael Hogben (Bob the child), Shaun Lawton (Zimmermann), Johanna Hofer (Heinrich's Mother), Carl Duering (Detective)

Martin Sheen
in "Eagle's Wing" © *Sam Goldwyn*

Sam Neill, Isabelle Adjani
in "Possession"
© *Limelight*

Oleg Yankovsky, Domiziana Giordano
in "Nostalghia"
© *Grange Communications*

Rudolf Hrusinsky in "Mysterious
Castle in the Carpathians" © *IFEX*

PHAROS OF CHAOS (Buhler Films) Directors, Wolf-Eckart Buhler, Manfred Blank; Photography, Bernd Fiedler; Editor, Manfred Blank; Producer, Wolf-Eckart Buhler; Not rated; 119 minutes; October release. A documentary profile of actor Sterling Hayden.

ONE MAN'S WAR (New Yorker) Producer, Jean-Marc Henchoz; Director, Edgardo Cozarinsky; Executive Producer, Alain Dahan; Screenplay, Edgardo Cozarinsky from "Parisian Diaries" by Ernst Junger; Editors, Christine Aya, Veronique Auricoste; Music, Hans Pfitzner, Richard Strauss, Arnold Schonberg, Franz Schreker; Junger's Voice, Niels Arestrup; In color; Not rated 105 minutes; October release. "A frightening descent into the garbage can of history."

SANS SOLEIL (New Yorker) Written, Directed, Photographed and Edited by Chris Marker; Producer, Anatole Dauman for Argos Films; Narrator, Alexandra Stewart; Not rated; 100 minutes; October release. Mr. Marker's views of people.

NOSTALGHIA (Grange Communications) Director, Andrei Tarkovsky; Screenplay, Andrei Tarkovsky, Tonino Guerra; Photography, Giuseppe Lanci; Art Director, Andrea Krisanti; Editors, Amedeo Salfa, Erminia Marani; Costumes, Lina Nerli Taviani; Assistant Directors, Norman Mozzato, Larissa Tarkovsky; Music, Verdi, Beethoven, Russian Folk Songs; In color, black and white; Italian with English subtitles; Not rated; 120 minutes; October release. CAST: Oleg Yankovsky (Gortchakov), Domiziana Giordano (Eugenia), Erland Josephson (Domenico), Patrizia Terreno (Gortchakov's Wife), Laura De Marchi (Maid), Delia Boccardo (Domenico's Wife), Milena Vukotic (Civil Servant), Alberto Canepa (Farmer)

THE ASSISTANT (International Film Exchange) Director, Zoro Zahon; Screenplay, Ondrej Sulaj, Zoro Zahon; From novel by Ladislav Ballek; Photography, Jozef Simoncic; Music, Svetozar Stur; Editor, Maximilian Remen; In color; Not rated; 94 minutes; October release. CAST: Gabor Konz (Volent), Elo Romancik (Riecan), Ildiko Pecsi (Mrs. Riecan), Marta Sladeckova (Eva), Milan Kis (Filadelfi), Ivan Mistrik (Dobrik), Jozef Ropog (Torok), Hana Talpova (Vilma), Julius Satinsky (Dr. Lielik), Roman Mecznarowski (Blascak)

SIGNUM LAUDIS (IFEX) Director, Martin Holly; Screenplay, Vladimir Kalina, Jiri Krizan; Photography, Frantisek Uldrich; Music, Zdenek Liska; In Eastmancolor; Not rated; 85 minutes; October release. CAST: Vlado Muller (Hoferik), Ilja Prachar (General), Jan Skopecek (Reischl-Dad), Jiri Zahajsky (Lorisch), Josef Blaha (Konig)

YOU TAKE THE KIDS (IFEX) Direction, Story and Screenplay, Marie Polednakova; Photography, Petr Polak; Design, Jiri Matolin; Music, Vaclav Zahradnik; Editor, Miroslav Hajek; In color; Not rated; 86 minutes; October release. CAST: Julius Stainsky (Albert), Jana Sulcova (Katerina), Marek Dvorak (Bertik), Marta Buchtikova (Kacenka), Lukas Machart (Matysek), Vaclav Postranecky (Michal), Eliska Balzerova (Dasa)

THE MYSTERIOUS CASTLE IN THE CARPATHIANS (IFEX) Director, Oldrich Lipsky; Screenplay, Jiri Brdecka, Oldrich Lipsky; Based on novel of same title by Jules Verne; Photography, Viktor Ruzicka; Design, Jan Zazvorka; Music, Lubos Fiser; Editor, Miroslav Hajek; In color; Not rated; 90 minutes; October release. CAST: Michal Docolomansky (Count Teleke), Jan Hartl (Forester), Milos Kopecky (Baron Gorc), Rudolf Hrusinsky (Prof. Orfanik), Vlastimil Brodsky (Valet), Augustin Kuban (Toma), Evelyna Steimarova (Salsa Verde), Jaroslava Kretschmerova (Myriota)

THE STEEPLE-CHASE (IFEX) Director, Jaroslav Soukup; Screenplay, Miroslav Vaic, Jafoslav Soukup; Photography, Richard Valenta; Design, Bojumil Novy; Music, Zdenek Bartak, Jr.; Editor, Jiri Brozek; In color; Not rated; 90 minutes; October release. CAST: Ladislav Mrkvicka (Sochor), Pavel Zednicek (Pecenac), Gabriela Csvaldova (Helena), Milan Klasek (Actor), Josef Vetrovec (Director), Jiri Tomek (Janousek), Miroslav Masopust (Tyml), Ivo Niederle (Official), Dana Syslova (Jarka), Ferdinand Kruta (Vanysek)

SHORTCUTS (IFEX) Director, Jiri Menzel; Screenplay, Bohumil Hrabal, Jiri Menzel; Photography, Jaromir Sofr; Art Director, Zbynek Hloch; Editor, Jiri Brozek; Music, Jiri Sust; In color; Not rated; 94 minutes; October release. CAST: Jiri Schmitzer (Francin), Magda Vasaryova (Marja), Jaromir Hanzlik (Pepin), Rudolf Hrusinsky (Dr. Gruntorad), Oldrich Vlach (Ruzicka), Frantisek Rehak (Vejvoda), Petr Cepek (de Giorgi), Miloslav Stibich (Bernadek), Alois Liskutin (Sefl), Pavel Vondruska (Lustig), Jaroslava Kretschmerova (Bookkeeper), Oldrich Vizner (Barber)

Ildiko Pecsi, Elo Romancik
in "The Assistant" © *IFEX*

Ladislav Mrkvicka
in "The Steeple-Chase" © *IFEX*

Zdena Studenkova, Vlastimil Harapes
in "Beauty and the Beast" © IFEX

Faye Dunaway, John Gielgud
in "The Wicked Lady"
© *Dawn Property Co.*

BEAUTY AND THE BEAST (IFEX) Direction and Screenplay, Juraj Herz; Story, Frantisek Hrubin, Ota Hofman; Photography, Jiri Machane; Design, Vladimir Labsky; Music, Petr Hapka; In color; Not rated; 83 minutes; October release. CAST: Zdena Studenkova (Beauty), Vaclav Voska (Merchant), Vlastimil Harapes (Beast), Jana Brejchova (Gabinka), Zuzana Kocurikova (Malinka), Karel Augusta (Herbalist), Josef Langmiler (Goldsmith), Josef Laufer (Count), Milan Hein (Prince)

THE WICKED LADY (MGM/UA) Producers, Menahem Golan, Yoram Globus; Director, Michael Winner; Screenplay, Leslie Arliss, Michael Winner; Additional Dialogue, Gordon Glennon, Aimee Stuart; From book by Magdalen King-Hall; Music, Tony Banks; Photography, Jack Cardiff; Editor, Arnold Crust; Art Director, John Blezard; Costumes, John Bloomfield; Assistant Director, Ron Purdie; Choreographer, Madeleine Inglehearn; In color; Rated R; 98 minutes; October release. CAST: Faye Dunaway (Lady Barbara Skelton), Alan Bates (Capt. Jerry Jackson), John Gielgud (Hogarth), Denholm Elliott (Sir Ralph Skelton), Prunella Scales (Lady Kingsclere), Oliver Tobias (Kit), Glynis Barber (Caroline), Joan Hickson (Aunt Agatha), Helena McCarthy (Moll), Mollie Maureen (Doll), Derek Francis (Lord Kingsclere), Marina Sirtis (Jackson's Girl), Nicholas Gecks (Ned), Hugh Millais (Uncle Martin), Guinevere John (Landlady), John Savident (Squire), Dermot Walsh (Marwood), Marc Sinden (Dolman), Glynis Brooks (Ned's Wife), Mark Burns (Charles II), Teresa Codling (Nell Gwynne)

GIRL WITH A SEASHELL (International Film Exchange) Director, Jiri Svoboda; Story, Jaromira Kolarova; Screenplay, Miloslav Vydra; Photography, Andrej Barla; Art Director, Milan Nejedly; Music, Petr Hapka; In color; Not rated; 90 minutes; October release. CAST: Dita Kaplanova (Vendula), Evelyna Steimarova (Mother), Ladislav Frej (Father), Regina Razlova (Brabec's Second Wife), Dana Medricka (Mrs. Humlova), Petr Bosak (Jenik), Martin Zavadil (Libor), Emma Cerna (Warden)

THE WIND IN MY POCKET (IFEX) Direction and Story, Jaroslav Soukup; Screenplay, Jaroslav Soukup, Miroslav Valc; Photography, Jaromir Sofr; Design, Bohumil Novy; Music, Zdenek Bartak, Jr.; Editor, Jifi Brozek; In color; Not rated; 81 minutes; October release. CAST: Lukas Vaculik (Ondrej), Sagvan Tofi (Cinda), Ivana

Andrlova (Helena), Karel Augusta (Madr), Karel Vochoc (Andrej's Father), Bronislav Poloczek (Palec), Zora Kesslerova (Ilonka), Karolina Sluneckova (Ondrej's Mother), Ilonka Svobodova (Jaruska), Jiri Kaluzny (Franta), Ferdinand Kruta (Brejcha)

RUSALKA (IFEX) Direction and Screenplay, Petr Weigl; Photography, Jiri Kadanka; Sets, Milos Cervinka; Music, Antonin Dvorak; In color; Not Rated; 110 minutes; October release.

HOW TO DROWN DR. MRACEK (IFEX) Director, Vaclav Vorlicek; Story, Petr Markov; Screenplay, Milos Macourek, P. Markov, V. Vorlicek; Photography, Vladimir Novotny; Music, Vitezslav Hadl; Producer, Barrandov Studio in 1974; Not rated; 105 minutes; October release. CAST: Libuse Safrankova (Jana), Jaromir Hanzlik (Dr. Mracek), Zdenek Rehor (Alois), Vladimir Mensik (Karel), Frantisek Filipovsky (Bertie), Milos Kopecky (Wassermann), Eva Trejtnarova (Polly), Mila Myslikova (Matylda), Stella Zazvorkova (Associate Prof.), Cestmir Randa (Albert)

MORGIANA (IFEX) Director, Juraj Herz; Screenplay, Juraj Herz, Vladimir Bor; From novel "Jessie and Morgiana" by Alexander Grin; Photography, Jaroslav Kucera; Music, Lubos Fiser; In color; Not rated; 106 minutes; October release. CAST: Iva Janzurova (Clara/Victoria), Josef Abrham (Mark), Peter Cepek (Glenar), Nina Diviskova (Otylie), Josef Somr (Drunkard), Jiri Kodet (Bessant), Ivan Paluch (Charles), Jiri Lir (Officer), Vaclav Vondracek (Concierge), Marie Drahokoupilova (Elisabeth), Jana Sedlmajerova (Eve)

A FISTFUL OF TALONS (Transmedia) Producer, Pal Ming; Director, Sun Chung; Screenplay, Wong Ping Yiu; In color; Rated R; 89 minutes; October release. CAST: Billy Chong, Hwang In Shik, Pai Ying, Liu Hao I, Chang Shan, Cheng Kay Ying, Chiang Tao

KUNG-FU WARLORDS PART II (World Northal) Producer, Runme Shaw; Director, Chang Chen; In color; Rated R; October release. Starring Alexander Fu Sheng

MAKING OUT (SRC) Producer, Wolf C. Hartwig; Director, Walter Boos; Screenplay, Gunther Heeler; Photography, Klaus Werner; Editor, George Stiehle; Set Design, Laslo Varga; German with English-dubbed soundtrack; In color; Rated R; 94 minutes; October release. CAST: Jessie St. Clair, Nona Phillips, Sandra Gayle, Brigette Lee, Karja Benet

Karel Augusta, Lukas Vaculik, Sagvan Tofi
in "The Wind in My Pocket"
© IFEX

Josef Abrham, Iva Janzurova
in "Morgiana"
© IFEX

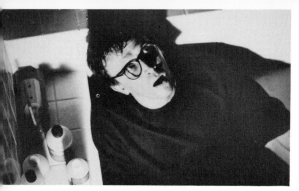

Peter Weller
in "Of Unknown Origin"
© *Warner Bros.*

DEADLY EYES (Warner Bros.) Producers, Paul Kahnert, Charles Eglee; Executive Producers, Gordon Arnold, Jeff Schechtman; Director, Robert Clouse; Screenplay, Charles Eglee; Based on novel by James Herbert; Photography, Rene Verzier; Editor, Ron Wisman; Special Effects, Allan Apone; In color; Rated R; 93 minutes; October release. CAST: Sam Groom (Paul), Sara Botsford (Kelly), Scatman Crothers (George), Lisa Langlois (Trudy), Cec Linder (Dr. Spenser), James B. Douglas (Mel), Lesleh Donaldson (Martha)

DRACULA BLOWS HIS COOL (Martin Films) Executive Producer, Martin Friedman; Director, Carlo Ombra; Screenplay, Grunbach & Rosenthal; Additional Dialogue, Don Arthur; Photography, Heinz Holscher; Music, Gerhard Heinz; In color; German with English subtitles; Rated R; 90 minutes; October release. CAST: Gianni Garko (Stan/Count Stanislaus), Betty Verges (Countess Olivia), Giacomo Rizzo (Mario), Linda Grondier (Linda), Bea Fiedler, Ralf Wolter, Alexander Grill, Herta Worell, Tobias Meister, Ellen Umlauf, Herbert Stiny, Laurence Kaesermann

WHEN THE MOUNTAINS TREMBLE (Skylight Pictures) Producer, Peter Kinoy; Directors, Pamela Yates, Thomas Sigel; Storyteller, Rigoberta Menchu; Editor, Peter Kinoy; Photography, Thomas Sigel; Music, Ruben Blades; In DuArt Color; Not rated; 83 minutes; October release. The story of a Guatemalan woman (Rigoberta Menchu) who was transformed from an impoverished, migratory peasant to a leading voice in shaping the destiny of her people.

BITTER CANE (Cinema Guild) Produced and presented by Haiti Films; Director, Jacques Arcelin; Narration, Jean-Claude Martineau; In color; Not rated; 75 minutes; October release. An analytical documentary about Haitian refugees.

BEYOND REASONABLE DOUBT (Satori) Producer, John Barnett; Director, John Laing; Screenplay, David Yallop from his book; Photography, Alun Bollinger; Editor, Michael Horton; Music, Dave Fraser; Art Director, Kai Hawkins; In color; Not rated; 111 minutes; November release. CAST: David Hemmings (Inspector Hutton), John Hargreaves (Arthur Allan Thomas), Tony Barry (Det. Hughes), Martyn Sanderson (Len), Grant Tilly (David), Diana Rowan (Vivien), Ian Watkin (Kevin), Terence Cooper (Paul), Marshall Napier (Constable Wyllie), John Bach (Det. Jeffries), Bruce Allpress (Det. Keith), Bruno Lawrence (Pat), Peter Hayden (Graham), Mark Hadlow (Bruce), Robert Shannon (Mickey), Kate Harcourt (Mrs. Eyre)

"Cross Country"
© *New World*

MONKEY GRIP (Cinecom International) Producer, Patricia Lovell; Director, Ken Cameron; Screenplay, Ken Cameron, Helen Garner; Editor, David Huggett; Music, Bruce Smeaton, Mark McEntee, Christina Amphlett; In color; Not rated 101 minutes; November release. CAST: Noni Hazelhurst (Nora), Colin Friels (Javo), Alice Garner (Gracie), Harold Hopkins (Willie), Candy Raymond (Lillian), Michael Caton (Clive), Tim Burns (Martin), Christina Amphlett (Angela), Don Miller-Robinson (Gerald), Lisa Peers (Rita), Cathy Downes (Eve)

SUSANA (Plexus) Director, Luis Bunuel; Screenplay, Jaime Salvador; Based on novel by Manuel Reachi; Spanish with English subtitles; Mexico 1951; Not rated; 82 minutes; November release. CAST: Rosita Quintana (Susana), Fernand Soler (Don Guadalupe), Luis Lopez Somoza (His Son), Victor Manuel Mendoza (Foreman), Matilde Palau (Wife and Mother), Maria Gentil Arcos (Maid)

THE QUIET DUEL (Daiei) Director, Akira Kurosawa; Screenplay, Akira Kurosawa, Senkichi Taniguchi; Based on play by Kazuo Kikuta; Photography, Shoichi Aizaka; Music, Akira Ifukube; Japanese with English subtitles; Producers, Hisao Ichikawa, Shojiro Motoki; Not rated; 95 minutes; November release (Japan 1949). CAST: Toshiro Mifune (Kyoji), Takashi Shimura (Kyonosuke), Miki Sanio (Misao), Kenjiro Uemura (Susumu), Chieko Nakakita (Takiko), Norjko Sengoku (Rui), Junnosuke Miyazaki (Cpl.), Isamu Yamaguchi (Patrolman), Hiroko Machida (Nurse)

IN FOR TREATMENT (Werkteater) Producer, Het Werkteater; Director, Erik van Zuylen, Maria Kok; Screenplay, by actors; Dutch with English subtitles; Photography, Rene van den Berg; Editor, Hans van Dongen; Not rated; 95 minutes; Not rated; 95 minutes; November release (1979 in Holland). CAST: Helmert Woudenberg (Mr. de Waal), Frank Groothof (Frank), Hans Man I'nt Veld (Dr. Hageman), Marja Kok (Mrs. de Waal), Daria Mohr (Anja), Herman Vinck (Frank's Father), Ivan Wolffers (Co-Assistant), Joop Admiraal (Patient), Olga Zuiderhoek, Shireen Strooker, Gerard Thoolen (Nurses)

OF UNKNOWN ORIGIN (Warner Bros.) Executive Producer, Pierre David; Producer, Claude Heroux; Screenplay, Brian Taggert; Based on "The Visitor" by Chaucey G. Parker; Director, George P. Cosmatos; Music, Ken Wannberg; Photography, Rene Verzier; Editor, Robert Silvi; Designer, Anne Pritchard; Assistant Directors, John Fretz, Frank Ruszczynski, Michael Sarao; Art Director, Rosemarie McSherry; Costumes, Paul-Andre Guerin; In color; Rated R; 102 minutes; November release. CAST: Peter Weller (Bart), Jennifer Dale (Lorrie), Lawrence Dane (Eliot), Kenneth Welsh (James), Louis Del Grande (Clete), Shannon Tweed (Meg), Keith Knight (Salesman), Maury Chaykin (Dan), Leif Anderson (Peter), Jimmy Tapp (Meg's Father), Gayle Garfinkle (Janis), Earl Pennington (Thompson), Bronwen Mantel (Florence), Monik Nantel (Secretary), Jacklin Webb (News Vendor)

CROSS COUNTRY (New World) Executive Producers, Ronald I. Cohen, James Beach; Producers, Pieter Kroonenburg, David J. Patterson; Director, Paul Lynch; Associate Producers, Paul Rose, Adrian Scrope; Screenplay, Logan N. Danforth, William Gray; Based on novel by Herbert Kastle; Music, Chris Rea; Photography, Rene Verzier; Designer, Michel Proulx; Editor, Nick Rotundo; A Yellowbill presentation in color; Rated R; 95 minutes; November release. CAST: Richard Beymer (Evan), Nina Axelrod (Lois), Michael Ironside (Det. Sgt. Roersch), Brent Carver (John), David Conner (Rico), George Sperdakos (Welles), Michael Kane (Harry), August Schellenberg (Cosgrove), Paul Bradley (Overland), Roberta Weiss (Alma), Anna Vitre (Judith)

CITY OF THE WALKING DEAD (21st Century) Released previously as "Nightmare City," "Nightmare."

MAKE THEM DIE SLOWLY (Aquarius) Executive Producer, Antonio Crescenzi; Direction and Screenplay, Umberto Lenzi; Photography, Giovanni Bergamini; Editor, Enzo Meniconi; Music, Budy/Maglione; Italian with English subtitles; In color; Not rated; 91 minutes; November release. CAST: John Morghen, Lorainne de Selle, Brian Redford, Zora Kerowa, Walter Lloyd, Robert Kerman, John Bartha, Meg Fleming, R. Bolla, Venantino Venantini, (El Indio) Rinoon

THE SWORD OF THE BARBARIANS (Cannon) Executive Producer, Ettore Spagnuollo; Producer, Pino Buricchi; Director, Michael E. Lemick; Screenplay, Pietro Regnoli; Photography, Giancarlo Ferrando; Editor, Alessandro Lucidi; Music, Franco Campanino; Assistant Director, Ettore Arena; Design, Franco Cuppini; Special Effects, John Corridori; In color; Rated R; 88 minutes; November release. CAST: Peter MacCoy (Sangral), Margareta Rance, Yvonne Fraschetti, Anthony Freeman, Sabrina Siani (Golden Goddess), Ziomaria Rodriguez, Al Huang

TENDRES COUSINES (Crown International) ("Tender Cousins") Producers, Stephan Films, Filmedis; Producer, Veral Belmont; Director, David Hamilton; Screenplay, Josiane Leveque, Claude D'Anna; Story, Pascal Laine; Assistant Directors, Alain Maline, Christine Raspillere, Philippe Gautier; Photography, Bernard Daillencourt; Art Director, Eric Simon; Editor, Jean-Bernard Bonis; Music, Jean-Marie Senia; French with English subtitles; In color; Rated R; 90 minutes; November release. CAST: Elisa Cervier (Claire), Jean-Yves Chatelais (Charles), Pierre Chantepie (Mathieu), Evelyne Dandry (Adele), Laure Dechasnel (Clementine), Valerie Dumas (Poune), Anne Fontaine (Justine), Jean-Louis Fortuit (Antoine), Anja Shute (Julia), Thierry Tevini (Julien), Pierre Vernier (Edouard), Macha Meril (Agnes), Catherine Rouvel (Mme. LaCroix), Jean Rougerie (M. LaCroix), Hannes Kaetner (Professeur), Gaelle Legrand (Mathilde), Fanny Meunire (Angele), Silke Rein (Liselotte), Jean-Pierre Rambal (Le Facteur), Carmen Weber (Madeleine)

THE EYES, THE MOUTH (Triumph) Producer, Enzo Porcelli with Enea Ferrario; Director, Marco Bellocchio; Story and Screenplay, Mr. Bellocchio with Vincenzo Cerami; Photography, Giuseppe Lanci; Editor, Sergio Nuti; Music, Nicola Piovani; Italian with English subtitles; In color; Rated R; 100 minutes; December release. CAST: Lou Castel (Giovanni), Angela Molina (Wanda), Emanuelle Riva (Mother), Michel Piccoli (Uncle Nigi), Antonio Piovanelli (Father of Wanda), Giampaolo Saccorola (Agostino), Viviana Toni (Adele), Antonio Petrocelli (Doctor)

THE KNIGHT (Zespoly Filmowe) Direction and Screenplay, Lech Majewski; Polish with English subtitles; Photography, Czeslaw Swirta; Music, Zdislaw Szostak; In color; Not rated; 87 minutes; December release. CAST: Piotr Skarga (Knight), Daniel Olbrychski (Herophant), Andrzej Hudziak (Youngest Monk), Katarzyna Kozak (Princess), Czeslaw Meissner (Monk 1), Stanislaw Holly (Old Monk), Pawel Sanakiewicz (Crispin), Piort Machalica (Vieslav)

WAR AND PEACE (TeleCulture) Producers, Eberhardt Junkersdorf, Theo Hinz; German with English subtitles; by Heinrich Boll, Volker Schlondorff, Alexander Kluge, Stefan Aust, Axel Angstfeld; Fiction sequences written by Mr. Boll; Based on "From the Standpoint of the Infantry" by Mr. Kluge; Photography, Franz Rath, Igor Luther, Werner Luring, Thomas Mauch, Bernd Mosblech; Editor, Dagmar Hirtz, Beate Mainka-Jellinghaus, Carola Mai, Barbara von Weitershausen; English version and post production, Barry Brown; Narrator, Axel-Torg Gros; In color; Not rated; 85 minutes; December release. CAST: Jurgen Prochnow (Kevin), Gunther Kaufmann (Mac), Manfred Zapatka (Nikotai), Karl-Heinz Merz (Ivan), Heinz Bennent (Joe), Edgar Selge (Oscar), Angela Winkler (Margot), Michael Gahr (Albert), Hans-Michael Rehberg (General), Dieter Traier (Interviewer)

ZIGGY STARDUST AND THE SPIDERS FROM MARS (20th Century-Fox International Classics) Director, D. A. Pennebaker; Photography, James Desmond, Mike Davis, Nick Doob, Randy Franken, D. A. Pennebaker; Editor, Lorry Whitehead; Produced by MainMan in association with Pennebaker Inc.; A Miramax release; Rated PG; 91 minutes; December release. A documentary of a 1973 David Bowie concert at the Hammersmith Odeon in London. Original title "Bowie '73 with the Spiders from Mars."

WUTHERING HEIGHTS (Plexus) Producer, Oscar Dancigers; Director, Luis Bunuel; Screenplay, Mr. Bunuel, Arduino Maiuri, Julio Alejandro de Castro; Based on Emily Bronte's novel of same title; Spanish with English subtitles; Photography, Augustin Jiminez; Editor, Carlos Savage; Music, Wagner adapted by Raul Lavista; In color; Not rated; 90 minutes; December release. CAST: Irasema Dilian (Catalina), Jorge Mistral (Alejandro), Lilia Prado (Isabel), Ernesto Alonso (Eduardo)

THE KEEP (Paramount) Producers, Gene Kirkwood, Howard W. Koch, Jr.; Direction and Screenplay, Michael Mann; Based on novel by F. Paul Wilson; Executive Producer, Colin M. Brewer; Designer, John Box; Photography, Alex Thomson; Editor, Dov Hoenig; Music, Tangerine Dream; Associate Producers, Theresa Curtin, Richard Brams, Gavin MacFadyen; Assistant Directors, Roger Simons, Ray Corbett; Costumes, Anthony Mendleson; Art Directors, Herbert Westbrook, Alan Tomkins; In Metrocolor and Dolby Stereo; Rated R; 96 minutes; December release. CAST: Scott Glenn (Glaeken Trismegestus), Alberta Watson (Eva), Jurgen Prochnow (Woermann), Robert Prosky (Father Fonescu), Gabriel Byrne (Kempffer), Ian McKellen (Dr. Cuza), Morgan Sheppard (Alexandru), Royston Tickner (Tomescu), Michael Carter (Radu), Phillip Joseph (Oster), John Vine (Lutz), Jona Jones (Otto), Wolf Kahler (S.S. Adjutant), Rosalie Crutchley (Josefa), Frederick Warder, Bruce Payne (Border Guards), David Cardy (Alexandru's Son), Philip Bloomfield (Josefa's Son), Yashar Adem (Carlos)

Jean-Yves Chatelais, Elisa Cervier
in "Tendres Cousines"
© Crown Intl.

WAR OF THE WIZARDS (21st Century) Formerly "The Phoenix"; Producer, Frank Wong; Directors, Richard Caan, Sam Arikawa; Screenplay, F. Kenneth Lin; Photography, Mike Tomioka; Music, Lawrence Borden; Special Effects, Sam Arikawa; Taiwanese in color; Rated PG; 72 minutes; December release. CAST: Richard Kiel, Charles Lang, Betty Noonan

ON THE RUN (Cineworld) Executive Producer, Bill Anderson; Producer-Director, Mende Brown; Screenplay, Michael Fisher; Photography, Paul Onorato; Editor, Richard Hindley; Music, Laurie Lewis; Assistant Director, Martin Coeh; Associate Producer, Tony Walker; In color; Not rated; 101 minutes; December release. CAST: Paul Winfield (Harry), Rod Taylor (Payette), Beau Cox (Paul), Shirley Cameron, Ray Meagher, Danny Adcock

WAGNER (Alan Landsburg) A London Trust Cultural Production; Producer, Alan Wright; Director, Tony Palmer; Executive Producers, Derek Brierley, Endre Florian; Associate Producers, Agnes Cs. Havas, Simon Channing-Williams; Screenplay, Charles Wood; Photography, Vittorio Storaro; Designer, Kenneth Carey; Costumes, Shirley Russell; Editor, Graham Bunn; Art Directors, Terry Pritchard, Andras Langmar; In color; Not rated; 208 minutes; December release. CAST: Richard Burton (Wagner), Vanessa Redgrave (Cosima), Gemma Craven (Minna), Laszlo Galffi (Ludwig II), John Gielgud (Pfistermeister), Ralph Richardson (Pfordten), Laurence Olivier (Pfeufer), Ekkehardt Schall (Liszt), Ronald Pickup (Nietzsche), Miguel Herz-Kestranek (Hans von Bulow), Richard Pasco (Wesendonck), Marthe Keller (Mathilde Wesendonck), Gwyneth Jones (Malvina), Peter Hofmann (Schnorr von Carolsfeld), Franco Nero (Crespi), Joan Greenwood (Frau Dangl), William Walton (Friedrich August II), Corin Redgrave (Dr. Pusinelli), Barbara Leigh-Hunt (Queen Mother), Joan Plowright (Mrs. Taylor), Christopher Gable (Cornelius), Cyril Cusack (Sulzer)

GROWING UP (Central Motion Pictures) Director, Chen Kun-ho; Mandarin with English subtitles; In color; Not rated; 100 minutes; December release. No other credits available. The account of an illegitimate boy's growth to manhood.

Vanessa Redgrave, Richard Burton
in "Wagner"

Brooke Adams   Alan Alda   Ann-Margret   Adam Baldwin   Sandra Bernhard   Ernest Borgnine

BIOGRAPHICAL DATA

(Name, real name, place and date of birth, school attended)

AAMES, WILLIE (William Upton): 1961.

ABBOTT, DIAHNNE: NYC, 1945.

ABBOTT, JOHN: London, June 5, 1905.

ABEL, WALTER: St. Paul, MN, June 6, 1898, AADA.

ABRAHAM, F. MURRAY: Pittsburgh, PA, Oct. 24, 1939. UTx.

ADAMS, BROOKE: NYC, 1949. Dalton.

ADAMS, DON: NYC, 1927.

ADAMS, EDIE (Elizabeth Edith Enke): Kingston, PA, Apr. 16, 1929. Juilliard, Columbia.

ADAMS JULIE (Betty May): Waterloo, Iowa, Oct. 17, 1928. Little Rock Jr. College.

ADAMS, MAUD (Maud Wikstrom): Lulea, Sweden.

ADDAMS, DAWN: Felixstowe, Suffolk, Eng., Sept. 21, 1930. RADA.

ADDY, WESLEY: Omaha, NB, Aug. 4, 1913. UCLA.

ADJANI, ISABELLE: Paris, 1955.

ADLER, LUTHER: NYC, May 4, 1903.

ADRIAN, IRIS (Iris Adrian Hostetter): Los Angeles, May 29, 1913.

AGAR, JOHN: Chicago, Jan. 31, 1921.

AGUTTER, JENNY: London, 1953.

AHERNE, BRIAN: Worcestershire, Eng., May 2, 1902. Malvern College, U. of London.

AIELLO, DANNY: June 20, 1935,NYC.

AIMEE, ANOUK: Paris, Apr. 27, 1934. Bauer-Therond.

AKINS, CLAUDE: Nelson, GA, May 25, 1936. Northwestern U.

ALBERGHETTI, ANNA MARIA: Pesaro, Italy, May 15, 1936.

ALBERT, EDDIE (Eddie Albert Heimberger): Rock Island, IL, Apr. 22, 1908. U. of Minn.

ALBERT, EDWARD: LOS Angeles, Feb. 20, 1951. UCLA.

ALBRIGHT, LOLA: Akron, OH, July 20, 1925.

ALDA, ALAN: NYC, Jan. 28, 1936. Fordham.

ALDA, ROBERT (Alphonso D'Abruzzo): NYC, Feb. 26, 1914. NYU.

ALDERSON, BROOKE: Dallas, Tx.

ALEJANDRO, MIGUEL: NYC, Feb. 21, 1958.

ALEXANDER, JANE (Quigley): Boston, MA, Oct. 28, 1939. Sarah Lawrence.

ALLEN, KAREN: Carrollton, IL. Oct. 5, 1951. UMd.

ALLEN, NANCY: NYC 1950.

ALLEN, REX: Wilcox, AZ, Dec. 31, 1922.

ALLEN, STEVE: New York City, Dec. 26, 1921.

ALLEN, WOODY (Allen Stewart Konigsberg): Brooklyn, Dec. 1, 1935.

ALLYSON, JUNE (Ella Geisman): Westchester, NY, Oct. 7, 1917.

ALVARADO, TRINI: NYC, 1967.

AMECHE, DON (Dominic Amichi): Kenosha, WI, May 31, 1908.

AMES, ED: Boston July 9, 1929.

AMES, LEON (Leon Wycoff): Portland, IN, Jan. 20, 1903.

AMOS, JOHN: Newark, NJ, Dec. 27, 1940. Colo. U.

ANDERSON, JUDITH: Adelaide, Australia, Feb. 10, 1898.

ANDERSON, LYNN: Grand Forkes, ND; Sept. 26, 1947. UCLA.

ANDERSON, MELODY: Canada 1955, Carlton U.

ANDERSON, MICHAEL, JR.: London, Eng., 1943.

ANDERSSON, BIBI: Stockholm, Nov. 11, 1935. Royal Dramatic Sch.

ANDES, KEITH: Ocean City, NJ, July 12, 1920. Temple U., Oxford.

ANDRESS, URSULA: Switz., Mar. 19, 1936.

ANDREWS, ANTHONY: London, 1948.

ANDREWS, DANA: Collins, MS, Jan. 1, 1909. Sam Houston Col.

ANDREWS, EDWARD: Griffin, GA, Oct. 9, 1914. U. VA.

ANDREWS, HARRY: Tonbridge, Kent, Eng., Nov. 10, 1911.

ANDREWS, JULIE (Julia Elizabeth Wells): Surrey, Eng., Oct. 1, 1935.

ANGEL, HEATHER: Oxford, Eng., Feb. 9, 1909. Wycombe Abbey.

ANN-MARGRET (Olsson): Valsjobyn, Sweden, Apr. 28, 1941. Northwestern U.

ANSARA, MICHAEL: Lowell, MA, Apr. 15, 1922. Pasadena Playhouse.

ANTHONY, TONY: Clarksburg, WV, Oct 16, 1937. Carnegie Tech.

ANTON, SUSAN: Yucaipa, CA. Oct. 12, 1950. Bernardino Col.

ANTONELLI, LAURA: Pola, Italy.

ARCHER, JOHN (Ralph Bowman): Osceola, NB, May 8, 1915. USC.

ARDEN, EVE (Eunice Quedens): Mill Valley, CA, Apr. 30, 1912.

ARKIN, ALAN: NYC, Mar. 26, 1934. LACC.

ARNAZ, DESI: Santiago, Cuba, Mar. 2, 1915. Colegio de Dolores.

ARNAZ, DESI, JR.: Los Angeles, Jan. 19, 1953.

ARNAZ, LUCIE: Hollywood, July 17, 1951.

ARNESS, JAMES (Aurness): Mineapolis, MN, May 26, 1923. Beloit College

ARTHUR, BEATRICE: NYC, May 13, 1926. New School.

ARTHUR, JEAN: NYC, Oct. 17, 1905.

ARTHUR, ROBERT (Robert Arthaud): Aberdeen, WA, June 18, 1925. U. Wash.

ASHLEY, ELIZABETH (Elizabeth Ann Cole): Ocala, FL, Aug. 30, 1939.

ASSANTE, ARMAND: NYC, Oct. 4, 1949. AADA.

ASTAIRE, FRED (Fred Austerlitz): Omaha, NB, May 10, 1899.

ASTIN, JOHN: Baltimore, MD, Mar. 30, 1930. U. Minn.

ASTIN, PATTY DUKE: (see Patty Duke)

ASTOR, MARY (Lucile V. Langhanke): Quincy, IL, May 3, 1906. Kenwood-Loring School.

ATHERTON, WILLIAM: Orange, CT, July 30, 1947. Carnegie Tech.

ATKINS, CHRISTOPHER: Rye, NY, Feb. 21, 1961.

ATTENBOROUGH, RICHARD: Cambridge, Eng., Aug. 29, 1923. RADA.

AUBERJONOIS, RENE: NYC, June 1, 1940. Carnegie Tech.

AUDRAN, STEPHANE: Versailles, Fr., 1933.

AUGER, CLAUDINE: Paris, Apr. 26, 1942. Dramatic Cons.

AULIN, EWA: Stockholm, Sweden, Feb. 14, 1950.

AUMONT, JEAN PIERRE: Paris, Jan. 5, 1909. French Nat'l School of Drama.

AUTRY, GENE: Tioga, TX, Sept. 29, 1907.

AVALON, FRANKIE (Francis Thomas Avallone): Philadelphia, Sept. 18, 1939.

AYKROYD, DAN: Ottawa, Can., 1952.

AYRES, LEW: Minneapolis, MN, Dec. 28, 1908.

AZNAVOUR, CHARLES (Varenagh Aznourian): Paris, May 22, 1924.

BACALL, LAUREN (Betty Perske): NYC, Sept. 16, 1924. AADA.

BACKUS, JIM: Cleveland, Ohio, Feb. 25, 1913. AADA.

BADDELEY, HERMIONE: Shropshire, Eng., Nov. 13, 1906 Margaret Morris School.

BAILEY, PEARL: Newport News, VA, March 29, 1918.

BAIN, BARBARA: Chicago, Sept. 13, 1934. U. ILL.

BAIO, SCOTT: Brooklyn, 1961.

BAKER, BLANCHE: NYC Dec. 20, 1956.

BAKER, CARROLL: Johnstown, PA, May 28, 1931. St. Petersburg Jr. College.

BAKER, DIANE: Hollywood, CA, Feb. 25, 1938. USC.

BALABAN, ROBERT: Chicago, Aug. 16, 1945. Colgate.

BALDWIN, ADAM: Chicago, IL. 1962.

BALIN, INA: Brooklyn, Nov. 12, 1937. NYU.

BALL, LUCILLE: Celaron, NY, Aug. 6, 1910. Chataqua Musical Inst.

BALSAM, MARTIN: NYC, Nov. 4, 1919. Actors Studio.

BANCROFT, ANNE (Anna Maria Italiano): Bronx, NY, Sept. 17, 1931. AADA.

BANNEN, IAN: Airdrie, Scot., June 29, 1928.

BARBEAU, ADRIENNE: Sacramento, CA. June 11, 1945. Foothill Col.

BARDOT, BRIGITTE: Paris, Sept. 28, 1934.

BARRAULT, MARIE-CHRISTINE: Paris, 1946.

BARRETT, MAJEL (Hudec): Columbus, OH, Feb. 23. Western Reserve U.

BARRON, KEITH: Mexborough, Eng., Aug. 8, 1936. Sheffield Playhouse.

BARRY, GENE (Eugene Klass): NYC, June 14, 1921.

BARRYMORE, DREW: Los Angeles, Feb. 22, 1975.

BARRYMORE, JOHN BLYTH: Beverly Hills, CA, June 4, 1932. St. John's Military Academy.

BARTHOLOMEW, FREDDIE: London, Mar. 28, 1924.

BARYSHNIKOV, MIKHAIL: Riga, Latvia, Jan. 27, 1948.

BASEHART, RICHARD: Zanesville, OH, Aug. 31, 1914.

BASINGER, KIM: Athens, GA. 1954. Neighborhood Playnouse.

BATES, ALAN: Allestree, Derbyshire, Eng., Feb. 17, 1934. RADA.

BAUER, STEVEN (Rocky Echevarrio): Cuba, 1956.

BAXTER, ANNE: Michigan City, IN, May 7, 1923. Ervine School of Drama.

BAXTER, KEITH: South Wales, Apr. 29, 1933. RADA.

BEAL, JOHN (J. Alexander Bliedung): Joplin, MO, Aug. 13, 1909. PA. U.

BEATTY, NED: Louisville, KY. 1937.

BEATTY, ROBERT: Hamilton, Ont., Can., Oct. 19, 1909. U. of Toronto.

BEATTY, WARREN: Richmond, VA, March 30, 1937.

BECK, MICHAEL: Horseshoe Lake, AR, 1948.

BEDELIA, BONNIE: NYC, Mar. 25, 1948. Hunter Col.

BEDI, KABIR: India, 1945.

BEERY, NOAH, JR.: NYC, Aug. 10, 1916. Harvard Military Academy.

BELAFONTE, HARRY: NYC, Mar. 1, 1927.

BELASCO, LEON: Odessa, Russia, Oct. 11, 1902.

BEL GEDDES, BARBARA: NYC, Oct. 31, 1922.

BELL, TOM: Liverpool, Eng., 1932.

BELLAMY, RALPH: Chicago, June 17, 1904.

BELLER, KATHLEEN: NYC, 1957.

BELMONDO, JEAN PAUL: Paris, Apr. 9, 1933.

BENEDICT, DIRK (Niewoehner): White Sulphur Springs, MT. March 1, 1945. Whitman Col.

BENJAMIN, RICHARD: NYC, May 22, 1938. Northwestern U.

BENNENT, DAVID: Lausanne, Sept. 9, 1966.

BENNETT, BRUCE (Herman Brix): Tacoma, WA, May 19, 1909. U. Wash.

BENNETT, JILL: Penang, Malay, Dec. 24, 1931.

BENNETT, JOAN: Palisades, NJ, Feb. 27, 1910. St. Margaret's School.

BENSON, ROBBY: Dallas, TX, Jan. 21, 1957.

BERENSON, MARISSA: NYC, Feb. 15, 1947.

BERGEN, CANDICE: Los Angeles, May 9, 1946. U. PA.

BERGEN, POLLY: Knoxville, TN, July 14, 1930. Compton Jr. College.

BERGER, HELMUT: Salzburg, Aus., 1945.

BERGER, SENTA: Vienna, May 13, 1941. Vienna Sch. of Acting.

BERGER, WILLIAM: Austria, Jan. 20, 1928. Columbia.

BERGERAC, JACQUES: Biarritz, France, May 26, 1927. Paris U.

BERLE, MILTON (Milton Berlinger): NYC, July 12, 1908. Professional Children's School.

BERLIN, JEANNIE: Los Angeles, Nov. 1, 1949.

BERLINGER, WARREN: Brooklyn, Aug. 31, 1937. Columbia.

BERNARDI, HERSCHEL: NYC, 1923.

BERNHARD, SANDRA: Arizona 1956.

BERRI, CLAUDE (Langmann): Paris, July 1, 1934.

BERTO, JULIET: Grenoble, France, Jan. 1947.

BEST, JAMES: Corydon, IN, July 26, 1926.

BETTGER, LYLE: Philadelphia, Feb. 13, 1915. AADA.

BEYMER, RICHARD: Avoca, IA, Feb. 21, 1939.

BIEHN, MICHAEL: Ariz. 1957.

BIKEL, THEODORE: Vienna, May 2, 1924. RADA.

BIRNEY, DAVID: Washington, DC, Apr. 23, 1939. Dartmouth, UCLA.

BIRNEY, REED: Alexandria, VA., Sept. 11, 1954. Boston U.

BISHOP, JOEY (Joseph Abraham Gottlieb): Bronx, NY, Feb. 3, 1918.

BISHOP, JULIE (formerly Jacqueline Wells): Denver, CO, Aug. 30, 1917. Westlake School.

BISSET, JACQUELINE: Waybridge, Eng., Sept. 13, 1944.

BIXBY, BILL: San Francisco, Jan. 22, 1934. U. CAL.

BLACK, KAREN (Ziegler): Park Ridge, IL, July 1, 1942. Northwestern.

BLAINE, VIVIAN (Vivian Stapleton): Newark, NJ, Nov. 21, 1923.

BLAIR, BETSY (Betsy Boger): NYC, Dec. 11, 1923.

BLAIR, JANET (Martha Jane Lafferty): Blair, PA, Apr. 23, 1921.

BLAIR, LINDA: Westport, CT, Jan. 22, 1959.

BLAKE, AMANDA (Beverly Louise Neill): Buffalo, NY, Feb. 20, 1921.

BLAKE, ROBERT (Michael Gubitosi): Nutley, NJ, Sept. 18, 1933.

BLAKELY, SUSAN: Frankfurt, Germany 1950. U. TEX.

BLAKLEY, RONEE: Stanley, ID, 1946. Stanford U.

BLOOM, CLAIRE: London, Feb. 15, 1931. Badminton School.

BLYTH, ANN: Mt. Kisco, NY, Aug. 16, 1928. New Wayburn Dramatic School.

BOCHNER, HART: Toronto, 1956. U San Diego.

BOGARDE, DIRK: London, Mar. 28, 1918. Glasgow & Univ. College.

BOLGER, RAY: Dorchester, MA, Jan. 10, 1903.

BOLKAN, FLORINDA (Florinda Soares Bulcao): Ceara, Brazil, Feb. 15, 1941.

BOND, DEREK: Glasgow, Scot., Jan. 26, 1920. Askes School.

BONO, SONNY (Salvatore): Feb. 16, 1935.

BOONE, PAT: Jacksonville, FL, June 1, 1934. Columbia U.

BOOTH, SHIRLEY (Thelma Ford): NYC, Aug. 30, 1907.

BORGNINE, ERNEST (Borgnino): Hamden, CT, Jan. 24, 1918. Randall School.

BOTTOMS, JOSEPH: Santa Barbara, CA, Aug. 30, 1954.

BOTTOMS, TIMOTHY: Santa Barbara, CA, Aug. 30, 1951.

BOULTING, INGRID: Transvaal, So. Africa, 1947.

BOVEE, LESLIE: Bend, OR, 1952.

BOWIE, DAVID: (David Robert Jones) Brixton, South London, Eng. Jan. 8, 1947.

BOWKER, JUDI: Shawford, Eng., Apr. 6, 1954.

BOXLEITNER, BRUCE: Elgin, IL., 1950.

BOYLE, PETER: Philadelphia, PA, 1937. LaSalle Col.

| Gary Busey | Ellen Burstyn | David Carradine | Kate Capshaw | Bill Cosby | Lindsay Crouse |

BRACKEN, EDDIE: NYC, Feb. 7, 1920. Professional Children's School.

BRADY, SCOTT (Jerry Tierney): Brooklyn, Sept. 13, 1924. Bliss-Hayden Dramatic School.

BRAGA, SONIA: Maringa, Brazil, 1951.

BRAND, NEVILLE: Kewanee, IL, Aug. 13, 1920.

BRANDO, JOCELYN: San Francisco, Nov. 18, 1919. Lake Forest College, AADA.

BRANDO, MARLON: Omaha, NB, Apr. 3, 1924. New School.

BRANDON, CLARK: NYC 1959.

BRANTLEY, BETSY: Rutherfordton, NC, 1955. London Central Sch. of Drama.

BRAZZI, ROSSANO: Bologna, Italy, Sept. 18, 1916. U. Florence.

BRIAN, DAVID: NYC, Aug. 5, 1914. CCNY.

BRIDGES, BEAU: Los Angeles, Dec. 9, 1941. UCLA.

BRIDGES, JEFF: Los Angeles, Dec. 4, 1949.

BRIDGES, LLOYD: San Leandro, CA, Jan. 15, 1913.

BRISEBOIS, DANIELLE: Brooklyn, June 28, 1969.

BRITT, MAY: (Maybritt Wilkins): Sweden, March 22, 1936.

BRITTANY, MORGAN: (Suzanne Caputo): Los Angeles, 1954.

BRODIE, STEVE (Johnny Stevens): Eldorado, KS, Nov. 25, 1919.

BROLIN, JAMES: Los Angeles, July 18, 1940. UCLA.

BROMFIELD, JOHN (Farron Bromfield): South Bend, IN, June 11, 1922. St. Mary's College.

BRONSON, CHARLES (Buchinsky): Ehrenfield, PA, Nov. 3, 1920.

BROWN, BLAIR: Washington, DC, 1948; Pine Manor.

BROWN, BRYAN: Panania, Aust., 1947.

BROWN, GEORG STANFORD: Havana, Cuba, June 24, 1943. AMDA.

BROWN, JAMES: Desdemona, TX, Mar. 22, 1920. Baylor U.

BROWN, JIM: St. Simons Island, NY, Feb. 17, 1935. Syracuse U.

BROWN, TOM: NYC, Jan. 6, 1913. Professional Children's School.

BROWNE, CORAL: Melbourne, Aust., July 23, 1913.

BROWNE, LESLIE: NYC, 1958.

BRYNNER, YUL: Sakhalin Island, Japan, July 11, 1915.

BUCHHOLZ, HORST: Berlin, Ger., Dec. 4, 1933. Ludwig Dramatic School.

BUETEL, JACK: Dallas, TX, Sept. 5, 1917.

BUJOLD, GENEVIEVE: Montreal, Can., July 1, 1942.

BURKE, PAUL: New Orleans, July 21, 1926. Pasadena Playhouse.

BURNETT, CAROL: San Antonio, TX, Apr. 26, 1933. UCLA.

BURNS, CATHERINE: NYC, Sept. 25, 1945. AADA.

BURNS, GEORGE (Nathan Birnbaum): NYC, Jan. 20, 1896.

BURR, RAYMOND: New Westminster, B.C., Can., May 21, 1917. Stanford, U. CAL., Columbia.

BURSTYN, ELLEN (Edna Rae Gillooly): Detroit, MI, Dec. 7, 1932.

BURTON, LeVAR: Los Angeles, CA. Feb. 16, 1958. UCLA.

BURTON, RICHARD (Richard Jenkins): Pontrhydyfen, S. Wales, Nov. 10, 1925. Oxford.

BUSEY, GARY: Tulsa, OK, 1944.

BUTTONS, RED (Aaron Chwatt): NYC, Feb. 5, 1919.

BUZZI, RUTH: Wequetequock, RI, July 24, 1936. Pasadena Playhouse.

BYGRAVES, MAX: London, Oct. 16, 1922. St. Joseph's School.

BYRNES, EDD: NYC, July 30, 1933. Haaren High.

CAAN, JAMES: Bronx, NY, Mar. 26, 1939.

CABOT, SUSAN: Boston, July 6, 1927. CAESAR, SID: Yonkers, NY, Sept. 8, 1922.

CAESAR, SID: Yonkers, NY, Sept. 8, 1922.

CAGNEY, JAMES: NYC, July 17, 1899. Columbia.

CAGNEY, JEANNE: NYC, Mar. 25, 1919. Hunter.

CAINE, MICHAEL (Maurice Michelwhite): London, Mar. 14, 1933.

CAINE, SHAKIRA (Baksh): Guyana, Feb. 23, 1947. Indian Trust Col.

CALHOUN, RORY (Francis Timothy Durgin): Los Angeles, Aug. 8, 1922.

CALLAN, MICHAEL (Martin Calinieff): Philadelphia, Nov. 22, 1935.

CALVERT, PHYLLIS: London, Feb. 18, 1917. Margaret Morris School.

CALVET, CORRINE (Corrine Dibos): Paris, Apr. 30, 1929. U. Paris.

CAMP, COLLEEN: San Francisco, 1953.

CAMPBELL, GLEN: Delight, AR, Apr. 22, 1935.

CANALE, GIANNA MARIA: Reggio Calabria, Italy, Sept. 12.

CANNON, DYAN (Samille Diane Friesen): Tacoma, WA, Jan. 4, 1935.

CANTU, DOLORES: 1957, San Antonio, TX.

CAPERS, VIRGINIA: Sumter, SC, 1925. Juilliard.

CAPSHAW, KATE: Ft. Worth, TX. UMo.

CAPUCINE (Germaine Lefebvre): Toulon, France, Jan. 6, 1935.

CARA, IRENE: NYC, Mar. 18, 1958.

CARDINALE, CLAUDIA: Tunis, N. Africa, Apr. 15, 1939. College Paul Cambon.

CAREY, HARRY, JR.: Saugus, CA, May 16, 1921. Black Fox Military Academy.

CAREY, MACDONALD: Sioux City, IA, Mar. 15, 1913. U. of Wisc., U. Iowa.

CAREY, PHILIP: Hackensack, NJ, July 15, 1925. U. Miami.

CARMEN, JULIE: Mt. Vernon, NY, Apr. 4, 1954.

CARMICHAEL, IAN: Hull, Eng., June 18, 1920. Scarborough Col.

CARNE, JUDY (Joyce Botterill): Northampton, Eng., 1939. Bush-Davis Theatre School.

CARNEY, ART: Mt. Vernon, NY, Nov. 4, 1918.

CARON, LESLIE: Paris, July 1, 1931. Nat'l Conservatory, Paris.

CARPENTER, CARLETON: Bennington, VT, July 10, 1926. Northwestern.

CARR, VIKKI (Florence Cardona): July 19, 1942. San Fernando Col.

CARRADINE, DAVID: Hollywood, Dec. 8, 1936. San Francisco State.

CARRADINE, JOHN: NYC, Feb. 5, 1906.

CARRADINE, KEITH: San Mateo, CA, Aug. 8, 1951. Colo. State U.

CARRADINE, ROBERT: San Mateo, CA, 1954.

CARREL, DANY: Tourane, Indochina, Sept. 20, 1936. Marseilles Cons.

CARRIERE, MATHIEU: West Germany 1950.

CARROLL, DIAHANN (Johnson): NYC, July 17, 1935. NYU.

CARROLL, MADELEINE: West Bromwich, Eng., Feb. 26, 1902. Birmingham U.

CARROLL, PAT: Shreveport, LA, May 5, 1927. Catholic U.

CARSON JOHN DAVID: 1951, Calif. Valley Col.

CARSON, JOHNNY: Corning, IA, Oct. 23, 1925. U. of Neb.

CARSTEN, PETER (Ransenthaler): Weissenberg, Bavaria, Apr. 30, 1929. Munich Akademie.

CASH, ROSALIND: Atlantic City, NJ, Dec. 31, 1938. CCNY.

CASON, BARBARA: Memphis, TN, Nov. 15, 1933. U. Iowa.

CASS, PEGGY (Mary Margaret): Boston, May 21, 1925.

CASSAVETES, JOHN: NYC, Dec. 9, 1929. Colgate College, AADA.

CASSEL, JEAN-PIERRE: Paris, Oct. 27, 1932.

CASSIDY, DAVID: NYC, Apr. 12, 1950.

CASSIDY, JOANNA: Camden, NJ, 1944. Syracuse U.

CASTELLANO, RICHARD: Bronx, NY, Sept. 3, 1934.

CAULFIELD, JOAN: Orange, NJ, June 1, 1922. Columbia U.

CAULFIELD, MAXWELL: Glasgow, Scot., Nov. 23, 1959.

CAVANI, LILIANA: Bologna, Italy, Jan. 12, 1937. U. Bologna.

CELI, ADOLFO: Sicily, July 27, 1922, Rome Academy.

CHAKIRIS, GEORGE: Norwood, OH, Sept. 16, 1933.

CHAMBERLAIN, RICHARD: Beverly Hills, CA, March 31, 1935. Pomona.

CHAMPION, MARGE: Los Angeles, Sept. 2, 1925.

CHANNING, CAROL: Seattle, Jan. 21, 1921. Bennington.

CHANNING, STOCKARD (Susan Stockard): NYC, 1944. Radcliffe.

CHAPIN, MILES: NYC, Dec. 6, 1954. HB Studio.

CHAPLIN, GERALDINE: Santa Monica, CA, July 31, 1944. Royal Ballet.

CHAPLIN, SYDNEY: Los Angeles, Mar. 31, 1926. Lawrenceville.

CHARISSE, CYD (Tula Ellice Finklea): Amarillo, TX, Mar. 3. 1922. Hollywood Professional School.

CHASE, CHEVY (Cornelius Crane Chase): NYC, Oct. 8, 1943.

CHER (Cherlin Sarkesian): May 20, 1946, El Centro, CA.

CHIARI, WALTER: Verona, Italy, 1930.

CHRISTIAN, LINDA (Blanca Rosa Welter): Tampico, Mex., Nov. 13, 1923.

CHRISTIE, JULIE: Chukua, Assam, India, Apr. 14, 1941.

CHRISTOPHER, DENNIS (Carelli): Philadelphia, PA, 1955. Temple U.

CHRISTOPHER, JORDAN: Youngstown, OH, Oct. 23, 1940. Kent State.

CILENTO, DIANE: Queensland, Australia, Oct. 5, 1933. AADA.

CLAPTON, ERIC: London, Mar. 30, 1945.

CLARK, DANE: NYC, Feb. 18, 1915. Cornell, Johns Hopkins U.

CLARK, DICK: Mt. Vernon, NY, Nov. 30, 1929. Syracuse U.

CLARK, MAE: Philadelphia, Aug. 16, 1910.

CLARK, PETULA: Epsom, England, Nov. 15, 1932.

CLARK, SUSAN: Sarnid, Ont., Can., Mar. 8. 1940. RADA

CLAYBURGH, JILL: NYC, Apr. 30, 1944. Sarah Lawrence.

CLERY, CORRINNE: Italy, 1950.

CLOONEY, ROSEMARY: Maysville, KY, May 23, 1928.

COBURN, JAMES: Laurel, NB, Aug. 31, 1928. LACC.

COCA, IMOGENE: Philadelphia, Nov. 18, 1908.

COCO, JAMES: NYC, Mar. 21, 1929.

CODY, KATHLEEN: Bronx, NY, Oct. 30, 1953.

COLBERT, CLAUDETTE (Lily Chauchoin): Paris, Sept. 15, 1903. Art Students League.

COLE, GEORGE: London, Apr. 22, 1925.

COLEMAN, GARY: Zion, IL., 1968.

COLLINS, JOAN: London, May 21, 1933. Francis Holland School.

COLLINS, STEPHEN: Des Moines, IA, Oct 1, 1947. Amherst.

COMER, ANJANETTE: Dawson, TX, Aug. 7, 1942. Baylor, Tex. U.

CONANT, OLIVER: NYC, Nov. 15, 1955. Dalton.

CONAWAY, JEFF: NYC, Oct. 5, 1950. NYC.

CONNERY, SEAN: Edinburgh, Scot., Aug. 25, 1930.

CONNORS, CHUCK (Kevin Joseph Connors): Brooklyn, Apr. 10, 1921. Seton Hall College.

CONNORS, MIKE (Krekor Ohanian): Fresno, CA, Aug. 15, 1925. UCLA.

CONRAD, WILLIAM: Louisville, KY, Sept. 27, 1920.

CONVERSE, FRANK: St. Louis, MO, May 22, 1938. Carnegie Tech.

CONVY, BERT: St. Louis, MO, July 23, 1935. UCLA.

CONWAY, KEVIN: NYC, May 29, 1942.

CONWAY, TIM (Thomas Daniel): Willoughby, OH, Dec. 15, 1933. Bowling Green State.

COOK, ELISHA, JR.: San Francisco, Dec. 26, 1907. St. Albans.

COOPER, BEN: Hartford, CT, Sept. 30, 1932. Columbia U.

COOPER, JACKIE: Los Angeles, Sept. 15, 1921.

CORBETT, GRETCHEN: Portland, OR, Aug. 13, 1947. Carnegie Tech.

CORBY, ELLEN (Hansen): Racine, WI, June 13, 1913.

CORCORAN, DONNA: Quincy, MA, Sept. 29, 1942.

CORD, ALEX (Viespi): Floral Park, NY, Aug. 3, 1931. NYU, Actors Studio.

CORDAY, MARA (Marilyn Watts): Santa Monica, CA, Jan. 3, 1932.

COREY, JEFF: NYC, Aug. 10, 1914. Fagin School.

CORLAN, ANTHONY: Cork City, Ire., May 9, 1947. Birmingham School of Dramatic Arts.

CORLEY, AL: Missouri, 1956. Actors Studio.

CORNTHWAITE, ROBERT: St. Helens, OR. Apr. 28, 1917. USC.

CORRI, ADRIENNE: Glasgow, Scot., Nov. 13, 1933. RADA.

CORTESA, VALENTINA: Milan, Italy, Jan. 1, 1925.

COSBY, BILL: Philadelphia, July 12, 1937. Temple U.

COSTER, NICOLAS: London, Dec. 3, 1934. Neighborhood Playhouse.

COTTEN, JOSEPH: Petersburg, VA, May 13, 1905.

COURTENAY, TOM: Hull, Eng., Feb. 25, 1937. RADA.

COURTLAND, JEROME: Knoxville, TN, Dec. 27, 1926.

CRAIG, JAMES (James H. Meador): Nashville, TN, Feb. 4, 1912. Rice Inst.

CRAIG, MICHAEL: India, Jan. 27, 1929.

CRAIN, JEANNE: Barstow, CA, May 25, 1925.

CRAWFORD, BRODERICK: Philadelphia, Dec. 9, 1911.

CREMER, BRUNO: Paris, 1929.

CRENNA, RICHARD: Los Angeles, Nov. 30, 1926. USC.

CRISTAL, LINDA (Victoria Moya): Buenos Aires, Feb. 25, 1934.

CROSBY, HARRY: Los Angeles, CA, Aug. 8, 1958.

CROSBY, KATHRYN GRANT: (see Kathryn Grant)

CROSBY, MARY FRANCES: Calif., Sept. 14, 1959.

CROSS, BEN: London, 1948. RADA.

CROSS, MURPHY (Mary Jane): Laurelton, MD, June 22, 1950.

CROUSE, LINDSAY ANN: NYC, May 12, 1948. Radcliffe.

CROWLEY, PAT: Olyphant, PA, Sept. 17, 1932.

CRUISE, TOM: Syracuse, NY, 1962.

CRYSTAL, BILLY: NYC, 1948.

CULLUM, JOHN: Knoxville, TN, Mar. 2, 1930. U. Tenn.

CULP, ROBERT: Oakland, CA., Aug. 16, 1930. U. Wash.

CULVER, CALVIN: Canandaigua, NY, 1943.

CUMMINGS, CONSTANCE: Seattle, WA, May 15, 1910.

CUMMINGS, QUINN: Hollywood, Aug. 13, 1967.

CUMMINGS, ROBERT: Joplin, MO, June 9, 1910. Carnegie Tech.

CUMMINS, PEGGY: Prestatyn, N. Wales, Dec. 18, 1926. Alexandra School.

CURTIN, JANE: Cambridge, MA; Sept. 6, 1947.

CURTIS, JAMIE LEE: Los Angeles, CA., Nov. 21, 1958.

CURTIS, KEENE: Salt Lake City, UT, Feb. 15, 1925. U. Utah.

CURTIS, TONY (Bernard Schwartz): NYC, June 3, 1924.

CUSACK, CYRIL: Durban, S. Africa, Nov. 26, 1910. Univ. Col.

CUSHING, PETER: Kenley, Surrey, Eng., May 26, 1913.

DAHL, ARLENE: Minneapolis, Aug. 11, 1928. U. Minn.

DALLESANDRO, JOE: Pensacola, FL, Dec. 31, 1948.

DALTON, TIMOTHY: Wales, 1945. RADA.

DALTREY, ROGER: London, Mar. 1, 1945.

DALY, TYNE: NYC, 1947. AMDA.

| Bo
Derek | Paul
Dooley | Linda
Evans | James
Farentino | Sally
Field | Peter
Gallagher |

DAMONE, VIC (Vito Farinola): Brooklyn, June 12, 1928.

D'ANGELO, BEVERLY: Columbus, OH., 1954.

DANIELS, WILLIAM: Bklyn, Mar. 31, 1927. Northwestern.

DANNER, BLYTHE: Philadelphia, PA. Bard Col.

DANO, ROYAL: NYC, Nov. 16, 1922. NYU.

DANSON, TED. Flagstaff, AZ, 1949. Stanford, Carnegie Tech.

DANTE, MICHAEL (Ralph Vitti): Stamford, CT, 1935. U. Miami.

DANTON, RAY: NYC, Sept. 19, 1931. Carnegie Tech.

DARBY, KIM: (Deborah Zerby): North Hollywood, CA, July 8, 1948.

DARCEL, DENISE (Denise Billecard): Paris, Sept. 8, 1925. U. Dijon.

DARREN, JAMES: Philadelphia, June 8, 1936. Stella Adler School.

DARRIEUX, DANIELLE: Bordeaux, France, May 1, 1917. Lycee LaTour.

DARYL, HANNAH: Chicago, IL, 1960. UCLA.

DA SILVA, HOWARD: Cleveland, OH, May 4, 1909. Carnegie Tech.

DAVIDSON, JOHN: Pittsburgh, Dec. 13, 1941. Denison U.

DAVIES, RUPERT: Liverpool, Eng., 1916.

DAVIS, BETTE: Lowell, MA, Apr. 5, 1908. John Murray Anderson Dramatic School.

DAVIS, BRAD: Fla., 1950. AADA.

DAVIS, MAC: Lubbock, TX, 1942.

DAVIS, NANCY (Anne Frances Robbins): NYC July 8, 1921. Smith Col.

DAVIS, OSSIE: Cogdell, GA, Dec. 18, 1917. Howard U.

DAVIS, SAMMY, JR.: NYC, Dec. 8, 1925.

DAVIS, SKEETER (Mary Francis Penick): Dry Ridge, KY. Dec. 30, 1935.

DAY, DENNIS (Eugene Dennis McNulty): NYC, May 21, 1917. Manhattan College.

DAY, DORIS (Doris Kappelhoff): Cincinnati, Apr. 3, 1924.

DAY, LARAINE (Johnson): Roosevelt, UT, Oct. 13, 1917.

DAYAN, ASSEF: Israel, 1945. U. Jerusalem.

DEAN, JIMMY: Plainview, TX, Aug. 10, 1928.

DeCARLO, YVONNE (Peggy Yvonne Middleton): Vancouver, B.C., Can., Sept. 1, 1922. Vancouver School of Drama.

DEE, FRANCES: Los Angeles, Nov. 26, 1907. Chicago U.

DEE, JOEY (Joseph Di Nicola): Passaic, NJ, June 11, 1940. Patterson State College.

DEE, RUBY: Cleveland, OH, Oct. 27, 1924. Hunter Col.

DEE, SANDRA (Alexandra Zuck): Bayonne, NJ, Apr. 23, 1942.

DeFORE, DON: Cedar Rapids, IA, Aug. 25, 1917. U. Iowa.

DeHAVEN, GLORIA: Los Angeles, July 23, 1923.

DeHAVILLAND, OLIVIA: Tokyo, Japan, July 1, 1916. Notre Dame Convent School.

DELL, GABRIEL: Barbados, BWI, Oct. 7, 1930.

DELON, ALAIN: Sceaux, Fr., Nov. 8, 1935.

DELORME, DANIELE: Paris, Oct. 9, 1927. Sorbonne.

DeLUISE, DOM: Brooklyn, Aug. 1, 1933. Tufts Col.

DEMONGEOT, MYLENE: Nice, France, Sept. 29, 1938.

DENEUVE, CATHERINE: Paris, Oct. 22, 1943.

DeNIRO, ROBERT: NYC, Aug. 17, 1943, Stella Adler.

DENISON, MICHAEL: Doncaster, York, Eng., Nov. 1, 1915. Oxford.

DENNER, CHARLES: Tarnow, Poland, May 29, 1926.

DENNIS, SANDY: Hastings, NB, Apr. 27, 1937. Actors Studio.

DEPARDIEU, GERARD: Chateauroux, Fr., Dec. 27, 1948.

DEREK, BO (Mary Cathleen Collins): Long Beach, CA, Oct. 1956.

DEREK, JOHN: Hollywood, Aug. 12, 1926.

DERN, BRUCE: Chicago, June 4, 1936. U PA.

DEWHURST, COLLEEN: Montreal June 3, 1926. Lawrence U.

DEXTER, ANTHONY (Walter Reinhold Alfred Fleischmann): Talmadge, NB, Jan. 19, 1919. U. Iowa.

DeYOUNG, CLIFF: Los Angeles, CA, Feb. 12, 1945. Cal State.

DHIEGH, KHIGH: New Jersey, 1910.

DIAMOND, NEIL: NYC, Jan. 24, 1941. NYU.

DICKINSON, ANGIE: Kulm, ND, Sept. 30, 1932. Glendale College.

DIETRICH, MARLENE (Maria Magdalene von Losch): Berlin, Ger., Dec. 27, 1901. Berlin Music Academy.

DILLER, PHYLLIS: Lima, OH, July 17, 1917. Bluffton College.

DILLMAN, BRADFORD: San Francisco, Apr. 14, 1930. Yale.

DILLON, MATT: Larchmont, NY, Feb. 18, 1964, AADA.

DILLON, MELINDA: Hope, AR, Oct. 13, 1939. Goodman Theatre School.

DIVINE (Glenn) Baltimore, MD, 1946.

DOBSON, TAMARA: Baltimore, MD, 1947. MD. Inst. of Art

DOMERGUE, FAITH: New Orleans, June 16, 1925.

DONAHUE, TROY (Merle Johnson): NYC, Jan. 27, 1937. Columbia U.

DONAT, PETER: Nova Scotia, Jan. 20, 1928. Yale.

DONNELL, JEFF (Jean Donnell): South Windham, ME, July 10, 1921. Yale Drama School.

DOOHAN, JAMES: Vancouver, BC, Mar. 3, Neighborhood Playhouse.

DOOLEY, PAUL: Parkersburg, WV, Feb. 22, 1928. U. WV.

DORS, DIANA (Fluck): Swindon, Wilshire, Eng., Oct. 23, 1931. London Academy of Music.

DOUGLAS, DONNA: Baton Rouge, LA. 1935.

DOUGLAS, KIRK (Issur Danielovitch): Amsterdam, NY, Dec. 9, 1916. St. Lawrence U.

DOUGLAS, MICHAEL: Hollywood, Sept. 25, 1944. U. Cal.

DOURIF, BRAD: Huntington, WV, Mar. 18, 1950. Marshall U.

DOVE, BILLIE: NYC, May 14, 1904.

DOWN, LESLEY-ANN: London, Mar. 17, 1954.

DRAKE, BETSY: Paris, Sept. 11, 1923.

DRAKE, CHARLES (Charles Rupert): NYC, Oct. 2, 1914. Nichols College.

DREW, ELLEN (formerly Terry Ray): Kansas City, MO, Nov. 23, 1915.

DREYFUSS, RICHARD: Brooklyn, NY, Oct. 19, 1947.

DRIVAS, ROBERT: Chicago, Oct. 7, 1938. U. Chi.

DRU, JOANNE (Joanne LaCock): Logan, WV, Jan. 31, 1923. John Robert Powers School.

DUBBINS, DON: Brooklyn, NY, June 28.

DUFF, HOWARD: Bremerton, WA, Nov. 24, 1917.

DUFFY, PATRICK: Montana, 1949. U. Wash.

DUKE, PATTY: NYC, Dec. 14, 1946.

DULLEA, KEIR: Cleveland, NJ, May 30, 1936. Neighborhood Playhouse, SF State Col.

DUNAWAY, FAYE: Bascom, FL, Jan. 14, 1941, Fla. U.

DUNCAN, SANDY: Henderson, TX, Feb. 20, 1946. Len Morris Col.

DUNNE, IRENE: Louisville, KY, Dec. 20, 1898. Chicago College of Music.

DUNNOCK, MILDRED: Baltimore, Jan. 25, 1900. Johns Hopkins and Columbia U.

DUPEREY, ANNY: Paris, 1947.

DURBIN, DEANNA (Edna): Winnipeg, Can., Dec. 4, 1921.

DURNING, CHARLES: Highland Falls, NY, Feb. 28, 1933. NYU.

DUSSOLLIER, ANDRE: Annecy, France, Feb. 17, 1946.

DUVALL, ROBERT: San Diego, CA, 1930. Principia Col.

DUVALL, SHELLEY: Houston, TX, July 7, 1949.

EASTON, ROBERT: Milwaukee, Nov. 23, 1930. U. Texas.

EASTWOOD, CLINT: San Francisco, May 31, 1930. LACC.

EATON, SHIRLEY: London, 1937. Aida Foster School.

EBSEN, BUDDY (Christian, Jr.): Belleville, IL, Apr. 2, 1910. U. Fla.

ECKEMYR, AGNETA: Karlsborg, Swed., July 2. Actors Studio.

EDEN, BARBARA (Moorhead): Tucson, AZ, Aug. 23, 1934.

EDWARDS, VINCE: NYC, July 9, 1928. AADA.

EGAN, RICHARD: San Francisco, July 29, 1923. Stanford U.

EGGAR, SAMANTHA: London, Mar. 5, 1939.

EICHHORN, LISA: Reading, PA, 1952. Queens Ont. U. RADA.

EKBERG, ANITA: Malmo, Sweden, Sept. 29, 1931.

EKLAND, BRITT: Stockholm, Swed., 1942.

ELIZONDO, HECTOR: NYC, Dec. 22, 1936.

ELLIOTT, DENHOLM: London, May 31, 1922. Malvern College.

ELLIOTT, SAM: Sacramento, CA, 1944. U. Ore.

ELY, RON (Ronald Pierce): Hereford, TX, June 21, 1938.

ERDMAN, RICHARD: Enid, OK, June 1, 1925.

ERICKSON, LEIF: Alameda, CA, Oct. 27, 1911. U. Calif.

ERICSON, JOHN: Dusseldorf, Ger., Sept. 25, 1926. AADA.

ESMOND, CARL: Vienna, June 14, 1906. U. Vienna.

EVANS, DALE (Francis Smith): Uvalde, TX, Oct. 31, 1912.

EVANS, GENE: Holbrook, AZ, July 11, 1922.

EVANS, LINDA (Evenstad): Conn., Nov. 19, 1943.

EVANS, MAURICE: Dorchester, Eng., June 3, 1901.

EVERETT, CHAD (Ray Cramton): South Bend, IN, June 11, 1936.

EWELL, TOM (Yewell Tompkins): Owensboro, KY, Apr. 29, 1909. U. Wisc.

FABARES, SHELLEY: Los Angeles, Jan. 19, 1944.

FABIAN (Fabian Forte): Philadelphia, Feb. 6, 1940.

FABRAY, NANETTE (Ruby Nanette Fabares): San Diego, Oct. 27, 1920.

FAIRBANKS, DOUGLAS JR.: NYC, Dec. 9, 1907. Collegiate School.

FAIRCHILD, MORGAN: (Patsy McClenny) Dallas, TX., 1950. UCLA.

FALK, PETER: NYC, Sept. 16, 1927. New School.

FARENTINO, JAMES: Brooklyn, Feb. 24, 1938. AADA.

FARINA, SANDY (Sandra Feldman): Newark, NJ, 1955.

FARR, DEREK: London, Feb. 7, 1912.

FARR, FELICIA: Westchester, NY, Oct. 4, 1932. Penn State Col.

FARRELL, CHARLES: Onset Bay, MA, Aug. 9, 1901. Boston U.

FARROW, MIA: Los Angeles, Feb. 9, 1945.

FAULKNER, GRAHAM: London, Sept. 26, 1947. Webber-Douglas.

FAWCETT, FARRAH: Corpus Christie, TX. Feb. 2, 1947. TexU.

FAYE, ALICE (Ann Leppert): NYC, May 5, 1912.

FEINSTEIN, ALAN: NYC, Sept. 8, 1941.

FELDON, BARBARA (Hall): Pittsburgh, Mar. 12, 1941. Carnegie Tech.

FELLOWS, EDITH: Boston, May 20, 1923.

FERRELL, CONCHATA: Charleston, WV, Mar. 28, 1943. Marshall U.

FERRER, JOSE: Santurce, P.R., Jan. 8, 1909. Princeton U.

FERRER, MEL: Elberon, NJ, Aug. 25, 1917. Princeton U.

FERRIS, BARBARA: London, 1943.

FERZETTI, GABRIELE: Italy, 1927. Rome Acad. of Drama.

FIELD, SALLY: Pasadena, CA, Nov. 6, 1946.

FIGUEROA, RUBEN: NYC 1958.

FINNEY, ALBERT: Salford, Lancashire, Eng., May 9, 1936. RADA.

FIRTH, PETER: Bradford, Eng., Oct. 27, 1953.

FISHER, CARRIE: Los Angeles, CA, Oct. 21, 1956. London Central School of Drama.

FISHER, EDDIE: Philadelphia, Aug. 10, 1928.

FITZGERALD, GERALDINE: Dublin, Ire., Nov. 24, 1914. Dublin Art School.

FLANNERY, SUSAN: Jersey City, NJ, July 31, 1943.

FLAVIN, JAMES: Portland, ME, May 14, 1906. West Point.

FLEMING, RHONDA (Marilyn Louis): Los Angeles, Aug. 10, 1922.

FLEMYNG, ROBERT: Liverpool, Eng., Jan. 3, 1912. Haileybury Col.

FLETCHER, LOUISE: Birmingham, AL, July 1934.

FOCH, NINA: Leyden, Holland, Apr. 20, 1924.

FOLDI, ERZSEBET: Queens, NY, 1967.

FONDA, JANE: NYC, Dec. 21, 1937. Vassar.

FONDA, PETER: NYC, Feb. 23, 1939. U. Omaha.

FONTAINE, JOAN: Tokyo, Japan, Oct. 22, 1917.

FORD, GLENN (Gwyllyn Samuel Newton Ford): Quebec, Can., May 1, 1916.

FORD, HARRISON: Chicago, IL, July 13, 1942. Ripon Col.

FOREST, MARK (Lou Degni): Brooklyn, Jan. 1933.

FORREST, STEVE: Huntsville, TX, Sept. 29, 1924. UCLA.

FORSLUND, CONNIE: San Diego, CA, June 19, 1950, NYU.

FORSTER, ROBERT (Foster, Jr.): Rochester, NY, July 13, 1941. Rochester U.

FORSYTHE, JOHN: Penn's Grove, NJ, Jan. 29, 1918.

FOSTER, JODIE (Ariane Munker): Bronx, NY, Nov. 19, 1962. Yale.

FOX, EDWARD: London, 1937, RADA.

FOX, JAMES: London, 1939.

FOXWORTH, ROBERT: Houston, TX, Nov. 1, 1941. Carnegie Tech.

FOXX, REDD: St. Louis, MO, Dec. 9, 1922.

FRANCIOSA, ANTHONY (Papaleo): NYC, Oct. 25, 1928.

FRANCIS, ANNE: Ossining, NY, Sept. 16, 1932.

FRANCIS, ARLENE (Arlene Kazanjian): Boston, Oct. 20, 1908. Finch School.

FRANCIS, CONNIE (Constance Franconero): Newark, NJ, Dec. 12, 1938.

FRANCISCUS, JAMES: Clayton, MO, Jan. 31, 1934. Yale.

FRANCKS, DON: Vancouver, Can., Feb. 28, 1932.

FRANK, JEFFREY: Jackson Heights, NY, 1965.

FRANKLIN, PAMELA: Tokyo, Feb. 4, 1950.

FRANZ, ARTHUR: Perth Amboy, NJ, Feb. 29, 1920. Blue Ridge College.

FRAZIER, SHEILA: NYC, 1949.

FREEMAN, AL, JR.: San Antonio, TX, 1934. CCLA.

FREEMAN, MONA: Baltimore, MD, June 9, 1926.

FREY, LEONARD: Brooklyn, Sept. 4, 1938. Neighborhood Playhouse.

FULLER, PENNY: Durham, NC, 1940. Northwestern U.

FURNEAUX, YVONNE: Lille, France, 1928. Oxford U.

GABEL, MARTIN: Philadelphia, June 19, 1912. AADA.

GABOR, EVA: Budapest, Hungary, Feb. 11, 1920.

GABOR, ZSA ZSA (Sari Gabor): Budapest, Hungary, Feb. 6, 1918.

GALLAGHER, PETER: Armonk, NY, 1956, Tufts U.

GAM, RITA: Pittsburgh, PA, Apr. 2, 1928.

GARBER, VICTOR: Montreal, Can., Mar. 16, 1949.

GARBO, GRETA (Greta Gustafson): Stockholm, Sweden, Sept. 18, 1905.

| Ruth Gordon | Joel Grey | Melanie Griffith | Harry Hamlin | Kathryn Harrold | John Houseman |

GARDENIA, VINCENT: Naples, Italy, Jan. 7, 1922.

GARDNER, AVA: Smithfield, NC, Dec. 24, 1922. Atlantic Christian College.

GARFIELD, ALLEN: Newark, NJ, Nov. 22, 1939. Actors Studio.

GARLAND, BEVERLY: Santa Cruz, CA, Oct. 17, 1930. Glendale Col.

GARNER, JAMES (James Baumgarner): Norman, OK, Apr. 7, 1928. Okla. U.

GARNER, PEGGY ANN: Canton, OH, Feb. 3, 1932.

GARR, TERI: Lakewood, OH, 1952.

GARRETT, BETTY: St. Joseph, MO, May 23, 1919. Annie Wright Seminary.

GARRISON, SEAN: NYC, Oct. 19, 1937.

GARSON, GREER: Ireland, Sept. 29, 1906.

GASSMAN, VITTORIO: Genoa, Italy, Sept. 1, 1922. Rome Academy of Dramatic Art.

GAVIN, JOHN: Los Angeles, Apr. 8, 1935. Stanford U.

GAYNOR, JANET: Philadelphia, Oct. 6, 1906.

GAYNOR, MITZI (Francesca Marlene Von Gerber): Chicago, Sept. 4, 1930.

GAZZARA, BEN: NYC, Aug. 28, 1930. Actors Studio.

GEARY, ANTHONY: Utah, 1948.

GEESON, JUDY: Arundel, Eng., Sept. 10, 1948. Corona.

GERARD, GIL: Little Rock, AR, 1940.

GERE, RICHARD: Philadelphia, PA, Aug. 29, 1949. U. Mass.

GERROLL, DANIEL: London, Oct. 16, 1951. Central.

GHOLSON, JULIE: Birmingham, AL, June 4, 1958.

GHOSTLEY, ALICE: Eve, MO, Aug. 14, 1926. Okla U.

GIANNINI, GIANCARLO: Spezia, Italy, Aug. 1, 1942. Rome Acad. of Drama.

GIBSON, MEL: Oneonta, NY., 1951. NIDA.

GIELGUD, JOHN: London, Apr. 14, 1904. RADA.

GILFORD, JACK: NYC, July 25.

GILLIS, ANNE (Alma O'Connor): Little Rock, AR, Feb. 12, 1927.

GILLMORE, MARGALO: London, May 31, 1897. AADA.

GILMORE, VIRGINIA (Sherman Poole): Del Monte, CA, July 26, 1919. U. Calif.

GINGOLD, HERMIONE: London, Dec. 9, 1897.

GIROLAMI, STEFANIA: Rome, Italy, 1963.

GISH, LILLIAN: Springfield, OH, Oct. 14, 1896.

GLASER, PAUL MICHAEL: Boston, MA, 1943. Boston U.

GLASS, RON: Evansville, IN, 1946.

GLEASON, JACKIE: Brooklyn, Feb. 26, 1916.

GLENN, SCOTT: Pittsburgh, PA, Jan. 26, 1942; William and Mary Col.

GLOVER, JOHN: Kingston, NY, Aug. 7, 1944.

GODDARD, PAULETTE (Levy): Great Neck, NY, June 3, 1911.

GOLDBLUM, JEFF: Pittsburgh, PA, Oct. 22, 1952. Neighborhood Playhouse.

GOLDEN, ANNIE: NYC, 1952.

GONZALES-GONZALEZ, PEDRO: Aguilares, TX, Dec. 21, 1926.

GOODMAN, DODY: Columbus, OH, Oct. 28, 1915.

GORDON, GALE (Aldrich): NYC, Feb. 2, 1906.

GORDON, KEITH: NYC, Feb. 3, 1961.

GORDON, RUTH: (Jones): Wollaston, MA, Oct. 30, 1896. AADA.

GORING, MARIUS: Newport, Isle of Wight, 1912. Cambridge, Old Vic.

GORMAN, CLIFF: Jamaica, NY, Oct. 13, 1936. NYU.

GORSHIN, FRANK: Apr. 5, 1933.

GORTNER, MARJOE: Long Beach, CA, 1944.

GOSSETT, LOUIS: Brooklyn, May 27, 1936. NYU.

GOULD, ELLIOTT (Goldstein): Brooklyn, Aug. 29, 1938. Columbia U.

GOULD, HAROLD: Schenectady, NY, Dec. 10, 1923. Cornell.

GOULET, ROBERT: Lawrence, MA, Nov. 26, 1933. Edmonton.

GRANGER, FARLEY: San Jose, CA, July 1, 1925.

GRANGER, STEWART (James Stewart): London, May 6, 1913. Webber-Douglas School of Acting.

GRANT, CARY (Archibald Alexander Leach): Bristol, Eng., Jan. 18, 1904.

GRANT, DAVID MARSHALL: Westport, CT, 1955. Yale.

GRANT, KATHRYN (Olive Grandstaff): Houston, TX, Nov. 25, 1933. UCLA.

GRANT, LEE: NYC, Oct. 31, 1930. Juilliard.

GRANVILLE, BONITA: NYC, Feb. 2, 1923.

GRAVES, PETER (Aurness): Minneapolis, Mar. 18, 1926. U. Minn.

GRAY, COLEEN (Doris Jensen): Staplehurst, NB, Oct. 23, 1922. Hamline U.

GRAY, LINDA: Santa Monica, CA; Sept. 12, 1941.

GRAYSON, KATHRYN (Zelma Hedrick): Winston-Salem, NC, Feb. 9, 1922.

GREENE, ELLEN: NYC, Feb. 22, Ryder Col.

GREENE, LORNE: Ottawa, CAN., Feb. 12, 1915. Queens U.

GREENE, RICHARD: Plymouth, Eng., Aug. 25, 1914. Cardinal Vaughn School.

GREENWOOD, JOAN: London, Mar. 4, 1919. RADA.

GREER, JANE: Washington, DC, Sept. 9, 1924.

GREER, MICHAEL: Galesburg, IL, Apr. 20, 1943.

GREGORY, MARK: Rome, Italy. 1965.

GREY, JOEL (Katz): Cleveland, OH, Apr. 11, 1932.

GREY, VIRGINIA: Los Angeles, Mar. 22, 1917.

GRIEM, HELMUT: Hamburg, Ger. U. Hamburg.

GRIFFITH, ANDY: Mt. Airy, NC, June 1, 1926. UNC.

GRIFFITH, MELANIE: NYC, Aug. 9, 1957. Pierce Col.

GRIMES, GARY: San Francisco, June 2, 1955.

GRIMES, TAMMY: Lynn, MA, Jan. 30, 1934. Stephens Col.

GRIZZARD, GEORGE: Roanoke Rapids, NC, Apr. 1, 1928. UNC.

GRODIN, CHARLES: Pittsburgh, PA, Apr. 21, 1935.

GROH, DAVID: NYC, May 21, 1939. Brown U., LAMDA.

GUARDINO, HARRY: Brooklyn, Dec. 23, 1925. Haaren High.

GUINNESS, ALEX: London, Apr. 2, 1914. Pembroke Lodge School.

GUNN, MOSES: St. Louis, MO, Oct. 2, 1929. Tenn. State U.

GUTTENBERG, STEVEN: Brooklyn, NY, Aug. 1958. UCLA.

GWILLIM, DAVID: Plymouth, Eng., Dec. 15, 1948. RADA.

HACKETT, BUDDY (Leonard Hacker): Brooklyn, Aug. 31, 1924.

HACKMAN, GENE: San Bernardino, CA, Jan. 30, 1931.

HADDON, DALE: Montreal, CAN., May 26, 1949. Neighborhood Playhouse.

HAGMAN, LARRY: (Hageman): Texas, 1931. Bard Col.

HALE, BARBARA: DeKalb, IL, Apr. 18, 1922. Chicago Academy of Fine Arts.

HALEY, JACKIE EARLE: Northridge, CA, 1963.

HALL, ALBERT: Boothton, AL, Nov. 10, 1937. Columbia.

HALL, ANTHONY MICHAEL: NYC, 1968.

HAMILL, MARK: Oakland, CA, Sept. 25, 1952. LACC.

HAMILTON, GEORGE: Memphis, TN, Aug. 12, 1939. Hackley.

HAMILTON, MARGARET: Cleveland, OH, Dec. 9, 1902. Hathaway-Brown School.

HAMILTON, NEIL: Lynn, MA, Sept. 9, 1899.

HAMLIN, HARRY: Pasadena, CA, 1952. Yale.

HAMPSHIRE, SUSAN: London, May 12, 1941.

HARDIN, TY (Orison Whipple Hungerford II): NYC, June 1, 1930.

HAREWOOD, DORIAN: Dayton, OH, Aug. 6. U Cinn.

HARMON, MARK: Los Angeles, CA, 1951; UCLA.

HARPER, VALERIE: Suffern, NY, Aug. 22, 1940.

HARRINGTON, PAT: NYC, Aug. 13, 1929. Fordham U.

HARRIS, BARBARA (Sandra Markowitz): Evanston, IL, 1937.

HARRIS, ED: Tenafly, NJ, 1950.

HARRIS, JULIE: Grosse Point, MI, Dec. 2, 1925. Yale Drama School.

HARRIS, RICHARD: Limerick, Ire., Oct. 1, 1930. London Acad.

HARRIS, ROSEMARY: Ashby, Eng., Sept. 19, 1930. RADA.

HARRISON, GREG: Catalina Island, CA, 1950; Actors Studio.

HARRISON, NOEL: London, Jan. 29, 1936.

HARRISON, REX: Huyton, Cheshire, Eng., Mar. 5, 1908.

HARROLD, KATHRYN: Tazewell, VA. 1950. Mills Col.

HARTMAN, DAVID: Pawtucket, RI, May 19, 1935. Duke U.

HARTMAN, ELIZABETH: Youngstown, OH, Dec. 23, 1941. Carnegie Tech.

HASSETT, MARILYN: Los Angeles, CA, 1949.

HAUER, RUTGER: Amsterdam, Hol. 1944.

HAVER, JUNE: Rock Island, IL, June 10, 1926.

HAWN, GOLDIE: Washington, DC, Nov. 21, 1945.

HAYDEN, LINDA: Stanmore, Eng. Aida Foster School.

HAYDEN, STERLING (John Hamilton): Montclair, NJ, March 26, 1916.

HAYES, HELEN: (Helen Brown): Washington, DC, Oct. 10, 1900. Sacred Heart Convent.

HAYS, ROBERT: San Diego, CA, 1948; SD State Col.

HAYWORTH, RITA: (Margarita Cansino): NYC, Oct. 17, 1918.

HEARD, JOHN: Washington, DC, Mar. 7, 1946. Clark U.

HEATHERTON, JOEY: NYC, Sept. 14, 1944.

HECKART, EILEEN: Columbus, OH, Mar. 29, 1919. Ohio State U.

HEDISON, DAVID: Providence, RI, May 20, 1929. Brown U.

HEGYES, ROBERT: NJ, May 7, 1951.

HEMINGWAY, MARIEL: Nov. 22, 1961.

HEMMINGS, DAVID: Guilford, Eng. Nov. 18, 1938.

HENDERSON, MARCIA: Andover, MA, July 22, 1932. AADA.

HENDRY, GLORIA: Jacksonville, FL, 1949.

HENNER, MARILU: Chicago, IL. Apr. 4, 1952.

HENREID, PAUL: Trieste, Jan. 10, 1908.

HENRY, BUCK (Zuckerman): NYC, 1931. Dartmouth.

HENRY, JUSTIN: Rye, NY, 1971.

HEPBURN, AUDREY: Brussels, Belgium, May 4, 1929.

HEPBURN, KATHARINE: Hartford, CT, Nov. 8, 1907. Bryn Mawr.

HERRMANN, EDWARD: Washington, DC, July 21, 1943. Bucknell, LAMDA.

HERSHEY, BARBARA: see Seagull, Barbara Hershey.

HESTON, CHARLTON: Evanston, IL, Oct. 4, 1922. Northwestern U.

HEWITT, MARTIN: Claremont, CA, 1960; AADA.

HEYWOOD, ANNE (Violet Pretty): Birmingham, Eng., Dec. 11, 1932.

HICKMAN, DARRYL: Hollywood, CA, July 28, 1930. Loyola U.

HICKMAN, DWAYNE: Los Angeles, May 18, 1934. Loyola U.

HILL, ARTHUR: Saskatchewan, CAN., Aug. 1, 1922. U. Brit. Col.

HILL, STEVEN: Seattle, WA, Feb. 24, 1922. U. Wash.

HILL, TERENCE (Mario Girotti): Venice, Italy, Mar. 29, 1941. U. Rome.

HILLER, WENDY: Bramhall, Cheshire, Eng., Aug. 15, 1912. Winceby House School.

HILLIARD, HARRIET: (See Harriet Hilliard Nelson)

HINGLE, PAT: Denver, CO, July 19, 1923. Tex. U.

HIRSCH, JUDD: NYC, Mar. 15, 1935. AADA.

HODGE, PATRICIA: Lincolnshire, Eng., 1946. LAMDA.

HOFFMAN, DUSTIN: Los Angeles, Aug. 8, 1937. Pasadena Playhouse.

HOLBROOK, HAL (Harold): Cleveland, OH, Feb. 17, 1925. Denison.

HOLLIMAN, EARL: Tennessas Swamp, Delhi, LA, Sept. 11, 1928. UCLA.

HOLM, CELESTE: NYC, Apr. 29, 1919.

HOMEIER, SKIP (George Vincent Homeier): Chicago, Oct. 5, 1930. UCLA.

HOOKS, ROBERT: Washington, DC, Apr. 18, 1937. Temple.

HOPE, BOB: London, May 26, 1903.

HOPPER, DENNIS: Dodge City, KS, May 17, 1936.

HORNE, LENA: Brooklyn, June 30, 1917.

HORTON, ROBERT: Los Angeles, July 29, 1924. UCLA.

HOUGHTON, KATHARINE: Hartford, CT, Mar. 10, 1945. Sarah Lawrence.

HOUSEMAN, JOHN: Bucharest, Sept. 22, 1902.

HOUSER, JERRY: Los Angeles, July 14, 1952. Valley Jr. Col.

HOUSTON, DONALD: Tonypandy, Wales, 1924.

HOVEY, TIM: Los Angeles, June 19, 1945.

HOWARD, KEN: El Centro, CA, Mar. 28, 1944. Yale.

HOWARD, RON: Duncan, OK, Mar. 1, 1954. USC.

HOWARD, RONALD: Norwood, Eng., Apr. 7, 1918. Jesus College.

HOWARD, TREVOR: Kent, Eng., Sept. 29, 1916. RADA.

HOWELLS, URSULA: London, Sept. 17, 1922.

HOWES, SALLY ANN: London, July 20, 1930.

HUDDLESTON, MICHAEL: Roanoke, VA., AADA.

HUDSON, ROCK (Roy Scherer Fitzerald): Winnetka, IL, Nov. 17, 1924.

HUFFMAN, DAVID: Berwin, IL, May 10, 1945.

HUGHES, BARNARD: Bedford Hills, NY, July 16, 1915. Manhattan Col.

HUGHES, KATHLEEN (Betty von Gerkan): Hollywood, CA, Nov. 14, 1928. UCLA.

HULCE, THOMAS: Plymouth, MI, Dec. 6, 1953. N.C.Sch. of Arts.

HUNNICUT, GAYLE: Ft. Worth, TX, Feb. 6, 1943. UCLA.

HUNT, LINDA: Morristown, NJ, Apr. 2, 1945. Goodman Theatre.

HUNT, MARSHA: Chicago, Oct. 17, 1917.

HUNTER, KIM (Janet Cole): Detroit, Nov. 12, 1922.

HUNTER, TAB (Arthur Gelien) NYC, July 11, 1931.

HUPPERT, ISABELLE: Paris, Fr., Mar. 16, 1955.

HURT, MARY BETH (Supinger): Marshalltown, IA., 1948. NYU.

HURT, WILLIAM: Washington, D.C., Mar. 20, 1950. Tufts, Julliard.

HUSSEY, RUTH: Providence, RI, Oct. 30, 1917. U. Mich.

HUSTON, JOHN: Nevada, MO, Aug. 5, 1906.

HUTTON, BETTY (Betty Thornberg): Battle Creek, MI, Feb. 26, 1921.

HUTTON, LAUREN (Mary): Charleston, SC, Nov. 17, 1943. Newcomb Col.

| Kate
Jackson | Page
Johnson | Nastassja
Kinski | Aron
Kincaid | Jessica
Lange | Ron
Leibman |

HUTTON, ROBERT (Winne): Kingston, NY, June 11, 1920. Blair Academy.

HUTTON, TIMOTHY: Malibu, CA, Aug. 16, 1960.

HYDE-WHITE, WILFRID: Gloucestershire, Eng., May 13, 1903. RADA.

HYER, MARTHA: Fort Worth, TX, Aug. 10, 1924. Northwestern U.

INGELS, MARTY: Brooklyn, NY, Mar. 9, 1936.

IRELAND, JOHN: Vancouver, B.C., CAN., Jan. 30, 1914.

IRONS, JEREMY: Cowes, Eng. Sept. 19, 1948. Old Vic.

IVES, BURL: Hunt Township, IL, June 14, 1909. Charleston ILL. Teachers College.

JACKSON, ANNE: Alleghany, PA, Sept. 3, 1926. Neighborhood Playhouse.

JACKSON, GLENDA: Hoylake, Cheshire, Eng., May 9, 1936. RADA.

JACKSON, KATE: Birmingham, AL. Oct. 29, 1948. AADA.

JACKSON, MICHAEL: Gary Ind., Aug. 29, 1958.

JACOBI, DEREK: Leytonstone, London, Eng. Oct. 22, 1938. Cambridge.

JACOBI, LOU: Toronto, CAN., Dec. 28, 1913.

JACOBS, LAWRENCE-HILTON: Virgin Islands, 1954.

JACOBY, SCOTT: Chicago, Nov. 19, 1956.

JAECKEL, RICHARD: Long Beach, NY, Oct. 10, 1926.

JAFFE, SAM: NYC, Mar. 8, 1892.

JAGGER, DEAN: Lima, OH, Nov. 7, 1903. Wabash College.

JAGGER, MICK: July 26, 1943.

JAMES, CLIFTON: NYC, May 29, 1921. Ore. U.

JARMAN, CLAUDE, JR.: Nashville, TN, Sept. 27, 1934.

JASON, RICK: NYC, May 21, 1926. AADA.

JEAN, GLORIA (Gloria Jean Schoonover): Buffalo, NY, Apr. 14, 1927.

JEFFREYS, ANNE (Carmichael): Goldsboro, NC, Jan 26, 1923. Anderson College.

JEFFRIES, LIONEL: London, 1927, RADA.

JERGENS, ADELE: Brooklyn, Nov. 26, 1922.

JETT, ROGER (Baker): Cumberland, MD., Oct. 2, 1946. AADA.

JOHN, ELTON: (Reginald Dwight) Middlesex, Eng., Mar. 25, 1947. RAM.

JOHNS, GLYNIS: Durban, S. Africa, Oct. 5, 1923.

JOHNSON, CELIA: Richmond, Surrey, Eng., Dec. 18, 1908. RADA.

JOHNSON, PAGE: Welch, WV, Aug. 25, 1930. Ithaca.

JOHNSON, RAFER: Hillsboro, TX, Aug. 18, 1935. UCLA.

JOHNSON, RICHARD: Essex, Eng., 1927. RADA.

JOHNSON, ROBIN: Brooklyn, NY: May 29, 1964.

JOHNSON, VAN: Newport, RI, Aug. 28, 1916.

JONES, CHRISTOPHER: Jackson, TN, Aug. 18, 1941. Actors Studio.

JONES, DEAN: Morgan County, AL, Jan. 25, 1936. Actors Studio.

JONES, JACK: Bel-Air, CA, Jan. 14, 1938.

JONES, JAMES EARL: Arkabutla, MS, Jan. 17, 1931. U. Mich.

JONES, JENNIFER (Phyllis Isley): Tulsa, OK, Mar. 2, 1919. AADA.

JONES, SAM J.: Chicago, IL, 1954.

JONES, SHIRLEY: Smithton, PA, March 31, 1934.

JONES, TOM (Thomas Jones Woodward): Pontypridd, Wales, June 7, 1940.

JONES, TOMMY LEE: San Saba, TX, Sept. 15, 1946. Harvard.

JORDAN, RICHARD: NYC, July 19, 1938. Harvard.

JOURDAN, LOUIS: Marseilles, France, June 18, 1920.

JULIA, RAUL: San Juan, PR, Mar. 9, 1940. U PR.

JURADO, KATY (Maria Christina Jurado Garcia): Guadalajara, Mex., 1927.

KAHN, MADELINE: Boston, MA, Sept. 29, 1942. Hofstra U.

KANE, CAROL: Cleveland, OH, 1952.

KAPLAN, JONATHAN: Paris, Nov. 25, 1947. NYU.

KAPOOR, SHASHI: Bombay 1940.

KATT, WILLIAM: Los Angeles, CA, 1955.

KAUFMANN, CHRISTINE: Lansdorf, Graz, Austria, Jan. 11, 1945.

KAYE, DANNY: (David Daniel Kominski): Brooklyn, Jan. 18, 1913.

KAYE, STUBBY: NYC, Nov. 11, 1918.

KEACH, STACY: Savannah, GA, June 2, 1941. U. Cal., Yale.

KEATON, DIANE (Hall): Los Angeles, CA, Jan. 5, 1946. Neighborhood Playhouse.

KEATS, STEVEN: Bronx, NY, 1945.

KEDROVA, LILA: Greece, 1918.

KEEL, HOWARD (Harold Keel): Gillespie, IL, Apr. 13, 1919.

KEELER, RUBY (Ethel): Halifax, N.S., Aug. 25, 1909.

KEITH, BRIAN: Bayonne, NJ, Nov. 15, 1921.

KEITH, DAVID: Knoxville, Tn., 1954. UTn.

KELLER, MARTHE: Basel, Switz., 1945. Munich Stanislavsky Sch.

KELLERMAN, SALLY: Long Beach, CA, June 2, 1938. Actors Studio West.

KELLEY, DeFOREST: Atlanta, GA, Jan. 20, 1920.

KELLY, GENE: Pittsburgh, Aug. 23, 1912. U. Pittsburgh.

KELLY, JACK: Astoria, NY, Sept. 16, 1927. UCLA.

KELLY, NANCY: Lowell, MA, Mar. 25, 1921. Bent!ey School.

KEMP, JEREMY: Chesterfield, Eng., 1935, Central Sch.

KENNEDY, ARTHUR: Worcester, MA, Feb. 17, 1914. Carnegie Tech.

KENNEDY, GEORGE: NYC, Feb. 18, 1925.

KENNEDY, LEON ISAAC: Cleveland, OH., 1949.

KERR, DEBORAH: Helensburg, Scot., Sept. 30, 1921. Smale Ballet School.

KERR, JOHN: NYC, Nov. 15, 1931. Harvard, Columbia.

KHAMBATTA, PERSIS: Bombay, Oct. 2, 1950.

KIDDER, MARGOT: Yellow Knife, CAN., Oct. 17, 1948. UBC.

KIER, UDO: Germany, Oct. 14, 1944.

KILEY, RICHARD: Chicago, Mar. 31, 1922. Loyola.

KINCAID, ARON (Norman Neale Williams III): Los Angeles, June 15, 1943. UCLA.

KING, ALAN (Irwin Kniberg): Brooklyn, Dec. 26, 1927.

KING, PERRY: Alliance, OH, Apr. 30. Yale.

KINGSLEY, BEN (Krishna Bhanji): Snaiton, Yorkshire, Eng., Dec. 31, 1943.

KINSKI, NATASSJA: Germany, Jan. 24, 1960.

KITT, EARTHA: North, SC, Jan. 26, 1928.

KLEMPERER, WERNER: Cologne, Mar. 22, 1920.

KLUGMAN, JACK: Philadelphia, PA, Apr. 27, 1925. Carnegie Tech.

KNIGHT, ESMOND: East Sheen, Eng., May 4, 1906.

KNIGHT, SHIRLEY: Goessel, KS, July 5, 1937. Wichita U.

KNOWLES, PATRIC (Reginald Lawrence Knowles): Horsforth, Eng., Nov. 11, 1911.

KNOX, ALEXANDER: Strathroy, Ont., CAN., Jan. 16, 1907.

KNOX, ELYSE: Hartford, CT, Dec. 14, 1917. Traphagen School.

KOENIG, WALTER: Chicago, IL, Sept. 14. UCLA.

KOHNER, SUSAN: Los Angeles, Nov. 11, 1936. U. Calif.

KORMAN, HARVEY: Chicago, IL, Feb. 15, 1927. Goodman.

KORVIN, CHARLES (Geza Korvin Karpathi): Czechoslovakia, Nov. 21. Sorbonne.

KOSLECK, MARTIN: Barkotzen, Ger., Mar. 24, 1907. Max Reinhardt School.

KOTTO, YAPHET: NYC, Nov. 15, 1937.

KREUGER, KURT: St. Moritz, Switz., July 23, 1917. U. London.

KRISTEL, SYLVIA: Amsterdam, Hol., Sept. 28, 1952.

KRISTOFFERSON, KRIS: Brownsville, TX, June 22, 1936, Pomona Col.

KRUGER, HARDY: Berlin Ger., April. 12, 1928.

KULP, NANCY: Harrisburg, PA, 1921.

KUNTSMANN, DORIS: Hamburg, 1944.

KWAN, NANCY: Hong Kong, May 19, 1939. Royal Ballet.

LACY, JERRY: Sioux City, IA, Mar. 27, 1936. LACC.

LADD, CHERYL: (Stoppelmoor): Huron, SD, July 12, 1951.

LADD, DIANE: (Ladnier): Meridian, MS, Nov. 29, 1932. Tulane U.

LAHTI, CHRISTINE: Detroit, MI, Apr. 4, 1950; U Mich.

LAMARR, HEDY (Hedwig Kiesler): Vienna, Sept. 11, 1913.

LAMAS, LORENZO: Los Angeles, Jan. 1958.

LAMB, GIL: Minneapolis, June 14, 1906. U. Minn.

LAMOUR, DOROTHY (Mary Dorothy Stanton): New Orleans, LA.; Dec. 10, 1914. Spence School.

LANCASTER, BURT: NYC, Nov. 2, 1913. NYU.

LANCHESTER, ELSA (Elsa Sullivan): London, Oct. 28, 1902.

LANDAU, MARTIN: Brooklyn, NY, 1931. Actors Studio.

LANDON, MICHAEL (Eugene Orowitz): Collingswood, NJ, Oct. 31, 1936. USC.

LANDRUM, TERI: Enid, OK., 1960.

LANE, ABBE: Brooklyn, Dec. 14, 1935.

LANE, DIANE: NYC, Jan. 1963.

LANGAN, GLENN: Denver, CO, July 8, 1917.

LANGE, HOPE: Redding Ridge, CT, Nov. 28, 1933. Reed Col.

LANGE, JESSICA: Minnesota, Apr. 20, 1949. U. Minn.

LANGTON, PAUL: Salt Lake City, UT, Apr. 17, 1913. Travers School of Theatre.

LANSBURY, ANGELA: London, Oct. 16, 1925. London Academy of Music.

LANSING, ROBERT (Brown): San Diego, CA, June 5, 1929.

LAURE, CAROLE: Montreal, Can., 1951.

LAURIE, PIPER (Rosetta Jacobs): Detroit, MI, Jan. 22, 1932.

LAW, JOHN PHILLIP: Hollywood, Sept. 7, 1937. Neighborhood Playhouse, U. Hawaii.

LAWFORD, PETER: London, Sept. 7, 1923.

LAWRENCE, BARBARA: Carnegie, OK, Feb. 24, 1930. UCLA.

LAWRENCE, CAROL (Laraia): Melrose Park, IL, Sept. 5, 1935.

LAWRENCE, VICKI: Inglewood, CA, 1949.

LAWSON, LEIGH: Atherston, Eng., July 21, 1945, RADA.

LEACHMAN, CLORIS: Des Moines, IA, Apr. 30, 1930. Northwestern U.

LEAUD, JEAN-PIERRE: Paris, 1944.

LEDERER, FRANCIS: Karlin, Prague, Czech., Nov. 6, 1906.

LEE, CHRISTOPHER: London, May 27, 1922. Wellington College.

LEE, MARK: Australia, 1958.

LEE, MICHELE (Dusiak): Los Angeles, June 24, 1942. LACC.

LEIBMAN, RON: NYC, Oct. 11, 1937. Ohio Wesleyan.

LEIGH, JANET (Jeanette Helen Morrison): Merced, CA, July 6, 1926. College of Pacific.

LEMMON, JACK: Boston, Feb. 8, 1925. Harvard.

LENZ, RICK: Springfield, IL, Nov. 21, 1939. U. Mich.

LEONARD, SHELDON (Bershad): NYC, Feb. 22, 1907, Syracuse U.

LEROY, PHILIPPE: Paris, Oct. 15, 1930. U. Paris.

LESLIE, BETHEL: NYC, Aug. 3, 1929. Brearley School.

LESLIE, JOAN (Joan Brodell): Detroit, Jan. 2o, 1925. St. Benedict's.

LESTER, MARK: Oxford, Eng., July 11, 1958.

LEVELS, CALVIN: Cleveland, OH, 1954.

LEWIS, JERRY: Newark, NJ, Mar. 16, 1926.

LIGON, TOM: New Orleans, LA, Sept. 10, 1945.

LILLIE, BEATRICE: Toronto, Can., May 29, 1898.

LINCOLN, ABBEY (Anna Marie Woolridge): Chicago, Aug. 6, 1930.

LINDFORS, VIVECA: Uppsala, Sweden, Dec. 29, 1920. Stockholm Royal Dramatic School.

LISI, VIRNA: Rome, 1938.

LITHGOW, JOHN: Rochester, NY, Oct. 19, 1945. Harvard.

LITTLE, CLEAVON: Chickasha, OK, June 1, 1939. San Diego State.

LOCKE, SONDRA: Shelbyville, TN, 1947.

LOCKHART, JUNE: NYC, June 25, 1925. Westlake School.

LOCKWOOD, GARY: Van Nuys, CA, Feb. 21, 1937.

LOCKWOOD, MARGARET: Karachi, Pakistan, Sept. 15, 1916. RADA.

LOLLOBRIGIDA, GINA: Subiaco, Italy, July 4, 1927. Rome Academy of Fine Arts.

LOM, HERBERT: Prague, Czechoslovakia, 1917. Prague U.

LOMEZ, CELINE: Montreal, Can., 1953.

LONDON, JULIE (Julie Peck): Santa Rosa, CA, Sept. 26, 1926.

LONOW, MARK: Brooklyn, NY.

LOPEZ, PERRY: NYC, July 22, 1931. NYU.

LORD, JACK (John Joseph Ryan): NYC, Dec. 30, 1928. NYU.

LOREN, SOPHIA (Sofia Scicolone): Rome, Italy, Sept. 20, 1934.

LOUISE, TINA (Blacker): NYC, Feb. 11, 1934, Miami U.

LOVELACE, LINDA: Bryan, TX, 1952.

LOWE, ROB: Virginia, 1964

LOWITSCH, KLAUS: Berlin, Apr. 8, 1936. Vienna Academy.

LOY, MYRNA (Myrna Williams): Helena, MT, Aug. 2, 1905. Westlake School.

LUCAS, LISA: Arizona, 1961.

LULU: Glasglow, Scot., 1948.

LUND, JOHN: Rochester, NY, Feb. 6, 1913.

LUPINO, IDA: London, Feb. 4, 1916. RADA.

LYDON, JAMES: Harrington Park, NJ, May 30, 1923.

LYNLEY, CAROL (Jones): NYC, Feb. 13, 1942.

LYNN, JEFFREY: Auburn, MA, 1909. Bates College.

LYON, SUE: Davenport, IA, July 10, 1946.

LYONS, ROBERT F.: Albany, NY. AADA.

MacARTHUR, JAMES: Los Angeles, Dec. 8, 1937. Harvard.

MacGINNIS, NIALL: Dublin, Ire., Mar. 29, 1913. Dublin U.

MacGRAW, ALI: NYC, Apr. 1, 1938. Wellesley.

MacLAINE, SHIRLEY (Beatty): Richmond, VA, Apr. 24, 1934.

MacMAHON, ALINE: McKeesport, PA, May 3, 1899. Barnard College.

MacMURRAY, FRED: Kankakee, IL, Aug. 30, 1908. Carroll Col.

MACNEE, PATRICK: London, Feb. 1922.

MacNICOL, PETER: Dallas, TX, Apr. 10, UMN.

MacRAE, GORDON: East Orange, NJ, Mar. 12, 1921.

MADISON, GUY (Robert Moseley): Bakersfield, CA, Jan. 19, 1922. Bakersfield Jr. College.

MAHARIS, GEORGE: Astoria, NY, Sept. 1, 1928. Actors Studio.

MAHONEY, JOCK (Jacques O'-Mahoney): Chicago, Feb. 7, 1919. U. of Iowa.

Tim
Matheson

Elizabeth
McGovern

Tony
Musante

Jeanne
Moreau

Don
Nute

Glynnis
O'Connor

MAJORS, LEE: Wyandotte, MI, Apr. 23, 1940. E. Ky. State Col.

MAKEPEACE, CHRIS: Toronto, Can., 1964.

MALDEN, KARL (Mladen Sekulovich): Gary, IN, Mar. 22, 1914.

MALET, PIERRE: St. Tropez, Fr., 1955.

MALONE, DOROTHY: Chicago, Jan. 30, 1925. S. Methodist U.

MANN, KURT: Roslyn, NY, July 18, 1947.

MANOFF, DINAH: NYC, Jan. 25, 1958. CalArts.

MANZ, LINDA: NYC, 1961.

MARAIS, JEAN: Cherbourg, France, Dec. 11, 1913. St. Germain.

MARGO (Maria Marguerita Guadalupe Boldoay Castilla): Mexico City, May 10, 1917.

MARGOLIN, JANET: NYC, July 25, 1943. Walden School.

MARIN, JACQUES: Paris, Sept. 9, 1919. Conservatoire National.

MARINARO, ED: NYC, 1951. Cornell.

MARSHALL, BRENDA (Ardis Anderson Gaines): Isle of Negros, P.I., Sept. 29, 1915. Texas State College.

MARSHALL, E. G.: Owatonna, MN, June 18, 1910. U. Minn.

MARSHALL, PENNY: Bronx, NY, Oct. 15, 1942. U. N. Mex.

MARSHALL, WILLIAM: Gary, IN, Aug. 19, 1924. NYU.

MARTIN, DEAN (Dino Crocetti): Steubenville, OH, June 17, 1917.

MARTIN, DEAN PAUL: Los Angeles, CA, 1952. UCLA.

MARTIN, MARY: Weatherford, TX, Dec. 1, 1914. Ward-Belmont School.

MARTIN, STEVE: Waco, TX, 1946. UCLA.

MARTIN, TONY (Alfred Norris): Oakland, CA, Dec. 25, 1913. St. Mary's College.

MARVIN, LEE: NYC, Feb. 19, 1924.

MASON, JAMES: Huddersfield, Yorkshire, Eng., May 15, 1909. Cambridge.

MASON, MARSHA: St. Louis, MO, Apr. 3, 1942. Webster Col.

MASON, PAMELA (Pamela Kellino): Westgate, Eng., Mar. 10, 1918.

MASSEN, OSA: Copenhagen, Den., Jan. 13, 1916.

MASSEY, DANIEL: London, Oct. 10, 1933. Eton and King's Col.

MASTERSON, PETER: Angleton, TX, June 1, 1934. Rice U.

MASTROIANNI, MARCELLO: Fontana Liri, Italy, Sept. 28, 1924.

MATHESON, TIM: Glendale, CA, Dec. 31, 1947. CalState.

MATTHAU, WALTER (Matuschanskayasky): NYC, Oct. 1, 1920.

MATTHEWS, BRIAN: Philadelphia, PA, Jan. 24, 1953. St. Olaf.

MATURE, VICTOR: Louisville, KY, Jan. 29, 1915.

MAY, ELAINE (Berlin): Philadelphia, Apr. 21, 1932.

MAYEHOFF, EDDIE: Baltimore, July 7. Yale.

MAYO, VIRGINIA (Virginia Clara Jones): St. Louis, MO, Nov. 30, 1920.

McCALLUM, DAVID: Scotland, Sept. 19, 1933. Chapman Col.

McCAMBRIDGE, MERCEDES: Jolliet, IL, Mar. 17, 1918. Mundelein College.

McCARTHY, ANDREW: NYC, 1963, NYU.

McCARTHY, KEVIN: Seattle, WA, Feb. 15, 1914. Minn. U.

McCLORY, SEAN: Dublin, Ire., Mar. 8, 1924. U. Galway.

McCLURE, DOUG: Glendale, CA, May 11, 1935. UCLA.

McCOWEN, ALEC: Tunbridge Wells, Eng., May 26, 1925. RADA.

McCREA, JOEL: Los Angeles, Nov. 5, 1905. Pomona College.

McDERMOTT, HUGH: Edinburgh, Scot., Mar. 20, 1908.

McDOWALL, RODDY: London, Sept. 17, 1928. St. Joseph's.

McDOWELL, MALCOLM (Taylor): Leeds, Eng., June 15, 1943. LAMDA.

McENERY, PETER: Walsall, Eng., Feb. 21, 1940.

McFARLAND, SPANKY: Dallas, TX, 1936.

McGAVIN, DARREN: Spokane, WA, May 7, 1922. College of Pacific.

McGILLIS, KELLY: Newport Beach, CA, 1958. Juilliard.

McGOVERN, ELIZABETH: Evanston, IL, July 18, 1961. Juilliard.

McGUIRE, BIFF: New Haven, CT, Oct. 25, 1926. Mass. State Col.

McGUIRE, DOROTHY: Omaha, NE, June 14, 1918.

McHATTIE, STEPHEN: Antigonish, NS, Feb. 3. AcadiaU, AADA.

McKAY, GARDNER: NYC, June 10, 1932. Cornell.

McKEE, LONETTE: Detroit, MI, 1954.

McKENNA, VIRGINIA: London, June 7, 1931.

McKEON, DOUG: New Jersey, 1966.

McKUEN, ROD: Oakland, CA, Apr. 29, 1933.

McLERIE, ALLYN ANN: Grand Mere, Can., Dec. 1, 1926.

McNAIR, BARBARA: Chicago, Mar. 4, 1939. UCLA.

McNALLY, STEPHEN (Horace McNally): NYC, July 29, 1913. Fordham U.

McNICHOL, KRISTY: Los Angeles, CA, Sept. 11, 1962.

McQUEEN, ARMELIA: North Carolina, Jan. 6, 1952. Bklyn Consv.

McQUEEN, BUTTERFLY: Tampa, FL, Jan. 8, 1911. UCLA.

McQUEEN, CHAD: Los Angeles, CA, 1961. Actors Studio.

MEADOWS, AUDREY: Wuchang, China, 1919. St. Margaret's.

MEADOWS, JAYNE (formerly, Jayne Cotter): Wuchang, China, Sept. 27, 1920. St. Margaret's.

MEDWIN, MICHAEL: London, 1925. Instut Fischer.

MEEKER, RALPH (Ralph Rathgeber): Minneapolis, Nov. 21, 1920. Northwestern U.

MEISNER, GUNTER: Bremen, Ger., Apr. 18, 1926. Municipal Drama School.

MEKKA, EDDIE: Worcester, MA, 1932. Boston Cons.

MELATO, MARIANGELA: Milan, Italy, 1941. Milan Theatre Acad.

MELL, MARISA: Vienna, Austria, Feb. 25, 1939.

MERCADO, HECTOR JAIME: NYC, 1949. HB Studio.

MERCOURI, MELINA: Athens, Greece, Oct. 18, 1915.

MEREDITH, BURGESS: Cleveland, OH, Nov. 16, 1908. Amherst.

MEREDITH, LEE (Judi Lee Sauls): Oct., 1947. AADA.

MERKEL, UNA: Covington, KY, Dec. 10, 1903.

MERRILL, DINA (Nedinia Hutton): NYC, Dec. 9, 1925. AADA.

MERRILL, GARY: Hartford, CT, Aug. 2, 1915. Bowdoin, Trinity.

METZLER, JIM: Oneonda, NY. Dartmouth Col.

MICHELL, KEITH: Adelaide, Aus., Dec. 1, 1926.

MIDLER, BETTE: Paterson, NJ, Dec. 1, 1944.

MIFUNE, TOSHIRO: Tsingtao, China, Apr. 1 1920.

MILES, SARAH: Ingatestone, Eng., Dec. 31, 1941. RADA.

MILES, SYLVIA: NYC, Sept. 9, 1932.

MILES, VERA (Ralston): Boise City, OK, Aug. 23, 1929. UCLA.

MILFORD, PENELOPE: Winnetka, IL.

MILLAND, RAY (Reginald Truscott-Jones): Neath, Wales, Jan. 3, 1908. King's College.

MILLER, ANN (Lucille Ann Collier): Chireno, TX, Apr. 12, 1919. Lawler Professional School.

MILLER, BARRY: NYC, 1958.

MILLER, JASON: Long Island City, NY, Apr. 22, 1939. Catholic U.

MILLER, LINDA: NYC, Sept. 16, 1942. Catholic U.

MILLER, MARVIN: St. Louis, July 18, 1913. Washington U.

MILLS, HAYLEY: London, Apr. 18, 1946. Elmhurst School.

MILLS, JOHN: Suffolk, Eng., Feb. 22, 1908.

MILNER, MARTIN: Detroit, MI, Dec. 28, 1931.

MIMIEUX, YVETTE: Los Angeles, Jan. 8, 1941. Hollywood High.

MINNELLI, LIZA: Los Angeles, Mar. 12, 1946.

MIOU-MIOU: Paris, Feb. 22, 1950.

MITCHELL, CAMERON: Dallastown, PA, Nov. 4, 1918. N.Y. Theatre School.

MITCHELL, JAMES: Sacramento, CA, Feb. 29, 1920. LACC.

MITCHUM, JAMES: Los Angeles, CA, May 8, 1941.

MITCHUM, ROBERT: Bridgeport, CT, Aug. 6, 1917.

MONTALBAN, RICARDO: Mexico City, Nov. 25, 1920.

MONTAND, YVES (Yves Montand Livi): Mansummano, Tuscany, Oct. 13, 1921.

MONTGOMERY, BELINDA: Winnipeg, Can., July 23, 1950.

MONTGOMERY, ELIZABETH: Los Angeles, Apr. 15, 1933. AADA.

MONTGOMERY, GEORGE (George Letz): Brady, MT, Aug. 29, 1916. U. Mont.

MOON, KEITH: London, Aug. 23, 1947.

MOOR, BILL: Toledo, OH, July 13, 1931. Northwestern.

MOORE, CONSTANCE: Sioux City, IA, Jan. 18, 1919.

MOORE, DICK: Los Angeles, Sept. 12, 1925.

MOORE, DUDLEY: London, Apr. 19, 1935.

MOORE, FRANK: Bay-de-Verde, Newfoundland, 1946.

MOORE, KIERON: County Cork, Ire., 1925. St. Mary's College.

MOORE, MARY TYLER: Brooklyn, Dec. 29, 1936.

MOORE, ROGER: London, Oct. 14, 1927. RADA.

MOORE, TERRY (Helen Koford): Los Angeles, Jan. 7, 1929.

MOREAU, JEANNE: Paris, Jan. 23, 1928.

MORENO, RITA (Rosita Alverio): Humacao, P.R., Dec. 11, 1931.

MORGAN, DENNIS (Stanley Morner): Prentice, WI, Dec. 10, 1910. Carroll College.

MORGAN, HARRY (HENRY) (Harry Bratsburg): Detroit, Apr. 10, 1915. U. Chicago.

MORGAN, MICHELE (Simone Roussel): Paris, Feb. 29, 1920. Paris Dramatic School.

MORIARTY, CATHY: Bronx, NY, 1961.

MORIARTY, MICHAEL: Detroit, MI, Apr. 5, 1941. Dartmouth.

MORISON, PATRICIA: NYC, 1915.

MORLEY, ROBERT: Wiltshire, Eng., May 26, 1908. RADA.

MORRIS, GREG: Cleveland, OH, 1934. Ohio State.

MORRIS, HOWARD: NYC, Sept. 4, 1919. NYU.

MORSE, DAVID: Hamilton, MA, 1953.

MORSE, ROBERT: Newton, MA, May 18, 1931.

MOSS, ARNOLD: NYC, Jan. 28, 1910. CCNY.

MULLIGAN, RICHARD: NYC, Nov. 13, 1932.

MURPHY, GEORGE: New Haven, CT, July 4, 1902. Yale.

MURPHY, MICHAEL: Los Angeles, CA, 1949.

MURRAY, BILL: Evanston, IL, Sept. 21, 1950. Regis Col.

MURRAY, DON: Hollywood, July 31, 1929. AADA.

MURRAY, KEN (Don Court): NYC, July 14, 1903.

MUSANTE, TONY: Bridgeport, CT, June 30, 1936. Oberlin Col.

NABORS, JIM: Sylacauga, GA, June 12, 1932.

NADER, GEORGE: Pasadena, CA, Oct. 19, 1921. Occidental College.

NAPIER, ALAN: Birmingham, Eng., Jan. 7, 1903. Birmingham University.

NATWICK, MILDRED: Baltimore, June 19, 1908. Bryn Mawr.

NAUGHTON, JAMES: Middletown, CT, Dec. 6, 1945. Yale.

NEAL, PATRICIA: Packard, KY, Jan. 20, 1926. Northwestern U.

NEFF, HILDEGARDE (Hildegard Knef): Ulm, Ger., Dec. 28, 1925. Berlin Art Academy.

NELL, NATHALIE: Paris, Oct. 1950.

NELLIGAN, KATE: London, Ont., Can., 1951. U Toronto.

NELSON, BARRY (Robert Nielsen): Oakland, CA, 1920.

NELSON, DAVID: NYC, Oct. 24, 1936. USC.

NELSON, GENE (Gene Berg): Seattle, WA, Mar. 24, 1920.

NELSON, HARRIET HILLIARD (Peggy Lou Snyder): Des Moines, IA, July 18, 1914.

NELSON, LORI (Dixie Kay Nelson): Santa Fe, NM, Aug. 15, 1933.

NELSON, RICK (Eric Hilliard Nelson): Teaneck, NJ, May 8, 1940.

NELSON, WILLIE: Texas, Apr. 30, 1933.

NETTLETON, LOIS: Oak Park, IL. Actors Studio.

NEWHART, BOB: Chicago, IL, Sept. 5, 1929. Loyola U.

NEWLEY, ANTHONY: Hackney, London, Sept. 21, 1931.

NEWMAN, BARRY: Boston, MA, Mar. 26, 1938. Brandeis U.

NEWMAN, PAUL: Cleveland, OH, Jan. 26, 1925. Yale.

NEWMAR, JULIE (Newmeyer): Los Angeles, Aug. 16, 1935.

NEWTON-JOHN, OLIVIA: Cambridge, Eng., Sept. 26, 1948.

NICHOLAS, PAUL: London, 1945.

NICHOLS, MIKE (Michael Igor Peschkowsky); Berlin, Nov. 6, 1931. U. Chicago.

NICHOLSON, JACK: Neptune, NJ, Apr. 22, 1937.

NICKERSON, DENISE: NYC, 1959.

NICOL, ALEX: Ossining, NY, Jan. 20, 1919. Actors Studio.

NIELSEN, LESLIE: Regina, Saskatchewan, Can., Feb. 11, 1926. Neighborhood Playhouse.

NIMOY, LEONARD: Boston, MA, Mar. 26, 1931. Boston Col., Antioch Col.

NOLAN, KATHLEEN: St. Louis, MO, Sept. 27, 1933. Neighborhood Playhouse.

NOLAN, LLOYD: San Francisco, Aug. 11, 1902. Stanford U.

NOLTE, NICK: Omaha, NE, 1941. Pasadena City Col.

NORRIS, CHRISTOPHER: NYC, Oct. 7, 1943. Lincoln Square Acad.

NORRIS, CHUCK (Carlos Ray): Ryan, OK, 1939.

NORTH, HEATHER: Pasadena, CA, Dec. 13, 1950. Actors Workshop.

NORTH, SHEREE (Dawn Bethel): Los Angeles, Jan. 17, 1933. Hollywood High.

NORTON, KEN: Aug. 9, 1945.

NOVAK, KIM (Marilyn Novak): Chicago, Feb. 18, 1933. LACC.

NUREYEV, RUDOLF: Russia, Mar. 17, 1938.

NUTE, DON: Connellsville, PA, Mar. 13. Denver U.

NUYEN, FRANCE (Vannga): Marseilles, France, July 31, 1939. Beaux Arts School.

O'BRIAN, HUGH (Hugh J. Krampe): Rochester, NY, Apr. 19, 1928. Cincinnati U.

O'BRIEN, CLAY: Ray, AZ, May 6, 1961.

O'BRIEN, EDMOND: NYC, Sept. 10, 1915. Fordham, Neighborhood Playhouse.

O'BRIEN, MARGARET (Angela Maxine O'Brien): Los Angeles, Jan. 15, 1937.

O'CONNELL, ARTHUR: NYC, Mar. 29, 1908. St. John's.

O'CONNOR, CARROLL: Bronx, NY, Aug. 2, 1925. Dublin National Univ.

O'CONNOR, DONALD: Chicago, Aug. 28, 1925.

O'CONNOR, GLYNNIS: NYC, Nov. 19, 1956. NYSU.

O'CONNOR, KEVIN: Honolulu, HI, May 7, U. Hi.

O'HANLON, GEORGE: Brooklyn, NY, Nov. 23, 1917.

O'HARA, MAUREEN (Maureen FitzSimons): Dublin, Ire., Aug. 17, 1920. Abbey School.

O'HERLIHY, DAN: Wexford, Ire., May 1, 1919. National U.

O'KEEFE, MICHAEL: Paulland, NJ, 1955, NYU, AADA.

OLIVIER, LAURENCE: Dorking, Eng., May 22, 1907. Oxford.

Dennis
Patrick

Lee
Purcell

Cliff
Robertson

Gena
Rowlands

O'LOUGHLIN, GERALD S.: NYC, Dec. 23, 1921. U. Rochester.

OLSON, NANCY: Milwaukee, WI, July 14, 1928. UCLA.

O'NEAL, GRIFFIN: Los Angeles, 1965.

O'NEAL, PATRICK: Ocala, FL, Sept. 26, 1927. U. Fla.

O'NEAL, RON: Utica, NY, Sept. 1, 1937. Ohio State.

O'NEAL, RYAN: Los Angeles, Apr. 20, 1941.

O'NEAL, TATUM: Los Angeles, Nov. 5, 1963.

O'NEIL, TRICIA: Shreveport, LA, Mar. 11, 1945. Baylor U.

O'NEILL, JENNIFER: Rio de Janeiro, Feb. 20, 1949. Neighborhood Playhouse.

O'SULLIVAN, MAUREEN: Byle, Ire., May 17, 1911. Sacred Heart Convent.

O'TOOLE, ANNETTE: Houston, TX, 1953. UCLA.

O'TOOLE, PETER: Connemara, Ire., Aug. 2, 1932. RADA.

PACINO, AL: NYC, Apr. 25, 1940.

PAGE, GERALDINE: Kirksville, MO, Nov. 22, 1924. Goodman School.

PAGE, TONY (Anthony Vitiello): Bronx, NY, 1940.

PAGET, DEBRA (Debralee Griffin): Denver, Aug. 19, 1933.

PAIGE, JANIS (Donna Mae Jaden): Tacoma, WA, Sept. 16, 1922.

PALANCE, JACK (Walter Palanuik): Lattimer, PA, Feb. 18, 1920. UNC.

PALMER, BETSY: East Chicago, IN, Nov. 1, 1929. DePaul U.

PALMER, GREGG (Palmer Lee): San Francisco, Jan. 25, 1927. U. Utah.

PALMER, LILLI: Posen, Austria, May 24, 1914. Ilka Gruning School.

PAMPANINI, SILVANA: Rome, Sept. 25, 1925.

PAPAS, IRENE: Chiliomodion, Greece, Mar. 9, 1929.

PARE, MICHAEL: Brooklyn, NY, 1959.

PARKER, ELEANOR: Cedarville, OH, June 26, 1922. Pasadena Playhouse.

PARKER, FESS: Fort Worth, TX, Aug. 16, 1927. USC.

PARKER, JAMESON: 1947. Beloit Col.

PARKER, JEAN (Mae Green): Deer Lodge, MT, Aug. 11, 1912.

PARKER, SUZY (Cecelia Parker): San Antonio, TX, Oct. 28, 1933.

PARKER, WILLARD (Worster Van Eps): NYC, Feb. 5, 1912.

PARKINS, BARBARA: Vancouver, Can., May 22, 1943.

PARSONS, ESTELLE: Lynn, MA, Nov. 20, 1927. Boston U.

PARTON, DOLLY: Sevierville, TN, Jan. 19, 1946.

PATRICK, DENNIS: Philadelphia, Mar. 14, 1918.

PATTERSON, LEE: Vancouver, Can., Mar. 31, 1929. Ontario Col.

PAVAN, MARISA (Marisa Pierangeli): Cagliari, Sardinia, June 19, 1932. Torquado Tasso College.

PEACH, MARY: Durban, S. Africa, 1934.

PEARL, MINNIE (Sarah Cannon): Centerville, TN, Oct. 25, 1912.

PEARSON, BEATRICE: Denison, TX, July 27, 1920.

PECK, GREGORY: La Jolla, CA, Apr. 5, 1916. U. Calif.

PELIKAN, LISA: Paris, July 12. Juilliard.

PENHALL, BRUCE: Balboa, CA, 1958.

PEPPARD, GEORGE: Detroit, Oct. 1, 1928. Carnegie Tech.

PERKINS, ANTHONY: NYC, Apr. 14, 1932. Rollins College.

PERREAU, GIGI (Ghislaine): Los Angeles, Feb. 6, 1941.

PERRINE, VALERIE: Galveston, TX, Sept. 3, 1944. U. Ariz.

PESCOW, DONNA: Brooklyn, NY, 1954.

PETERS, BERNADETTE (Lazzara): Jamaica, NY, Feb. 28, 1948.

PETERS, BROCK: NYC, July 2, 1927. CCNY.

PETERS, JEAN (Elizabeth): Canton, OH, Oct. 15, 1926. Ohio State U.

PETTET, JOANNA: London, Nov. 16, 1944. Neighborhood Playhouse.

PFEIFFER, MICHELLE: Santa Ana, CA, 1957.

PHILLIPS, MacKENZIE: Hollywood, CA, 1960.

PHILLIPS, MICHELLE (Holly Gilliam): NJ, June 4, 1944.

PICERNI, PAUL: NYC, Dec. 1, 1922. Loyola U.

PIDGEON, WALTER: East St. John, NB, Can., Sept. 23, 1897.

PINE, PHILLIP: Hanford, CA, July 16, 1925. Actors' Lab.

PISIER, MARIE-FRANCE: Vietnam, May 10, 1944. U. Paris.

PLACE, MARY KAY: Port Arthur, TX, Sept., 1947. U. Tulsa.

PLAYTEN, ALICE: NYC, Aug. 28, 1947. NYU.

PLEASENCE, DONALD: Workshop, Eng., Oct. 5, 1919. Sheffield School.

PLESHETTE, SUZANNE: NYC, Jan. 31, 1937. Syracuse U.

PLOWRIGHT, JOAN: Scunthorpe, Brigg, Lincolnshire, Eng., Oct. 28, 1929. Old Vic.

PLUMMER, AMANDA: NYC, Mar. 23, 1957. Middlebury Col.

PLUMMER, CHRISTOPHER: Toronto, Can., Dec. 13, 1927.

PODESTA, ROSSANA: Tripoli, June 20, 1934.

POITIER, SIDNEY: Miami, FL, Feb. 27, 1924.

POLITO, LINA: Naples, Italy, Aug. 11, 1954.

POLLARD, MICHAEL J.: Pacific, NJ, May 30, 1939.

PORTER, ERIC: London, Apr. 8, 1928. Wimbledon Col.

POWELL, JANE (Suzanne Burce): Portland, OR, Apr. 1, 1928.

POWELL, ROBERT: London, June 1, 1944.

POWER, TARYN: Los Angeles, CA, 1954.

POWERS, MALA (Mary Ellen): San Francisco, Dec. 29, 1921. UCLA.

POWERS, STEFANIE (Federkiewicz): Hollywood, CA, Oct. 12, 1942.

PRENTISS, PAULA (Paula Ragusa): San Antonio, TX, Mar. 4, 1939. Northwestern U.

PRESLE, MICHELINE (Micheline Chassagne): Paris, Aug. 22, 1922. Rouleau Drama School.

PRESNELL, HARVE: Modesto, CA, Sept. 14, 1933. USC.

PRESTON, ROBERT (Robert Preston Meservey): Newton Highlands, MA, June 8, 1913. Pasadena Playhouse.

PRICE, VINCENT: St. Louis, May 27, 1911. Yale.

PRIMUS, BARRY: NYC, Feb. 16, 1938. CCNY.

PRINCE, WILLIAM: Nicholas, NY, Jan. 26, 1913. Cornell U.

PRINCIPAL, VICTORIA: Fukuoka, Japan, Mar. 3, 1950. Dade Jr. Col.

PROCHNOW, JURGEN: Germany, 1941.

PROVAL, DAVID: Brooklyn, NY, 1943.

PROVINE, DOROTHY: Deadwood, SD, Jan. 20, 1937. U. Wash.

PROWSE, JULIET: Bombay, India, Sept. 25, 1936.

PRYOR, RICHARD: Peoria, IL, Dec. 1, 1940.

PURCELL, LEE: Cherry Point, NC, June 15, 1947. Stephens.

PURCELL, NOEL: Dublin, Ire., Dec. 23, 1900. Irish Christian Brothers.

PURDOM, EDMUND: Welwyn Garden City, Eng., Dec. 19, 1924. St. Ignatius College.

PYLE, DENVER: Bethune, CO, 1920.

QUAYLE, ANTHONY: Lancashire, Eng., Sept. 7, 1913. Old Vic School.

QUINE, RICHARD: Detroit, MI, Nov. 12, 1920.

QUINLAN, KATHLEEN: Mill Valley, CA, Nov. 19, 1954.

QUINN, AIDAN: Chicago, IL, 1959.

QUINN, ANTHONY: Chihuahua, Mex., Apr. 21, 1915.

RADNER, GILDA: Detroit, MI, June 28, 1946.

RAFFERTY, FRANCES: Sioux City, IA, June 16, 1922. UCLA.

RAFFIN, DEBORAH: Los Angeles, Mar. 13, 1953. Valley Col.

RAINES, ELLA (Ella Wallace): Snoqualmie Falls, WA, Aug. 6, 1921. U. Wash.

RAMPLING, CHARLOTTE: Surmer, Eng., Feb. 5, 1946. U. Madrid.

RAMSEY, LOGAN: Long Beach, CA, Mar. 21, 1921. St. Joseph.

RANDALL, TONY: Tulsa, OK, Feb. 26, 1920. Northwestern U.

RANDELL, RON: Sydney, Australia, Oct. 8, 1920. St. Mary's Col.

RASULALA, THALMUS (Jack Crowder): Miami, FL, Nov. 15, 1939. U. Redlands.

RAY, ALDO (Aldo DeRe): Pen Argyl, PA, Sept. 25, 1926. UCLA.

RAYE, MARTHA (Margie Yvonne Reed): Butte, MT, Aug. 27, 1916.

RAYMOND, GENE (Raymond Guion): NYC, Aug. 13, 1908.

REAGAN, RONALD: Tampico, IL, Feb. 6, 1911. Eureka College.

REASON, REX: Berlin, Ger., Nov. 30, 1928. Pasadena Playhouse.

REDDY, HELEN: Australia, Oct. 25, 1942.

REDFORD, ROBERT: Santa Monica, CA, Aug. 18, 1937. AADA.

REDGRAVE, CORIN: London, July 16, 1939.

REDGRAVE, LYNN: London, Mar. 8, 1943.

REDGRAVE, MICHAEL: Bristol, Eng., Mar. 20, 1908. Cambridge.

REDGRAVE, VANESSA: London, Jan. 30, 1937.

REDMAN, JOYCE: County Mayo, Ire., 1919. RADA.

REED, DONNA (Donna Mullenger): Denison, IA, Jan. 27, 1921. LACC.

REED, OLIVER: Wimbledon, Eng., Feb. 13, 1938.

REED, REX: Ft. Worth, TX, Oct. 2, 1939. LSU.

REEMS, HARRY (Herbert Streicher): Bronx, NY, 1947. U. Pittsburgh.

REEVE, CHRISTOPHER: NJ, Sept. 25, 1952. Cornell, Juilliard.

REEVES, STEVE: Glasgow, MT, Jan. 21, 1926.

REID, ELLIOTT: NYC, Jan. 16, 1920.

REINER, CARL: NYC, Mar. 20, 1922. Georgetown.

REINER, ROBERT: NYC, 1945. UCLA.

REMICK, LEE: Quincy, MA. Dec. 14, 1935. Barnard College.

RETTIG, TOMMY: Jackson Heights, NY, Dec. 10, 1941.

REVILL, CLIVE: Wellington, NZ, Apr. 18, 1930.

REY, FERNANDO: La Coruna, Spain, 1917.

REYNOLDS, BURT: Waycross, GA, Feb. 11, 1935. Fla. State U.

REYNOLDS, DEBBIE (Mary Frances Reynolds): El Paso, TX, Apr. 1, 1932.

REYNOLDS, MARJORIE: Buhl, ID, Aug. 12, 1921.

RHOADES, BARBARA: Poughkeepsie, NY, 1947.

RICH, IRENE: Buffalo, NY, Oct. 13, 1891. St. Margaret's School.

RICHARDS, JEFF (Richard Mansfield Taylor): Portland, OR, Nov. 1. USC.

RICKLES, DON: NYC, May 8, 1926. AADA.

RIEGERT, PETER: NYC, Apr. 11, 1947. U Buffalo.

RIGG, DIANA: Doncaster, Eng., July 20, 1938. RADA.

RITTER, JOHN: Burbank, CA, Sept. 17, 1948. U. S. Cal.

ROBARDS, JASON: Chicago, July 26, 1922. AADA.

ROBERTS, ERIC: Biloxi, MS, 1956. RADA.

ROBERTS, RALPH: Salisbury, NC, Aug. 17, 1922. UNC.

ROBERTS, TANYA: (Leigh): NYC, 1965.

ROBERTS, TONY: NYC, Oct. 22, 1939. Northwestern U.

ROBERTSON, CLIFF: La Jolla, CA, Sept. 9, 1925. Antioch Col.

ROBERTSON, DALE: Oklahoma City, July 14, 1923.

ROBINSON, CHRIS: Nov. 5, 1938, West Palm Beach, FL. LACC.

ROBINSON, JAY: NYC, Apr. 14, 1930.

ROBINSON, ROGER: Seattle, WA, May 2, 1941. USC.

ROBSON, FLORA: South Shields, Eng., Mar. 28, 1902. RADA.

ROCHEFORT, JEAN: Paris, 1930.

ROGERS, CHARLES "BUDDY": Olathe, KS, Aug. 13, 1904. U. Kan.

ROGERS, GINGER (Virginia Katherine McMath): Independence, MO, July 16, 1911.

ROGERS, ROY (Leonard Slye): Cincinnati, Nov. 5, 1912.

ROGERS, WAYNE: Birmingham, AL, Apr. 7, 1933. Princeton.

ROLAND, GILBERT (Luis Antonio Damaso De Alonso): Juarez, Mex., Dec. 11, 1905.

ROLLINS, HOWARD E., JR.: 1951, Baltimore, MD.

ROMAN, RUTH: Boston, Dec. 23, 1922. Bishop Lee Dramatic School.

ROME, SIDNE: Akron, OH. Carnegie-Mellon.

ROMERO, CESAR: NYC, Feb. 15, 1907. Collegiate School.

ROONEY, MICKEY (Joe Yule, Jr.): Brooklyn, Sept. 23, 1920.

ROSS, DIANA: Detroit, MI, Mar. 26, 1944.

ROSS, KATHARINE: Hollywood, Jan. 29, 1943. Santa Rosa Col.

ROSSELLINI, ISABELLA: Rome, June 18, 1952.

ROSSITER, LEONARD: Liverpool, Eng., Oct. 21, 1926.

ROUNDTREE, RICHARD: New Rochelle, NY, Sept. 7, 1942. Southern Ill.

ROURKE, MICKEY: Miami, FL, 1950.

ROWLANDS, GENA: Cambria, WI, June 19, 1936.

RUBIN, ANDREW: New Bedford, MA, June 22, 1946. AADA.

RUDD, PAUL: Boston, MA, May 15, 1940.

RULE, JANICE: Cincinnati, OH, Aug. 15, 1931.

RUPERT, MICHAEL: Denver, CO, Oct. 23, 1951. Pasadena Playhouse.

RUSH, BARBARA: Denver, CO, Jan. 4, 1929. U. Calif.

RUSSELL, JANE: Bemidji, MI, June 21, 1921. Max Reinhardt School.

RUSSELL, JOHN: Los Angeles, Jan. 3, 1921. U. Calif.

RUSSELL, KURT: Springfield, MA, Mar. 17, 1951.

RUTHERFORD, ANN: Toronto, Can., Nov. 2, 1917.

RUYMEN, AYN: Brooklyn, July 18, 1947. HB Studio.

SACCHI, ROBERT: Bronx, NY, 1941. NYU.

SAINT, EVA MARIE: Newark, NJ, July 4, 1924. Bowling Green State U.

ST. JACQUES, RAYMOND (James Arthur Johnson): CT.

ST. JAMES, SUSAN (Suzie Jane Miller): Los Angeles, Aug. 14. Conn. Col.

ST. JOHN, BETTA: Hawthorne, CA, Nov. 26, 1929.

ST. JOHN, JILL (Jill Oppenheim): Los Angeles, Aug. 19, 1940.

SALDANA, THERESA: Brooklyn, NY, 1955.

SALMI, ALBERT: Coney Island, NY, 1925. Actors Studio.

SALT, JENNIFER: Los Angeles, Sept. 4, 1944. Sarah Lawrence Col.

SANDS, TOMMY: Chicago, Aug. 27, 1937.

SAN JUAN, OLGA: NYC, Mar. 16, 1927.

SARANDON, CHRIS: Beckley, WV, July 24, 1942. U. WVa., Catholic U.

SARANDON, SUSAN (Tomalin): NYC, Oct. 4, 1946. Catholic U.

SARGENT, RICHARD (Richard Cox): Carmel, CA, 1933. Stanford.

SARRAZIN, MICHAEL: Quebec City, Can., May 22, 1940.

SAVAGE, JOHN (Youngs): Long Island, NY, Aug. 25, 1949. AADA.

SAVALAS, TELLY (Aristotle): Garden City, NY, Jan. 21, 1925. Columbia.

SAVOY, TERESA ANN: London, July 18, 1955.

SAXON, JOHN (Carmen Orrico): Brooklyn, Aug. 5, 1935.

SCALIA, JACK: Bensonhurst, NY, 1951.

SCARWID, DIANA: Savannah, GA. AADA, Pace U.

SCHEIDER, ROY: Orange, NJ, Nov. 10, 1935. Franklin-Marshall.

SCHELL, MARIA: Vienna, Jan. 15, 1926.

SCHELL, MAXIMILIAN: Vienna, Dec. 8, 1930.

SCHNEIDER, MARIA: Paris, Mar. 27, 1952.

SCHRODER, RICKY: Staten Island, NY, Apr. 13, 1970.

SCHWARZENEGGER, ARNOLD: Austria, 1947.

SCHYGULLA, HANNA: Katlowitz, Poland. 1943.

SCOFIELD, PAUL: Hurstpierpoint, Eng., Jan. 21, 1922. London Mask Theatre School.

SCOTT, DEBRALEE: Elizabeth, NJ, Apr. 2.

SCOTT, GEORGE C.: Wise, VA, Oct. 18, 1927. U. Mo.

229

Susan Sarandon	John Shea	Kathleen Turner	James Victor	Rachel Ward	Michael York

SCOTT, GORDON (Gordon M. Werschkul): Portland, OR, Aug. 3, 1927. Oregon U.

SCOTT, MARTHA: Jamesport, MO, Sept. 22, 1914. U. Mich.

SCOTT, RANDOLPH: Orange County, VA, Jan. 23, 1903. UNC.

SCOTT-TAYLOR, JONATHAN: Brazil, 1962.

SEAGULL, BARBARA HERSHEY (Herzstein): Hollywood, Feb. 5, 1948.

SEARS, HEATHER: London, 1935.

SECOMBE, HARRY: Swansea, Wales, Sept. 8, 1921.

SEGAL, GEORGE: NYC, Feb. 13, 1934. Columbia.

SELLARS, ELIZABETH: Glasgow, Scot., May 6, 1923.

SELWART, TONIO: Watenberg, Ger., June 9, 1906. Munich U.

SERNAS, JACQUES: Lithuania, July 30, 1925.

SEYLER, ATHENE (Athene Hannen): London, May 31, 1889.

SEYMOUR, ANNE: NYC, Sept. 11, 1909. American Laboratory Theatre.

SEYMOUR, JANE (Joyce Frankenberg): Hillingdon, Eng., Feb. 15, 1951.

SHARIF, OMAR (Michel Shalboub): Alexandria, Egypt, Apr. 10, 1932. Victoria Col.

SHARKEY, RAY: Brooklyn, NY, 1952. HB Studio.

SHATNER, WILLIAM: Montreal, Can., Mar. 22, 1931. McGill U.

SHAW, SEBASTIAN: Holt, Eng., May 29, 1905. Gresham School.

SHAW, STAN: Chicago, IL, 1952.

SHAWLEE, JOAN: Forest Hills, NY, Mar. 5, 1929.

SHAWN, DICK (Richard Shulefand): Buffalo, NY, Dec. 1, 1929. U. Miami.

SHEA, JOHN V.: North Conway, NH, Apr. 14, 1949. Bates, Yale.

SHEARER, MOIRA: Dunfermline, Scot., Jan. 17, 1926. London Theatre School.

SHEEDY, ALLY: NYC, June 13, 1962. USC.

SHEEN, MARTIN (Ramon Estevez): Dayton, OH, Aug. 3, 1940.

SHEFFIELD, JOHN: Pasadena, CA, Apr. 11, 1931. UCLA.

SHEPARD, SAM (Rogers): Ft. Sheridan, IL, Nov. 5, 1943.

SHEPHERD, CYBIL: Memphis, TN, Feb. 18, 1950. Hunter, NYU.

SHIELDS, BROOKE: NYC, May 31, 1965.

SHIRE, TALIA: Lake Success, NY. Yale.

SHORE, DINAH (Frances Rose Shore): Winchester, TN, Mar. 1, 1917. Vanderbilt U.

SHOWALTER, MAX (formerly Casey Adams): Caldwell, KS, June 2, 1917. Pasadena Playhouse.

SIDNEY, SYLVIA: NYC, Aug. 8, 1910. Theatre Guild School.

SIGNORET, SIMONE (Simone Kaminker): Wiesbaden, Ger., Mar. 25, 1921. Solange Sicard School.

SILVERS, PHIL (Philip Silversmith): Brooklyn, May 11, 1911.

SIMMONS, JEAN: London, Jan. 31, 1929. Aida Foster School.

SIMON, SIMONE: Marseilles, France, Apr. 23, 1910.

SIMPSON, O. J. (Orenthal James): San Francisco, CA, July 9, 1947. UCLA.

SINATRA, FRANK: Hoboken, NJ, Dec. 12, 1915.

SINCLAIR, JOHN (Gianluigi Loffredo): Rome, Italy, 1946.

SINDEN, DONALD: Plymouth, Eng., Oct. 9, 1923. Webber-Douglas.

SKALA, LILIA: Vienna. U. Dresden.

SKELTON, RED (Richard): Vincennes, IN, July 18, 1910.

SKERRITT, TOM: Detroit, MI, 1935. Wayne State U.

SMITH, ALEXIS: Penticton, Can., June 8, 1921. LACC.

SMITH, CHARLES MARTIN: Los Angeles, CA, 1954. CalState U.

SMITH, JACLYN: Houston, TX, Oct. 26, 1947.

SMITH, JOHN (Robert E. Van Orden): Los Angeles, Mar. 6, 1931. UCLA.

SMITH, KATE (Kathryn Elizabeth): Greenville, VA, May 1, 1909.

SMITH, KENT: NYC, Mar. 19, 1907. Harvard U.

SMITH, LOIS: Topeka, KS, Nov. 3, 1930. U. Wash.

SMITH, MAGGIE: Ilford, Eng., Dec. 28, 1934.

SMITH, ROGER: South Gate, CA, Dec. 18, 1932. U. Ariz.

SMITHERS, WILLIAM: Richmond, VA, July 10, 1927. Catholic U.

SNODGRESS, CARRIE: Chicago, Oct. 27, 1946. UNI.

SOLOMON, BRUCE: NYC, 1944. U. Miami, Wayne State U.

SOMERS, SUZANNE (Mahoney): San Bruno, CA, Oct. 16, 1946. Lone Mt. Col.

SOMMER, ELKE (Schletz): Berlin, Nov. 5, 1940.

SORDI, ALBERTO: Rome, Italy, 1919.

SORVINO, PAUL: NYC, 1939. AMDA.

SOTHERN, ANN (Harriet Lake): Valley City, ND, Jan. 22, 1907. Washington U.

SOUL, DAVID: Aug. 28, 1943.

SPACEK, SISSY: Quitman, TX, Dec. 25, 1949. Actors Studio.

SPANO, VINCENT: Brooklyn, NY, Oct. 18, 1962.

SPENSER, JEREMY: Ceylon, 1937.

SPRINGER, GARY: NYC, July 29, 1954. Hunter Col.

SPRINGFIELD, RICK: Australia, 1950.

STACK, ROBERT: Los Angeles, Jan. 13, 1919. USC.

STADLEN, LEWIS J.: Brooklyn, Mar. 7, 1947. Neighborhood Playhouse.

STAFFORD, NANCY: Ft. Lauderdale, FL.

STALLONE, SYLVESTER: NYC, July 6, 1946. U. Miami.

STAMP, TERENCE: London, 1940.

STANDER, LIONEL: NYC, Jan. 11, 1908. UNC.

STANG, ARNOLD: Chelsea, MA, Sept. 28, 1925.

STANLEY, KIM (Patricia Reid): Tularosa, NM, Feb. 11, 1925. U. Tex.

STANWYCK, BARBARA (Ruby Stevens): Brooklyn, July 16, 1907.

STAPLETON, JEAN: NYC, Jan. 19, 1923.

STAPLETON, MAUREEN: Troy, NY, June 21, 1925.

STEEL, ANTHONY: London, May 21, 1920. Cambridge.

STEELE, TOMMY: London, Dec. 17, 1936.

STEENBURGEN, MARY: Newport, AR, 1953. Neighborhood Playhouse.

STEIGER, ROD: Westhampton, NY, Apr. 14, 1925.

STERLING, JAN (Jane Sterling Adriance): NYC, Apr. 3, 1923. Fay Compton School.

STERLING, ROBERT (William Sterling Hart): Newcastle, PA, Nov. 13, 1917. U. Pittsburgh.

STERN, DANIEL: Bethesda, MD, 1957.

STEVENS, ANDREW: Memphis, TN, June 10, 1955.

STEVENS, CONNIE (Concetta Ann Ingolia•): Brooklyn, Aug. 8, 1938. Hollywood Professional School.

STEVENS, KAYE (Catherine): Pittsburgh, July 21, 1933.

STEVENS, MARK (Richard): Cleveland, OH, Dec. 13, 1920.

STEVENS, STELLA (Estelle Eggleston): Hot Coffee, MS, Oct. 1, 1936.

STEVENSON, PARKER: CT, 1953.

STEWART, ALEXANDRA: Montreal, Can., June 10, 1939. Louvre.

STEWART, ELAINE: Montclair, NJ, May 31, 1929.

STEWART, JAMES: Indiana, PA, May 20, 1908. Princeton.

STEWART, MARTHA (Martha Haworth): Bardwell, KY, Oct. 7, 1922.

STIMSON, SARA: Helotes, TX, 1973.

STOCKWELL, DEAN: Hollywood, Mar. 5, 1936.

STOCKWELL, JOHN: Texas, 1961. Harvard.

STORM, GALE (Josephine Cottle): Bloomington, TX, Apr. 5, 1922.

STRAIGHT, BEATRICE: Old Westbury, NY, Aug. 2, 1916. Dartington Hall.

STRASBERG, SUSAN: NYC, May 22, 1938.

STRASSMAN, MARCIA: New Jersey, 1949.

STRAUD, DON: Hawaii, 1943.

STRAUSS, PETER: NY, 1947.

STREEP, MERYL (Mary Louise): Basking Ridge, NJ, Sept. 22, 1949. Vassar, Yale.

STREISAND, BARBRA: Brooklyn, Apr. 24, 1942.

STRITCH, ELAINE: Detoit, MI, Feb. 2, 1925. Drama Workshop.

STRODE, WOODY: Los Angeles, 1914.

STRUTHERS, SALLY: Portland, OR, July 28, 1948. Pasadena Playhouse.

SULLIVAN, BARRY (Patrick Barry): NYC, Aug. 29, 1912. NYU.

SUMMER, DONNA (LaDonna Gaines): Boston, MA, Dec. 31, 1948.

SUTHERLAND, DONALD: St. John, New Brunswick, Can., July 17, 1934. U. Toronto.

SVENSON, BO: Goteborg, Swed., Feb. 13, 1941. UCLA.

SWEET, BLANCHE: Chicago, 1896.

SWINBURNE, NORA: Bath, Eng., July 24, 1902. RADA.

SWIT, LORETTA: Passaic, NJ, Nov. 4. AADA.

SYLVESTER, WILLIAM: Oakland, CA, Jan. 31, 1922. RADA.

SYMS, SYLVIA: London, June 1, 1934. Convent School.

T, MR. (Lawrence Tero): Chicago, 1952.

TABORI, KRISTOFFER (Siegel): Los Angeles, Aug. 4, 1952.

TAKEI, GEORGE: Los Angeles, CA, Apr. 20. UCLA.

TALBOT, LYLE (Lysle Hollywood): Pittsburgh, Feb. 8, 1904.

TALBOT, NITA: NYC, Aug. 8, 1930. Irvine Studio School.

TAMBLYN, RUSS: Los Angeles, Dec. 30, 1934.

TANDY, JESSICA: London, June 7, 1909. Dame Owens' School.

TAYLOR, DON: Freeport, PA, Dec. 13, 1920. Penn State U.

TAYLOR, ELIZABETH: London, Feb. 27, 1932. Byron House School.

TAYLOR, KENT (Louis Weiss): Nashua, IA, May 11, 1906.

TAYLOR, ROD (Robert): Sydney, Aust., Jan. 11, 1929

TAYLOR-YOUNG, LEIGH: Wash., DC, Jan. 25, 1945. Northwestern.

TEAGUE, ANTHONY SKOOTER: Jacksboro, TX, Jan. 4, 1940.

TEEFY, MAUREEN: Minneapolis, MN, 1954; Juilliard.

TEMPLE, SHIRLEY: Santa Monica, CA, Apr. 23, 1927.

TERRY-THOMAS (Thomas Terry Hoar Stevens): Finchley, London, July 14, 1911. Ardingly College.

TERZIEFF, LAURENT: Paris, June 25, 1935.

THACKER, RUSS: Washington, DC, June 23, 1946, Montgomery Col.

THAXTER, PHYLLIS: Portland, ME, Nov. 20, 1921. St. Genevieve.

THELEN, JODI: St. Cloud, MN., 1963.

THOMAS, DANNY (Amos Jacobs): Deerfield, MI, Jan. 6, 1914.

THOMAS, MARLO (Margaret): Detroit, Nov. 21, 1938. USC.

THOMAS, PHILIP: Columbus, OH, May 26, 1949. Oakwood Col.

THOMAS, RICHARD: NYC, June 13, 1951. Columbia.

THOMPSON, JACK (John Payne): Sydney, Aus., 1940. U. Brisbane.

THOMPSON, MARSHALL: Peoria, IL, Nov. 27, 1925. Occidental.

THOMPSON, REX: NYC, Dec. 14, 1942.

THOMPSON, SADA: Des Moines, IA, Sept. 27, 1929. Carnegie Tech.

THULIN, INGRID: Solleftea, Sweden, Jan. 27, 1929. Royal Drama Theatre.

TICOTIN, RACHEL: Bronx, NY, 1958.

TIERNEY, GENE: Brooklyn, Nov. 20, 1920. Miss Farmer's School.

TIERNEY, LAWRENCE: Brooklyn, Mar. 15, 1919. Manhattan College.

TIFFIN, PAMELA (Wonso): Oklahoma City, Oct. 13, 1942.

TODD, RICHARD: Dublin, Ire., June 11, 1919. Shrewsbury School.

TOLO, MARILU: Rome, Italy, 1944.

TOMLIN, LILY: Detroit, MI, Sept. 1, 1939. Wayne State U.

TOPOL (Chaim Topol): Tel-Aviv, Israel, Sept. 9, 1935.

TORN, RIP: Temple, TX, Feb. 6, 1931. U. Tex.

TORRES, LIZ: NYC, 1947. NYU.

TOTTER, AUDREY: Joliet, IL, Dec. 20, 1918.

TRAVERS, BILL: Newcastle-on-Tyne, Engl, Jan. 3, 1922.

TRAVIS, RICHARD (William Justice): Carlsbad, NM, Apr. 17, 1913.

TRAVOLTA, JOEY: Englewood, NJ, 1952.

TRAVOLTA, JOHN: Englewood, NJ, Feb. 18, 1954.

TREMAYNE, LES: London, Apr. 16, 1913. Northwestern, Columbia, UCLA.

TREVOR, CLAIRE (Wemlinger): NYC, March 8, 1909.

TRINTIGNANT, JEAN-LOUIS: Pont-St. Esprit, France, Dec. 11, 1930. Dullin-Balachova Drama School.

TRUFFAUT, FRANCOIS: Paris, Feb. 6, 1932.

TRYON, TOM: Hartford, CT, Jan. 14, 1926. Yale.

TSOPEI, CORINNA: Athens, Greece, June 21, 1944.

TUCKER, FORREST: Plainfield, IN, Feb. 12, 1919. George Washington U.

TURNER, KATHLEEN: Springfield, MO, June 19, 1954. UMd.

TURNER, LANA (Julia Jean Mildred Frances Turner): Wallace, ID, Feb. 8, 1921.

TUSHINGHAM, RITA: Liverpool, Eng., 1940.

TUTIN, DOROTHY: London, Apr. 8, 1930.

TUTTLE, LURENE: Pleasant Lake, IN, Aug. 20, 1906. USC.

TWIGGY (Lesley Hornby): London, Sept. 19, 1949.

TYLER, BEVERLY (Beverly Jean Saul): Scranton, PA, July 5, 1928.

TYRRELL, SUSAN: San Francisco, 1946.

TYSON, CICELY: NYC, Dec. 19.

UGGAMS, LESLIE: NYC, May 25, 1943.

ULLMANN, LIV: Tokyo, Dec. 10, 1938. Webber-Douglas Acad.

USTINOV, PETER: London, Apr. 16, 1921. WEstminster School.

VACCARO, BRENDA: Brooklyn, Nov. 18, 1939. Neighborhood Playhouse.

VALLEE, RUDY (Hubert): Island Pond, VT, July 28, 1901. Yale.

VALLI, ALIDA: Pola, Italy, May 31, 1921. Rome Academy of Drama.

VALLONE, RAF: Riogio, Italy, Feb. 17, 1916. Turin U.

VAN CLEEF, LEE: Somerville, NJ, Jan. 9, 1925.

VAN DE VEN, MONIQUE: Holland, 1957.

VAN DEVERE, TRISH (Patricia Dressel): Englewood Cliffs, NJ, Mar. 9, 1945. Ohio Wesleyan.

VAN DOREN, MAMIE (Joan Lucile Olander): Rowena, SD, Feb. 6, 1933.

VAN DYKE, DICK: West Plains, MO, Dec. 13, 1925.

VAN FLEET, JO: Oakland, CA, 1922.

VAN PATTEN, DICK: NYC, Dec. 9, 1928.

VAN PATTEN, JOYCE: NYC, Mar. 9, 1934.

VAUGHN, ROBERT: NYC, Nov. 22, 1932. USC.

VEGA, ISELA: Mexico, 1940.

VENNERA, CHICK: Herkimer, NY, Mar. 27, 1952. Passadena Playhouse.

VENORA, DIANE: Hartford, Ct., 1952. Juilliard.

VENTURA, LINO: Parma, Italy, July 14, 1919.

VENUTA, BENAY: San Francisco, Jan. 27, 1911.

VERDON, GWEN: Culver City, CA, Jan. 13, 1925.

VEREEN, BEN: Miami, FL, Oct. 10, 1946.

VICTOR, JAMES: (Lincoln Rafael Peralta Diaz) Santiago, D.R., July 27, 1939. Haaren HS/NYC.

VILLECHAIZE, HERVE: Paris, Apr. 23, 1943.

VINCENT, JAN-MICHAEL: Denver, CO, July 15, 1944. Ventura.

VIOLET, ULTRA (Isabelle Collin-Dufresne): Grenoble, France.

VITALE, MILLY: Rome, Italy, July 16, 1938. Lycee Chateaubriand.

VOHS, JOAN: St. Albans, NY, July 30, 1931.

VOIGHT, JON: Yonkers, NY, Dec. 29, 1938. Catholic U.

VOLONTE, GIAN MARIA: Milan, Italy, Apr. 9, 1933.

VON SYDOW, MAX: Lund, Swed., July 10, 1929. Royal Drama Theatre.

WAGNER, LINDSAY: Los Angeles, June 22, 1949.

WAGNER, ROBERT: Detroit, Feb. 10, 1930.

WAHL, KEN: Chicago, IL, 1957.

WAITE, GENEVIEVE: South Africa, 1949.

WALKEN, CHRISTOPHER: Astoria, NY, Mar. 31, 1943. Hofstra.

WALKER, CLINT: Hartford, IL, May 30, 1927. USC.

WALKER, NANCY (Ann Myrtle Swoyer): Philadelphia, May 10, 1921.

WALLACH, ELI: Brooklyn, Dec. 7, 1915. CCNY, U. Tex.

WALLACH, ROBERTA: NYC, Aug. 2, 1955.

WALLIS, SHANI: London, Apr. 5, 1941.

WALSTON, RAY: New Orleans, Nov. 22, 1917. Cleveland Playhouse.

WALTER, JESSICA: Brooklyn, NY, Jan. 31, 1940. Neighborhood Playhouse.

WANAMAKER, SAM: Chicago, June 14, 1919. Drake.

WARD, BURT (Gervis): Los Angeles, July 6, 1945.

WARD, RACHEL: London, 1957.

WARD, SIMON: London, 1941.

WARDEN, JACK: Newark, NJ, Sept. 18, 1920.

WARNER, DAVID: Manchester, Eng., 1941. RADA.

WARREN, JENNIFER: NYC, Aug. 12, 1941. U. Wisc.

WARREN, LESLEY ANN: NYC, Aug. 16, 1946.

WARREN, MICHAEL: South Bend, IN, 1946. UCLA.

WARRICK, RUTH: St. Joseph, MO, June 29, 1915. U. Mo.

WASHBOURNE, MONA: Birmingham, Eng., Nov. 27, 1903.

WASHINGTON, DENZEL: Mt. Vernon, NY, Dec. 28, 1954. Fordham.

WASSON, CRAIG: Ontario, OR, Mar. 15, 1954. UOre.

WATERSTON, SAM: Cambridge, MA, Nov. 15, 1940. Yale.

WATLING, JACK: London, Jan. 13, 1923. Italia Conti School.

WATSON, DOUGLASS: Jackson, GA, Feb. 24, 1921. UNC.

WAYNE, DAVID (Wayne McKeehan): Travers City, MI, Jan. 30, 1914. Western Michigan State U.

WAYNE, PATRICK: Los Angeles, July 15, 1939. Loyola.

WEATHERS, CARL: New Orleans, LA, 1948. Long Beach CC.

WEAVER, DENNIS: Joplin, MO, June 4, 1924. U. Okla.

WEAVER, MARJORIE: Crossville, TN, Mar. 2, 1913. Indiana U.

WEAVER, SIGOURNEY (Susan): NYC, 1949. Stanford, Yale.

WEBBER, ROBERT: Santa Ana, CA, Sept. 14, 1925. Compton Jr. Col.

WEDGEWORTH, ANN: Abilene, TX, Jan. 21, 1935. U. Tex.

WELCH, RAQUEL (Tejada): Chicago, Sept. 5, 1940.

WELD, TUESDAY (Susan): NYC, Aug. 27, 1943. Hollywood Professional School.

WELDON, JOAN: San Francisco, Aug. 5, 1933. San Francisco Conservatory.

WELLES, GWEN: NYC, Mar. 4.

WELLES, ORSON: Kenosha, WI, May 6, 1915. Todd School.

WERNER, OSKAR: Vienna, Nov. 13, 1922.

WESTON, JACK (Morris Weinstein): Cleveland, OH, Aug. 21, 1915.

WHITAKER, JOHNNY: Van Nuys, CA, Dec. 13, 1959 .

WHITE, CAROL: London, Apr. 1, 1944.

WHITE, CHARLES: Perth Amboy, NJ, Aug. 29, 1920. Rutgers U.

WHITE, JESSE: Buffalo, NY, Jan. 3, 1919.

WHITMAN, STUART: San Francisco, Feb. 1, 1929. CCLA

WHITMORE, JAMES: White Plains, NY, Oct. 1, 1921. Yale.

WHITNEY, GRACE LEE: Detroit, MI, Apr. 1, 1930.

WIDDOES, KATHLEEN: Wilmington, DE, Mar. 21, 1939.

WIDMARK, RICHARD: Sunrise, MN, Dec. 26, 1914. Lake Forest.

WILCOX-HORNE, COLIN: Highlands, NC, Feb. 4, 1937. U. Tenn.

WILDE, CORNEL: NYC, Oct. 13, 1915. CCNY, Columbia.

WILDER, GENE (Jerome Silberman): Milwaukee, WI, June 11, 1935. U. Iowa.

WILLIAMS, BILLY DEE: NYC, Apr. 6, 1937.

WILLIAMS, CINDY: Van Nuys, CA, Aug. 22, 1947. LACC.

WILLIAMS, DICK A.: Chicago, IL, Aug. 9, 1938.

WILLIAMS, EMLYN: Mostyn, Wales, Nov. 26, 1905. Oxford.

WILLIAMS, ESTHER: Los Angeles, Aug. 8, 1921.

WILLIAMS, GRANT: NYC, Aug. 18, 1930. Queens College.

WILLIAMS, ROBIN: Chicago, IL, July 21, 1952.

WILLIAMS, TREAT (Richard): Rowayton, CT. 1952.

WILLIAMSON, FRED: Gary, IN, Mar. 5, 1938. Northwestern.

WILSON, DEMOND: NYC, Oct. 13, 1946. Hunter Col.

WILSON, FLIP (Clerow Wilson): Jersey City, NJ, Dec. 8, 1933.

WILSON, LAMBERT: Paris, 1959.

WILSON, NANCY: Chillicothe, OH, Feb. 20, 1937.

WILSON, SCOTT: Atlanta, GA, 1942.

WINDE, BEATRICE: Chicago, Jan. 6.

WINDOM, WILLIAM: NYC, Sept. 28, 1923. Williams Col.

WINDSOR, MARIE (Emily Marie Bertelson): Marysvale, UT, Dec. 11, 1924. Brigham Young U.

WINFIELD, PAUL: Los Angeles, 1940. UCLA.

WINGER, DEBRA: Cleveland, OH, 1956.

WINKLER, HENRY: NYC, Oct. 30, 1945. Yale.

WINN, KITTY: Wash., D.C., 1944. Boston U.

WINTERS, JONATHAN: Dayton, OH, Nov. 11, 1925. Kenyon Col.

WINTERS, ROLAND: Boston, Nov. 22, 1904.

WINTERS, SHELLEY (Shirley Schrift): St. Louis, Aug. 18, 1922. Wayne U.

WINWOOD, ESTELLE: Kent, Eng., Jan. 24, 1883. Lyric State Academy.

WITHERS, GOOGIE: Karachi, India, Mar. 12, 1917. Italia Conti.

WITHERS, JANE: Atlanta, GA, Apr. 12, 1926.

WOODLAWN, HOLLY (Harold Ajzenberg): Juana Diaz, PR, 1947.

WOODS, JAMES: Vernal, UT, Apr. 18, 1947. MIT.

WOODWARD, JOANNE: Thomasville, GA, Feb. 27, 1930. Neighborhood Playhouse.

WOOLAND, NORMAN: Dusseldorf, Ger., Mar. 16, 1910. Edward VI School.

WOPAT, TOM: Lodi, WI, 1950.

WORONOV, MARY: Brooklyn, Dec. 8, 1946. Cornell.

WORTH, IRENE: (Hattie Abrams) June 23, 1916, Neb. UCLA.

WRAY, FAY: Alberta, Can., Sept. 15, 1907.

WRIGHT, TERESA: NYC, Oct. 27, 1918.

WYATT, JANE: Campgaw, NJ, Aug. 10, 1911. Barnard College.

WYMAN, JANE (Sarah Jane Fulks): St. Joseph, MO, Jan. 4, 1914.

WYMORE, PATRICE: Miltonvale, KS, Dec. 17, 1926.

WYNN, KEENAN: NYC, July 27, 1916. St. John's.

WYNN, MAY (Donna Lee Hickey): NYC, Jan. 8, 1930.

WYNTER, DANA (Dagmar): London, June 8, 1927. Rhodes U.

YORK, DICK: Fort Wayne, IN, Sept. 4, 1928. De Paul U.

YORK, MICHAEL: Fulmer, Eng., Mar. 27, 1942. Oxford.

YORK, SUSANNAH: London, Jan. 9, 1941. RADA.

YOUNG, ALAN (Angus): North Shield, Eng., Nov. 19, 1919.

YOUNG, LORETTA (Gretchen): Salt Lake City, Jan. 6, 1912. Immaculate Heart College.

YOUNG, ROBERT: Chicago, Feb. 22, 1907.

ZACHARIAS, ANN: Stockholm, Sw., 1956.

ZADORA, PIA: Forest Hills, NY. 1954.

ZETTERLING, MAI: Sweden, May 27, 1925. Ordtuery Theatre School.

ZIMBALIST, EFREM, JR.: NYC, Nov. 30, 1918. Yale.

| Rod | Dolores | Raymond | David | Pat | Gloria |
| Cameron | Del Rio | Massey | Niven | O'Brien | Swanson |

1983 OBITUARIES

ROBERT (BOBBY) AGNEW, 84, Kentucky-born leading man and later assistant director, died of kidney failure Nov. 8, 1983 in Palm Springs, CA. where he had been in retirement for a number of years. After entering films in 1919, he appeared in over 40 productions, including "Passion Flower," "Clarence," "Blue-beard's Eighth Wife," "Only 38," "Wine of Youth," "Tessie," "Racing Blood," "Wild Oats Lane," "College Hero," "Prince of Headwaiters," "The Fourth Commandment," "Heart of Salome," "Wandering Girls," "Slightly Used," "The Heart of Broadway," "Midnight Taxi," and his last sound pictures were "Extravagance," "The Woman Racket," "Naughty Flirt" and "Gold Diggers of 1933." He is survived by his widow and a daughter.

ROBERT ALDRICH, 65, Rhode Island-born director-producer, died of kidney failure in his Los Angeles, Ca., home on Dec. 5, 1983. He made 29 feature films beginning in 1953 with "The Big Leaguer," followed by such as "Apache," "Vera Cruz," "Kiss Me Deadly," "The Big Knife," "Autumn Leaves," "The Garment Jungle," "Attack!," "The Ride Back," "The Last Sunset," "Whatever Happened to Baby Jane?," "Four for Texas," "Hush, Hush, Sweet Charlotte," "The Dirty Dozen," "The Flight of the Phoenix," "The Legend of Lylah Clare," "The Killing of Sister George," "Too Late the Hero," "Ulzana's Raid," "Emperor of the North," "The Longest Yard," "Hustle," "The Choirboys," and his last "All the Marbles." He is survived by his widow, and four children by his first wife.

PETER ARNE, 62, British character actor, was found bludgeoned to death in his London apartment Aug. 1, 1983. His film credits include "The Purple Plain," "Cockleshell Heroes," "Tarzan and the Lost Safari," "Scent of Mystery," "Conspiracy of Hearts," "The Model Murder Case," "Khartoum," "Battle Beneath the Earth," "The Return of the Pink Panther," "Straw Dogs," "The Moonraker" and "Arrangement in Tangier." No reported survivors.

SYDNEY BOX, 76, British-born Academy Award winning producer, died May 25, 1983 in Perth, Australia, where he retired in 1967. He produced more than 100 films, including "The Seventh Veil" (his "Oscar" winner), "The Years Between," "Holiday Camp," "Jassy," "The Smugglers," "The Brothers," "Bear Murderer," "Don't Take It to Heart," "Broken Journey," "Daybreak," "Facts of Love," "A Girl in a Million," "So Long at the Fair," "The Prisoner," "Quartet," "Trio," "The Years Between," "The Man Within," "The Truth about Women." He also wrote many of his own screenplays, and more than 50 one-act plays. His widow survives.

LUIS BUNUEL, 83, Spanish-born director-screenwriter, died July 29, 1983 of cirrhosis of the liver in Mexico City where he had lived since 1947. His films include "The Golden Age," "The Forgotten," "Viridiana," "Land without Bread," "The Exterminating Angel," "Diary of a Chambermaid," "Simon of the Desert," "Belle de Jour," "The Milky Way," "Tristana," "Specter of Freedom," "That Obscure Object of Desire," and his Academy Award winning "The Discreet Charm of the Bourgeoisie!" Surviving are his widow, and two sons, Jean-Louis and Rafael, both filmmakers.

ROD CAMERON, 73, Canadian-born Ron Cox, screen and tv actor, died Dec. 21, 1983 after a long illness in Gainesville, Ga., where he had retired. After appearing as a stuntman, he was featured or starred in over 50 films. His credits include "The Quarterback," "Christmas in July," "Northwest Mounted Police," "Night of January 16," "Midnight Angel," "Priorities on Parade," "The Fleet's In," "Wake Island," "Forest Rangers," "Gung Ho!," "Honeymoon Lodge," "Riding High," "No Time for Love," "Salome Where She Danced," "Pirates of Monterey," "Belle Star's Daughter," "Stampede," "Oh! Susanna," "Stage to Tucson," "The Jungle," "Commandos Strike at Dawn," "Southwest Passage," "Sea Hornet," "Ride the Man Down," "Requiem for a Gunfighter," "Gun Hawk," "Bounty Killer," "The Last Movie," and "Evil Knievel." He appeared in the tv series "City Detective" and "State Trooper." No reported survivors.

JUDY CANOVA, 66, Florida-born singer, comedian and actress, died of cancer Aug. 5, 1983 in Hollywood, Ca. Began her career yodeling, singing and playing guitar with her brother and sister in a nightclub act in NYC, and made her Broadway debut in "Ziegfeld Follies of 1936." She was hostess of the "Judy Canova Radio Show" for 12 years. Her films include "Going Highbrow," "In Caliente," "Artists and Models," "Thrill of a Lifetime," "Scatterbrain," "Sis Hopkins," "Puddin' Head," "Sleepytime Gal," "Joan of the Ozarks," "True to the Army," "Chatterbox," "Louisiana Hayride," "Honeychile," "Oklahoma Annie," "Wac from Walla Walla," "Carolina Cannonball," "Adventures of Huckleberry Finn." Surviving are two daughters, Julieta England, and actress Diana Canova.

ROBERT CHRISTIAN, 42, California-born stage and screen actor, died of cancer in NYC on Jan. 27, 1983. As a child actor, he appeared on such tv shows as "The Andy Griffith Show" and "Amos 'n' Andy." His film credits include "Prince of the City," "Bustin' Loose," "The Seduction of Joe Tynan," "And Justice for All." His mother survives.

PETER COFFIELD, 38, Illinois-born stage, tv and film actor, died Nov. 19, 1983 after a long illness in NYC. Among his film appearances were "Only When I Laugh," "Legacy of Fear" and "Washington Behind Closed Doors." On tv he had appeared in "The Adams Chronicles," "Family," "Beacon Hill," "Cry Rape," "The Chinese Prime Minister" and "Legacy of Fear." Surviving are his mother, two sisters and two brothers.

MICHAEL CONRAD, 58, NY-born film-stage-tv actor, died of cancer Nov. 22, 1983 in Los Angeles, CA. His screen credits include "Requiem for a Heavyweight," "The Longest Yard," "Castle Keep," and "They Shoot Horses, Don't They?" He had received two Emmy Awards for his portrayal of Sgt. Phillip Freemason Esterhaus on tv's "Hill Street Blues" series. His fourth wife survives.

ANTHONY COSTELLO, 42, stage, film and tv actor, artist and novelist, died Aug. 15, 1983 after a long illness in Hollywood, CA. He had appeared in such films as "Blue," "The Molly Maguires," "Will Penny," "Doctors' Wives," "The Laughing Policeman," and "Night Moves." No reported survivors.

233

BUSTER CRABBE, 75, born Clarence Linden Crabbe in Oakland, CA, died of a heart attack Apr. 23, 1983 at his home in Scottsdale, AZ. As a handsome Olympics swimming champion, he received Hollywood's attention and was signed for films. He appeared in approximately 180 films, including "King of the Jungle," "Search for Beauty," "Sweetheart of Sigma Chi," "Tarzan the Fearless," "The Thundering Herd," "Badge of Honor," "Hold 'Em Yale!," "Wanderer of the Wasteland," "Spaceship to the Unknown," "Desert Gold," "Lady Be Careful," "Nevada," "Rose Bowl," Flash Gordon series, "Murder Goes to College," "King of Gamblers," "Thrill of a Lifetime," Red Barry series, "Million Dollar Legs," Buck Rogers series, "Jungle Man," Billy the Kid series, "Wildcat," "Queen of Broadway," "Frontier Outlaw," "Nabonga," "Devil Riders," "Gentlemen with Guns," "Prairie Badmen," "Swamp Fire," "Bounty Killer," Kaspa the Lion Man series, Thuda the Jungleman series, and "Arizona Raiders." On tv he appeared in the series "Capt. Gallant of the French Foreign Legion." His wife of 50 years, and a son and daughter survive.

GEORGE CUKOR, 83, NYC-born director, died of a stroke and heart attack Jan. 24, 1983 in Los Angeles, CA. After a successful career in the legitimate theatre, he accepted a call to Hollywood as a co-director for "All Quiet on the Western Front" in 1929. He stayed on and became one of film's most distinguished directors of more than 50 pictures, starring the most popular and talented actresses. His credits include, among others, "Royal Family of Broadway," "Tarnished Lady," "A Bill of Divorcement," "Our Betters," "Dinner at 8," "Little Women," "David Copperfield," "Sylvia Scarlett," "Romeo and Juliet," "Camille," "Holiday," "Zaza," "The Women," "Susan and God," "The Philadelphia Story," "A Woman's Face," "Two-Faced Woman," "Keeper of the Flame," "Gaslight," "Winged Victory," "A Double Life," "Adam's Rib," "Born Yesterday," "A Star Is Born," "Les Girls," "Song without End," "My Fair Lady" (for which he received an Oscar), "Pat and Mike," "Heller in Pink Tights," and his last in 1981 "Rich and Famous." In 1975 he received an Emmy for tv's "Love among the Ruins." In 1978 he was honored with a gala at NY's Lincoln Center. A bachelor, he left no immediate survivors.

DOROTHY CUMMING, 84, actress, died of pneumonia in NYC on Dec. 10, 1983. Among her credits are "The Cheat," "Twenty-one," "Nellie, the Beautiful Cloak Model," "The Manicure Girl," "Coast of Folly," "The New Commandment," "Dancing Mothers," "Mlle. Modiste," "For Wives Only," "Butterflies in the Rain," "The King of Kings," "In Old Kentucky," "Our Dancing Daughters," "Kitty," and "The Divine Lady." A son survives.

MARCEL DALIO, 83, Paris-born Israel Mosche Blauschild, died Nov. 20, 1983 in his native city. With his wife, he fled France ahead of the invading Germans who used his portrait on posters as a typical Jew. He settled in Hollywood and appeared in numerous films, repeating his success in France. He returned to Paris in the 1960's. His credits include "Grand Illusion," "Kiss of Fire," "Pepe le Moko," "Unholy Partners," "Pied Piper," "Casablanca," "Tonight We Raid Calais," "The Constant Nymph," "Desert Song," "Song of Bernadette," "Pin Up Girl," "Wilson," "To Have and Have Not," "A Bell for Adano," "Sirocco," "The Damned," "Snowbound," "Rules of the Game," "Snows of Kilimanjaro," "The Happy Time," "Gentlemen Prefer Blondes," "Flight to Tangier," "Sabrina," "Anything Goes," "Miracle in the Rain," "Pillow Talk," "Can-Can," "How to Steal a Million," "Tender Scoundrel," "How Sweet It Is." No reported survivors.

LEORA DANA, 60 stage, tv and screen actress, died of cancer Dec. 13, 1983 in her native New York City. After Broadway success, she appeared in such films as "3:10 to Yuma," "Kings Go Forth," "Some Came Running," "Pollyanna," "A Gathering of Eagles," "Norman Vincent Peale Story," "The Group," "Boston Strangler," "Tora! Tora! Tora!," "Change of Habit," "Shoot the Moon" and "Baby It's You." She appeared as Sylvie in the tv series "Another World," and in "The Adams Chronicles." A sister survives. She was divorced from actor Kurt Kasznar.

JOHNNY SCAT DAVIS, 73, musician, singer, bandleader and actor, died of a heart attack while camping with his son near Pecos, TX. He appeared in 14 films including "Varsity Show," "Brother Rat," "Sarong Girl" and "Knickerbocker Holiday." Survivors include his widow, a son and two daughters.

LOUIS DE FUNES, 68, died of a heart attack Jan. 27, 1983 in Nantes, France. He was a comedian who in 1968 was voted France's favorite actor in a public-opinion poll. He began his career in 1945, subsequently appearing in over 100 comedies. He achieved stardom in 1963 in "Pouic-Pouic," followed by "Fufu," his policeman series: "Le Gendarme de St. Tropez," "The Policeman in New York," "The Policeman Gets Married," and his last film "The Policeman and the Policewoman." His greatest box-office successes were "The Big Gadabout," "The Folly of Greatness," and "The Adventures of Rabbi Jacob." His widow and two sons survive.

DOLORES DEL RIO 78, actress, died Apr. 11, 1983 of natural causes in her home in Newport Beach, CA. Her exceptional beauty and talent made her a star in Hollywood and her native Mexico, after her debut in 1925 in "Joanna." Her other credits include "What Price Glory," "Resurrection," "Ramona," "Loves of Carmen," "Gateway of the Moon," "The Trail of '98," "The Red Dance," "Revenge," "Evangeline," "The Bad One," "Girl of the Rio," "Bird of Paradise," "Flying Down to Rio," "Wonder Bar," "Madame du Barry," "In Caliente," "The Bank Dick," "Accused," "Journey into Fear," "Maria Candelaria," "The Fugitive," "Dona Perfecta," "Torero!," "La Cucaracha," "Flaming Star," "Soldiers and Pancho Villa," "Cheyenne Autumn," "Once upon a Time," "Rio Blanco" and "The Children of Sanchez." She was born Lolita Dolores Martinez Asunsolo Lopez Negrette, and at 15 married Jaime Del Rio. Her third husband, producer Lewis Riley, was with her when she died. She was also divorced from director Cedric Gibbons.

WILLIAM DEMAREST, 91, Minnesota-born character actor on stage, tv and film, died Dec. 28, 1983 of a heart attack in his home in Palm Springs, CA. His career began as a child in vaudeville, followed by Broadway, and he moved to Hollywood in 1936. Among his more than 100 films are "Don't Tell the Wife," "Old San Francisco," "The Jazz Singer," "A Girl in Every Port," "The Escape," "Butter and Egg Man," "Many Happy Returns," "Diamond Jim," "Hands across the Table," "Hit Parade," "Big City," "Rebecca of Sunnybrook Farm," "While New York Sleeps," "Gracie Allen Murder Case," "Mr. Smith Goes to Washington," "The Farmer's Daughter," "The Great McGinty," "Tin Pan Alley," "Little Men," "Lady Eve," "Dressed to Kill," "Sullivan's Travels," "My Favorite Spy," "Pardon My Sarong," "Stage Door Canteen," "Hail the Conquering Hero," "Along Came Jones," "Miracle of Morgan's Creek," "Sorrowful Jones," "Jolson Sings Again," "It's a Mad, Mad, Mad World," "Viva Las Vegas," "That Darn Cat." On tv he was in "Wells Fargo," "The Millionaire," "Love and Marriage," and his most popular Uncle Charley in "My Three Sons." He retired in 1971. His widow survives.

JACK DEMPSEY, 87, Colorado-born former heavyweight champion of the world, and former actor, died of a heart ailment May 31, 1983 in NYC. After winning the championship, he went to Hollywood where he met and married his second wife, silent star Estelle Taylor. Together they appeared in "Manhattan Madness." He later appeared in "The Prizefighter and the Lady," "Off Limits," "Requiem for a Heavyweight" and "The Legendary Champions." He is survived by his fourth wife and her daughter whom he adopted. By his third wife, singer Hannah Williams, two daughters survive.

HOWARD DIETZ, 86, lyricist and former MGM executive, died July 30, 1983 of Parkinson's disease in his native NYC. He had written words for over 500 songs, most of them with Arthur Schwartz. Mr. Dietz devised the familiar MGM trademark from the lion mascot of his alma mater, Columbia University. He is survived by his second wife, one daughter by his first wife, and two step-children.

FIFI D'ORSAY, 79, the "French Bombshell" of 1930's films, died of cancer Dec. 2, 1983 in Woodland Hills, CA. Born Yvonne Lussier in Montreal, Canada, she went to NYC in 1923 and got a job as a chorus girl, and in 1929 made her movie debut in "They Had to See Paris." The phrase "ooh-la-la" became her trademark as a French flirt, and she appeared in 23 films, including "Hot for Paris," "Women Everywhere," "On the Level," "Those Three French Girls," "Mr. Lemon of Orange," "Women of All Nations," "Young as You Feel," "Life of Jimmy Dolan," "Going Hollywood," "Wonder Bar," "Three Legionnaires," "The Gangster," "What a Way to Go!," "Just Imagine," "Silk Stockings," "Wild and Wonderful" and "Assignment to Kill," her last in 1968. No reported survivors.

JOSEPHINE DUNN, 76, former screen actress, died of cancer during April of 1983 in her home in Thousand Oaks, CA. After her film debut in 1926's "Fascinating Youth," she appeared in "Love's Greatest Mistake," "Fireman, Save My Child," "Get Your Man," "The Singing Fool," "Excess Baggage," "Melody Lane," "Big Time," "A Most Immoral Lady," "Safety in Numbers," "Madonna of the Streets," "Two Kinds of Women," "One Hour with You," "Big City Blues," "Second Honeymoon," "Forbidden Company," "Surrender at Dawn," "Between Fighting Men." She was married to the late Allen Case, and leaves no survivors.

WILLIAM DAVID ELLIOTT, 49, actor, died Sept. 30, 1983 in Los Angeles, CA. Screen credits include "A Change of Habit," "On a Clear Day You Can See Forever," and "Where Does It Hurt?" On tv he had been a regular on the series "Adam 12" and "Bridget Loves Bernie." Divorced from Dionne Warwick, he is survived by two sons, his mother, a brother and a sister.

FAYE EMERSON, 65, Louisiana-born former actress and tv personality, died of cancer Mar. 9, 1983 in her home on Majorca. Her film career began in 1941 in "Bad Men of Missouri," followed by "The Nurse's Secret," "9 Lives Are Not Enough," "Manpower," "Blues in the Night," "Juke Box Girl," "Murder in the Big House," "Secret Enemies," "Air Force," "Desert Song," "Destination Tokyo," "Uncertain Glory," "Between Two Worlds," "Mask of Dimitrios," "The Very Thought of You," "Hollywood Canteen," "Hotel Berlin," "Her Kind of Man," "Nobody Lives Forever," "Main Street to Broadway" and "Guilty Bystander." She began her own tv show "Faye Emerson's Wonderful Town" in 1949 and became a popular tv personality, inspiring the nickname for the Emmy Awards. She was divorced from Elliott Roosevelt and Skitch Henderson. A son by her first marriage, William Crawford III, survives.

PAUL FIX, 82, NY-born character actor on film and tv, died of kidney failure Oct. 14, 1983 in Santa Monica, CA. His career in films began in 1928 in "The First Kiss," followed by more than 300 pictures, including "Lucky Star," "The Good Bad Girl," "Dancers in the Dark," "The Last Mile," "Back Street," "Road to Glory," "Winterset," "After the Thin Man," "Border Cafe," "King of Gamblers," "Souls at Sea," "Penitentiary," "Undercover Doctor," "News Is Made at Night," "Mutiny on the Blackhawk," "Behind Prison Gates," "Black Friday," "The Great Plane Robbery," "Jail House Blues," "Sherlock Holmes and the Secret Weapon," "Pittsburgh," "Fighting Seabees," "Tall in the Saddle," "Back to Bataan," "Red River," "Wake of the Red Witch," "What Price Glory," "Hondo," "Johnny Guitar," "The High and the Mighty," "Blood Alley," "The Bad Seed," "Giant," "Night Passage," "To Kill a Mockingbird," "Shenandoah," "Welcome to Hard Times," "El Dorado." He was Micah Torrance in the tv series "The Rifleman." A daughter survives.

LYNNE FONTANNE, either 95 or 100 according to varying records, actress, died July 30, 1983 at her home in Genesee Depot, WI. With her husband, the late Alfred Lunt, they were one of the greatest husband-and-wife acting teams in the theatre. They appeared in only three films, "Second Youth," "The Guardsman" and "Stage Door Canteen." They had appeared on tv in "The Magnificent Yankees" for which they both received Emmy Awards. No reported survivors.

EDDIE FOY, JR., 78, former vaudevillian, stage, tv and screen actor, died of cancer July 15, 1983 in Woodland Hills, CA. Among his screen credits are "Queen of the Night Clubs," "Myrt and Marge," "Women in the Wind," "Frontier Marshal," "Lillian Russell," "A Fugitive from Justice," "Rookies on Parade," "Yankee Doodle Dandy," "Powder Town," "Dixie Dugan," "And the Angels Sing," "Wilson," "The Farmer Takes a Wife," "Lucky Me," "The Pajama Game," "Bells Are Ringing," "Gidget Goes Hawaiian." He also appeared in many tv comedies. Surviving are a son, actor Eddie Foy III, two sisters and two brothers.

EDUARD FRANZ, 80, Milwaukee-born actor on film, tv and stage, died after a long illness on Feb. 10, 1983 in Los Angeles, CA. After Broadway success, he went to Hollywood in 1947 and his credits include "The Iron Curtain," "Wake of the Red Witch," "Outpost in Morocco," "Oh You Beautiful Doll," "Whirlpool," "The Magnificent Yankee," "Molly," "The Great Caruso," "Desert Fox," "One Minute to Zero," "Everything I Have Is Yours," "The Jazz Singer," "Beachhead," "Sign of the Pagan," "White Feather," "Lady Godiva," "The Ten Commandments," "Day of the Badman," "A Certain Smile," "Story of Ruth," "Francis of Assisi," "Hatari," "The President's Analyst" and "The Twilight Zone." He was a regular on tv's "World of Giants" and "Breaking Point." His widow survives.

CHRISTOPHER GEORGE, 54, Michigan-born film and tv actor, died of a heart attack Nov. 28, 1983 in Los Angeles, CA. His screen credits include "El Dorado," "In Harm's Way," "The Delta Factor," "Chisum," "Day of the Animals," "Grizzly," "Tiger by the Tail" and "The Exterminator." He appeared regularly on tv's "Rat Patrol" and "The Immortal." His widow, actress Lynda Day George, a son and a daughter survive.

IRA GERSHWIN, 86, Manhattan-born lyricist brother of George, died Aug. 17, 1983 at his home in Beverly Hills, CA. With George, he wrote music and lyrics for such films as "Shall We Dance," "Goldwyn Follies," "Lady Be Good," "Girl Crazy," "Broadway Rhythmn," "Ziegfeld Follies of 1946," "The Shocking Miss Pilgrim," "Three for the Show," "Funny Face," "Porgy and Bess." After his brother's death he collaborated with other composers. Surviving are his widow and a sister.

GAVIN GORDON, 82, Mississippi-born screen and tv actor, died Apr. 7, 1983 after a long illness in Canoga Park, CA. Among his many screen credits are "His First Command," "Romance," "The Silver Horde," "The Great Meadow," "Shipmates," "Two against the World," "Man against Woman," "Bitter Tea of Gen. Yen," "Female," "The Scarlet Empress," "Bordertown," "Bride

of Frankenstein," "Page Miss Glory," "As You Like It," "The Toast of New York," "Centennial Summer," "The Vagabond King," "The Matchmaker," "The Bat," "Johnny Tremaine," and "Pocketful of Miracles." A cousin survives.

JOAN HACKETT, 49, Manhattan-born screen, tv and stage actress, died of cancer Oct. 8, 1983 in Encino, CA. She made her film debut in 1966 in "The Group," followed by "Will Penny," "The Last of Sheila," "Terminal Man," "Escape Artist," "The Rivals," and "Only When I Laugh" for which she received an Oscar nomination. She was divorced from actor Richard Mulligan, and is survived by a sister and a brother.

JAMES HAYTER, 75, India-born screen and stage actor, died March 27, 1983 in Spain where he had been living. Among his film credits are "Sensation," "Sailors Three," "Nicholas Nickleby," "Blue Lagoon," "Tom Brown's School Days," "Robin Hood," "Four Sided Triangle," "Pickwick Papers," "Beau Brummel," "A Day to Remember," "Land of the Pharoahs," "Abandon Ship!," "The Captain's Table," "The 39 Steps" and "Stranger in the House." His widow and seven children survive.

CAROLYN JONES, 50, Texas-born screen and television actress, died of cancer Aug. 3, 1983 at her home in Los Angeles, CA. Among her many film credits are "House of Wax," "The Big Heat," "Shield for Murder," "Desiree," "The Seven Year Itch," "The Tender Trap," "The Opposite Sex," "Bachelor Party" (for which she received an Oscar nomination), "Marjorie Morningstar," "A Hole in the Head," "Career," "Ice Palace," "How the West Was Won," and "A Ticklish Affair." She was best known for her Morticia in the tv series "The Addams Family." She is survived by her third husband, and by a sister.

BRONISLAW KAPER, 81, composer, died Apr. 26, 1983 in Hollywood, CA. He received a 1953 Oscar for his score for "Lili." No reported survivors.

MIKE KELLIN, 61, Connecticut-born stage, film and tv actor, died of cancer Aug. 26, 1983 in Nyack, NY. His screen credits include "So Young, So Bad," "At War with the Army," "Hurricane Smith," "Lonely Hearts," "The Wackiest Ship in the Army," "The Great Impostor," "Hell Is for Heroes," "The Incident," "Banning," "Invitation to a Gunfighter," "Boston Strangler," "The Riot," "The Phynx," "On the Yard," "Next Stop Greenwich Village" and "Midnight Express." Surviving are his widow, actress Sally Moffet, a daughter, and three stepsons.

JOHN LeMESURIER, 71, British character actor, died Nov. 15, 1983 in Ramsgate, Kent, Eng. He had appeared in over 100 films, including "Law and Disorder," "Too Many Crooks," "Happy Is the Bride," "Jack the Ripper," "Man in a Cocked Hat," "School for Scoundrels," "Follow a Star," "The Mouse on the Moon," "Masquerade," "Moonspinners," "The Wrong Box," "The Magic Christian" and "The Garnett Saga." No reported survivors.

JACQUELINE LOGAN, 78, Texas-born, silent film leading lady, died Apr. 4, 1983 in Melbourne, FL. After her 1921 debut in "A Perfect Crime," she appeared in 57 other films, including "Ebb Tide," "Mr. Billings Spends His Dime," "Salomy Jane," "The Light That Failed," "Manhattan," "If Marriage Fails," "Thank You," "The King of Kings," "Blood Ship," "Wise Wife," "Stocks and Blondes," "The Cop," "Power," and "Middle Watch." A stepson survives.

RICHARD LOO, Hawaii-born screen and tv actor, died of cardio-pulmonary arrest on Nov. 20, 1983 in Los Angeles, CA. After his film debut in "Dirigible" (1931), he appeared in over 140 other pictures, and on many tv shows including a featured role in the "Kung Fu" series. His movies include "Bitter Tea of General Yen," "War Lord," "The Good Earth," "Island of Lost Men," "Bombs over Burma," "The Falcon Strikes Back," "Jack London," "The Purple Heart," "Keys of the Kingdom," "Story of Dr. Wassell," "God Is My Co-Pilot," "China Sky," "Tokyo Rose," "Malaya," "Five Fingers," "Soldier of Fortune," "Back to Bataan," "Love Is a Many Splendored Thing," "Around the World in 80 Days," "The Quiet American," "The Sand Pebbles," "Marcus Welby, M.D." He is survived by his second wife, and two daughters.

RAYMOND MASSEY, 86, Canada-born versatile actor on stage, screen and tv, died of pneumonia July 29, 1983 in Los Angeles, CA. After London and Broadway success, he began a memorable film career in 1931. His pictures include "Face at the Window," "Scarlet Pimpernel," "Prisoner of Zenda," "Fire over England," "Drums," "Abe Lincoln in Illinois" (for which he received an Oscar nomination), "Reap the Wild Wind," "Desperate Journey," "Woman in the Window," "Arsenic and Old Lace," "Hotel Berlin," "God Is My Co-Pilot," "Stairway to Heaven," "Possessed," "Mourning Becomes Electra," "The Fountainhead," "David and Bathsheba," "Desert Song," "Prince of Players," "East of Eden," "Seven Angry Men," "The Naked and the Dead," "The Great Impostor," "How the West Was Won," and

"Mackenna's Gold." From 1961–66 he starred with Richard Chamberlain in the popular tv series "Dr. Kildare." He was married three times, and is survived by two sons, Daniel an actor, and Geoffrey, a daughter, actress Anna, and a stepdaughter.

JOHN McHUGH, 69, Montana-born film and stage actor, died of a heart attack Jan. 13, 1983 in Las Vegas, NV. He began his career in Hollywood in 1921 as Jack McHugh, a freckle-faced member of the "Our Gang" series. In the following years, he appeared in over 200 juvenile comedies, including the "Buster Brown" series, "Big Boy" series, and "Jack McHugh" series. His first talking picture was "Chinatown Nights," followed by "Mayor of Hell," "This Day and Age" and "Wild Boys of the Road." Over all, he had appeared in over 300 films. No reported survivors.

DAVID NIVEN, 73, Scotland-born actor and novelist, died of amyotrophic lateral sclerosis (also known as Lou Gehrig's disease) in Chateau d'Oex, Switzerland. After service in the British army, he went to Hollywood in 1934 and subsequently appeared in such films as "Splendor," "Dodsworth," "Charge of the Light Brigade," "Prisoner of Zenda," "Dawn Patrol," "Bluebeard's Eighth Wife," "Wuthering Heights," "Raffles," "Spitfire," "Stairway to Heaven," "Magnificent Doll," "The Elusive Pimpernel," "Bonnie Prince Charlie," "Enchantment," "Kiss in the Dark," "Toast of New Orleans," "The Moon Is Blue," "Court Martial," "The Bishop's Wife," "Around the World in 80 Days," "The Little Hut," "My Man Godfrey," "Separate Tables" (for which he won an Oscar), "Please Don't Eat the Daisies," "Guns of Navarone," "The Best of Enemies," "Kremlin Letter," "Rough Cut," "A Man Called Intrepid," and "The Sea Wolves." On tv he was the host of "The David Niven Show" (1959–64), and starred in "The Rogues" series. In addition to his second wife, he is survived by two sons by his first wife, and two adopted daughters during his second marriage.

MARIAN NIXON, 78, Minnesota-born screen star, died of complications from open heart surgery on Feb. 13, 1983 in Los Angeles, CA. After her 1925 debut in the Tom Mix picture "Riders of the Purple Sage," she appeared in over 50 films, including "What Happened to Jones," "What Was I," "Devil's Island," "Taxi Taxi," "Out All Night," "Chinese Parrot," "How to Handle Women," "Red Lips," "Geraldine," "Rainbow Man," "Say It with Songs," "Show of Shows," "General Crack," "Courage," "The Pay-Off," "Scarlet Pages," "Women Go on Forever," "College Lovers," "Charlie Chan's Chance," "Rebecca of Sunnybrook Farm," "Winner Take All," "Madison Square Garden," "The Best of Enemies," "Pilgrimage," "The Line Up," "Strictly Dynamite," "Face in the Sky," "Chance at Heaven," "We're Rich Again," "Sweepstakes Annie," "Tango," "Captain Calamity" and "The Dragnet." After her marriage to director Willian Seitner in 1934 she retired to raise a family. After his death, she was married to actor Ben Lyon who died in 1979. Surviving are a son and a daughter.

SIMON OAKLAND, 61, NYC-born character actor on stage, film and tv, died Aug. 29, 1983 after a long illness in his home in Cathedral City, CA. After Broadway success, he appeared in such films as "The Brothers Karamazov," "I Want to Live," "Psycho," "Murder Inc.," "Who's That Lady?," "West Side Story," "Follow That Dream," "The Raiders," "Ready for the People," "Satan Bug," "Sand Pebbles," "The Plainsman," "Tony Rome," "Bullitt," "On a Clear Day You Can See Forever." He was a regular on tv's "Baa Baa Black Sheep," "Toma" and "Kolchak, The Night Stalker" series. He leaves his wife and a daughter.

PAT O'BRIEN, 83, Milwaukee-born character actor, died Oct. 15, 1983 of a heart attack following prostate surgery in Santa Monica, CA. Of his more than 100 feature films, his best known are "Front Page," "Flying High," "Final Edition," "Arm of the Law," "Virtue," "Destination Unknown," "Bureau of Missing Persons," "College Coach," "Personality Kid," "Here Comes the Navy," "Flirtation Walk," "Gambling Lady," "Devil Dogs of the Air," "Oil for the Lamps of China," "Page Miss Glory," "The Irish in Us," "Ceiling Zero," "China Clipper," "The Great O'-Malley," "Angels with Dirty Faces," "Fighting 69th," "Knute Rockne All American," "Submarine Zone," "Broadway," "Bombardier," "The Iron Major," "Secret Command," "Fighting Father Dunne," "Fireball," "The People against O'Hara," "The Last Hurrah," "Some Like It Hot," "Okinawa," "The End" and "Ragtime." Surviving are his wife of 52 years, former actress Eloise Taylor, a daughter, and three adopted children.

RICHARD O'BRIEN, 65, character actor on stage and tv, died of cancer March 29, 1983 in his home in Los Angeles, CA. He had appeared in some 200 pictures, including "Looking for Mr. Goodbar," "The Andromeda Strain," "Get Patty Hearst," "Flash Gordon" and "Shock Treatment." Two brothers survive.

ESTELLE OMENS, 55, Chicago-born actress on stage, screen and tv, died Dec. 4, 1983 in her North Hollywood home. After her 1968 film debut in "The Secret Cinema," she had roles in "Dog Day Afternoon," "Law and Disorder," "Loving Couples," "Looker" and "Stir Crazy." She is survived by her husband, writer Frank Gregory.

PATRICK O'MOORE, 74, Dublin-born stage, screen and tv actor, died Dec. 10, 1983 following surgery in Van Nuys, CA. His film credits, beginning in 1941, include "Smilin' Through," "Stage Door Canteen," "Desperate Journey," "Sahara," "Between Two Worlds," "The Horn Blows at Midnight," "Moss Rose," "The Two Mrs. Carrolls," "Bulldog Drummond Strikes Back," "Kind Lady," "Son of Dr. Jekyll," "Bwana Devil," "Ride a Violent Mile," "Desert Hell," "The Rookie," "How To Succeed in Business . . .," "My Fair Lady." He appeared on numerous TV shows. He is survived by his widow.

GALE PAGE, 72, nee Sally Rutter, film actress, died of cancer Jan. 8, 1983 in her Santa Monica, CA home. After her 1938 debut in "Crime School," her credits include "The Amazing Dr. Clitterhouse," "Four Daughters," "Heart of the North," "You Can't Get Away with Murder," "Daughters Courageous," "Naughty but Nice," "Four Wives," "A Child Is Born," "They Drive by Night," "Knute Rockne," "Four Mothers," "The Time of Your Life," "Anna Lucasta," "About Mrs. Leslie." No reported survivors.

HARRIET PARSONS, 76, Iowa-born former child actress, writer, and one of Hollywood's few female producers, died of cancer Jan. 2, 1983 in Santa Monica, CA. She had a weekly radio program, and often substituted for her mother on the "Louella Parsons Show" and "Hollywood Hotel." Her more notable film productions include "The Enchanted Cottage," "Night Song," "Never a Dull Moment," "Clash by Night" and "Susan Slept Here." She was the widow of actor King Kennedy, and is survived by a daughter.

THELMA PELISH, 55, character actress on stage, screen and tv, died Mar. 6, 1983 in Woodland Hills, CA. Her screen credits include "The Pajama Game," "Splendor in the Grass," "Sweet Charity," "Every Which Way but Loose," "Scream" and "Flicks." A sister survives.

SLIM PICKENS, 64, born Louis Bert Lindley, Jr. in Kingsboro, CA, died of pneumonia after brain surgery on Dec. 8, 1983 in Modesto, CA. Former rodeo star, he appeared in many westerns, and his more than 300 credits include "Rocky Mountain," "Will Rogers Story," "Thunderbirds," "The Sun Shines Bright," "The Outcast," "The Last Command," "The Great Locomotive Chase," "Stranger at My Door," "When Gangland Strikes," "Tonka," "Escort West," "One-Eyed Jacks," "Savage Sam," "Dr. Strangelove," "Major Dundee," "In Harm's Way," "Up from the Beach," "Stagecoach," "Flim Flam Man," "Will Penny," "Never a Dull Moment," "The Cowboys," "The Apple Dumpling Gang," "The Howling," "Honeysuckle Rose." His widow and two daughters survive.

LeROY PRINZ, 88, Missouri-born dance director and choreographer, died of natural causes Sept. 15, 1983 in Wadsworth, CA. During his 25-year career in Hollywood, he worked on more than 200 feature films, including "Sign of the Cross," "The Crusades," "Little Miss Marker," "Yankee Doodle Dandy," "Desert Song," "This Is the Army," "Night and Day," several of the Crosby-Hope "Road" features, "Rhapsody in Blue," "My Wild Irish Rose," "April in Paris," "The Ten Commandments," "Sayonara" and "South Pacific." No reported survivors.

RALPH RICHARDSON, 80, beloved English stage and screen actor, died of digestive ailments Oct. 10, 1983 in London. During his career of 63 years, he appeared more frequently on stage (his first love) than in films. Prominent among his film performances were roles in "The Man Who Could Work Miralces," "Divorce of Lady X," "The Citadel," "Four Feathers," "The Avengers," "Anna Karenina," "The Fallen Idol," "The Heiress," "Breaking the Sound Barrier," "The Holly and the Ivy," "Richard III," "Oscar Wilde," "Our Man in Havana," "Exodus," "Long Day's Journey into Night," "Doctor Zhivago," "Khartoum," and "Oh! What a Lovely War!" He is survived by his second wife, actress Meriel Forbes-Robertson, and their son.

MAURICE RONET, 55, French actor, died Mar. 14, 1983 after a long illness in Paris. Among his 70 film credits are "The Seven Deadly Sins," "Desperate Decision," "He Who Must Die," "Frantic," "Time Out for Love," "The Victors," "Fire Within," "Circle of Love," "Enough Rope," "Lost Command," "Birds in Peru," "Elevator for the Scaffold," "The Scandal," "La Femme Infidele," and "La Balance." He was married to Josephine Chaplin, the youngest daughter of Charles Chaplin.

SELENA ROYLE, 78, retired stage and screen actress, died Apr. 23, 1983 in Guadalajara, Mexico after a short illness. A native of NYC, she began her career on Broadway but moved to Hollywood where she appeared in such films as "Stage Door Canteen," "The Sullivans," "30 Seconds over Tokyo," "Mrs. Parkington," "The Harvey Girls," "Night and Day," "Till the End of Time," "The Courage of Lassie," "Cass Timberlane," "Joan of Arc," "A Date with Judy," "Bad Boy," "The Heiress," "The Big Hangover," "Come Fill the Cup" and "Murder Is My Beat." With her late husband, actor George Renavent, she had lived in Mexico for 30 years. A sister survives.

TAMARA SHAYNE, 80, Russia-born actress of film and stage, died Oct. 23, 1983 of a heart attack in Los Angeles, CA. She made her film debut in 1939 in "Ninotchka," followed by such pictures as "Mission to Moscow," "The Jolson Story," "Pirates of Monterey," "It Happened in Brooklyn," "Northwest Outpost," "The Snake Pit," "Walk a Crooked Mile," "The Red Danube," "Black Magic," "Jolson Sings Again," "Thieves' Highway," "Anastasia" and "Romanoff and Juliet." After the death of her husband, character actor Akim Tamiroff, she retired to Palm Springs. No reported survivors.

NORMA SHEARER, 80, Canada-born film star, died of bronchial pneumonia in Woodland Hills, CA. After a few minor parts in NYC productions, she was signed by Louis B. Mayer and Irving Thalberg and moved to Hollywood in 1923. She married Thalberg in 1927 who unfortunately died at the age of 37. She received an Oscar for her performance in "The Divorcee" (1930). Other credits include "The Trial of Mary Dugan," "The Last of Mrs. Cheyney," "Let Us Be Gay," "A Free Soul," "Private Lives," "Smilin' Through," "Strange Interlude," "Rip Tide," "The Barretts of Wimpole Street," "Romeo and Juliet," "Marie Antoinette," "Idiot's Delight," "The Women," "Escape," "We Were Dancing" and "Her Cardboard Lover." In 1942 she met and married ski instructor Martin Arrouge and retired. He survives, as do her son and daughter by her first marriage.

MARTHA SLEEPER 72, Illinois-born stage and film actress, died of a heart attack Mar. 25, 1983 in her home in Beaufort, NC. She began her career as a child in Hal Roach comedies, later appearing in "Danger Street," "Voice of the Storm," "Our Blushing Brides," "War Nurse," "Madam Satan," "Ten Cents a Dance," "Confessions of a Co-Ed," "Huddle," "Rasputin and the Empress," "Penthouse," "Broken Dreams," "Spitfire," "West of the Pecos," "Tomorrow's Youth," "The Scoundrel," "Rhythm on the Range" and "The Bells of St. Mary's." Her husband survives.

WALTER SLEZAK, 80, Vienna-born character actor on stage, film and tv, fatally shot himself Apr. 21, 1983 at his home in Flower Hill, NY. He was depressed over a series of illnesses, and had been in retirement for several years. Before coming to the U.S., he was a popular actor and singer in Germany. His film credits include "Once Upon a Honeymoon," "This Land Is Mine," "Fallen Sparrow," "Lifeboat," "Step Lively," "Till We Meet Again," "Salome Where She Danced," "Sinbad the Sailor," "The Pirate," "Inspector General," "Bedtime for Bonzo," "Call Me Madam," "Steel Cage," "The Miracle," "The Gazebo," "Come September," "The Wonderful World of the Brothers Grimm," "A Very Special Favor" and "Caper of the Golden Bulls." Surviving are his widow, a son, and two daughters, one of whom is actress Erika Slezak.

ARTHUR SPACE, 74, stage, screen and tv actor, died of cancer Jan. 13, 1983 in his Hollywood home. His many credits include "Riot Squad," "Tortilla Flat," "Wilson," "Leave Her to Heaven," "Our Vines Have Tender Grapes," "Black Beauty," "Cockeyed Miracle," "The Guilt of Janet Ames," "Her Husband's Affairs," "I Love Trouble," "The Fuller Brush Man," "Fighter Squadron," "Mr. Belvedere Goes to College," "Miss Grant Takes Richmond," "The Fuller Brush Girl," "The Good Humor Man," "Her First Romance," "Tomahawk," "Rainbow 'Round My Shoulder," "Fargo," "Foxfire," "The Spirit of St. Louis," "Lassie Come Home," "Twilight of the Gods" and "The Shakiest Gun in the West." He is survived by his two daughters.

FAY SPAIN, 50, film and tv actress, died of cancer during May 1983 in California. After her screen debut in "The Crooked Circle" (1957), she appeared in "The Abductors," "Teenage Doll," "God's Little Acre," "Al Capone," "The Private Lives of Adam and Eve," "Black Gold,""Thunder Island," "Flight to Fury," "The Gentle Rain," "Welcome to Hard Times" and "The Grove." Surviving are her husband, Philip Westbrook, a son and four stepchildren.

SHEPPERD STRUDWICK (also known as John Shepperd), 75, North Carolina-born actor on stage, screen and tv, died of cancer Jan. 15, 1983 in NYC. He had appeared in over 50 films, including, "Marie Antoinette," "Flight Command," "Remember the Day," "Belle Star," "The Loves of Edgar Allan Poe," "Rings on Her Fingers," "Pride of the Marines," "Joan of Arc," "Fighter Squadron," "The Red Pony," "All the King's Men," "A Place in the Sun," "Eddie Duchin Story," "Autumn Leaves," "Sad Sack," "Girl on the Run" and "Slaves." He is survived by his widow, and a son from a previous marriage.

GLORIA SWANSON, 84, Chicago-born Gloria May Josephine Svensson, actress on stage and tv, and one of Hollywood's most enduring stars, died of a heart ailment Apr. 4, 1983 in NYC. She began her career at 14 as an extra, and soon gained featured roles and leads in Mack Sennett comedies, and stardom under director Cecil B. DeMille. Her films, both silent and talking, include "Don't Change Your Husband," "For Better For Worse," "Male and Female," "Why Change Your Wife," "The Great Moment," "Affairs of Anatol," "Beyond the Rocks," "Prodigal Daughters," "Bluebeard's 8th Wife," "Zaza," "Manhandled," "Her Love Story," "Wages of Virtue," "Mme. Sans Gene," "Stage Struck," "Untamed Lady," "Sadie Thompson," "The Tresspasser," "Queen Kelly," "What a Widow," "Indiscreet," "Tonight or Never," "Music in the Air," "Father Takes a Wife," "Sunset Boulevard," "3 for Bedroom C," "When Comedy Was King," "Black Point," and "Airport 1975." For 16 years she became involved in several businesses and sculptured. She is survived by her sixth husband, writer William Dufty, and two daughters. She was cremated.

VAUGHN TAYLOR, 72, actor on stage, screen and tv, died of a cerebral hemorrhage May 3, 1983 in Los Angeles, CA. His film credits include "Up Front," "It Should Happen to You," "Decision at Sundown," "Party Girl," "Andy Hardy Comes Home," "Cat on a Hot Tin Roof," "Warlock," "Blue Denim," "Psycho," "Diamond Head," "Carpetbaggers" "The Unsinkable Molly Brown," "In Cold Blood," "Fever Heat," "The Ballad of Cable Hogue." No reported survivors.

JOAN VALERIE, Wisconsin-born actress, died of pneumonia after an automobile collision Jan. 30, 1983 in Long Beach, CA. Among her more than 40 films are "A Trip to Paris," "Submarine Patrol," "Tail Spin," "Daytime Wife," "Young as You Feel," "Free, Blonde and 21," "Lillian Russell," "Girl in 313," "The Great Profile," "Michael Shayne," "Rio Rita," and "Jeannie." A daughter survives.

DOODLES WEAVER, 71, born Winstead Sheffield Weaver in Los Angeles, died Jan. 17, 1983 apparently of self-inflicted gunshot wounds at his home in Burbank, CA. He had been a comedian on screen and television. His film credits include "Behind the Headlines," "Topper," "Pied Piper," "Since You Went Away," "Story of Dr. Wassell," "San Antonio," "Gentlemen Prefer Blondes," "Pocketful of Miracles," "The Birds," "The Rounders," "Zebra in the Kitchen," "Rosie," "Road to Nashville" and "Bigfoot." He was married four times. A son survives.

ALICE WHITE, 78, New Jersey-born leading lady, died of a stroke Feb. 19, 1983 in her Los Angeles home. She had appeared in almost 40 films before her retirement in 1950. Her credits include "American Beauty," "The Private Life of Helen of Troy," "Gentlemen Prefer Blondes" (1928), "Harold Teen," "Broadway Daddies," "Hot Stuff," "Naughty Baby," "Sweet Mama," "Sweethearts on Parade," "Playing Around," "Murder at Midnight," "Luxury Liner," "King for a Night," "Jimmy the Gent," "Gift of Gab," "Sweet Music," "Big City," "Night of January 16th," "Girls Town" and "Flamingo Road." She was married and divorced twice. No reported survivors.

JOHN WILLIAMS, 80, British-born actor on stage, screen and tv, died from an aneurism May 5, 1983 in La Jolla, CA. After success on London and Broadway stages, he began his successful film career in 1938 with "Emil," followed by "Somewhere in France," "A Woman's Vengeance," "Sabrina," "Kind Lady," "Thunder in the East," "Student Prince," "Dial 'M' for Murder," "To Catch a Thief," "Solid Gold Cadillac," "D-Day," "Island in the Sun," "Will Success Spoil Rock Hunter?," "Witness for the Prosecution," "Visit to a Small Planet," "Dear Brigitte," "None but the Brave," "Harlow," "Double Trouble," "A Flea in Her Ear," "Coming Home," "Hot Lead and Cold Feet" and "The Swarm." His wife survives him.

TENNESSEE WILLIAMS, 71, Pulitzer-Prize-winning playwright and screenwriter, choked to death on a bottle cap in his NYC hotel suite on Aug. 13, 1983. He was born Thomas Lanier Williams in Columbus, Mississippi. His screenplays include "The Glass Menagerie," "A Streetcar Named Desire," "The Rose Tattoo," "Baby Doll," "Suddenly Last Summer," "The Fugitive Kind" and "Boom!" He was the original author of the above and also of "Cat on a Hot Tin Roof," "Summer and Smoke," "The Roman Spring of Mrs. Stone," "Sweet Bird of Youth," "Period of Adjustment," "Night of the Iguana" and "This Property Is Condemned." A sister and brother survive. Interment was in St. Louis, Mo.

239

241

249

256